Charlot

Charlot

Charlie Chaplin, France, and Transnational Stardom

MELVYN STOKES

OXFORD
UNIVERSITY PRESS

Oxford University Press is a department of the University of Oxford.
It furthers the University's objective of excellence in research, scholarship,
and education by publishing worldwide. Oxford is a registered trade mark of
Oxford University Press in the UK and in certain other countries.

Published in the United States of America by Oxford University Press
198 Madison Avenue, New York, NY 10016, United States of America.

Library of Congress Cataloging-in-Publication Data

ISBN 9780199354221 (pbk.)
ISBN 9780199354214 (hbk.)

DOI: 10.1093/9780197839294.001.0001

Paperback printed by Marquis Book Printing, Canada
Hardback printed by Lightning Source, Inc., United States of America

The manufacturer's authorized representative in the EU for product safety is
Oxford University Press España S.A. of Parque Empresarial San Fernando de Henares,
Avenida de Castilla, 2 – 28830 Madrid (www.oup.es/en or product.safety@oup.com).
OUP España S.A. also acts as importer into Spain of products made by the manufacturer.

For Nahed and Sarah

with all my love
In memory of my dear parents, Alice and Bernard Stokes

Contents

Acknowledgments

In 2004, together with a French colleague, Raphaëlle Costa de Beauregard, I wrote a chapter in a book I was editing with Richard Maltby that focused on the reception of American films outside the United States. Our chapter was titled "The Reception of American Films in France, c. 1910–1920." Researching it opened my eyes to the wealth and vibrancy of early French film culture. Fascinated by this, I later wrote an article on the career of D. W. Griffith's highly racist movie *The Birth of a Nation* in France—where it was twice banned from exhibition by the authorities. Casting around for a larger project, I finally settled on the reception and career of Charlie Chaplin ("Charlot") in France.

Looking back over the researching and writing of this book, it is a pleasure both to recognize and express immense gratitude for all the help I have received along the way. Like many other writers on Chaplin, I owe a huge debt of gratitude to David Robinson's 1984 biography and Charles (Chuck) Maland's 1989 study of the evolution of Chaplin's star image in the United States. Other works that helped greatly from the start include biographies of Chaplin by Georges Sadoul (1978) and Kenneth S. Lynn (1997), Richard Abel's two fine anthologies of French film theory and criticism covering the period 1907–39 (1988), and Timothy J. Lyons's 1979 guide to Chaplin resources that referenced some of the extensive French writing on Chaplin.

The staff of many libraries have helped greatly in the researching of this book. These include the Bibliothèque Nationale–François Mitterrand and the Bibliothèque du Film at the Cinémathèque in Paris, the Reuben Library of the British Film Institute, the British Library, the University College London Library, and the University of London Library. I would also like to express my gratitude to my institution, University College London, for providing support over the years, including a sabbatical that finally enabled me to finish the book.

I am most grateful for their help to Norman Hirschy, executive editor at Oxford University Press, and Zara Cannon-Mohammed, the book's editor. Leigh Priest prepared the index with her usual skill and accuracy.

An early version of part of chapter 6 was published in Iwan Morgan and Philip John Davies, eds., *Hollywood and the Great Depression: American Film, Politics and Society in the 1930s* (Edinburgh University Press, 2016). It has been extensively rewritten and expanded and appears here with the kind permission of the editors. An early version of part of chapter 7 was published in Christof Decker and Astrid Böger, eds., *Transnational Mediations: Negotiating Popular Culture Between Europe and the United States* (Universitätsverlag Winter, 2015). It too has been considerably expanded and rewritten and appears here by kind permission of the editors.

Finally, I owe more than I can ever repay to Nahed and Sarah. This book is dedicated to them.

Introduction

In February 1916, English music-hall performer turned movie actor Charles Chaplin left Los Angeles for New York to join his brother Sydney. In his autobiography, Chaplin claimed that it was on this five-day rail journey that he first became conscious of his new and overwhelming popularity. Arriving in Amarillo, Texas, at seven in the evening, he was greeted by the town's mayor and a large, enthusiastic crowd. The telegram Chaplin had sent Sydney providing details of his journey had been leaked to the press by telegraph operators: people stood alongside the railroad tracks at many points of the trip, and there were enthusiastic crowds waiting at the stations in Kansas City and Chicago. Spending the night in Chicago, Chaplin received a telegram from the chief of police in New York asking him to get off his train at 125th Street rather than Grand Central Station, where large crowds were already beginning to assemble. In his autobiography, published almost half a century later, Chaplin claimed he had been very ambivalent over this sudden fame: he had, he recalled, "wanted to enjoy it all without reservation" but "kept thinking the world had gone crazy! If a few slapstick comedies could arouse such excitement, was there not something bogus about all celebrity?"[1]

It is unlikely, whatever he later wrote, that Chaplin felt such a degree of ambivalence at the time. Moreover, in another passage of his autobiography, he contradicted the assertion that he had realized his immense popularity only during his 1916 trip to New York. The First World War had begun in August 1914. Around this time, Chaplin noted, he had asked Mack Sennett to raise his salary at the Keystone Film Company to one thousand dollars a week. When Sennett objected that this was more than he himself earned, Chaplin recalled telling him, "the public doesn't line up outside the box office when your name appears as they do for mine."[2] But it was only after he moved to the Essanay Studio in January 1915 that there occurred what David Robinson calls "the great Chaplin explosion."[3] Journalist Charles J. McGuirk agreed. Once Chaplin arrived to work at the Essanay Studio in Chicago, he wrote in the second of a two-part profile titled "Chaplinitis" in the summer of 1915, "the world went mad. From New York to San Francisco, from Maine to

Charlot. Melvyn Stokes, Oxford University Press. © Oxford University Press 2026.
DOI: 10.1093/9780197839294.003.0001

California, came the staccato tapping of the telegraph key. 'Who is this man Chaplin? What are his ambitions? What's his theory of humor? Is he married, or single? How does he like American life? Does he eat eggs for breakfast? Is he conceited?' The newspapers wanted to know; the country had risen and demanded information."[4]

The growing links between the press and cinema expressed themselves in ways involving other motion picture actors. Mary Pickford, for example, had a daily syndicated column in many newspapers in 1915.[5] What distinguished "Chaplinitis" was its scale and reach. Newspapers and magazines responded to the apparently insatiable interest in Chaplin with a plethora of articles and stories. "A poet," McGuirk remarked, "can always sell a Chaplin poem; a writer finds a market for a Chaplin story."[6] Many newspapers published cartoons and comic strips inspired by his screen character. Encouraged by public fascination with the films, "Chaplinitis" spread way beyond the media. There were Chaplin songs: Lupino Lane sang "The Charlie Chaplin Walk" in a revue. There were Chaplin dances (McGuirk mentioned that "a Chaplin chorus of show-girls, each one costumed a la Chaplin, was the latest hit on Broadway"). There were Chaplin imitators, both legitimate (Bob Hope won a Chaplin look-alike contest in Cleveland, Ohio) and illegitimate (Billy Ritchie and other film and stage actors shamelessly appropriated Chaplin's screen persona for themselves). In June 1915, *Motion Picture Magazine* reported that the popularity of Chaplin-style mustaches was increasing. Business was quick to exploit this Chaplin craze: one British observer noted that there were "Chaplin ties, Chaplin shirts, Chaplin cocktails, Chaplin yachts." There were also Chaplin postcards, dolls, and toys. (One manufacturer offered a "Charlie Chaplin Squirt Ring" for fifteen cents.)[7]

Chaplin's fame was all the more remarkable because crediting or "naming" film actors was itself only a very recent development in American cinema. The earliest motion pictures in the United States formed part of what Tom Gunning has called the "cinema of attractions": they focused on showing what film could record and reveal.[8] They were principally documentaries, travelogues, newsreels, reproductions of sporting events, and "trick" films using camera angles and editing to create illusory effects.[9] Even when they endeavored to tell a narrative story, the camera would usually be fixed at some distance from the performers, making it hard to identify actors from shots of their whole bodies.[10] With no screen credits to identify them or the characters they played, most early screen actors remained anonymous.[11] This situation began to change for two reasons. The establishment of the first storefront movie theater, or "nickelodeon," in Pittsburgh in 1905 gave American cinema for the first time its own exhibition venue. Thousands of other nickelodeons opened in the years that followed.[12] To keep pace with the vastly increased demand for films (nickelodeons changed their programs on a frequent, sometimes daily basis) movie production became more and more industrialized. Film acting, hitherto casual work performed either by amateurs or by stage actors in search of temporary employment, became a more regular occupation. Several production companies developed their own corps of actors who appeared repeatedly in their films.[13] The second reason was the almost simultaneous move away from the "cinema of attractions" toward making films that foregrounded narrative, whether in the form of comedy or drama.[14]

For most of the twentieth century, there was a large measure of agreement among film writers over how movie actors in the United States first came to be named, the first step toward the creation of stars. The change was seen as the consequence of an economic struggle for control of the new motion picture industry. The Motion Picture Patents Company (MPPC) had been formed in 1908 when a number of companies, including Edison and Biograph, pooled their patents in order to try to dominate movie production. They were resisted by independent companies such as Carl Laemmle's Independent Motion Picture Corporation (IMP). The members of the MPPC preferred to identify their principal actors as corporate products (the "Biograph Girl/Boy"). They believed that naming individual actors would encourage them to demand higher salaries. In 1910, however, Laemmle persuaded the current "Biograph Girl," Florence Lawrence, to join IMP in return for named credits and a higher salary. He publicized this coup in March 1910 in an ad in the cinema trade journal *Moving Picture World* that denied a report supposedly circulating in St. Louis that Lawrence had been killed in a streetcar accident. Lawrence—allegedly the first film actor to be named—was not only "whole and sound," the ad claimed, but she had moved from Biograph to IMP and the release of her first film for her new studio was imminent. In the wake of this publicity coup, members of the MPPC—with Biograph as the slowest to react—also began to publicize their own "stars."[15]

Much of this story has now been exposed as fiction. Members of the MPPC had started to publicize the names of their actors before Lawrence's defection (which had actually taken place six months earlier).[16] There was evidence that moviegoers, encouraged by the fact that certain actors were now appearing regularly in films—as well as by changing conventions in filming that made them more recognizable through medium and close-up shots[17]—were beginning to show greater interest in them. The first magazine for movie fans, *Motion Picture Story Magazine*, appeared in February 1911 and was followed by *Photoplay* in 1912.[18] Newspapers and magazines were covering movie actors more and more. The first press books (publicity guides for exhibitors) appeared in 1913.[19] Yet the film star in the modern sense had not fully emerged. This, Richard deCordova argued, reflected the limited discourse surrounding movie actors. In essence, they were "picture personalities," defined only in terms of the roles they played on the screen and the publicity for these films. Newspapers, periodicals, and fan magazines limited their coverage to screen personas, avoiding any coverage of private lives.[20] "Information as to matrimonial alliances and other purely personal matters will not be answered," *Photoplay* primly informed its readers in March 1912.[21] It was only when restrictions of this kind were abandoned, deCordova maintained, and publicity began to concentrate on the *private* lives of film actors rather than their on-screen characters, that real stars finally appeared. During 1913, coverage of this variety began to grow.[22] Chaplin's arrival in Los Angeles in December 1913 and the shooting of his first Keystone film at the end of January 1914 were perfectly timed to help make him one of the first true stars of American cinema.

The Chaplin craze of 1915 emerged while the actor was shooting films for his new studio, Essanay. The thirty-six films he made for Keystone between January and November 1914 introduced the figure of the Little Tramp to the screen and laid the foundations of Chaplin's reputation. Of the twelve films he made for Essanay in 1915, only the last (*A Night at the Show*) did not feature Chaplin in his Tramp persona, which had rapidly become iconic. Other stars emerged at roughly the same time and developed their own screen characters: Mary Pickford, for example, often described as "Little Mary" after initially being identified in this way through an intertitle in D. W. Griffith's *The Little Teacher* (Biograph, 1909), was hailed by film writer Benjamin Hampton (1931) as the first star.[23] But Chaplin was an auteur as well as an actor: from the release of *Twenty Minutes of Love* in May 1914 he directed most of the Keystone movies in which he appeared and all of his Essanay films.[24]

Fans' enthusiasm for Chaplin's films and curiosity about the man himself prompted a virtual feeding frenzy in the media, as newspaper reporters, magazine writers, and cinema trade press commentators publicized Chaplin's background and private life as well as his movies. But, as already noted, Chaplin's cultural influence spread far beyond the media. He was perceived as a celebrity as well as an actor. Businesses hastened to cash in on his fame, commodifying his screen persona. Whatever the claims of other stars, Richard Koszarski argues that Chaplin dominated the period from 1915 to 1928 "as both a creative force within the industry and a cultural icon of unparalleled visibility."[25]

Chaplin's stardom, of course, would last much longer than this. While he would make his final appearance as the non-talking Little Tramp in *Modern Times* (1936)—the only major star of American cinema to resist for so long the advent of the talkies—he would continue playing a principal character in films until the 1950s. "Because stardom depends on winning and maintaining the good graces of an audience," observes Charles J. Maland, "and because public taste and cultural values shift over time, nearly every star's career is a story of his or her rise and fall. Chaplin's career is no exception."[26] Maland's own work (1989) on Chaplin's evolving star image followed on from Richard Dyer's pioneering book *Stars*, originally published in 1979. Grounded in both British cultural studies and the structuralist approach adopted by Christian Metz and others in France, Dyer argued that stardom could be explored from two perspectives that were separate but related: "the sociological and the semiotic." The sociological approach focused on stars "as a remarkable, and probably influential or symptomatic, social phenomenon, as well as being an aspect of film's 'industrial' nature." The semiotic approach emphasized that stars' images are collections of signs that are themselves constructed "across a range of media texts" that include promotion, publicity, and criticism/commentaries as well as films themselves. The two approaches "are mutually interdependent": sociological analysis is possible only through engagement with how stars are created across media texts, while semiotic inquiry needs to acknowledge that "all texts are social facts," formed in specific historical circumstances.[27] A second influence on Maland's study of Chaplin's star image was the literary reception theory advanced by Hans Robert Jauss. To Jauss, literary work derived meaning only to the extent that successive audiences responded to it. Such responses were heavily conditioned by the "horizon of expectations" of the audience concerned (itself much influenced by changing social, political, and aesthetic factors), the current reactions of critics and commentators, and the impact of the general reception of earlier work on what comes later. To Maland, Jauss's ideas on literature were equally applicable to the changing reception of Chaplin's films.[28]

Chaplin's star image in the United States, according to Maland, was made up "of the changing qualities and traits associated with Charles Spencer Chaplin and the changing qualities and traits associated with the characters Chaplin played in his films, particularly his Charlie [Little Tramp] persona." It was constructed and reconstructed through the interplay of three factors. First, the ways in which Chaplin contributed to that image "through his actions, words, and films." Second, the influence wielded by "reviewers, press publicists, editorialists, moralists and censorship groups, government agencies, and intellectuals." Third, broader historical developments in the United States, including those internal to Hollywood (such as the conversion to sound) and "external political and social events," including the 1930s Depression and the Cold War. These developments not only had their impact on Chaplin personally but also shaped the critical discourse surrounding him and his work.[29]

The first film persona displayed by Chaplin, Maland argues, "was often mean, crude, and brutish."[30] It could be disruptive, even violent, and was attacked for its "vulgarity" by elitist spokesmen for the genteel tradition in American culture.[31] Aware of these criticisms, and determined not to alienate the growing middle-class audience for the movies, Chaplin responded by refining his screen persona. The Little Tramp soon attracted sympathy for the pathos of his failed romances and the resilience with which he coped with constant disappointment.[32] The favorable attention Chaplin received from critics and the growing support he attracted from American intellectuals helped to some extent to insulate his star image from resentment surrounding his increasingly high salaries.[33] In spite of poor reviews for the two films he released in 1919—*Sunnyside* and *A Day's Pleasure*—and the publicity surrounding his divorce from his first wife, Mildred Harris, in 1920, there was sufficient support in the press and among intellectuals for Chaplin's star image to remain high as the 1920s began.[34] The new decade saw Chaplin return to form as a filmmaker with a series of movies beginning with *The Kid* (1921).[35] *A Woman of Paris* (1923), in which he assumed only a minor acting role, increased his reputation as a serious film director.[36] Through his own writings, dealings with the press, and increasing personal interaction with young intellectuals, Chaplin helped safeguard his star image as a serious artist in a category of his own.[37] After the critical and commercial success of *The Gold Rush* (1925), however, that image was challenged by a series of factors, including the allegations over his sexual demands made by Chaplin's second wife, Lillita Louise McMurray (better known under her stage name of Lita Grey), in her divorce complaint of 1927, major tax problems, the aesthetic issues created by the coming of sound, and the impact after 1929 of the economic depression.[38]

The issues raised over this second divorce, which reflected the deep cultural divisions in the United States during the 1920s, posed the most crucial threat to Chaplin's star image.[39] Yet he was supported by defenders in the press and cinema trade magazines, as well as by artists and intellectuals, and in the end his reputation suffered "surprisingly little" damage.[40] By the late 1920s, Maland points out, Chaplin had created an "aesthetic contract" with his audiences: he promised them a consistent pantomimic central character, as well as "romance tinged with pathos, inventive humor, and some serious themes or concerns."[41] The last of these characteristics was about to become much more important.

Chaplin's world tour of 1931–32, Maland suggests, prompted his first serious engagement with the Depression and the political issues it had raised.[42] His next film, *Modern Times*, created controversy for its critique of Depression-era economic, social, and political conditions. With its release, Chaplin's own star image became "inextricably associated in the public mind with politics."[43] Increasingly ambitious to comment on economic, social, and political issues, he would abandon the figure of the Little Tramp and finally embrace talking films.[44] *The Great Dictator* (1940) was a satirical attack on fascism. It stretched Chaplin's "aesthetic contract" with his audience considerably: the silent, pantomimic figure of his films up to *Modern Times* had gone, and the romance and pathos that formed a major part of his star image had sharply diminished.[45]

With the success of *The Great Dictator*, Chaplin's career reached a peak. He was invited to recite his final speech from the film at a gala in Washington on the eve of President Franklin D. Roosevelt's third inauguration in January 1941.[46] After this, it was mainly downhill. During the Second World War, he became not simply antifascist but also pro-USSR, campaigning for aid to Russia and the opening of a "second front" in Europe.[47] In personal terms, the wartime years were disastrous for Chaplin: he became sexually involved with a young woman, Joan Barry, who subsequently filed a paternity suit against him. After the intervention of the FBI, Chaplin was also charged with violating the Mann Act (1910) by paying to transport Barry across state lines for "immoral purposes." In April 1944, he was found not guilty of contravening the Mann Act. At a second paternity trial in April 1945 (the first resulted in no verdict), the jury decided in favor of Barry. The press covered the three trials in lurid detail, and Chaplin's star image suffered considerably as a result.[48]

In 1947, *Monsieur Verdoux* was released, offering a fictionalized take on the life of a French mass-murderer. As well as attempting to make a comedy based on a Bluebeard theme, the movie offered "a progressive critique of capitalism." This film, Maland argues, violated the aesthetic contract sustaining Chaplin's stardom. Together with the negative publicity from the Barry affair, it alienated much of the American audience that had worshiped him as a star.[49] Worse was to come. Chaplin continued to defend left-wing individuals and causes, making him particularly vulnerable in the early stages of the Cold War. He was attacked as a communist fellow-traveler in some parts of the American press and subpoenaed to appear before the House Committee on Un-American Activities (HUAC). Although ultimately never called by HUAC to give testimony, Chaplin was criticized by politicians for his left-wing views, his reputation as a seducer of young American women, and his status as an alien who had never acquired American citizenship.[50]

Under constant attack—and investigated by the FBI, the Internal Revenue Service, and the Immigration and Naturalization Service[51]—Chaplin tried to row back from his support for left-wing causes, reminded his fans of the Little Tramp by rereleasing *City Lights* (1931), and returned to his vaudeville roots by incorporating autobiographical elements into his new film, *Limelight* (1952).[52] All to no avail. In September 1952, in mid-Atlantic on his way to attend the premières of *Limelight* in Europe, his permit to reenter the United States was revoked by Attorney General James McGranery on the grounds of "moral turpitude."[53] Chaplin, a fallen Hollywood star, would spend the rest of his life as an exile in Europe, although he would ultimately experience what Maland terms a "guarded restoration," making a brief return visit to the United States in 1972 to receive an honorary Oscar.[54]

As a study of the development of Chaplin's star image, Maland's book is a classic. Yet its analysis is confined to the United States.[55] Chaplin was a star in countries all over the world. The beginning of his career was well-timed to profit from the growing success of the American film industry. In the early days of the nickelodeons, most motion pictures seen in the United States came from Europe, especially France, with the Pathé company dominating the American movie market. By September 1910, when Chaplin sailed from Britain to the United States for the first time as part of Fred Karno's traveling company of music-hall entertainers, that dominance had been undercut through a combination of aggressive business tactics on the part of the Thomas Edison–created MPPC and a growing nationalistic discourse from American reformers that tagged French films as "alien" and "foreign." By January 1914, when Chaplin began making films for Keystone Studios, imported films had been to a considerable degree excluded from the American market.[56] Seven months later, World War I broke out, crippling production in European studios. In the immediate months and years that followed, American productions established hegemony over the European and world movie market that would endure, at least in peacetime, until today. Chaplin and other actors who would play a crucial role in the initial expansion of the American movie industry abroad—including Pearl White, Mary Pickford, Douglas Fairbanks, William S. Hart, and Sessue Hayakawa—were all international as well as American stars.

After his performance in *The Cheat* (1915), Sessue Hayakawa was hailed by French writer Colette as a "genius." (French film critic Louis Delluc bracketed Hayakawa with Chaplin as the "two masterpieces" of American cinema.)[57] A reporter who visited Pearl White's home in 1920 was impressed by the broad transnational nature of her fan mail. "I had never seen such an enormous, worldwide representation of attention," he wrote. "There were letters bearing the stamps of countries I had never heard of."[58] In the 1910s, comments David Robinson, "the public of the entire world had elevated Charles Chaplin to a status and idolatry no artist in any medium had ever known before."[59] By 1924, it was estimated that Chaplin's *The Kid* (1921) had played in fifty countries around the world. "Have you ever calculated by how many people you are loved?" demanded Hungarian film writer Béla Balázs in an open letter to Chaplin in 1927. "If you take, very modestly, only half of the movie audiences in all the countries where your films have produced laughter and tears, you'll probably reach well over half a billion."[60] Chaplin's huge foreign audience—which meant that his films commonly grossed more abroad than in the United States—also impacted his filmmaking, since one of his reasons for resisting dialogue for so long was that speaking English could alienate non-English-speaking moviegoers.[61]

Scholarly studies into the reception of "American" stars[62]—and the development of their star images—abroad are a relatively recent development. In 1989, Helen Taylor studied the ways in which British as well as American fans identified with and created meanings from the character of Scarlett O'Hara (Vivien Leigh) in *Gone With the Wind* (1939). In 1994, Jackie Stacey analyzed the role of Hollywood's female stars in how British women remembered the 1940s and 1950s, and in 2002 Annette Kuhn published her investigations into British cultural memory of 1930s moviegoing (including memories of favorite American stars).[63] In 2007, Daisuke Miyao wrote about the "international stardom" of Sessue Hayakawa, locating that stardom in relation to the response of spectators and critics in Europe and Japan as well as the United States.[64] During the 2010s, as "transnationalism" became an increasingly salient way of approaching the study of history, a number of film scholars began to adopt this approach in their work on stardom. In 2013, for example, Russell Meeuf published a book on the ways in which John Wayne's construction of masculinity in his films made him popular across much of the world and (with Raphael Raphael) an edited book of essays analyzing transnational stardom in which most of the film and media stars under discussion came originally from outside the United States.[65]

While Charlie Chaplin was hugely popular across much of the world, there are relatively few studies of his stardom outside the United States. C. Brian Morris, for example, has analyzed Chaplin's critics and supporters in Spain in the two decades before the outbreak of the civil war, and David Selbourne has written about the left-wing tributes to Chaplin organized by Indians in Calcutta after the news of his death in December 1977.[66] But the only country apart from the United States in which historians have so far written extensively about his reception and stardom is Germany. Sabine Hake and Joseph Garncarz have debated the extent of Chaplin's popularity among intellectuals and different social classes in Weimar Germany.[67] And in 2011, Norbert Aping produced a well-researched book in German that would be republished in 2024 in English as *Charlie Chaplin and the Nazis: The Long German Campaign Against the Artist.*[68]

As a result of the First World War and the collapse of the German Empire, Aping notes, it was not until August 1921 that the first Chaplin film (*The Rink,* 1916) arrived in the cinemas of what was now the Weimar Republic. It and subsequent films proved wildly popular with German audiences, and, as earlier in the United States, a media storm emerged focusing on Chaplin himself, together with associated merchandising and, inevitably, Chaplin impersonators.[69] But, as Aping shows, there were also dissenting voices. Nationalists criticized the release in November 1921 of Chaplin's antiwar movie *Shoulder Arms* (1918), accusing it of smearing the German army and calling (unsuccessfully) for a boycott of all Chaplin films.[70] In 1926, when *The Gold Rush* (1925) arrived in Germany, it received many enthusiastic reviews and demonstrated popularity with cinemagoers generally by doing extremely well at the box office, but it was attacked by sympathizers of the new Nazi Party (founded in 1920) for Chaplin's supposed Jewish roots and his on-screen image as a social misfit. Yet, as Aping points out, the Nazi Party was still only one faction in 1926—and it did little to challenge the success of Chaplin's next film, *The Circus*, when it arrived in Germany in 1928.[71]

By contrast, in the years that followed, Nazis would become increasingly strident in their criticism.[72] When Chaplin himself visited Berlin in 1931, Nazi propaganda journals attacked him "on a massive scale," and Nazis may also have been involved in street demonstrations against him.[73] While Aping could find no evidence for allegations made by one of the local German distributors of *City Lights* (1931) that the Nazis disrupted screenings of the film and were responsible for bankrupting the company that distributed it, it is still the case that the Nazi press was very critical of Chaplin and his new film.[74] Two years later, at the end of January 1933, Adolf Hitler became German chancellor, and from May of that year, according to Aping, "no more public screenings of Chaplin films . . . could be traced" in Germany until after the demise of the Third Reich in 1945.[75] This did not, however, end Nazi attempts to undermine Chaplin's later films. There were German attempts to suggest that *Modern Times* had been a failure at its first performance in Paris. A similar tactic was employed against *The Great Dictator* (1940), coupled this time with suggestions that Chaplin had abandoned making the film and attempts by the Nazi government through diplomacy and putting pressure on Hollywood itself to try to prevent his satire on Hitler from being released.[76] It was only after the Second World War, Aping writes, that Chaplin finally "regained [in what was now a geographically divided Germany] the artistic recognition that had been widely paid to him during the Weimar Republic."[77]

Studying the evolution of the star image of American stars in other countries puts into perspective the images of those stars within the United States. It underlines the fact that what might seem natural and universal is often merely local and contingent. Cinemagoers, critical communities, commentators, and intellectuals construct and reconstruct star images in the light of their own social, cultural, and political identities and the historical circumstances in which they find themselves. Since these contexts within which meaning is created vary from nation to nation, star images reflect such differences. Other nations appropriated American stars, taking advantage of what Richard Dyer famously termed their "structured polysemy" to reinscribe them into their own society and culture.[78] If not every appropriation was as extreme as that carried out in the 1930s by Turkish exhibitors who reconstructed the Marx Brothers as "Three Buddies" living in Istanbul,[79] American stars were reinterpreted by members of other nations in ways that made them more representative of their own societies and cultures—and of the tensions and contradictions that characterized them.

This book explores the development of Chaplin's star image in France from the arrival of his first films there in March 1915 until the tributes paid to him at the Cannes Film Festival in May 1971, at the start of his eighty-third year, and his visit to Henri Langlois's Cinémathèque in Paris in September 1973.[80] There are five major reasons for choosing to study Chaplin and France. First, he was hugely popular with French moviegoers. Commenting from Europe in early 1917, American writer Harvey O'Higgins observed, "Chaplin is as preeminent a favorite in Paris... as he is here."[81] During a 1921 visit to the French capital, noted the novelist and critic Waldo Frank, he was mobbed by enthusiastic fans. A decade later, en route to Paris by train from Venice, French police—like their predecessors in New York fifteen years earlier—asked Chaplin to get off the train early to avoid the vast crowds that were waiting to greet him. (He refused.)[82] As time passed, enthusiasm for Chaplin and his films showed little sign of diminishing. *The Great Dictator* (1940), released as *Le Dictateur* in France in 1945, proved popular with French audiences. *Monsieur Verdoux* and *Limelight* (*Les feux de la rampe*, 1952), films that failed financially in the United States, proved much more successful in France.[83] So great was Chaplin's popularity in France over the years, indeed, that there would be persistent rumors that he had been born in the country, either in Fontainebleau, to the southeast of Paris, or in nearby Melun. At the height of the Cold War furor over Chaplin's political loyalties, after he had been refused permission to return to the United States, both MI5 and MI6, Britain's domestic and foreign intelligence services, were asked by the American authorities to investigate this possibility but could find no real evidence that Chaplin was born in France.[84]

The second reason was the glittering array of French intellectual and cultural talent who wrote seriously about Chaplin. A very partial list of those involved would include Colette, Jean Cocteau, Louis Delluc, Louis Aragon, Élie Faure, Philippe Soupault, Jean-Paul Sartre, Jean Epstein, René Clair, André Maurois, Jean Prévost, Jean Renoir, André Bazin, and Jean Mitry. These intellectuals, commentators, and cinéastes helped Chaplin secure and maintain an international reputation as an artist of the first rank. In 1921, for example, Delluc published the first book-length study of Chaplin's work in any language.[85] Together they created an evolving image of Chaplin as a star that was significantly different at many points from that in the United States. Their appreciation of Chaplin was all the more remarkable because—unlike many American commentators and intellectuals whom Chaplin consciously cultivated—few of them knew him personally. The main problem was language. Chaplin spoke no French, at least until he moved to Switzerland in 1952, and few French writers and artists spoke English.[86] Chaplin's relationship with French writer and polymath Jean Cocteau is a case in point. In 1936, shortly after the American première of *Modern Times*, Chaplin sailed for a vacation in the Far East. Cocteau was a passenger on the same ship and the two met on board. "I do not speak English; Chaplin does not speak French," Cocteau later recalled. "Yet we talked without the slightest difficulty." Chaplin remembered it differently; according to him, Cocteau's "secretary" (his Moroccan lover Marcel Khill) "acted as interpreter for us." Although their first conversation lasted until four in the morning, neither Cocteau nor Chaplin was keen to repeat the experience and, Chaplin claimed in his autobiography, the two men spent much of the rest of the return voyage avoiding each other.[87] On this occasion, Chaplin's recollection has a ring of truth. The few relationships he sustained for long periods with French people were with intellectuals, notably Louis Aragon, who spoke some English, or cinéastes, such as Robert Florey, who had lived for many years in the United States.[88]

The third reason is that the evolution of Chaplin's star image in France casts much light on how cinema was understood and theorized in France. It also offers considerable insight into the more general social, cultural, and political history of France. In the 1920s, Chaplin was cited by various writers and commentators on cinema as exemplifying new concepts such as *photogénie* and *cineplastics*, as a major factor in the emergence of surrealism, and as a symbol of the superiority of cinema over the live stage. With the advent of the "talkies"—which arrived later in France than in the United States[89]—he became a crucial figure for those, including Marcel Pagnol and René Clair, who argued over the aesthetic impact of the coming of sound. Later in the 1930s, he was compared to French directors such as Jean Renoir for his social realism. In terms of French history in general, Chaplin's visits to Paris in 1921 and 1931 prompted much discussion and debate on the new phenomenon of "celebrity" culture. His 1921 visit saw right-wing and left-wing journalists clashing over whether he agreed or disagreed with their respective views of the Bolshevik Revolution of 1917. While the political message of Chaplin's film *Modern Times* was confused, its reception and distribution in France coincided with—and illuminated—the left-wing surge that led to widespread industrial action and the election of a Popular Front government made up of socialists and radicals. Aspects of French anti-Americanism became evident through the surrealists' critique of the puritanism and conservative moralism of Chaplin's American critics at the time of his divorce from Lita Grey in 1927 and the efforts of French writers and intellectuals to defend him from attacks by U.S. anticommunists between 1947 and 1952.

The fourth reason is the wealth of the sources available. By the early 1920s, France had already developed a very rich film culture, based on cinemas and ciné-clubs, but also spreading across the print media. Specialist film journals existed, including *Ciné-Journal*, *La Cinématographie française*, *Cinéopse*, *Filma*, and *Le Courrier cinématographique* for the movie industry, *Le Film*, *Ciné-pour-tous*, *Cinéa*, and *Cinémagazine* for film enthusiasts and the general public.[90] Newspapers such as *Le Petit Journal*, *Le Matin*, *Le Temps*, *Le Journal*, *L'Intransigeant*, *Le Figaro*, *L'Humanité*, *Paris-Midi*, *Le Gaulois*, *Paris-Soir*, and *L'Echo de Paris* and the arts daily *Comoedia* published reviews and covered the lives of stars. A number of literary and art journals—*SIC*, *Nord-Sud*, *Le Crapouillot*, *Littérature*—and the satirical magazine *Le Canard enchaîné* also published reviews. Fan magazines appeared in the 1920s and 1930s—first *Ciné-Miroir* and *Mon-Ciné*, later *Cinémonde* and *Pour Vous*. Over time, most of these publications disappeared—including many newspapers during World War II. They were replaced by others—film periodicals *Les Cahiers du cinéma* and *Positif*, newspapers *Le Monde* and *Combat*. All of these publications published reviews of Chaplin's films and news about him and his life.

The fifth reason is the evidence that Chaplin himself was affected by a number of French influences. Clearly, at some point—perhaps during his 1909 or 1912 visits to France or, more likely, after his first arrival in the United States in the fall of 1910—he became aware of the work of French comedian Max Linder. Linder had made four hundred films for Pathé by 1914; in 1911, he secured (as Chaplin did later) the right to direct his own pictures. His comedies probably influenced Chaplin's own style of filmmaking. "Did they," writes Chaplin biographer Kenneth S. Lynn, "cause him to realize that the motion picture camera had not only enlarged the playing field of a slam-bang humor of incident, but could also enormously enhance a humor based on character? Did the gentlemanly deliberateness, for instance, with which Max removed his gloves, finger by finger, before popping an adversary on the nose teach Chaplin something about the ways in which a gentlemanly tramp might conduct himself?" To Lynn, the answer to both questions was clearly positive.[91] Chaplin himself seems to have accepted that Linder had an impact on his work. Famously, on May 12, 1917, he gave Linder (who had arrived in Hollywood in 1916) a photograph of himself with the dedication "To the one and only Max—The Professor—from his Disciple Charlie Chaplin."[92]

During his 1921 visit to Paris, Chaplin met Henri Letellier, a publisher and man-about-town whom he later used as the model for Pierre Revel in *A Woman of Paris* (*L'Opinion Publique*, 1923). The shots of the factory production lines in *Modern Times* (*Les Temps modernes*) drew much of their inspiration from René Clair's *À Nous la liberté* (1931). The nonsense song sung by Chaplin in *Modern Times*, as several French observers noted, was set to the music of a song that had been very popular in France: "Je cherche après Titine."[93] *Monsieur Verdoux*, of course, was loosely based on the career of French serial killer Henri Landru (1869–1922).[94]

The book that follows is divided into eight broadly chronological chapters. Chapter 1 shows how French moviegoers, critics, and intellectuals assimilated Chaplin into their own culture between 1915 and 1921. Chaplin was originally appropriated for French audiences by the decision taken in March 1915 by the distributor of his films, Jacques Haïk, to identify him in publicity and film titles as "Charlot" (Little Charlie). His films, moreover, often included French subtitles. Initially, he appealed to working-class and petit-bourgeois audiences in the cities where most French cinemas were located. But he also quickly won the support of pioneering film critics such as Louis Delluc. At various points during the First World War, Chaplin's star image was imperiled by carping in the press over his failure to fight on the Allied side and his wealth. Yet by 1918 he was beginning to attract strong support from the literary and intellectual avant-garde: Louis Aragon published his first poem under the title "Charlot sentimental" and Jean Cocteau hailed Chaplin as "our modern Guignol . . . [who] speaks to every age, every nation."[95]

Chapter 2 analyzes the impact of Chaplin's two brief visits to Paris in 1921. As already noted, so great was his popularity that journalists vied with each other to appropriate him as a supporter of their political standpoint. At the same time, there was considerable debate in the press over Chaplin's treatment as a "celebrity." Some regarded the idolization of a man who was only a screen comic as a sign of decadence; others placed it in the context of the high cultural value traditionally accorded actors in the live theater. While his French fans by this time seem to have been drawn from a broad cross-section of society, it was his appearance and the showing of *The Kid* (*Le Gosse*,

1921) at a charity gala to aid the recovery of the regions of eastern France devastated by war that first won him the support of sections of the French social and political elite.

The 1920s was the period in which Chaplin reached what was probably the peak of his popularity in the United States but also, as Maland notes, suffered the first major threats to his stardom.[96] The next two chapters analyze his evolving star image in France during these years. Chapter 3 begins with growing acclaim from French critics and increasing enthusiasm on the part of many intellectuals. Critic and filmmaker Louis Delluc, in his pioneering 1921 book on Chaplin and his work, presented him as an artistic innovator on a par with giants such as Beethoven in music, Shakespeare in the theater, and Velázquez in painting. This chapter will also suggest how the four longer movies made by Chaplin during the 1920s—*A Woman of Paris* (released in France as *L'Opinion publique*), *The Pilgrim* (*Le pèlerin*), *The Gold Rush* (*La Ruée vers l'or*), and *The Circus* (*Le Cirque*)—helped further enhance his reputation among French writers and critics.[97] Yet Chaplin's supporters in France also had to defend him against vigorous attacks in 1926–27 from writer-poet André Suarès, who accused him of too much cloying sentimentality and dismissed the idea that silent cinema in general could be seen as a new art form.

Chapter 4 begins with an analysis of what happened in the wake of the sensational sexual allegations made against Chaplin in Lita Grey's divorce complaint of 1927. While Chaplin was much criticized in America, he received strong support from intellectuals in France. "Hands Off Love," a manifesto written by Louis Aragon and signed by thirty-one surrealists (all of them male), defended Chaplin's right to sexual emancipation against the confining restraints of conventional marriage. This chapter discusses Chaplin's relationship with surrealism both before and after "Hands Off Love." It suggests that his films were a formative influence on the birth of both surrealism and its predecessor, Dadaism. By 1927, however, surrealism itself was being torn apart by political disputes, and as a collaborative movement—as opposed to an enduring cultural influence—it soon largely disappeared. Chaplin himself would be an unwitting observer of what might be seen as its last rites: at a press conference in Paris in October 1952, a group of international lettrists-situationists launched a protest attacking both Chaplin and surrealism as *passé*.

Chapter 5 analyzes Chaplin's visits to France in 1931—the first time he spent considerable time there. In contrast to his low-key arrival ten years earlier, a large and enthusiastic crowd of fans greeted him at the Gare de

Lyon. Far more than in 1921, he was welcomed by the French political establishment. He had lunch with Minister for Foreign Affairs Aristide Briand at the foreign office (newspapers noted that the crowd waiting to greet him there was the biggest since the Paris peace negotiations of 1919) and returned to the Quai d'Orsay a few days later to receive the Légion d'honneur. While this award was not without controversy, it confirmed Chaplin's acceptance by the political elite. His 1931 visit to France also demonstrated that—as perhaps the most famous film star in the world—he was much sought after by members of the international social elite. But while Chaplin was fêted politically and socially, the reception of his new film was more equivocal. *City Lights* had only a short run in Paris, and French reviewers in general were more critical of it than of earlier Charlot films. Chaplin, as always, had his defenders. But the reception of his latest film in France was also heavily influenced by an awareness of the arrival of the "talkies" and the sense on the part of many critics that the days of silent cinema—even that of Charlot— were numbered.

Chapter 6 deals with the response in France to the growing politicization of Chaplin's star image during the 1930s and early 1940s. French critics were aware that a number of American reviewers had attacked *Modern Times* for disseminating left-wing propaganda. In the main, however, French reviewers preferred to criticize it on aesthetic or structural grounds (Chaplin's continuing resistance to the spoken word, the episodic nature of the film) rather than for its political content. What gave *Modern Times* real resonance in France was its exposé of factory conditions; the movie was the sixth best performer at the French box office in 1936, and cinema trade press reports of its profits suggest that it was particularly successful in large, strike-hit industrial cities. Chaplin's next film, *The Great Dictator*, was in essence a satire on fascist leaders with its portrayal of Hynkel (Hitler) and Napaloni (Mussolini). Because of the French surrender in June 1940 and the German occupation, it would not be screened in France until early April 1945. By this time, the war in Europe was approaching its end—Hitler committed suicide on April 30, 1945, two days after Mussolini was killed by Italian partisans. French spectators, even if they found the combination of farce and political messaging at times confusing, demonstrated their continued enthusiasm for Chaplin by making *The Great Dictator* by far the most popular film released in France in 1945.

Chapter 7 analyzes French attitudes to Chaplin in the early postwar period. Chaplin's star image had declined in America during the war, in part because of scandal in his private life (the Joan Barry affair) and in part because his campaigning for a "second front" to help Russia had led to accusations of communist sympathies. When his next film, *Monsieur Verdoux*, was premièred in the United States in April 1947, it offended many critics with its anticapitalist critique. Chaplin himself came under increasing attack by American anticommunists during these early days of the Cold War. The controversy this generated, together with poor publicity for the film itself and the fact that, in *Monsieur Verdoux*, Chaplin was playing a character very far from the appealing persona of the Little Tramp, helped ensure the failure of the movie at the U.S. box office. Its French reception, however, proved very different.

The war and German occupation had cut the French off from news of developments in the United States, and most people were unaware of the effects of the Joan Barry affair on Chaplin's U.S. reputation. Nor were they generally as concerned over the domestic communist threat perceived in the United States. The French Communist Party (PCF) had emerged as heroes from the war for their active involvement in the Resistance movement against the Germans. It was one of the largest parties in the National Assembly, serving in postwar governments up to May 1947. Moreover, two major figures in the French film world stoutly defended the movie against American critics even before it had its Paris première. Director Jean Renoir defended Chaplin's right as an artist to change and evolve, and André Bazin, a rising star in the world of film criticism, hailed it as an artistic masterpiece.

As the final part of this chapter notes, Chaplin's American critics eventually prevailed, and from September 1952 he effectively became an exile from the country where all his movies had so far been made. At the end of October, he arrived in France for *Limelight*'s French opening and was warmly welcomed by fans, cinéastes, and politicians. In terms of critical response to the film itself, most French reviewers saw Chaplin's portrayal of a burned-out music-hall comedian as heavily influenced by his own early career on the stage as well as memories of the dawn-world age of silent comedy. Some critics, including Bazin, believed that *Limelight* would help liberate Chaplin as a filmmaker, making it easier for him to move away from his youthful Charlot persona.

Chapter 8 covers the French response to the two films Chaplin directed during his European exile (*A King in New York*, 1957, and *A Countess from Hong Kong*, 1967); the analysis of his moviemaking career by film theorist Jean Mitry; the major part played by France in reviving his international reputation in 1970–72, which included his being honored at the twenty-fifth anniversary of the Cannes Film Festival in May 1971; and the long relationship between Chaplin and Henri Langlois of the Cinémathèque Française symbolized by Chaplin's visit to the Cinémathèque in 1973 for a screening of *Monsieur Verdoux.*

1

The Birth of Charlot

Charlie Chaplin in France, 1915–21

March 1915 was grim in France. Many on both sides had believed that the war beginning in August 1914 would be over by Christmas. But the German invasion of eastern France had been halted by French and British forces at the Battle of the Marne (September 5–8, 1914). A last attempt by German and Allied armies to outflank each other in Flanders ground to a halt in November. By the beginning of 1915, the two sides were dug in along a four-hundred-mile front that stretched from the Swiss border to the English Channel. It had become a war of muddy trenches and barbed wire, of machine guns and artillery—a stalemate in which, despite periodic offensives, neither side could claim a distinct advantage.[1] It must have been obvious to most French people by this point that the war was likely to continue for some considerable time. Many families and communities had already been deeply affected by the conflict: the casualties of 1914 were proportionately the highest in the war. By the end of 1914, 265,000 French soldiers had been killed, but total battle casualties of all types had reached 385,000 as early as September 10.[2]

On Monday, March 15, 1915, the stories on the front pages of the main French newspapers were entirely war-related. After several days of fierce fighting, French forces had managed to reoccupy the village of Vauquois in the Argonne. North of Rheims, the Germans had attacked a front-line French trench and been repulsed. German artillery had bombarded Rheims itself, together with Soissons to the west and Ypres in the north.[3] Ironically, amid so much death and destruction, this was also the day that saw the first attempt to adapt the films produced in the United States by English comedian Charlie Chaplin for the French market. The new issue of the fortnightly cinema trade magazine *Ciné-Journal* published an advertisement announcing the imminent arrival in France from the Keystone company of a new cinematic talent called "Charlot," described as a "dramatic actor" and "irresistible comedian."[4]

Charlot. Melvyn Stokes, Oxford University Press. © Oxford University Press 2026.
DOI: 10.1093/9780197839294.003.0002

The ad had been placed by Jacques Haïk on behalf of the Western Import Company. Born in Tunis in 1893, Haïk had begun working for a British film company at the age of seventeen. By 1915, from his offices at 83, rue Lafayette in Paris, he was energetically running Western Import, which specialized in the importation into France of British and, increasingly, American movies. Haïk was an able and inventive film distributor.[5] He knew, of course, that in the years immediately before the outbreak of the war it had become traditional to make comic films based on the name of a single character. The Pathé-Frères' studio featured André Deed ("Boireau"), Max Linder ("Max"), Louis-Jacques Boucot ("Babylas," later "Pénard"), Charles Prince ("Rigadin"), and Sarah Duhamel ("Rosalie"), and Gaumont had released films by Léonce Perret ("Léonce") and Lucien Bataille ("Zigoto").[6] Haïk was following these precedents. But his decision to rebaptize Chaplin as Charlot—"Little Charlie"—was a stroke of commercial genius. It effectively rebranded Chaplin's films in France, giving him instant recognition in terms of film titles alone that was not the case either in the United States or Britain. It also inaugurated the process by which the French appropriated Chaplin for themselves and, to a significant extent, assimilated him into their own culture.

The name "Charlot" caught on with great rapidity. It became the affectionate nickname by which most French people thought of Chaplin from that point onward. The same issue of *Ciné-Journal* that saw the appearance of Haïk's ad also featured an ad by the distribution company Établissements L. Aubert announcing the exhibition of several Keystone films in what it called "the series of Mabels," named after their supposed star, Mabel Normand.[7] Several of these featured Chaplin and would later be repackaged with Charlot's name in the title. Établissements L. Aubert itself quickly moved to exploit Chaplin's near-instant popularity in France: the next issue of *Ciné-Journal* a fortnight later had them about to show *Charlot fait du cinéma*, the Keystone film released in the United States fifteen months earlier as *A Film Johnnie*.[8] The same issue contained an advertisement from another firm of distributors, the Société Adam et Cie, announcing the imminent release of three 1914 Chaplin Keystones of its own: *Le maillot du Charlot* (*The Fatal Mallet*), *Charlot acteur dramatique* (*The Masquerader*), and *Charlot et la somnambule* (*Caught in the Rain*). Six weeks later, it added a fourth film available for rental: *Charlot dentiste* (*Laughing Gas*).[9]

So quickly did Chaplin as Charlot find popularity among French cinemagoers that by the beginning of June 1915, announcing its forthcoming exclusive exhibition of *Charlot dans les coulisses* (*His New Job*, Essanay, 1915) in five cinemas across Paris, the Société Adam et Cie hailed him as "the biggest success of the season."[10] That success was partly a result of Chaplin's own talents and effective marketing by Haïk, but it was also the result of further attempts to domesticate and appropriate his films for the French market. Chaplin's films in France were appreciably different from those shown in the United States. In January 1916, for example, the firm of film distributors Société Adam et Cie listed eighteen Charlot films from 1914 as being available for rental. Some of the eighteen Keystones cannot be identified,[*] and others were either the same films or fragments of the same films, but eleven are clearly recognizable. In every case, the length advertised by Adam et Cie was appreciably longer than that of the original American productions (Table 1).

Table 1

French title	U.S. Title	U.S. length (feet)	Equivalent (in meters)	Meters actually advertised
Charlot pensionnaire (The Star Boarder)		1,020	310.896	330
Charlot peintre (The Face on the Bar-room Floor)		1,020	310.896	332
Charlot livreur de pianos (His Musical Career)		1,025	312.42	325
Charlot concierge (The New Janitor)		1,020	310.896	337
Nouvelle profession de Charlot (His New Profession)		1,015	309.372	334
Charlot et Mabel en promenade (Getting Acquainted)		1,025	312.42	335
Charlot au bal (Tango Tangles)		734	223.72	260
Charlot et son maillet (The Fatal Mallet)		1,120	341.77	350
Charlot et la somnambule (Caught in the Rain)		1,015	309.372	335
Charlot dentiste (Laughing Gas)		1,020	310.896	315
Charlot garçon de théâtre (The Property Man)		1,858	566.318	640[11]

* Analyzing the reception of Chaplin's films in France is complicated by two main factors. First, his early movies were not released in any systematic way. So, in the first few years, Keystone, Essanay, and Mutual films were screened in no particular order. They could be released at the same time in France even if the films themselves had been made several years apart. Second, some Chaplin films were released with different titles by different distributors. In this book, when a particular film is initially referenced, the French title is given first, followed in parentheses by the English title, production company, and year of first release. For alternative French titles, see the list in the filmography.

The differences in length were mainly accounted for by the insertion of French intertitles linking scenes together. As French film historian Georges Sadoul explained, "distributors [doubtless including Société Adam et Cie] added a large number of intertitles, made up of jokes and stupid puns, to increase the footage and rental rates."[12] (The cost of renting films in France was tied to the actual length of the films concerned.) This would remain a consistent feature of Chaplin's silent-era films released in France; in 1921, film critic Louis Delluc demanded the removal of "many inopportunely florid subtitles" with their silly jokes from *Le Gosse* (*The Kid*, First National, 1921).[13] Using intertitles in this way, however, also helped appropriate Chaplin for French audiences who would see "Charlot" inscribed in a familiar French-speaking world.[14]

The first Chaplin films also benefited from the impact of war on the French movie industry. At the beginning of the war, many actors, directors, and technicians were called up to fight for their country or otherwise to help the war effort. For those who remained, making newsreels was a priority, together with what Susan Hayward terms "patriotic melodramas that either demonized the German enemy . . . or glorified the sacrificial spirit of the ordinary French men and women."[15] Of the three most famous French film comedians of the prewar era, only Charles Prince ("Rigadin") managed to produce short comic films more or less continuously throughout the war. Both Max Linder, the best-known French comic of the time, and Léonce Perret, were temporarily sidelined into war-related occupations. Since neither was fit enough to join the army proper, Linder became a dispatch rider between Paris and the front, while Perret worked as an aide to nurses in Niort. At some point in 1915, Perret resumed filmmaking, now producing in the main short patriotic movies.[16]

Consequently, for several months at the beginning of the war, very few new French comedies were being released. At first this had no noticeable effect since, when war with Germany was declared at the beginning of August 1914, nearly all French cinemas closed down. As hopes of a quick end to the war faded in late 1914, some reopened in November on a part-time basis, and over the next few months, the total number of movie admissions grew rapidly: 788,000 in December 1914; 909,000 in March 1915, when the first "Charlots" arrived; 1,223,000 by May; and 1,604,000 by October 1915.[17] The fact that in a year the number of French moviegoers effectively doubled meant that Chaplin's films could profit from this growing demand at the same time as they themselves encouraged more people to go to the cinema.

To many French observers of the time, the astonishing thing about Chaplin was the breadth of his popularity. As early as December 1915, a critic puzzled over Charlot's ability "to entertain so much people so diverse, [and] to merit a popularity that leaves far behind the memory of the [contemporary French star] Gaby Deslys, and other elegant French beauties." All that was needed, he continued, was "[a] bowler hat that is much too small, a waistcoat so short that it leaves several visible centimeters of shirt, sack-like trousers, boots of immoderate length and width, a cheap cane, a tie without equal—all that to cover an unorthodox talent with unexpected brainwaves, improbable twists and stupefying falls, entertainments executed with the most British composure."[18]

Even hardened film critics were bowled over by Chaplin's films. The weekly reviewer for the recently established *La Cinématographie Française*, after watching a trade screening of a new version of *Charlot boxeur* (*The Champion*, Essanay, 1915) in November 1918, remarked, "all the blasé experts on cinema, which we are, laughed from beginning to end at this hilarious parody of a boxing match."[19] It was through Chaplin's films, indeed, that some critics had first been induced to write about cinema. Film critic Louis Delluc later confessed that he had initially "detested the cinema" and, before the war, had never gone "unless coerced and compelled to go." But in late 1916, his girlfriend and future wife, actress Eve Francis, persuaded him to see Cecil B. DeMille's *Forfaiture* (*The Cheat*, 1915). For Delluc, this "coup de foudre" (love at first sight) was confirmed a few weeks later when the pair saw Chaplin for the first time in *Le roman comique de Charlot et Lolotte* (*Tillie's Punctured Romance*, Keystone, 1914). Delluc was impelled to change career, from theater critic to reviewer and later director of movies.[20] After watching *Charlot cambrioleur* (a 1916 Essanay film called *Police*), Guillaume Danvers, who—unusually among French reviewers—was at times more critical of Charlot, ruefully hailed it as a film "stunning with verve . . . incredible pirouettes, unforeseen capers [all], let us say the word, logically brought about; all that makes a whole so beautifully constructed, so well framed, that the most difficult person can scarcely find anything to criticize."[21]

France was almost instantly afflicted with its own brand of "Chaplinitis." Almost everything about Chaplin became news. The French cinema trade press, as well as newspapers, reported his increasingly stellar salary, the films he was working on, his legal proceedings against studios and individuals,[22] and his participation—together with Mary Pickford, Douglas Fairbanks, and David W. Griffith—in the organization of the United Artists studio in 1919.[23]

They covered his marriage to seventeen-year-old Mildred Harris in 1918,[24] her pregnancy,[25] the death of their baby son and subsequent divorce.[26] Romances, real and fictional, came and went; in December 1918 the supposedly serious *La Cinématographie Française* declared that "around town, Charlie Chaplin is a handsome young man of 29 whose malicious eyes, black hair, naturally curled, and sympathetic smile have turned many heads." In April 1921, *Ciné-Journal* falsely reported that the "incorrigible" Chaplin was about to marry seventeen-year-old Mary May Collins.[27]

Even the work of Chaplin's brother Sydney—promptly christened "Julot" in France—or the fact that a llama in the Paris zoo had been named "Charlot"—was considered newsworthy.[28] Many of the stories—including that he was about to make a film about Beethoven, had "bought several planes and automobiles for his personal usage," and had pretended to be a waiter when Douglas Fairbanks invited Belgian philosopher Maurice Maeterlink to lunch—were absurdly false.[29] "There are few men," commented Henri Coutant of *Ciné-Journal*, "about whom has been published so contradictory information as on Charlot. You cannot believe the very natural exaggeration that takes possession of all columnists as soon as they come into contact with a 'star' and then there are the necessities of publicity that carry them easily along … on the fatal slope of hyperbole, paradox and fantasy."[30]

The "necessities of publicity" were especially relevant in the case of those "selling" Charlot to the public. In *Ciné-Journal* for September 15, 1915, the firm of distributors Agence Générale Cinématographique (AGC) published an ad contradicting a spurious and probably planted account of Chaplin's death. The ad was in essence publicity for Chaplin's new studio and a "plug" for his first post-Keystone film, *Charlot débute* (*His New Job*, Essanay, 1915). Chaplin, the ad explained, was "neither dead, nor mad nor ill"; he had merely moved from the Keystone Studio to Essanay. Part of the ad was a letter allegedly from Chaplin himself on Essanay-headed notepaper. Addressed to cinema managers and the public, and in suspiciously perfect French (a language Chaplin neither wrote nor understood), Charlot assured his worried fans that he had "not succeeded in convincing any insurance company that I have been the victim of an accident or that I have been killed." He invited anyone who did not believe that he was still around to watch him at work in the first of his new series of Essanay comedies. "If I don't make you laugh," Charlot—or more likely a studio publicist—commented, "I will agree to consider myself as dead, but not before."[31]

Charlot and His Imitators

As early as the beginning of July 1915, announcing the imminent appearance of *Charlot pensionnaire* (*The Star Boarder*, Keystone, 1914), Société Adam et Cie insisted that the movie featured "Charlot, the real Charlot, the one who creates laughter by himself and who does not copy anybody."[32] This hint that Chaplin was being criticized by some for copying other comedians in his films was unusual; in reality, most distributors' concern—as would rapidly become apparent—lay in the opposite direction. Just two weeks later, AGC advertised that its program for winter 1915 would include a new Charlot film produced by the Essanay studio every week. There was only one Charlot, the ad insisted, the one played by "Charlie Chaplin, the great American comedian," who was "always imitated" but "never equaled."[33] The same phrases would be repeated many times over the next few years, starting with the pioneering front-page ad (the first of many) devoted to Charlot in *Ciné-Journal* on October 1, 1915.[34] They underlined the fact that, from the beginning, others tried to cash in on Chaplin's immense popularity by imitating him.

In December 1916, for example, one cinema in the 17th arrondissement in Paris advertised the appearance of a new comic act, "Charlot II and his family," described as "a true masterpiece of the Charlot genre," containing "comedy, blows, sensations, falls, in short a film that will please everywhere and which will make young and old laugh."[35] Some of the screen imitators were imported films from America; movies featuring Billy Ritchie (1879–1921), an old Karno colleague and in some ways the most shameless of the Chaplin rip-offs and look-alikes, were already being distributed to Paris cinemas by A. Bonaz in early 1916.[36] Later, Établissements L. Aubert advertised a selection of comedies by "the entertainer Billy West" (1883–1975), a Russia-born actor who, with his baggy trousers, oversized shoes, ill-fitting jacket, and bowler hat, was a carbon copy of Charlot.[37] But France also produced its own versions of Chaplin on the screen, including "Georget" (advertised as "The man who made the whole world laugh");[38] Chalumeau, another actor very similar to Chaplin in dress and profile;[39] and Georges Biscot, who mimed Chaplin-type roles.[40] As *Ciné-Journal* noted in January 1919, "his imitators are numerous."[41] Sometimes it was not even necessary to imitate Chaplin: having his name anywhere helped sell things. In the summer of 1919, the firm L. Van Goitsenhoven distributed a film titled *Aristide double Charlot*, in which the connection with Chaplin was thin to the point of disappearance. The plot of the film revolved around "Charlot" having a cold and Aristide having to substitute for him. Charlot himself never appeared.[42]

Stage acts were also eager to cash in on the Charlot craze. In April 1916, an entertainer named Merin presented a "hilarious parody" of the screen Chaplin in a revue titled *Et après!* at the Eldorado Theater in Nice. The following month, a couple calling themselves Charlot and Josette appeared at the Apollo Music-Hall in Nantes with an act that imitated the celebrated film comedian.[43] In August 1917, "Charlot . . . with his company" appeared, also in Nantes, at the Theater Graslin. "But is it really Charlie Chaplin, of the Keystone?" demanded A. Dolbois in *Le Film*. "We are permitted to doubt it."[44] "Our correspondents tell us," remarked film critic E. Meignen in *Le Cinéma et l'Echo du Cinéma Réunis* in September 1917, "that several flesh and blood 'Charlots' who have not dared show themselves in Paris are playing in provincial music-halls and in the suburbs, each passing himself for the celebrated Charley [*sic*] Chaplin."[45] Six months earlier, *Ciné-Journal* had drawn attention to "a music-hall comedian, or rather an acrobat" who was performing in Bordeaux under the name "S. M. Charlot," even though he had "absolutely no relation to the cinema artist who works for Essanay, the American studio." While the real Charlot (who "has absolutely no intention . . . of coming to give performances in France") worked with Mabel Normand, the Bordeaux "Charlot" appeared with his own "Mabel"—a Mabel O'Brien.[46] In October 1917, when the same S. M. Charlot finally did dare come to the French capital to appear at the Casino of Paris, Georges Dureau, editor of *Ciné-Journal*, published a two-page editorial emphasizing that this stage comedian had "nothing in common with Charlie Chaplin" the screen actor. Promoting this fake "Charlot," Dureau insisted, was "a deception and the general public alone would bear the cost of the hoax."[47] Later, in June 1918, *Le Film* exulted that this imposter—allegedly a Spaniard—had been expelled from France.[48] In December 1919, the Alcazar Theater in Marseilles featured a review in which variety performer Fortuné Cadet appeared in a tableau in which—according to local correspondent Georges Baille—"he imitates Charlot to perfection." Such imitators, Baille observed, "arise spontaneously at all points of the globe."[49]

The desire to profit from the Charlot phenomenon also spilled over into other forms of media in France. In June 1916, the movie reviewer of *Le Film* noted that "animated silhouettes" of Charlot were being offered by Société Adam et Cie. Three weeks later, a "sensational" series of animated comic

"Charlot" cartoons were advertised by a company called Cosmopolis-Films as "made under the direction of Charlie Chaplin."[50] On July 8, an ad by this company in *Ciné-Journal* claimed that these "Charlie Chaplin" cartoons were based on "the admirable performer who is responsible for the Charlot series."[51] This ad was repeated on July 22. In the meantime, however, clearly exasperated by the number of people who were making use of his creation for their own profit, Jacques Haïk had finally taken action. The same issue of *Ciné-Journal* published a warning. Under the heading "Avis aux Exploitants" (Notice to cinema managers), was this announcement: "The name Charlot, registered in conformity with the law, is the exclusive property of Mr. Haïk, of Paris. It must only be used to announce films edited by the Keystone and Essanay companies, in which the actor Charlie Chaplin appears. The usage of the name **Charlot** is absolutely forbidden for all other films from any other company, and the cinema manager who makes use of it whether directly or indirectly lays himself open to the seizure of the film and judicial proceedings."[52]

Haïk's threat of legal action over the use of the name "Charlot" obviously gave Cosmopolis-Films much pause for thought, although they continued to insist that Chaplin himself had been responsible for their animated cartoons. A week later, when they released the first of the series, it was titled *Charles Chaplin et l'Éléphant Blanc* (*Charles Chaplin and the White Elephant*). The ad announcing the new film included a warning: "The name Charlot being the property of the Keystone and Essanay companies [which was untrue but saved face by ignoring Haïk], we warn cinema managers not to mention it on their programs when they show our animated films, produced by Charles Chaplin, the actor who has created the Charlot films. Not wishing to make people think that we are offering imitations, this artist will in future appear under his own name Charles Chaplin."[53] In September 1916, Guillaume Danvers of *Le Film* saw a short animated cartoon film made by Wallace A. Carlson for Essanay and shown in France as *Master Bob va voir Charlot* and described it as "very adroitly made and most amusing." Two years later, in November 1918, Établissements L. Aubert offered a cartoon titled *Charlie joue "Carmen"* (Charlie plays Carmen)—a clear rip-off of the 1916 Essanay film with the French title *Charlot joue Carmen*.[54] In February 1919, advertisements appeared in the trade press for a new series of cartoons featuring Charlot, Mabel (Normand), and Fatty (Arbuckle).[55]

Charlot and the War

There was constant speculation over Chaplin's national origins. *Filma* in 1919 authoritatively claimed that Charlot had been born in Paris in 1889, of an English father and a Spanish mother. A year earlier, in an article devoted to the question of his nationality, *Filma* had asserted that *both* his parents were Spanish, that he had been born in Madrid, and that his real name was Carlos Martinez Chaplin.[56] There were other claims. *Le Cinéma et L'Echo du Cinéma Réunis* reported in different issues in 1917 that Charlot had been born in Latin America[57] or was "a Jew of French origin."[58] Another source cited in the same journal three years later was correct in declaring that he was born in Britain but claimed that he was the child of poor Polish Jews and his real name was Levinski.[59] And while his British background would over the years become increasingly well-known—the distribution company AGC would often advertise the latest work of the "celebrated English comedian"[60]—there would continue to be sporadic reports in France that he had been born in Paris, Melun, or Fontainebleau and was really French.[61]

Nationality was, of course, a major issue during the First World War. If Chaplin really was French—or indeed British—why was he not fighting in the war? Some writers in both France and Britain criticized him for spending the war safely in California while making considerable amounts of money from his films. "Since he is English," declared a film critic for *Le Cinéma et l'Echo du Cinéma Réunis* as late as April 1918, "we do not despair of seeing him one day in the ranks of Tommies [ordinary British soldiers]."[62] A few months earlier, *Ciné-Journal* had falsely reported that Chaplin had indeed enlisted in the British army.[63] There were absurd stories that, despite his failure to join up, he was somehow supporting the Allies by proxy: *Filma* reprinted a story from a British newspaper of a Belgian warplane with a picture of Charlot "in one of his familiar poses" on the front. "And thus," it declared, "the celebrated artist is obliged to collaborate with the Allies, carrying terror and death to the German lines."[64] An equally eccentric story in *Filma* described how "Prince George of Battenberg, who occupies an important post in the British navy, has introduced screening rooms in all his ships. He shows above all films by Charlot and Max [Linder] whom his sailors prefer to everything else."[65] The story confused Prince Louis of Battenberg, who was the head of the Royal Navy when war broke out, with his young son George. Since Prince Louis was forced by anti-German sentiment to resign his post in October 1914, it was clearly wrong to claim that he had introduced floating cinemas into the wartime navy. Inaccurate as it may have been, however, the story did point toward the principal defense of Chaplin's status as a noncombatant: that his films boosted Allied morale by providing entertainment for soldiers in the trenches.[66] In 1918, *Le Courrier Cinématographique* described a free cinema in a rest camp along the Somme where the sound of artillery duels became muted and "Poilus" (French soldiers) greeted the films of Charlot, Max Linder, and Rigadin with "enormous, endless laughter."[67]

For those who believed Chaplin to be American, the same issue arose when the United States entered the war in April 1917. There would be many false reports in French cinema journals that Charlot had enlisted in the U.S. army.[68] It was reported elsewhere that his health did not permit him to join the army, that he was not making films during wartime, and that, instead, he had offered himself as a propagandist for the war—all false claims.[69] More accurately, it was asserted that he was campaigning vigorously—together with other stars—for war bonds.[70] The fact that he had just completed a ten-minute film titled *The Bond* (Mutual, 1916) as part of this campaign was also noted by *Le Cinéma et l'Echo du Cinéma Réunis*.[71] A report that he had delayed production of *Une vie de chien* (*A Dog's Life*, 1918), the first film under his new contract with First National, in order to help raise a million dollars for wounded American soldiers was wide of the mark, but another story—suggesting he had personally donated more to helped wounded servicemen than other movie actors—may have been correct.[72]

Charlot and His Critics

In addition to French criticism of Chaplin for his failure to fight on the Allied side in the war, there was palpable resentment at times over reports of his increasingly high salary. When the news of his new contract with the First National studio broke in the summer of 1917, *Filma* reported that Chaplin "gets a million dollars—or five million francs—for making twelve films a year." The same writer, acidly commenting on Chaplin's growing reputation for avarice, noted that the now wealthy actor was "still someone who is capable of asking for a rise to cover the growing cost of living."[73] "We calculate with some bitterness," observed another critic a few weeks later, "that according to the terms of his last contract, Charlot is earning 13,700 francs per day, for 365 days a year."[74] To put Chaplin's salary into perspective, the average wage per ten-hour day for a bricklayer or carpenter in Paris in June 1917 was 14 francs; for a metalworker on a standard wage it was between 13.25 and 13.75 francs. (For a semi-skilled female metalworker it was between 7.5 and 9.5 francs.) Ordinary workers were also under great financial pressure because of rampant inflation: between February and May 1917, prices in Paris rose by 14%. As a consequence, there were increasing numbers of strikes, cresting in January and the spring.[75]

To most French moviegoers, Chaplin's salary was the stuff of dreams. Yet there were also stories suggesting that he could get by on very little and that his main object was simply to outsmart the movie men. In August 1917, *Filma* published a story of an impresario who had offered Chaplin 5,000 francs per week. Chaplin demanded 5,125. After the contract was signed, the impresario wanted to know why he had asked for this small increase. Charlot replied, "these 125 francs represent my costs of living for a week." In November 1917, announcing *Charlot Chef de Rayon* (*The Floorwalker*, Mutual, 1916), the commercially astute AGC paid tribute to Chaplin's negotiating skills and subtly implied that the sum paid under his previous contract had been worth it. Its ad described *Chef de Rayon* as the first of "twelve extraordinary films" for which Charlot "had touched 'Mutual Film' for the imposing sum of four million francs (670,000 dollars)."[76]

Discussion of the sums Chaplin was paid to some degree grew out of attempts to come to grips with a new economic and cultural phenomenon: the advent of the movie star. In April 1919, *Ciné-Journal* argued that cinemagoers selected the films they went to see on the basis of who was in it: "the name of the star they love [the article specifically mentioned Chaplin] on its own can attract them."[77] When the large new Marivaux movie theater opened in Paris at 15, boulevard des Italiens in April 1919, it did so with "a veritable gala," including a "revue of the principal films of Charlot, the king of cinema."[78] From the beginning, Chaplin's films appealed to both young and old.[79] Very quickly he developed in France what several critics referred to as a "faithful public."[80] Cinema managers knew that showing a Charlot film would help fill their theaters; in many venues, it became the tradition to show a Charlot at the end of an evening's program, to finish the show with a "burst of mad laughter" that would send audiences away happy.[81] Knowing the appeal of Chaplin, the French production and distribution company Pathé-Frères had no hesitation in paying a million dollars for a year's rights to show his First National films in France. The same article in *La Cinématographie Française* that reported this also revealed how the hierarchy of the world of entertainment had been overturned by the rise of the film star. Opera singers and early recording artists such as Enrico Caruso had formerly earned the most; now "the salaries of Charles Chaplin surpass by a good deal those of Caruso."[82]

Another debate in which attitudes to Charlot played a significant part was that provoked by the increasing importance of American films in France as the war continued. By 1917, American films made up more than 50% of those shown in Paris cinemas. In July of that year, the French government issued a decree banning the importation of foreign films, though this was subsequently changed into a procedure for stricter control over such films.[83] Some critics adopted a nationalistic approach. "Charlot, Billa [*sic*—Billy West?], Fatty [Arbuckle] are on the majority of movie programs," commented Jean Noely in 1916, "representing there 'Anglo-American humor,' to the detriment of 'French verve,' so spiritually incarnated by [Charles] Prince ['Rigadin'], Max Linder, Léonce [Perret] and others, whom we see more rarely on our screens."[84] F. Camoin, resenting that Pathé-Frères, the French production and distribution company, was also circulating American films, wrote acidly in 1918, "Evidently, the Pathé establishments make sacrifices to the tastes of today and the program for this week is made up of foreign films, notably a comedy with Charlie Chaplin [*Une vie de chien; A Dog's Life*, First National, 1918]. What do you want? Charlot is inimitable, he pleases very much, he makes profits, it is consequently necessary to adopt him."[85]

Some critics believed that American filmmakers pandered only to the lowest tastes simply to make as much money as possible. Guillaume Danvers commented that U.S.-made "dramas are out-and-out comedies, for example [Thomas Ince's] *Civilization* [1916], and their comedies . . . worthy of tears!"[86] Yet Danvers, who specifically excluded Chaplin from his indictment of American comic films, also saw Charlot—despite occasional lapses—as greatly superior to most French productions. *Charlot au Music-Hall* (*A Night in the Show*, Essanay, 1915), he noted, was "hilarious and without longueurs. . . . we guffawed ten times more, a hundred times more than at the interminable [Jacques Feyder film] *Pied qui Etreint* [a 1916 parody of Louis Feuillade's serials such as *Les Vampires*] of lugubrious memory."[87] Rather than, like Danvers, seeing Chaplin as an exception to the mediocrity of American cinema, future surrealist Philippe Soupault regarded him as a leader of that cinema, who "with a tap of his walking stick . . . [gave] an extraordinary vigor . . . to American movies."[88] Critic Louis Delluc—so enthusiastic about American films that, by 1917, he was receiving letters accusing him of being paid by Hollywood—would similarly write in 1919 that Chaplin "sums up six years of [American] creative activity with his genius."[89]

Just as in the United States, of course, not everyone in France approved of Charlot. Film writers recognized that such people existed but explained them in different ways. It was alleged that they had no sense of humor; a commentator for *Ciné-Journal* observed in December 1915 that "morose spirits who wish absolutely to forbid laughter have contested the talent of Charles Chaplin." In 1918, Max Linder noted that "certain writers speak a little contemptuously of Charlot." Linder insisted that the "small minority" who "do not find him funny" were critical of Chaplin either because they did not know him well enough or had confused him "with vague imitators." In 1920, "Boisyvon" of *Le Film* described the "contradictory spirits" and "eternal malcontents" who were prone to give "a cool reception to Charlot, sighing greatly and declaring with a scornful air to their neighbor who bursts out laughing: 'How can you be amused by such clowning around?'"[90]

Dismissing Charlot as a clown, as Boisyvon demonstrates, was a means of patronizing him. It reduced him (and, by implication, cinema itself) to the status of a circus or fairground attraction. That he was "only" a clown was an accusation that would continue to be leveled against him for many years in France by those who disliked the excessive adulation directed at Charlot the movie star or disapproved of the public recognitions accorded him for his achievements by the French state. Movie reviewers responded to the accusation by defending Charlot, in Edmond Floury's words, as "[an] artist and not clown."[91] They also insisted that Chaplin's artistry increased as his work developed and became more complex.[92] In defending Chaplin as an artist in this way, of course, reviewers were also justifying cinema itself and their role in relation to it.

In terms of parallels with other American criticisms of Chaplin, there were very occasional echoes of genteel criticism of the early Chaplin films for the crudity of his behavior on-screen. *Le Courrier Cinématographique* printed a story—almost certainly apocryphal—of a young would-be comic called Paul Férir who "went to the cinema to begin his studies." In particular, he went to see "the man whom he already called his master, the famous English comedian Charlot." The lesson proved a profitable one, insisted the author of the column: "From the next day, one could see him spitting his cigarette-end in the face of passers-by, blowing his nose on the clothes of his neighbors, and doing a thousand other gracious things in the manner of Charlie Chaplin."[93] The ironic disapproval of Charlot's on-screen behavior by this writer was extremely unusual. A number of French reviewers did criticize some of Chaplin's films, but for different reasons.

In May 1916, Guillaume Danvers of *Le Film* hailed *Charlot et la somnambule* (*Caught in the Rain*, 1914) as "a Charlot, but not one of his best." Two months later, he similarly noted that *Charlot pensionnaire* (*The Star Boarder*) was "not one of the best Charlots," since it was hardly original. "We see again there," he wrote, "the shot of the magic lantern projecting the same snapshots taken indiscreetly by a small child. It's amusing, but it has already been done several times." *Charlot en famille* (an alternative title for *His Trysting Place*, Keystone, 1914), he declared, was "described as a comedy" but "throughout all the first part I found it rather heavy going." Danvers himself generally looked down on slapstick comedy, since he had great aspirations for cinema as an art form that would become a synthesis of all other arts.[94] After watching *Charlot au bal* (another title for *Tango Tangles*, Keystone, 1914) in June 1917, he confessed, "not liking this genre I was afraid of being unjust but I do not believe that similar tomfooleries are either the future nor the raison d'être of cinema." Whatever his reservations, however, Danvers was unable to prevent himself at times from being bowled over by Chaplin's sheer comic genius. After viewing the first episode of the series *Le roman comique de Charlot et Lolotte* (*Tillie's Punctured Romance*), he described it as "madly amusing." The third episode, he wrote, continued to create "mad laughter like its two predecessors."[95]

Like Danvers, a small number of other critics tried to use Chaplin's films to support their own agendas. Simounet of *Le Cinéma et l'Echo du Cinéma Réunis*, in common with Henri Diamant-Berger of *Le Film*, believed in the crucial importance of the scenario in tying a succession of shots together into a coherent narrative whole.[96] Simounet disliked *Charlot est encombrant* (another title for *Caught in the Rain*, Keystone, 1914) when he saw it in December 1916 because "all the scenario consists of a walk and a persistent coming-and-going of Charlot." A few months later, he condemned *Charlot concierge* for its "lack of depth . . . due to a scenario that is lacking in imagination." In July 1917, he found *Charlot et Mabel en promenade* (*Getting Acquainted*, Keystone, 1914) to be short of comic gaiety, with characters who "bustle about without expression." "Thanks to this fever of constant locomotion," Simounet wrote, "it is to look for the impossible if you wish to discover in the film the shadow of a scenario."[97] Some reviewers resented Chaplin for eclipsing most contemporary French comics. "There isn't only Charlie Chaplin under the vault of the skies," declared Paul Barrière of *Le Courrier*

Cinématographique in November 1919, "and I am not hypnotized by his pirouettes to the point of believing that he is the sole, the unique being.... Is it ... so difficult to discover also ... in France, comedians who, by their science of mad laughter, by their verve, their charm and their sentiment easily equal Charlot?"[98] Most French critics, however, were Charlot enthusiasts. They might find some Chaplin films better than others: "Voittout" of *Le Courrier Cinématographique* considered *Charlot en famille* (*His Trysting Place*) "certainly not one of the best," and "Intérim" of *Le Cinéma et l'Echo du Cinéma Réunis* thought *Agathe cherche un mari* (an alternative title for *The Star Boarder*) to be deficient in "the habitual verve of the worldwide Charlot." But criticisms they made were normally mild. (Edmond Floury, for example, suggested that *Le Rêve de Charlot* [*His Prehistoric Past*, Keystone, 1914] was "a little long" and needed cutting, while still praising it as an "excellent comic film.")[99]

Popular Audiences and Charlot

Since the popular audiences of early cinema formed only the most temporary of communities and left few if any traces of their presence, explaining the enthusiasm of many such audiences for Chaplin's films is no easy task. At least one film critic, Louis Delluc, declared that he was more concerned to describe audience reactions and responses than he was to set forth ideas of his own ("It is from the crowd actually that I gather the best impressions and the clearest judgments").[100] From Delluc we know that audiences drawn from different sections of society behaved differently in front of the screen. Those who patronized the new cinema palaces in western Paris, such as the Colisée on the Champs-Elysées, were drawn from the wealthier classes. (Delluc, tongue in cheek, described this "faithful and elegant clientele" as made up of "likeable idlers, artists, prostitutes, industrialists, and a vast majority of the high bourgeoisie.") These spectators preferred the cruder, blood-and-thunder serials, since they liked nothing better than to demonstrate their own superiority by "joking, chuckling, and engaging in other ferocious convulsions" as the film was shown. "An admirable comic film," Delluc noted, "a Charlie Chaplin perhaps, disappoints their need for devastating mockery." Delluc himself preferred the more working-class cinemas of the *faubourgs*, where audiences watched the films attentively and without talking. Yet he left little account of the reaction of these spectators to Charlot other than his comment, in an article on Chaplin and Sessue Hayakawa, "that I have never seen a cinema audience resist the enterprises of these two men."[101]

In May 1919, AGC published an advertisement in *La Cinématographie Française* that began with the words "Hullo, Charlie!" The ad went on to claim that this was the greeting shouted out in cinemas when the figure of "the incomparable Charlot" appeared on the screen.[102] So positive was the ad on this point that it was probably true, giving us a rare glimpse of how popular audiences of the time responded. We know that Chaplin's films and his Little Tramp persona, with its inspired combination of comic genius and pathos, made him popular all over the world. But to explain his appeal to working-class French audiences in particular, in the absence of written sources from spectators themselves, is no easy task. In 1982, Hans Robert Jauss, one of the founders of reader-response theory in literary studies, explained that literary works were understood and interpreted by their readers in accordance with a "horizon of expectations" created by similar works and readers' own social and cultural competencies. "A literary work," Jauss argued, "even when it appears to be new, does not present itself as something absolutely new in an informational vacuum, but predisposes its audience to a very specific kind of reception by announcements, overt and covert signs, familiar characteristics, or implicit allusions. It awakens memories of that which was already read, stirs particular emotions in the reader, and . . . arouses expectations."[103]

If we apply Jauss's concept of a "horizon of expectations" to Chaplin's films, it becomes clear that they were less novel to French audiences than might be assumed. One of the "familiar characteristics" was Chaplin's own acting style. In 1919, critic F. Camoin commented that Chaplin had "a funny originality because of his gestures and his facial expressions." Two years later, filmmaker and film theorist Jean Epstein went even further, describing his acting in terms of mental pathology. Chaplin, he asserted, "has created the overwrought hero. His entire performance consists of the reflex actions of a nervous, tired person. A bell or an automobile horn makes him jump, forces him to stand anxiously, his hand on his chest, because of the nervous palpitations of his heart. This isn't so much an example, rather a synopsis of his photogenic neurasthenia."[104]

Yet, as Rae Beth Gordon suggests in a fascinating article, such an acting style would already have been very familiar to Parisian audiences in particular from the most popular forms of popular entertainment before the movies: the cabaret and café concert (*caf' conc'*). Between 1865 and 1907, Gordon argues, performances in these venues "were characterized by a convulsive body language made up of frenetic, angular, and 'mechanical' movements accompanied by tics and grimaces." It was a language much influenced "by the medical discourse surrounding hysteria and epilepsy"—especially that associated with the movements of the patients of late nineteenth-century neurologist Jean-Martin Charcot at the Salpêtrière hospital in Paris—"and by popularized depictions of the nervous disorders in newspapers and magazines." When cabaret and music-hall performers moved into the new medium of cinema during its first twenty years of existence, they took with them "the aesthetics of [this] performance style." Gordon cites the comment by cinema historian Georges Sadoul that "the unforgettable sidekicks of Charlot . . . are the direct descendants of the types that [Ferdinand] Zecca [an early Pathé filmmaker] and his followers" appropriated from the "caf' conc." [105] Far from new, Charlot's performance style was already very familiar to his popular audiences in France from their experience of cabarets, café concerts, and early French film comedies.

Another factor that may have made Chaplin's comic style familiar to French popular audiences was the films of Gabriel Leuvielle (1883–1925), better known as Max Linder. Linder had been making films for Pathé since 1905. Playing the character "Max" in many movies between 1910 and 1914, at a superficial level he seemed very different from Chaplin's Tramp. His essential role was that of the *flâneur*, an idle man-about-town who gets into a series of scrapes that are mostly created by women or the consumption of alcohol. He was different from Charlot in terms of appearance. Although he also often carried a cane, he was better-dressed than Chaplin's Tramp, usually appearing as a dandy wearing a top hat, formal dress, and ordinary-size shoes. Yet many of his films included gags or plot lines very similar to those in Chaplin's later pictures. *Les débuts d'un patineur* (*The Skater's Debut*, 1907) anticipated some of the sequences of *Charlot patine* (*The Rink*, Mutual, 1916). In *Champion de boxe* (*Boxing Champion*, 1910), Max acted the part of a boxing referee who gets involved in the fight itself—a role reprised by Chaplin in *Charlot et Fatty dans le ring* (*The Knockout*, Keystone, 1914). The waiter played by Linder in *Max, maître d'hôtel* (*Max, Head-Waiter*, 1914) was very similar to Chaplin's waiter in *Charlot mitron* (*Dough and Dynamite*, Keystone, 1914) and the first part of *Charlot patine*. When inebriated, as in *Max, victime du quinquina* (*Max, Victim of Quinine*, 1911), Max could challenge those in positions of authority in much the same way as Chaplin's Tramp. Linder went to Hollywood in 1916 to work for Essanay, and he and Chaplin became friends.[106] Clearly, at some point—perhaps during his 1908 or 1912 visits to France or, more likely, after his first arrival in the United States in the fall of 1910—Chaplin had become aware of Linder's work and been influenced by it.

It may also be that working-class spectators were attracted to Chaplin films by his Tramp persona. One of the most perceptive analyses of that persona was advanced by Paul Gsell in *Démocratie Nouvelle*. This article seemed to the editors of *Ciné-Journal* so insightful that they republished it in full. "What constitutes the originality of Charlot," Gsell declared,

> is . . . first of all the silhouette that he has assumed. It is eccentric and comical; but if it provokes hilarity, it also reproduces in an exaggerated way a type that is common enough, that of the beggar who has pretensions to stylishness. Amongst the people of modest means, poverty tries to hide itself under a false garish elegance. The long curly hair of Charlot, his short moustaches hanging from his nose, his remarkable little hat, his checked trousers, are so many details that betray the desire to impress.
>
> The jacket closely buttoned is a subterfuge to hide the absence of waistcoat and underwear; it is destitution that obliges our man to be wasp-waisted.[107]

The physical appearance of Charlot suggested to Gsell the figure of the hopeful striver: the man who, however buffeted by the pressures of life, had not given up. He was still determined, in spite of a lack of financial means, to put on the best possible outward show and retain whatever shreds were left of personal dignity.

Ultimately, Gsell believed, the character played by Chaplin was not innately a crooked person despite the fact that

> he carries through life a complete indifference for scruples. He is a kind of modern Panurge [the knave from Rabelais's *Pantagruel*]. Lying, trickery and theft are his weaknesses. He is intelligent and adaptable. He makes use of prodigious resources of spirit to satisfy his desires, which are, in truth, quite modest. His awkward and clumsy manner is very useful to him for fooling people. . . .
>
> His character is consequently well-constructed: it is in essence that of the survivor. The type is very well-known in our democratic era, in Europe as in the United States. We are inclined to forgive him his indiscretions and even his misdeeds as a result of the good humor with which he commits

> them. And then, at bottom, we feel that this survivor is not bad. Charlot is
> a rogue only because life is difficult for him.... If fortune comes to smile on
> him, he "will turn over a new leaf" as the common people say.[108]

Painting the screen Charlot as a man victimized by environment and economic circumstances, desperately trying to cling to his self-respect while struggling to make his way in the world, Gsell sketched out a character with whom many working-class cinemagoers could sympathize and perhaps, in part at least, identify.

Chaplin's films may also have appealed to contemporary popular audiences because they reflected the broader forms and experiences of modern urban culture. In mid-March 1919, *La Cinématographie Française* published an article titled "The Crisis of the French Film" that was also a demographical survey of cinemagoing. It pointed out that, whereas there was one cinema for every four thousand inhabitants in the United States and eight thousand in Britain, the comparable French figure was one cinema for every thirty thousand inhabitants. It was not so much the relatively small numbers of such cinemas that was crucial: it was the location. The exhibition of films in France was dominated by Paris, with 1,325 cinemas in 1918, compared to 1,250 for the whole of the rest of France.[109] Many of these 1,250 provincial cinemas, of course, were also located in cities. The dominant French audiences for movies in general—and Chaplin's movies in particular—were city-based.

Vanessa Schwartz argued in *Spectacular Realities* (1999) that crowds of Parisians in the late 1890s and early 1900s were attracted by, enjoyed, and to a degree reinvented themselves through spectacles and entertainment that accompanied the rise of an expanding, mass consumer culture. Schwartz's analysis, which was significantly more positive than earlier critics of the alienating effects of commercial mass culture, including Max Horkheimer and Theodor W. Adorno, dealt with crowds' experience of the boulevards, popular press, displays of bodies in morgues, wax museums, panoramas, and early film.[110] A few years after the period analyzed by Schwartz, Chaplin's films became hugely popular in Paris. And while film critic Edmond Floury pointed out in a review of *Une idylle aux champs* (*Sunnyside*, First National, 1919) that "Charlot isn't always dedicated to the life of cities," nearly all of his early films were in fact set in an urban environment.[111]

The films that first made Chaplin popular in France were the thirty-six Keystone comedies he made between February and December 1914.[112]

Many of these films were set against a background of the kind of everyday recreational activities available in modern cities. Auto races of various kinds are shown in these films—the children's races in *Charlot est content de lui* (*Kid Auto Races at Venice*), the Vanderbilt Cup car race in *Charlot et Mabel au volant* (*Mabel at the Wheel*), and ordinary auto races in *Charlot et Mabel aux courses* (*Gentlemen of Nerve*). *Charlot et les saucisses* (*Mabel's Busy Day*) was set against a horse-racing background. Ballroom dancing was depicted in *Charlot danseur* (*Tango Tangles*) and *Le roman comique de Charlot et de Lolotte* (*Tillie's Punctured Romance*), prizefights in *Charlot et Fatty dans le ring* (*The Knockout*) and *Charlot et Mabel en ménage* (*Mabel's Married Life*), a small music hall in *Charlot garçon de théâtre* (*The Property Man*), a magic lantern show in *Charlot pensionnaire* (*The Star Boarder*), and a cheap cabaret show in *Charlot garçon de café* (*Caught in a Cabaret*). Finally, small cinemas or nickelodeons were represented in *Charlot fait du cinéma* (*A Film Johnny*) and *Charlot rival d'amour* (*Those Love Pangs*), and the cinematic apparatus (cameras and studios) needed to display such recreations to a mass audience in *Charlot grande coquette* (*The Masquerader*), *Charlot fait du cinéma* (*A Film Johnny*), and *Charlot est content de lui* (*Kid Auto Races at Venice*).

For viewers of today, these films are deeply nostalgic: they offer tantalizing glimpses of the urban social recreations of the past. For spectators of the time, especially in Paris, they created common ground between Chaplin as the Little Tramp and the familiar consumer culture of their own city. Working-class moviegoers may have been drawn to Chaplin's films in part at least because they recognized in the screen world he inhabited clear echoes of their own. That world, of course, was greatly under threat when the first Charlot films arrived in Paris. Many popular recreation activities had been closed down or greatly curtailed as a result of the First World War. Even the cinemas had gone dark for the initial four and a half months of the war. For the remainder of the conflict, most cinemas were open only on Saturdays and Sundays, with a small number also playing on Thursdays.[113] For French popular audiences of 1915 to 1918, Charlot was not simply a hugely gifted comedian, working at a time of extreme social stress and dislocation. His films reflected a world of innocent recreation and urban sociability, much of which had now declined or disappeared. Charlot's films, at least in part, may have pleased for the simple nostalgia they offered for an urban way of life that had seemingly been lost in the turmoil of war.

Charlot and the Avant-garde

In 1929, surrealist poet Robert Desnos claimed that it was "four or five years after the man in the street" that the French avant-garde had "discovered" Charlot and "taken him to its heart."[114] In reality, members of the literary and artistic avant-garde discovered Chaplin's films far more quickly than this. Novelist, literary critic, and later filmmaker Jean Epstein, for example, remembered watching his first Chaplin film in England in 1914. Poet and novelist Blaise Cendrars recalled seeing his first Charlot in Paris in 1915.[115] Polymath Jean Cocteau was clearly familiar with Charlot films at an early stage: Jane C. Desmond points out that he imagined both the Horse and the Little American Girl in his ballet *Parade*, first performed in May 1917, "as possessing characteristics reminiscent of Chaplin."[116] Yet while many members of the avant-garde may have come across Charlot at an early stage, it would take a while for their perceptions of him to find their way into print.[117] In March 1918, Louis Aragon published his first poem, an eccentric tribute to Chaplin titled "Charlot Sentimental," in *Le Film* at the invitation of Louis Delluc.[118] Six months later, also in *Le Film*, Aragon argued, "Charlie Chaplin fulfills the conditions I'd like to see insisted on [in cinema]. If you need a model, look to him. He alone has sought the intimate sense of cinema and, endlessly persevering in his endeavors, he has drawn comedy towards the absurd and the tragic with equal inspiration." "The best, unquestionably," wrote Cocteau in the spring of 1919, "is Charlie Chaplin."[119]

Among the more thoughtful film critics and the general French avant-garde of the time, there was a sense that Charlot brought something new to cinema. He had taken pantomime and, through his genius, transformed it for the screen. To both Aragon and Cocteau, his work had helped cinema to break with the theatrical tradition. There was also a striking recognition on the part of many observers that—in the then nonverbal medium of film— Charlot's work was somehow poetic. Reviewing *Charlot rentre tard* (*One A.M.*, Mutual, 1916), Delluc observed that "the familiar objects of Charlot's house are all pretexts for unbelievable follies based on close observation. The exact accord of the folly and the observation makes great poems out of eve-ryday things. And this foreign film is like a true poem."[120] Viewing *Une idylle aux champs* (*Sunnyside*, First National, 1919), another reviewer commented that "it is altogether a poem that is worthy of applause."[121] "Nobody has even realized that the sublime thing about Charlot is what we poets call poetry," wrote Philippe Soupault in 1920. To Élie Faure in 1921, most people did not perceive Chaplin as a poet because he was a clown, and "a poet is, by definition, a solemn person who brings us knowledge through the door of boredom." Nonetheless, Faure argued, Chaplin was "a poet, even a great poet, a creator of myths, symbols and ideas, the discoverer of a new and unknown world."[122]

Faure also thought Charlot's films expressed "the modern spirit" of the postwar period, seeing him as a "man, drunk with intelligence, dancing on the summits of despair."[123] To fully appreciate *Charlot musicien* (*The Vagabond*, Mutual, 1916), asserted Aragon, "it is indispensable to know and love Pablo Picasso's 'Blue Period' paintings, in which thin-hipped Harlequins look at too-erect women combing their hair, to have read Kant and Nietzsche, and to believe one's soul loftier than that of other men."[124] Cocteau saw Charlot as embodying the essence both of modern American civilization and of modern man himself. He was the "modern Guignol," speaking "to every age, every nation." Cocteau praised Chaplin for his contribution to making the "spirit of lightness" replace the "spirit of weight," breaking down the barriers of the past, freeing art from conservative restrictions and allowing the artist to use radically different approaches.[125] If writers studied Charlot, Cocteau claimed, they would learn how "to reach several different kinds of public simultaneously for different reasons."[126]

Re-editions: Charlot versus Charlot

January 1917 signaled the start of something new. "Voittout," the movie critic of *Le Courrier Cinématographique*, commented that distributors Adam et Cie were now offering *La nouvelle profession de Charlot* (*His New Profession*), a Keystone film that had been released originally in the United States in the summer of 1914. The movie, Voittout remarked, was "a re-edition, or so announces the program." Confessing that he had not seen the film before, Voittout commented that "it is necessary to believe that it caused a great stir in order to deserve being shown anew."[127] Two months later, the response of Edmund Floury, Voittout's successor at *Le Courrier Cinématographique*, to Adam et Cie's release of another Keystone film, *Charlot concierge* (*The New Janitor*, Keystone, 1914), was very similar. Floury mentioned in his column the "reappearance" of this movie, "whose success, it appears, had been legendary a few years ago." The version of the film now on offer, Floury noted, was "a re-edition, a rare thing in cinematography."[128] What seemed highly unusual in January and March soon became part of a pattern. In May, Adam et Cie advertised a third Keystone re-edition, *Charlot et Mabel en promenade* (*Getting Acquainted*, 1914) and in June an Essanay re-edition, *Charlot dans les coulisses* (*His New Job*, 1915).[129]

For the time being, Adam et Cie were the only major distributors offering re-editions. Their efforts showed there was a market for such films, but there were still enough new or recent Charlots being produced to meet most of the existing demand. On August 3, 1918, AGC advertised that it would be making available for rental between September 1918 and March 1919 seven new Charlot films, starting with *Charlot et le Comte* (*The Count*, Mutual, 1916) and finishing with *Charlot fait du ciné* (*Behind the Screen*, Mutual, 1916). A few weeks later, it promised to bring out one film "of the new Charlot series" each month until June 1919.[130] This "new series" was made up of the films Chaplin had produced for the Mutual studio between March 1916 and June 1917. Shortly afterward, the production and distribution company Pathé Frères announced it had acquired the rights to its own new series of Chaplin films: the movies he had shot for the First National studio from January 1918, beginning with *Une vie de chien* (*A Dog's Life*).[131]

For almost a year afterward, at least one new Charlot picture was released in France every month. By the summer of 1919, however, the supply of new Chaplin films was drying up. The twelve two-reeler Mutual films had been widely shown. Chaplin's own productivity, as his films grew longer, was tapering off. He had produced thirty-six films, mainly single-reelers, for Keystone in 1914; twelve films, mostly double-reelers, for Essanay in 1915; ten altogether for Essanay and Mutual in 1916; and four for Mutual in 1917. He released only two three-reelers for First National in 1918, and a further two films in 1919. In 1920, for the first time since the beginning of his movie career, he produced no films at all. At the same time, demand for Charlot films increased as the war finally came to an end in November 1918, millions of men were demobilized from the army, and cinemas started to return to their normal peacetime schedule of daily screenings.[132] As fewer and fewer new movies became available and Chaplin's own popularity among the French waxed rather than waned, distributors found they had to bridge this widening gap. The solution was to re-edit earlier Charlot films.

Adam et Cie continued with their re-editions of early Charlots. In January 1919, AGC announced a re-edition of the Essanay film *Charlot fait la noce* (*A Night Out*, 1915).[133] Other AGC re-editions followed: another Essanay,

Charlot dans le parc (*In the Park*, 1915) in June 1919 and the Keystone *Le roman comique de Charlot et de Lolotte* (*Tillie's Punctured Romance*, 1914) in November.[134] There clearly was a growing demand for such films. In June 1919, E. Tisson et Cie, a firm of distributors holding a concession for the south of France, Corsica, and French colonies in North Africa, advertised twenty-four re-editions of Keystone Charlots.[135] There was also a much shadier world of re-edited Chaplin films on offer. In July 1919, Kinéma-Locations of Paris advertised a series titled *Les Amours de Charlot* in six episodes of 365 meters apiece. Essentially, as AGC pointed out in a legal warning published in November, these were illegal copies or "forgeries" of the series *Le roman comique de Charlot et de Lolotte*, which AGC itself was about to release in re-edited form.[136] A few months later, more than ever aware of the lucrative market for Chaplin re-editions, AGC itself decided to go the whole hog. "In response to the desire of a large number of clients," it announced in July 1920, "the AGC is going soon to re-edit at a rate of one film per week the fifty best films made by the inimitable Charlot (Charlie Chaplin) to which it has exclusive rights. These new copies will be produced from the original negatives, which are in perfect condition, and their titles have been completely redone according to today's tastes."[137]

The fact that many re-edited versions of Chaplin's Keystone and Essanay films were still in circulation in 1919–20 at the same time as later Mutual and First National films provoked considerable interest within the critical community. As early as May 1918, after viewing a re-edition of *Charlot journaliste* (*Making a Living*, 1914), Chaplin's first Keystone film to be released, critic Louis Delluc described it as "a demonstration of the outdated and limited technique of early film comedy"—although he also hailed it as the movie that launched Charlot's career, revealing for the first time "the brightness of an actor not at all banal, with his charm, his authority, his strange and harmonious inspiration."[138] Other film critics saw the re-edited films as dated and old-fashioned. "O. Réol" of *Le Cinéma et l'Echo du Cinéma Réunis* thought that the new version of *Charlot et les saucisses* (*Mabel's Busy Day*, Keystone, 1914) "will add nothing to the glory of that excellent artiste" and was unimpressed by Chaplin's acrobatics in *Charlot marin* (*Shanghaied*, Essanay, 1915): "he is so much better than that!" The same writer, a few weeks later, saw the re-edition of *Charlot entre le bar et l'amour* (*His Favorite Pastime*, Keystone, 1914) as the exception that proved the rule, since it had "aged less than the others, the situations are amusing and the talent of Charlot is not entirely sacrificed to acrobatics."[139]

A debate broke out between French film critics over whether they preferred the first Charlots, now becoming available as re-editions, or Chaplin's later productions. Underpinning it was the issue of whether Chaplin was simply a brilliant comedian or, as his films evolved, had turned into something more complex—an artist—as well. "Some people prefer this first demonstration of the talent of the perfect comic that is Charlot," declared the critic of *La Cinématographie Française* in a review of the re-edited *Charlot vagabond* (*The Tramp*, Essanay, 1915). "Others do not wish to know more than his latest films. Who is right? . . . If I recognize the incomparable virtuosity of *Une vie de chien* [*A Dog's Life*], or *Charlot soldat* [*Shoulder Arms*, First Nation, 1918] and of *Une idylle aux champs* [*Sunnyside*, First National, 1919], in which Charlie Chaplin rises to the intellectual level of the greatest artists, I cannot however forget his [early] series 'Charlot' in which he is the incomparable humorous philosopher that we never tire of applauding."[140]

In his fine study of the evolution of Chaplin's stardom in the United States, Charles J. Maland argued that in order to blunt genteel criticism of the vulgarity and crudity of his early screen persona he began to refine that persona, showing the Tramp figure as unlucky in love yet coping resiliently with his disappointments.[141] This change was noted in France, even if critics were unaware of the rationale for it. "Des Angles" in *Le Courrier Cinématographique* hailed a "good re-edition" of *Charlot vagabond* (*The Tramp*, Essanay, 1915) as a film "in which for a moment the comic becomes sentimental and even moving." Edmond Floury in *Le Cinéma et l'Echo du Cinéma Réunis* offered similar praise for a re-edition of *Charlot violiniste* (*The Vagabond*, Mutual 1916), in which the very poor but self-sacrificing Charlot did finally get the girl in the end. "This amusing film," declared Floury, ". . . has the additional advantage of ending with a touch of sentiment in which Charlot proves to us that he is also a comedian capable of disturbing us after having made us laugh as usual."[142]

By the time the earliest of the First National films were released, however, a number of French critics were questioning Chaplin's movement away from his comedic roots. Commenting on a re-edition of *Charlot va dans le monde* (English title unidentified), the reviewer for *La Cinématographie Française* declared, "There are many people for whom these films are novelties and others who prefer the first films of Charlot to the great and recent comedies which, in spite of all their merits, are not as 'funny' as this example, for Charlot going into the world has only one ambition, to make us laugh whilst in other more recent films we find a psychology that wishes to be profound."

A few weeks later, writing about *Charlot brocanteur* (*The Pawnshop*), a re-edition of Chaplin's sixth film for Mutual, the same reviewer commented that "a [Chaplin] film that is already old is much more entertaining than certain recent comedies which have been more psychological than amusing."[143]

Some critics simply wished Charlot to remain the same. They found his early slapstick films much funnier than his later, more sentimental and psychologically nuanced ones. This was in part nostalgia: they looked back with fondness to the first Chaplin movies they had seen. One reviewer wrote that a re-edition of *Charlot papa* (*His Trysting Place*) rekindled memories of a film dating "from the time already distant when Charlie Chaplin had Mabel Normand for partner."[144] For another, *Charlot et Fatty dans le ring* (*The Knockout*) was "just like a friend of former times, a good old film we have re-seen with pleasure."[145] It was also a reflection of the widespread belief that these films had already attained classic status. "I cannot believe that it will one day be out of fashion," declared Edmond Floury of a new version of *Charlot boxeur* (*The Champion*, Essanay, 1915), "for the years cannot affect it, such gaiety cannot grow old."[146] Several reviewers emphasized that preview screenings of re-edited Charlots were greeted with continuous uproarious laughter from experienced critics (or *blasés*). "To hear the laughs," a reviewer for *Ciné-Journal* commented of the response of this kind to *Charlot entre le bar et l'amour* (*His Favorite Pastime*), "[is] to recognize the very real success it currently enjoys, yet I note that some of my colleagues have wrongly criticized this most justifiable series of re-editions."[147]

The disagreements between critics over the re-editions of Chaplin's films helped reinforce the impression that they were in a category by themselves, in many ways forming their own distinct genre. One Charlot was judged against another, his first films against the later ones. Some critics preferred the humor in his early, slapstick comedies. Others championed his latest films, regarding them as more sophisticated, character-led comedies. From the point of view of the latter reviewers, including Louis Delluc, the re-issues of Chaplin's earlier films with their cruder, more physical humor helped obscure his growing reputation as an artist of cinema. In the United States, as Maland shows, Chaplin's star image from 1916 onward profited from the attempt in the press—aided and abetted at times by Chaplin himself— to construct him as an aspiring artist.[148] French writers and avant-garde intellectuals were doing the same from early 1918 onward, although this time without any contact with Chaplin himself. Most of these commentators, unlike film reviewers, made little distinction between Charlot's earlier and later films. There is evidence that, by late 1920, a number of critics were following their lead, abandoning the debate on re-editions by accepting that Chaplin, from the beginning of his career, had been both a comic and an artist. A critic in *Ciné-Journal*, reviewing the Essanay production *Charlot marin* (*Shanghaied*), noted that "some scenes are acted with the skills of a comedian who has the talent of an artist." Another critic two months later hailed an "excellent" re-edition of *Charlot au spectacle* (*A Night in the Show*, 1915), another Essanay film, confidently insisting that it "will not harm the reputation of the marvelous artist whose reputation now grows in two different ways."[149]

Between 1919 and 1921, French cinemagoers who enjoyed Chaplin films had an enormous variety to choose from. In order to help potential spectators by informing them whether a film advertised was an old or a new Charlot, the critic for *Ciné Pour Tous* suggested it might be sensible to put dates on all Charlot films. Yet at the same time he also accepted that it would be necessary to carry on with re-editions of Chaplin's earlier films since, in France, the demand greatly outstripped the supply.[150] Some distribution companies still sought to differentiate their products by advertising them in slightly different ways. AGC, continuing to assert its exclusive rights to the Mutual films, insisted, "The extraordinary American entertainer has won fame under the pseudonym that is now so popular of Charlot. It is under this name that he will continue to appear in the programs of the Agence Générale Cinématographique. And it is thus that we have had last Monday, under the title of *Charlot patine* [*The Rink*, Mutual, 1916], the priceless vision of one of the most extraordinary comedies of the series."[151] Exactly three weeks earlier, Pathé Frères, having acquired the rights to distribute the First National films, had recognized the claims of the AGC by announcing, "The films of CHARLIE CHAPLIN have up until now been circulated in France under the pseudonym of: CHARLOT. But the new series of films by this incomparable artist, to which we have exclusive rights, will be distributed under the actual name of the artist: CHARLIE CHAPLIN."[152]

Clearly, these two large distribution companies recognized each other's position and sought to regularize their relationship. But it was not the Mutual and First National films that created most confusion in the minds of real or potential viewers. It was the large number of Keystone and Essanay productions that were still in circulation, either in original or re-edited form.[153] Some of these were legal; many were not. Almost all of these films were now offered under several different titles, making it more and more difficult for cinemagoers to tell them apart or to avoid seeing the same film in several different guises (see the filmography at the end of this book). In 1921, chaos still ruled in the exhibition of Chaplin films. It was against this background that Chaplin's latest film, *Le Gosse* (*The Kid*, First National, 1921)—his first since 1919—had its first showing in France. Its appearance coincided with Chaplin's own arrival in the country on his first visit for nine years. In 1909, he had spent a month in Paris, unknown and unacknowledged, as a member of Fred Karno's traveling troupe of entertainers. He had briefly visited France a second time, in the summer of 1912, again as part of a Karno tour. In 1921, he returned there as the best-known movie star in the world.

2

"Charlot Is in Paris": 1921

In the short book he published soon after he returned from his 1921 European trip—a book titled *My Trip Abroad* in the United States and *My Wonderful Visit* in Britain—Chaplin wrote that he had made a sudden decision to leave California in search of an "emotional holiday." He had already started filming a new movie about a pair of plumbers, provisionally titled *Come Seven*, which had to be closed down. Chaplin explained the circumstances that had led him so suddenly to embark on this trip. He was feeling "very tired, weak, and depressed" after a bout of influenza. After nine years away, he started to experience nostalgia for Britain—a nostalgia greatly encouraged by the steak-and-kidney pie served at a Pasadena dinner party he attended. His latest completed picture for First National Films, *The Kid* (1921), was about to be screened in London. Until now, Chaplin had never been present at the première of any of his films and, he confessed, he "sort of wanted to be patted on the back" and to be able to enjoy his success publicly.[1]

There may have been other reasons for making the trip to Europe that he did not divulge. Chaplin must have known that several of the other early stars of American cinema had already visited Paris and been fêted there. Fanny Ward, from Cecil B. DeMille's *Forfaiture* (*The Cheat*, 1915), led the way in August 1919.[2] Pearl White, heroine of the serial *Les Mystères de New York* (*The Perils of Pauline*, 1914), who had become very popular in France where she was known as "Pearl Vite" (Quick Pearl), was there in April 1920 and April–May 1921.[3] Roscoe "Fatty" Arbuckle, who had started work with Mack Sennett at Keystone several months before Chaplin arrived, was in Paris in November and December 1920.[4] Mary Pickford and Douglas Fairbanks, Chaplin's colleagues in the organization of the United Artists (UA) studio in Hollywood in 1919, had visited the French capital and attended a banquet held in their honor in July 1920.[5]

Chaplin may also have been very conscious that, unlike the others involved in founding UA, he had as yet—bound by the terms of his existing contract with First National—failed to produce anything for the new studio.[6] In the summer of 1921, the new studio advertised the opening of its Paris

Charlot. Melvyn Stokes, Oxford University Press. © Oxford University Press 2026.
DOI: 10.1093/9780197839294.003.0003

office, run by the highly entrepreneurial Guy Croswell Smith.[7] In August, it announced the first UA films to be exhibited in France: Fairbanks's *Le Signe de Zorro* (*The Sign of Zorro*), to be previewed on August 18 and available for rental from September 30, and Pickford's *Polyanna*, scheduled for preview on September 15 and rental from October 20.[8] Chaplin, who attended the première of Fairbanks's latest swashbuckler, *The Three Musketeers*, in New York before taking the boat for Europe, may have planned to help publicize UA's productions in Britain and France. There may have already been loose plans for the three UA stars to meet up again in France. Chaplin sailed for Cherbourg and Southampton on the White Star Line's *Olympic* on September 3. Fairbanks and Pickford left for Europe on the same ship eighteen days later.[9]

In personal terms, Chaplin was probably influenced in his decision to go to Europe by the desire to see again his childhood sweetheart, Hetty Kelly, whom he had written to affectionately in the summer of 1918. He would not discover until he was already in England that Hetty had died during the Spanish influenza pandemic in November 1918.[10] If Chaplin was nearly three years too late to renew his acquaintance with Hetty, he was fortunate in the timing of his trip in another respect: he was outside the United States when the Fatty Arbuckle scandal broke. Arbuckle was charged with the manslaughter of starlet Virginia Rappe at a drunken party in San Francisco on September 5, 1921.[11] Given the fact that Chapin had made six of his Keystone films with Fatty, the scandal might have damaged him if he had been in the United States during its early stages.[12]

Chaplin arrived in England after a brief stop at Cherbourg on September 6. He would stay for two weeks at the Ritz Hotel in London. Satiated with both the popular frenzy and the media circus that surrounded him, he decided abruptly to leave for Paris without advertising what he was doing. (He kept his apartment at the Ritz to throw journalists off the scent.) He arrived on the express from Calais at the Gare du Nord on Sunday evening, September 18, at 6.40. He stayed for five nights in suite 248 of Claridge's Hotel, close to the Champs-Elysées, leaving Paris by train for Berlin on Friday, September 23. However, he returned to Paris for several days the following week and—for a final time on this trip—flew from London on October 4 to present his new film, *The Kid* (*Le Gosse* in France), at a gala performance at the Trocadéro Theatre on the evening of Wednesday, October 5. He left Paris, again by air, on Friday, October 7, returning to Britain to sail again on the *Olympic*, which left Southampton bound for New York on October 10.[13]

1921 was a crucial year in the construction of Chaplin's star persona in France. In that year, Louis Delluc published the first book-length study of Chaplin's artistry to appear in any country. This was also the first year in which Chaplin visited France with all the accoutrements of modern movie stardom. He was pursued by journalists, photographers, and fans. In their response to him, many French observers and critics would construct a Chaplin of their own that went far beyond his roles on the screen. This chapter will examine three major aspects of Chaplin's visits to Paris in 1921. First, the manner in which he was constructed politically—and especially in connection with attempts to link him to Russian communism. Second, his exposure to French fandom and the manner in which French critics and commentators viewed the phenomenon of "Charlot." Third, the significance of his involvement in the Trocadéro première of *Le Gosse*.

Charlot Bolshevik

The most perceptive analyses of Chaplin's work and career in 1921 were by Louis Delluc, who published not only his book discussing Chaplin's film artistry but also a "mock" interview with Chaplin in which Chaplin's side of the conversation was left blank. Later, in *Cinéa* on October 14, Delluc warned his readers that most of the so-called interviews appearing in the press since Chaplin arrived in France were apocryphal.[14] Chaplin spoke no French, and relatively few French journalists spoke any English, so the possibilities of communication rested heavily on the presence of interpreters.[15] Some reporters who claimed to have interviewed Charlot clearly had not.[16] One, indeed, made a whole story out of the fact that he had *not* interviewed Chaplin (claiming that Chaplin was not prepared to answer the serious questions about his work the journalist had prepared).[17] Other reporters probably made things up—reading into "Chaplin" essentially what they wanted to. In one case, this provoked political controversy.

While Charles Maland comments that Chaplin's only major political involvement before 1921 had been his tour on behalf of Liberty Loans and the making of *Shoulder Arms*—both patriotic gestures that seemingly supported the existing wartime priorities of the American government—there must have been some suspicion in an America that had just emerged from the "Red Scare" of 1919–20 that he had hidden left-wing opinions. In his memoir on his European travels in 1921, Chaplin recalled that it was an American reporter at the Ritz Hotel in New York on the eve of his departure who first asked him if he was a Bolshevik. In *My Trip Abroad*, Chaplin claimed that he replied, "I am an artist. I am interested in life. Bolshevism is a new phase of life." When journalists continued to question him over Russia, Lenin, and Bolshevism, he retreated with the blanket statement "I am an artist, not a politician."[18] If Chaplin thought he could escape such issues on his visit to France, where the Communist Party had been founded in 1920 by dissident socialists who also took control of *L'Humanité*, the socialist newspaper founded by Jean Jaurès in 1904, he was mistaken. In France, moreover, the issue of whether Charlot had Bolshevik sympathies quickly became caught up in a kind of guerrilla warfare in the French press.

The warfare began with a long article by Max Massot published in the newspaper *Le Journal* on September 19.[19] In great detail, Massot described Charlot's arrival at the Gare du Nord and a subsequent interview with him that supposedly started at his hotel and continued as Charlot and the journalists concerned walked toward Montmartre. Chaplin apparently declared he was in Paris only for a rest, commented that he had visited Paris before at the time of the Steinheil affair in 1909[20] and performed at the Folies-Bergère, confessed that he would not be staying very long, and expressed satisfaction with the reception so far of *The Kid*. He went on to mention his admiration for Max Linder and give a brief bland comment on the Fatty Arbuckle case. So far, much of what he said was confirmed—or at least repeated—in other newspapers. But this so-called interview then began to spiral away in a different direction. First, Charlot (whom Massot had previously described as "not talkative") suddenly confessed he had a "romantic soul" that made him appreciate Paris seen through the fog. Subsequently, he began to ask questions of journalists about the state of France. He also expressed his sympathy "for our devastated regions" and for the "admirable example of faith [in their recovery] that we are giving the world." Massot then wrote: "The god Lenin forgive us! Charlot launched, with small brief gestures, amplified with his walking-stick, a tirade on the debilitating effects of Bolshevism."[21]

L'Humanité, in common with nearly all Paris newspapers, covered the arrival of Chaplin in Paris. A report from London dated September 18 noted, "Charlie Chaplin left on an impulse this afternoon for Paris from Victoria Station." A second article, published on September 20, could hardly ignore Massot. The anonymous communist writer hailed the coming of the "true" and "unique" flesh-and-blood Charlot to the French capital. He argued that the lack of pre-publicity for the visit "proves that Charlot does not lack modesty." But he also noted that Charlot had felt the need to subject "one of our colleagues" to "a terrible tirade" on the consequences of Bolshevism. Reviewing Chaplin's travel plans in Europe, therefore, he drily remarked, "Charlot who is thirteen times a millionaire will consequently not be going to Russia."[22]

Over the next few hours after this first response appeared, the editor and writers for *L'Humanité* clearly resented intensely the idea that the hugely popular Chaplin had effectively been appropriated by anticommunists. Next day, they launched a counterstroke. Under the headline "Charlot bolchevik," the newspaper regretted "having echoed the amusing claims of some of our bourgeois colleagues who have *more or less interviewed* [my italics] Charlot and generously attributed to him some political fantasies." "Far from being the fiery opponent of Bolshevism these good souls claimed," the story continued, "everyone in New York knows that Charlie Chaplin is one of the financial supporters of *Liberator*, the communist journal of Max Eastman, to the extent that the name of the celebrated artist had figured on a list of suspects produced in an America dominated by the most savage form of capitalism." *L'Humanité* offered apologies to Charlot for its earlier reports and promised to treat him justly "as the son of a worker that he is, in spite of his millions."[23]

L'Humanité's own attempted appropriation of Charlot provoked a lively debate. Clément Vautel, novelist and later a scriptwriter, noted in *Le Journal* that *L'Humanité* had earlier included "the king of cinema" among those it referred to as "dirty bourgeois." Vautel was extremely skeptical of the notion that supporting a communist journal "proved" in any meaningful sense that Chaplin was a communist. He claimed to know many wealthy middle-class people who did the same kind of thing without abandoning their "extreme moderation" in matters political, social, and philosophical. He refused to recognize them as convinced communist partisans until, like Tolstoy at the end of his life, they "renounced their wealth and left their castles to carry a pick on the shoulder in the army of the proletariat." Vautel pointed out that Chaplin, at home in California, lived the life of a rich bourgeois on his income of six million dollars a year. He insisted that he would believe Charlot was truly a communist only when he distributed all his fortune to the people. Even Chaplin's humor, Vautel argued, which was "simple, cordial, logical, based on selected observations [of] . . . daily life," had nothing in common with "the gloomy sectarians of Moscow."[24] A. Nangis in *La Libre*

Parole, a right-wing and Catholic newspaper, reproduced Vautel's article almost verbatim under the title "Charlot bolchevik." At the end, however, he added a chilling personal postscript. Nangis, in common with many right-wing French figures of the period, including Charles Maurras of the political movement Action Française, which reached the peak of its popularity after the First World War, was deeply antisemitic. In a classic smear, he linked Chaplin's alleged left-wing sympathies with his rumored Jewish origins. At the same time, he dismissed Chaplin as a mere entertainer. "What explains the communist subsidies paid by the millionaire clown," Nangis remarked, "is the Jewish origins that we ascribe to him."[25]

L'Humanité's annexation of Charlot was challenged at other points on the political spectrum. Jacques Barty, writing in the republican *L'Homme Libre*, which had been founded by Georges Clemenceau, sardonically observed that Chaplin—now "officially recognized" as a communist "by communist organizations"—would go to Russia, "where the wretched people evidently had great need of a comic who could potentially change their ideas."[26] A commentator in the right-wing *Le Figaro* sadly noted that "even if, as for many capitalists, it is out of fear that Mr. Chaplin pours out this manna to the revolutionaries, the side of Charlot that *Humanité* shows us is nonetheless less cheerful than the others."[27] Adrian Vély, in the right-wing and monarchist *Le Gaulois*, archly confessed that the story of "Charlot bolchevik" had inspired him to scribble out a scenario for a film starring Charlot while on the way to visit Charlot himself at his hotel. In this scenario, Charlot eats someone else's fruit (arguing that the earth and its products belong to everyone) and tries to kiss someone else's fiancée (on the grounds that communism means that women should be shared). He is chased by a policeman and a soldier ("infamous props of bourgeois capitalism"). A miracle then takes place. American president Warren G. Harding is overthrown and Charlot becomes the people's commissar. His first act is to give away his many millions. According to Vély's fictional account of their subsequent conversation, which suggests Charlot is far from being a communist, Chaplin himself liked the scenario but declared it necessary to change the ending.[28]

Reaction on the left to the notion of Chaplin as a communist varied from subtle doubt to complete outrage. Alfred Varella, writing in *Le Journal du Peuple*, commented that "the official organ of our party" had declared Charlot "a perfect communist," and so "we have no good reason to doubt it." However, most of the rest of his article was in fact devoted to doubting it, though Varella did concede that Chaplin was "a child of the people" who had known want and misery in his youth. Yet he also wondered whether "the fact of gaining thirteen million dollars in two years of playacting is easily reconcilable with . . . the anti-capitalist idea." Charlot ("the communist millionaire") would have to prove himself a communist by becoming "the revolutionary Molière of his time."[29]

Predictably, the most savage attacks on the idea of Charlot as a communist came in *Le Libertaire*, an anarchist newspaper, and *Le Peuple*, a syndicalist one. Pierre Mualdes in *Le Libertaire* snidely remarked that it was enough for the "good disciples" of *L'Humanité* "to be a communist in the manner of [Marcel] Cachin [a leader of the French party] by paying a little money to a progressive journal. It's priceless!" For Mualdes, the buffoonery of Charlot was preferable to that of Cachin: Charlot had not made his millions by pointless speeches or voting credits for war (which Cachin had done as a deputy in the French parliament). On the other hand, Mualdes made clear, the issue of whether Chaplin was a communist distracted attention from the real struggle of anarchists everywhere—and especially in Spain, Italy, America, and Russia—against "the savage repression of murderous governments."[30] In *Le Peuple*, two articles by journalist Saint-Eloi attacked the Communist Party of Cachin and its newspaper *L'Humanité*—which he consistently referred to as "the *Pravda* of Paris"[31] and accused of "altering the truth with a dash of Lenin sauce." According to Saint-Eloi, the communists apologized to Chaplin not "in spite of his millions" but mainly "because of" them. There were already enough comedians in the French Communist Party, he sardonically implied, referring specifically to Henri-Paul Gassier, Victor Méric, and many others who were unintentionally funny, that "Charlot bolchevik" was by no means out of place.[32]

The controversy over "Charlot bolchevik" was an early illustration of the transcultural reception of a star of American cinema. French journalists inscribed Chaplin into the context of the impact on France of the Bolshevik Revolution of October 1917 in Russia. This, together with the impact of the First World War, had led to a number of political changes in France, including the founding of the French Communist Party on Bolshevik lines at the Tours conference of December 1920.[33] Now, less than nine months later, French intellectuals and commentators were debating with considerable vigor Chaplin's supposed views on Bolshevism. This had very little to do with Chaplin himself; he may not even have known what was happening. But the controversy underscored two new factors. First, given Chaplin's status as an international celebrity—in 1921, he was probably the best-known film star in the world—associating him with particular views and opinions was perceived as a way of strengthening their popular appeal. Second, those who sought to use his star image in this way constructed a Chaplin in the light of their own priorities and cultural background. In France, as would become increasingly clear, "Charlot" was a signifier used to express French cultural and political concerns, at times in direct opposition to Chaplin's star image in the United States and frequently with little attention paid to his own ideas and values.

French Fandom

The emergence of the movie star was inseparable from the advent of movie fans. Chaplin had been familiar with fandom—created by the conjunction of moving pictures, newspaper publicity, and film magazines—since the up-surge of "Chaplinitis" in the summer of 1915. If he thought even for a moment he would escape it by traveling to Europe, he was quickly disabused. Newspapermen on board the *Olympic* cabled daily accounts of his prog-ress across the Atlantic. A large group of journalists "invaded" the liner, demanding to speak to Chaplin, when it stopped briefly at Cherbourg in France. Although the crowd meeting him at Southampton, the *Olympic*'s final destination, was small, his subsequent welcome was much warmer. Many people were waiting to see him at stations as his train passed by on its way to London. His arrival in the capital, David Robinson remarks, was "a triumph hardly paralleled [in Britain] in the twentieth century outside a few great royal or national events." Thousands of people filled the streets of the British capital as Chaplin was driven from Waterloo Station to the Ritz Hotel, where forty policemen were needed to clear a way through the dense crowd.[34] A large array of people outside the Ritz waited for Chaplin to show himself at the window of his suite. He would be able to revisit the scenes of his boyhood in south London—where he was also quickly recognized and another crowd began to form—only by leaving the hotel through the service entrance.[35]

Chaplin's accounts of his initial reception in Paris—both in *My Trip Abroad*, published a year later, and in his subsequent autobiography—made it seem very similar to what had happened in London. According to *My Trip Abroad*, he was met at the Gare du Nord with "a reportorial avalanche" and a crowd waiting to meet him outside the station that was "almost as large as the one in London." Still experiencing the effects of being seasick on the boat from Dover to Calais, he was "not equal to speaking nor answering questions." He was escorted to the customs house, where a helpful reporter suggested another way out. Disappointing the crowd, he leaped into a taxi and was driven straight to Claridge's Hotel, just off the Champs-Elysées. In his autobiography, published over forty years later, he recalled being greeted in Paris "by a large crowd and a cordon of police." He was "pushed and massaged" by the people around him but finally, with the police's help, "lifted and bundled into a taxi." The "excitement" generated by such "a stirring reception" left him feeling "exhausted."[36]

French newspapers at the time reported Charlot's arrival very differently. At one end of the spectrum was *Le Petit Parisien*, which insisted that Chaplin had arrived "strictly incognito" and that no one was waiting for him, or even recognized him, before he was driven immediately to Claridge's.[37] At the other was the above-mentioned article by Max Massot in *Le Journal*, which presented a mass of convincing details (including the fact that the train had arrived at platform 19) to suggest that Massot himself had been present at the scene.[38] Most of the newspapers, however, seem to have based their coverage on embroidered versions of a report by L'agence Radio. This described Charlot as wearing a gray overcoat *à martingale* (with a half-belt across the waist). It suggested that he *would* have escaped the station without being noticed had it not been for a young woman who recognized him ("Tiens! C'est Charlot!") and went to shake his hand. Chaplin resigned himself to being photographed and answering a series of questions: he was happy to be in France, which he had already visited before and performed on a stage there—though he could not remember precisely where; his only purpose in coming was to get to know Paris and the French better; he was not staying long but would return; and he was surprised by the allegations against Arbuckle, even the fact that he drank alcohol. Variations of this story appeared in *Le Petit Parisien* (effectively contradicting its own report that Chaplin had left the station unnoticed), *L'Echo de Paris*, *L'Eclair*, *L'Avenir*, *L'Homme Libre*, *Le Gaulois*, and *L'Action Française*.[39] *Le Journal*, *Le Matin*, *La République Française*, and *Le Petit Journal* also told the story of a railway man who rushed forward, welcoming Charlot warmly "in the name of France" and shaking him vigorously by the hand.[40]

The slowness of the French response to Chaplin was partly to do with the lack of comparable pre-publicity for his visit. (His decision to go to Paris was apparently made at the last moment, and he kept his room at the

Ritz to throw his British fans—and reporters on both sides of the English Channel—off the scent.) It also reflected the fact that he did not look at all like the screen Charlot. A writer for *L'Intransigeant* observed that, in the absence of Chaplin's trademark moustache, baggy trousers, and long shoes, many had difficulty recognizing him.[41] Clearly, it was a surprise—even a disappointment—to many French observers that Chaplin's screen persona was not the same as his everyday appearance. A reporter for *Paris-Midi* noted sadly that he wore "a bowler hat—but, alas, not the real little elastic bowler hat, another rather commonplace one—Charlot, clean-shaven, carried a cane—but, alas, not the true little plastic cane, also another one—and walked in little steps, steps which were not the same as the 'true' steps of Charlot. "[42] In place of the Tramp figure, here was a man dressed in a smart gray coat, wearing "a most fashionable bowler hat, carrying a small but rigid light yellow cane, laughing with all his white, symmetrical teeth."[43] Perhaps the greatest shock for many was the discovery that the real Chaplin, unlike Charlot, had no moustache. A journalist in *Le Peuple*, for example, noted that "the news, so unanticipated, that his famous little moustache was false, has made more noise than the response of Sinn Fein to Lloyd George or the session of the League of Nations Assembly."[44]

A number of French observers, however, clearly had less difficulty in identifying Chaplin as Charlot. One new aspect of cinema to emerge in the 1910s was the rise of fandom, with moviegoers not only watching the films of their favorite stars but also following their private lives through newspaper gossip columns and illustrated fanzines.[45] In the United States, the principal market for such coverage was female, and it is probable that the same was true in France.[46] It may be no accident, therefore, that it was a young woman who reportedly recognized Charlot on his arrival at the Gare du Nord. The reporter for *L'Echo de Paris* speculated, "for her, he is an old acquaintance: just imagine, she has known him—on the screen—since *Charlot dentiste* [*Laughing Gas*] and *Charlot champion de boxe* [*The Champion*], that is to say, since 1915!"[47] Significantly, it was a second young woman who recognized Chaplin when he visited the Café de la Rotonde in Montparnasse and a third who presented him with a bouquet of flowers as he was leaving Paris for Germany.[48]

French journalists and film critics hoped that Chaplin would be welcomed warmly in Paris, but without the scenes of excessive adulation that he—and other Hollywood stars—had experienced in London. "For heaven's sake," urged Georges Dureau, editor of *Ciné-Journal*, "let us not renew in Paris the scenes of epileptic enthusiasm which marked the arrival in London of Pearl White and the large worthy Fatty."[49] In its next issue, *Ciné-Journal*'s correspondent in London made it clear that the warmth of Chaplin's reception there greatly exceeded that for White and Arbuckle. "No emperor, exotic sovereign or potentate," declared G.-W. Smith, "has ever known a more frenzied welcome than Charlot. London went mad with enthusiasm."[50] Some French commentators pleaded with their readers to treat Chaplin with greater tact and sympathy. "He has not come," insisted Maurice Prax in *Le Petit Parisien*, "... to find himself blockaded in his hotel by a mass of fifty thousand admirers, all wanting to touch the sacred relics of his suit and to obtain interviews.... He has not come to be pursued by a pack of men and women gone wild.... He wants to see Paris and not the gawking onlookers of Paris.... Let us leave him in peace."[51]

It seemed to some observers that this wish for a more restrained welcome for Charlot in Paris than in England had been fulfilled. "Charlot has been in Paris for two days," reported *La Libre Parole*, "and he has not yet produced the very scandalous scenes which marked, in London, the passage of the celebrated clown." A. Aulard similarly noted in *Le Peuple* that his reception had been "sympathetic" but "less lively." Jean-Louis Croze of the daily arts newspaper *Comoedia* claimed that, unlike Londoners, Parisians did not clutch at Chaplin's clothes when he tried to get into his car, as the London crowds had done.[52] Just after Chaplin had left on his journey back to the United States, a journalist at *Le Matin* reflected on his stay in a Paris, "which welcomed him cordially, but where he has been able to stay with a little more tranquillity and do what he wishes, where he has at last been spared the indiscrete demonstrations that each of his deeds seemed automatically to trigger off in [supposedly more] phlegmatic England."[53]

Certainly, the crowd outside his hotel in Paris seemed, for most of the time, to be much smaller, more patient, and generally better behaved than in London. The day after Chaplin's arrival in Paris, Croze of *Comoedia* set off to visit him at Claridge's. He observed that there were two hundred people waiting outside the hotel, a crowd drawn from a wide social spectrum of "midinettes [shopgirls], store clerks, children's nurses, all mixed together with better-off men and even more distinguished women."[54] The crowd continued to grow throughout the day, wrote another reporter. By 9:00 a.m. on Chaplin's second full day in Paris, there were "several hundred people" standing opposite the hotel "in the hope—however fallacious—that they might be able to catch sight of the 'king of the screen.'"[55] At 7:00 p.m. on the third day, there were still "some two hundred people, of varied appearance, standing, patiently" there. A few moments later, a boy shouted "There he is!" as a car arrived. Chaplin got out, smiling at people on the left and right. The crowd followed him to the hotel, and as he passed into the entrance hall, there were many shouts of "Vive Charlot!" Chaplin responded to these acclamations by turning around and waving his acknowledgment.[56]

There were times during his three visits to Paris in 1921 when Chaplin was able to move around with reasonable freedom. He renewed his acquaintance with French boxer Georges Carpentier, whom he had met that summer in New York. *La Libre Parole* claimed, with some satisfaction, that Chaplin and Carpentier had strolled together down the Champs-Elysées, watched only by a little group of silent onlookers.[57] He met members of the avant-garde from both the United States and France. Waldo Frank had written *Our America* (1919), hailing what he saw as a great American cultural revival from the ashes of the genteel tradition. He and Chaplin had lunch and dinner; early one morning, they sat together on a bench on the Champs-Elysées, watching wagons heading off for market. Jacques Copeau was a playwright, director of the Théâtre du Vieux Colombier, and an editor of the *Nouvelle Revue Française*, which encouraged new French writers. Chaplin had supper with Copeau and his circle at Brasserie Lipp. He ate with members of the British aristocracy: Sir Philip Sassoon, Prime Minister Lloyd George's parliamentary private secretary; Sassoon's sister, Sybil, Lady Rocksavage; and her husband, George. The day after the gala at the Trocadéro, he mingled with the French and international elite at a lunch held at the Petit Trianon palace at Versailles, once the favorite refuge of Queen Marie Antoinette. Chaplin also did the same as many other tourists: he went to the Folies-Bergère music-hall (which he found "shabbier" than when he performed there in 1909), had a drink at the Café de La Rotonde in Montparnasse, and finished a long evening in Montmartre at the Lapin Agile bar-cabaret.[58]

There were also times, however, when Chaplin was hounded nearly as much as he had been in London. Cami, the cartoonist, had already exchanged drawings and photographs with Chaplin before the two met in Paris (and discovered that they were unable to communicate since neither spoke the other's language). In *Le Journal*, Cami recounted going up and down in an elevator at Claridge's with Chaplin and his "devoted" secretary Carlyle Robinson, trying to evade the curious and those seeking autographs.[59] Many newspaper photographers waited with the crowd outside the hotel, but as more and more penetrated the hotel itself, Chaplin bowed to the inevitable and agreed (together with Georges Carpentier) to a long photo shoot.[60] Away from the hotel, being recognized by a crowd could sometimes be a frightening experience. When Chaplin and Waldo Frank went to see the Fratellini brothers, the famous clowns in the Médrano Circus, the audience realized toward the end of their act that Chaplin was present. Frank later recalled:

> A score of gendarmes broke into the delirious maze of men and women, pressing on Chaplin as if they were hungry to devour him. The police . . . formed a phalanx about him and he was shuffled out into the Place Pigalle.
>
> But the cry *Charlot!* had got there first. The square, the boulevards that lead to it, turned into a magnetized mob; thousands came pouring, pushing, shouting. Men touched him; women tried to kiss him. At last, with his London-tailored garments reduced to the state of a rummage sale in the Bronx, Charlie was swept into a strategic taxi.[61]

The Paris edition of the *New York Herald* reported scenes of Chaplin being mobbed on the Left Bank and having to make his escape in a taxi with an insistent autograph-hunter still standing on the running-board.[62] More ominous, prefiguring in an eerie way what would happen to Diana, Princess of Wales, some seventy-six years later, there were stories in the press of Chaplin leaving Claridge's and being driven fast and erratically around the Arc de Triomphe to get away from pursuing cars and cyclists.[63]

At the start of Chaplin's stay in Paris, a number of newspapers reported that he was traveling "in the strictest incognito" to avoid publicity and crowds.[64] According to *La Liberté*, he was trying to move around freely, "like a monarch on vacation."[65] Very few French newspapers respected Charlot's supposed desire for anonymity. Most covered his presence in Paris as a page 1 story, dispatching what the satirical magazine *Le Canard enchaîné* referred to as "a veritable army of reporters" (some of whom spoke no English) and photographers to Claridge's Hotel.[66] By 1921, of course, there was nothing new about newspaper coverage of celebrities. Urbain Dhere of *Paris-Midi* saw Chaplin as the most recent arrival in the genealogy of celebrity. "The shoulders which carry Charlot in triumph," he wrote metaphorically, "are still fatigued from having hoisted boxers towards the sky. Before the turn of the boxers, it was that of aviators, who, themselves, replaced cyclists, tenors and generals."[67] Dhere's reference to boxers is interesting, since Georges Carpentier, having gallantly but unsuccessfully fought Jack Dempsey for the heavyweight championship of the world on July 2, 1921, was then at the peak of his popularity in France. The reunion of Carpentier and Chaplin (described by *Le Petit Parisien* as "the king of laughter and the prince of the ring"),[68] the photographs of them together, and their appearance on the balcony of Chaplin's room at Claridge's helped emphasize the celebrity in their respective fields of what J.-L. Croze referred to as these two *"wonder men."*[69] But if Carpentier was, as *Le Figaro* pointed out, as famous as Charlot in France, he could not compete with Charlot's international appeal.[70] As Dhere noted in *Paris-Midi*, Chaplin's European reception so far had been way beyond anything experienced before: "Never, in the memory either of man or historian, have we seen the crowd animated by a similar enthusiasm."[71]

After confirming Charlot's vast popularity, Dhere added that "never has a clown been acclaimed in this way."[72] In common with a number of journalists and some film critics, he appears to have had reservations about the challenge to cultural hierarchies posed by the emergence of slapstick comedians as film stars. D. Mosellan in *The Radical*, indeed, produced a fictional dialogue in which he reproached a friend—"un homme sérieux"—for joining in "this absurd admiration for the stars of cinema, old dishwashers, such as Fatty, who have now become clowns and millionaires."[73] The most systematic—and widely reproduced—defense of Chaplin in this respect was written by A. Aulard in *Le Peuple* under the title "The Popularity of Charlot: Is It a Sign of Decadence?" Aulard argued that civilized people had often shown a taste for actors, who made them laugh, cry, and reflect on life. This taste, rather than reflecting decadence, was a sign of "intellectual culture, of refined sensibility." Dismissing the idea that Chaplin was only a clown used to receiving kicks up the backside, Aulard reminded his readers that Molière himself had entertained audiences in similar ways. He went on in chauvinistic fashion to compare American and French moviegoers, to the great advantage of the latter. He dismissed most American spectators as "puerile," appreciating only the simplest slapstick humor. French spectators, he argued, were more sophisticated. Based on his personal observation of Parisian cinemagoers, Aulard insisted that what French viewers loved was not at all "the kick in the pants," "the brutal farce" of Chaplin's comedies but the "fine sensibility" and "the beautiful human sympathy" they displayed. He finished by arguing that "the popularity of this delicious clown, whom Hamlet would have loved, and who actually has something of Shakespeare in him, is consequently with us not a sign of decadence, but rather of moral nobility."[74]

Underpinning the efforts of French critics and commentators to define Chaplin's place in their own culture was an uneasy consciousness that a career such as his would have been impossible if he had been working in the French film industry. He would, Louis Forest maintained in *Le Matin*, have been damaged by the fact that he had not fought in the war. Once the war was over, he would have been hindered by the narrow nature of the French domestic market, and American filmmakers would have resisted the penetration of his films into the United States.[75] There was indeed another half-hearted attempt to claim Charlot as French—*Le Petit Parisien* reported that he had been born in Fontainebleau[76]—but most writers assumed that Chaplin himself was an American.[77] It was as an American star that they hailed his participation in the effort to rebuild France after the First World War.

Postwar Reconstruction and the Gala at the Trocadéro

Chaplin returned in 1921 to a France that was much changed from the time of his visit in 1912. The First World War had been a disaster for France, even though it and its allies had ultimately defeated Germany after four years of fighting; 1.4 million French soldiers had been killed and 3 million had been wounded, of which 1.1 million were permanently disabled.[78] On the Western Front, the war had been fought almost entirely on French territory. As John Horne notes, "Ten French departments [in the northeast of the country] had suffered extensive damage both from the fighting . . . and German occupation policies. Cultural monuments of national significance, such as Rheims cathedral, were devastated." The population of the whole area had fallen by almost half, and many villages had been totally obliterated. In the last stages of the war, the Germans had systematically destroyed factories and razed the land itself as they retreated.[79]

Efforts to rehabilitate these areas had been made since 1918, and Louis Loucheur was in charge of a government ministry charged solely with the task. The major problem Loucheur faced was the lack of funding available for reconstruction. The Treaty of Versailles had required Germany to make reparation payments to make good the damage of the war, but the only cash payment made had been in May 1921. In August, Loucheur and Walter Rathenau, a member of the Joseph Wirth government in Germany, concluded a draft agreement (the Wiesbaden accord) to replace cash reparations with reparations in kind. Called "réparations en nature" in France, these envisaged the direct delivery from Germany of "vast quantities of reconstruction material." The final version of the Wiesbaden agreement would not, however, be signed until October 6, 1921, and, Marc Trachtenberg notes, despite the hopes it stirred in France, it "was never actually put into effect."[80]

In default of German reparations, and recognizing the size of the challenge in reconstructing the devastated regions, the French government had shown itself prepared to accept assistance from any source, including private philanthropy. One organization that became involved in this work was the idealistic Comité américain des Regions dévastés (CARD). By agreement with the French government, CARD had assumed the primary responsibility for the "material and moral reconstruction" of four cantons chosen from the most ravaged part of the Department of the Aisne, the areas around Soisson, Coucy-le-Chateaux, and Vic-sur-Aisne.[81] Headed by André Tardieu, the first minister of liberated regions, as honorary president and with the support of the American ambassador Myron T. Herrick, CARD was largely run by American women, including Mrs. A. M. Dike as president and Miss Anne Morgan, banker J. P. Morgan's daughter, as vice president. By 1921 it could point to many successes, including the establishment of a construction workshop, employment exchange, thirty-two agricultural syndicates, twenty-eight public libraries, sixteen hostels, fourteen schools for infants, a hospital, a charitable center, sixty-two domestic science classes, sports clubs, and a stadium. The young women of CARD, wearing their sky-blue uniforms modeled, by special permission of Marshall Philippe Pétain, on those of the French infantry, were to be seen everywhere in the devastated parts of the Aisne driving cars, acting as nurses, and distributing toothbrushes. By the late summer of 1921, the organization had reportedly spent some twenty million francs and—even with financial aid from the French government—was on the point of running out of money.[82]

In this situation, the arrival of Charlie Chaplin in France must have seemed like a godsend. Anne Morgan became involved in organizing a charitable gala at the Trocadéro to raise money for CARD. She quickly realized that, because of the huge popularity of Charlot in France, persuading Chaplin to give her *The Kid* to show at the gala would aid considerably the committee's fundraising efforts—and that the financial success of the event would be guaranteed if Chaplin himself agreed to appear. But Chaplin was annoyed by the endless phone calls from Miss Morgan's secretary and the fact that, when he did finally agree to meet with Morgan herself, she was late. He readily agreed to give her *The Kid* but refused to appear with it. Morgan airily (and rather arrogantly) seems to have promised that Chaplin would be decorated by the French government if he took part, and Chaplin, without actually agreeing, seems to have indicated he might participate if this was the case. He then left for Germany.[83] Leaked stories in the French press claimed that he had promised Morgan he would attend the gala.[84] Chaplin was about to issue a denial when a telegram arrived from Morgan with an assurance that he would be decorated if he attended. Thus mollified, Chaplin agreed. In all probability, he expected to receive the Légion d'honneur. In practice, the decoration he received on the night of the gala from Minister of Beaux-Arts and Public Instruction André Bérard was the much less impressive ribbon of an Officier de l'Instruction Publique. Chaplin put the best face he could on this setback. In all probability, his real reward was the "society" lunch Morgan invited him to the next day at the Villa Trianon at Versailles.[85]

When Chaplin began making films in January 1914, the audience for those films—at least in much of the United States—had been primarily working class and often immigrant. He must have derived considerable satisfaction from the fact that, at the Trocadéro in 1921, the audience was largely made up of Paris high society, drawn from politics, diplomacy, arts, and the aristocracy, and the elite of the American colony, headed by the ambassador, Myron T. Herrick. Although the prices of tickets varied from five hundred francs for a box to a democratic five francs for an ordinary seat, most of the people there were clearly rather well-off.[86] The newspapers the next day printed lists of those present, which included Henri Letellier, the financier and publisher, whom Chaplin would later use as the basis for the character of Pierre Revel in *A Woman of Paris* (1923).[87] Chaplin shared a box with, among others, Anne Morgan and Cécile Sorel of the Comédie Française, wearing what Louis Delluc described as "a dress from the last Opera ball." Sorel, coming from a much older acting tradition, seems to have treated Chaplin in a distinctly patronizing way. (Delluc sardonically remarked, "French tact is also a region devastated by the war.")[88]

The program had been organized by impresario Firmin Gémier, with the help of his assistant, André Roubler.[89] It began with the performance of an overture by Berlioz, played by the Colonne Orchestra, which would continue playing throughout the evening. There followed *La France qui renaît*, a film made by the Ministry for the Devastated Regions. It showed the destruction wrought by the war and the efforts at reconstruction, including the "restoration of huge locks, of mining shafts, of manufacturing plants." It also covered the great efforts made to bring agricultural land back into cultivation, with pictures of a disabled workman plowing—a symbol, one newspaper noted, of the "many who have gone back to work the soil they fought for, despite physical disability."[90] To one French observer, it was "a moving witness to the profound vitality of our national stock"; to Chaplin, or so he would later recall, it was "a dreary documentary" that "went on endlessly up to the intermission."[91]

When the intermission itself was over, a second film was shown—*Le Rire dans les Ruines*—dealing with the work of the young women of CARD toward the physical education of children in the neighborhood of Soissons. Once this was over, American journalist H. Nobel Hall took the stage to introduce Chaplin. When Charlot himself walked on the stage, carrying a young girl (Mary Pickford's niece), the audience applauded loudly and enthusiastically. Chaplin clearly wanted to say something but was so moved he burst into tears. Nobel Hall excused him and introduced Douglas Fairbanks, who was also present at the gala. Fairbanks walked onto the stage to, in the words of one of the journalists present, "greet the crowd and show all his teeth."[92]

There followed the screening of Chaplin's latest film, *Le Gosse* (*The Kid*). Although this had already been shown to critics two weeks earlier (Louis Delluc had hailed it "as a mixture of Dickens and Rabelais. . . . It will draw vast attention to Chaplin, the principal actor of our time"),[93] it is likely that fewer than a handful of people in the Trocadéro audience had seen it before, and the effect seems to have been enormous. J.-L. Croze of *Comoedia* called it a "masterpiece" with an emotional quality that "will take you and pull you along."[94] Dealing with an "orphan child" (played by Jackie Coogan) and lost mother, it must have had a special resonance for the millions of grieving families in France in 1921—to whom it also offered a fantasy of everything coming out right in the end. As one reporter commented, it saw Charlot, "thanks to his captivating smile, soothe, a little, the tears of our poor little French kids."[95]

When *The Kid* had finished and the applause had died down, Chaplin was invited to the box of Minister Bérard to receive his decoration. He then stood up and made a brief speech saying that he and the motion picture industry were very happy to support the rehabilitation of France's devastated regions. He was applauded and the evening finished with Chaplin, who had already signed 250 programs at his hotel, signing many others to be auctioned off. The evening was a great financial success, with 230,000 francs raised for CARD. Of this, 30,000 francs was raised from the sale of items signed by Chaplin.[96]

Two days later, Chaplin left Paris by air on his way back to England and the boat for America.[97] He left behind a message translated into French that thanked "all those who welcomed me so warmly" and claiming that, while he would like to have stayed longer in France, he needed to get back to work.[98] Chaplin would not return to France for ten years; on his next visit, in 1931, he *would* finally receive the coveted Légion d'honneur. On his 1921 trip, he spent barely more than a week in Paris over a three-week period, since he traveled during this time both to Berlin and London. His visits to Paris began with a debate in the press over whether he was a Bolshevik. They ended with his being fêted by the French social and political elite both at the Trocadéro gala and afterward. In the intervening time, he had encountered many of his French fans. In this comparatively early period in the history of both fandom and the culture of celebrity, he tried—with varying degrees of success—to do the same things in Paris other tourists would have done. Whether he seriously hoped to move around Paris incognito, as he claimed, is a debatable point. After all, as Chaplin himself subsequently confessed, he had traveled to Europe at least in part to taste the fruits of his screen success. Speaking no French, he clearly had no idea of the discussion in the French press over whether the enthusiasm of his fans was a sign of decadence.

It is unclear to what extent, if at all, Chaplin was influenced by the plight of France's devastated regions. According to one (possibly fictional) report in *Le Journal*, soon after arriving in France he had expressed pity for those areas once occupied by the Germans.[99] (In his own account of his European trip, he would recall passing through them only at night on the train taking him to Germany.)[100] Chaplin may simply have seen participation in the gala on October 5 as a means of promoting his film in France (and gaining a decoration in the process). But his gesture was warmly appreciated; one newspaper claimed it demonstrated that "to the genius of a great artist it adds the goodwill of a warm heart."[101] The screening of *The Kid* at the gala proved a crucial moment in the development of Chaplin's reputation in France. His conduct did much to strengthen his stature in political circles and among the wealthier Parisians who earlier might have been indifferent to him. Conversely, the nature of his treatment as a celebrity and the "official" recognition he gained at the Trocadéro gala seem to have disturbed his more avant-garde supporters, including Philippe Soupault.[102]

3

Charlot in the 1920s

A Growing Reputation

For the remainder of the 1920s, Chaplin's reputation in France continued to grow. His work was hailed by critics as well as writers and intellectuals such as Élie Faure, a very young Jean-Paul Sartre, Lucien Fabre, Jean Prévost, and André Maurois. He made a film supposedly set in France itself, *L'Opinion publique* (*A Woman of Paris*, UA, 1923), in which, for the first time, he did not take a major role. (He appeared on-screen for only a few seconds as an inept railroad porter who smashes up a trunk.) For his three other longer films of the 1920s—*Le pélerin* (*The Pilgrim*, First National, 1922), *La Ruée vers l'or* (*The Gold Rush*, UA, 1925), and *Le Cirque* (*The Circus*, UA, 1928)—he returned to his Tramp persona.[1] Most film critics appreciated these longer movies as a further development of Chaplin's artistry. Yet between the release of *The Gold Rush* in France in September 1925 and *The Circus* in February 1928, Chaplin himself passed through a period in which he would be much criticized by some French writers, notably André Suarès and Paul Souday, while many others would spring to his defense.

Louis Delluc's *Charlot*

The first serious book-length study of Chaplin as an artist of the cinema to be published anywhere in the world appeared in France in 1921. Its author, Louis Delluc, had been born in Cadouin, a small town in southwest France, in 1890. Over the next few years his father, a pharmacist, moved the family first to Bordeaux and then, in 1903, to Paris. Delluc began his career as a precocious devotee of traditional culture: at fifteen he won a national poetry prize; at eighteen, published his first book of poems; by twenty he was a theater critic for the fortnightly *Comoedia illustré*.[2] On his own admission, he detested the cinema before the First World War.[3] But in 1916, at the urging of his girlfriend and future wife, actress Eve Francis, he went to see a series

Charlot. Melvyn Stokes, Oxford University Press. © Oxford University Press 2026.
DOI: 10.1093/9780197839294.003.0004

of Chaplin films and Cecil B. DeMille's *The Cheat* (1915). The experience was transformative. He was, Francis later wrote, "struck as by lightning. He had caught a glimpse of the incommensurable possibilities of film and he consecrated himself to its service."[4] Over the next few years, Delluc became a major force in nascent French film culture. In 1917, he joined the weekly magazine *Le Film*, founded by André Heuzé and Henri Diamant-Berger in 1914, as editor-in-chief. In 1918 he was the first film critic to have a weekly newspaper column (in *Paris-Midi*). He founded his own film journals, *Le Journal du Ciné-Club* in 1920 and *Cinéa* in 1921. In 1919–20, he produced scenarios for three films, two of which he also directed.[5] His first book on cinema, *Cinéma et Cie*, mainly a collection of revised reviews from *Le Film*, was published in 1919. A second, *Photogénie*, followed in 1920. *Charlot* was his third.

In *Charlot*, Delluc showed he was well aware of Chaplin's real biography: his birth in London in 1889, his quasi-Dickensian family knowing "illnesses and poverty and days of real hunger," his apprenticeship with Karno's troupe of pantomime players ("no better school"), and his early days in California.[6] But knowing the truth about "this Anglo-American mime" did not prevent Delluc from endowing him, almost wistfully, with some recognizably "French" qualities and suggesting that—somehow—he was linked to French history and culture. Chaplin's on-screen "mask" or persona, he argued, "is curiously Latin."[7] "With all his formulas of Cockney pantomime," he maintained, à propos of the visual appearance of Chaplin's films, "he gives us sometimes the charm, almost retrospective and classic, of the early French painters."[8] In relation to Chaplin's early, failed attempt at Essanay to produce "a really dramatic" (rather than humorous) film, Delluc claimed such a project "was to be expected, for he has in him that sort of French grace which gives him kinship with the drama of sentiment. He is own cousin of [Alexandre Dumas the elder's fictional hero] D'Artagnan."[9] When it came to Chaplin's rapid rise to worldwide eminence, only real-life French comparisons came to mind: the comedian's celebrity, Delluc observed, "eclipses the fame of Joan of Arc, Louis XIV, and Clemenceau. I can think only of Napoleon rivalling his notoriety."[10]

At the core of Delluc's 1921 book were the two longest chapters: the first dealing with Chaplin's methods of work, the second with what David Robinson terms "enraptured, impressionistic descriptions of the individual films."[11] In his chapter on Chaplin's working methods, rather than analyzing these himself, Delluc reprinted previously published articles by French comedian Max Linder, a friend of Chaplin, Elsie Codd, his secretary, and Chaplin himself. All three emphasized how brutally hard and professional was the work involved in bringing Charlot to the screen: the crucial role played by rehearsals, the painstaking way in which multiple takes of every sequence were shot, and, if only by implication, the key role of editing in shaping the final product. Linder, for example, claimed that Chaplin "spent two months in making a picture of 1,800 feet; he used for that more than 36,000 feet of negative; every scene was 'shot' twenty times; and with trials, and alterations and finishing touches, that meant about fifty rehearsals."[12]

The final part of Delluc's book made no real attempt to give a narrative account of Chaplin's movies. (Delluc tried to do so for *Charlot s'évade* [*The Adventurer*, Mutual, 1917] but confessed, "I give it up. I ask pardon. I've been trying to *tell* the funniest of Charlie's stories. I shan't do it again.")[13] Nor did it deal with all of Chaplin's films. As I noted in chapter 1, Delluc had reviewed a reissue of *Making a Living*, Chapin's very first film for Keystone, as already demonstrating "his charm, his authority, his strange and harmonious inspiration."[14] But he made clear in *Charlot* that he regarded the Keystone films—only four out of thirty-six were discussed in the book—as essentially preparatory rather than fully formed examples of Chaplin's art. By 1921, Delluc seems to have regarded Chaplin's earlier films in the same light as the first works by seventeenth-century playwright Jean-Baptiste Poquelin, better known as Molière, which he dismissed as "simple off-scourings."[15] *Charlot* covered twelve of Chaplin's fourteen Essanay productions and three of his first four movies produced for First National, but it was his Mutual films (nine of twelve were discussed) that Delluc perceived as the real turning point in his artistic career. This "dazzling sequence of pictures, satiric and tender, stinging and ardent," he wrote of films such as *Charlot chef de rayon* (The *Floorwalker*, 1916), *One A.M.*, *The Pawnshop*, *Charlot policeman* (*East Street*, 1917) and *Charlot voyage* (*The Immigrant*, 1917), marked "a decided opening out of Chaplin's genius." These films also demonstrated "technical progress" in "stage management," a movement away from the cruder ("custard-pie") traditions of English stage pantomime, and greater depth of characterization.[16]

Delluc had been among the first French critics to discern the strong vein of melancholy that accompanied and underpinned Chaplin's on-screen humor.[17] He developed this insight further in *Charlot*. "I stand amazed," he confessed, "at the immense sadness of Chaplin. This man will be lucky if he doesn't die in a madhouse." Delluc drew attention to the downheartedness of

Chaplin's violin playing in *The Vagabond*. ("He drives the gypsies to tears.") "And then he's a burglar [in *Police*]! And then on a journey [*The Tramp*]! And at the pawnbroker's [*The Pawnshop*]! But he's sad, he's sad." To Delluc, the "somber" nature of Chaplin's movie artistry was most obviously on display in two of his First National films, *A Dog's Life* and *Shoulder Arms*, both released for the first time in 1918. *A Dog's Life*, he insisted, was "a travesty woven of grief." Chaplin's Little Tramp was "down and out, and he gulps down the flavor of the dancing-hall, the band, the singer wailing her turn. He is hungry, hungry with all his being." Delluc suggested that here was "a real film" that "might well have the title of Pity." For its deft combination of sadness and humor, he hailed it as "the first complete work of art the cinema has. It is classical. It EXISTS."[18] *Shoulder Arms*, showing Charlot in the trenches of the First World War, had initially been seen by many as "in bad taste" when released a few days before the end of the conflict. Later, it had been broadly accepted as an amusing comedy. "But really," Delluc insisted, "it is not amusing, not a bit." Viewing the war "through Charlie's eyes" had produced "one of the most truthful [movies] that the War inspired. . . . The farcical atmosphere of the film, its amusing details and jokes . . . only accentuate the cruel nature of the fantasy." "When dogs are wretched they bay at the moon," Delluc wrote in a striking and expressive passage. "That war film of Chaplin bays most terribly at the moon." Through his "personal genius," the filmmaker had once again used humor to shed light on a gloomy and unhappy subject (the war) in a way that "justified all that one can expect from the cinema."[19]

Part of the purpose of Delluc's *Charlot* was to emphasize the significance of the cinema as a new, modern art. The comparisons he made between Chaplin and other cultural and historical figures underlined the importance he attached to both the star and the new art he represented. This was demonstrated on the very first page, where he compared Chaplin's creative artistry in the cinema to Beethoven's in music and suggested (with tongue mildly in cheek) that those unprepared to accept this read no further. If the first comparison Delluc made was between Chaplin and a great musical composer, he also identified parallels between his work and a range of artistic productions. There was, he maintained, a "family resemblance" between Chaplin's mask—the visual persona he created on-screen—and both traditional Japanese masks and the work of great European painters, especially Velázquez, Albrecht Dürer, and "Flemish primitive" artists. Delluc insisted there was nothing at all absurd in comparing Chaplin to great artists of the past, for what he considered most striking "in the latest presentations of this mask is how clearly it has taken on the quality of a painter's work." Yet the difference between Chaplin and early painters, he pointed out, was that "Charlie . . . is his own painter, his very own. For Charlie is the artist and the work of art at the same time, and he has accomplished something which . . . is possible only in the cinema: to paint and model and sculpt one's *own* body, one's *own* features, to make a transposition of art."[20]

Chaplin had turned himself on-screen into Charlot, an example of "living pictorial art."[21] For Delluc, the key word here was "living." In *Photogénie*, the book he had published a year earlier, one of Delluc's major concerns had been to distinguish cinema from photography. Unlike photography, cinema ("moving pictures") possessed the transformative power of motion in how it represented life. Charlot's often athletic movements on-screen were choreographed in the same way as modern dance. In *The Floorwalker*, Delluc observed, Chaplin "falls back on a dance . . . and in the subtlest of rhythms he blends the seductive arts of [improviser of movement to music Émile] Jacques[-]Dalcroze or [ballerina] Anna Pavlova or [innovative choreographer-dancer] Isadore [*sic*] Duncan."[22] Delluc also specifically compared Chaplin to Vaslav Nijinsky, the Russian dancer famed for his gravity-defying leaps. "Charlie Chaplin," he argued, "is an inventor in his art as Nijinsky in his." Yet Chaplin, Delluc insisted, was more significant: "Nijinsky . . . stands for only one epoch of the dance in all the history of the dance. But Charlie is the pioneer of the very first epoch of his art, and he is in some measure responsible for the plaything having become an art." Cinema in its early years had produced around a dozen "distinguished interpreters" (Delluc cited William S. Hart, Douglas Fairbanks, Sessue Hayakawa, and Lillian Gish, among others), but only one of them was "anything more than an interpreter." Chaplin's uniqueness was that he "interprets himself. And he sums up, not what is being done, like Nijinsky, but what is going to be done."[23]

From Delluc's perspective, all arts met in Chaplin, who was at the center of a dense web of cultural reference points. Like François Villon, the fifteenth-century poet who wrote primarily about his own low-life experiences, Delluc judged that Chaplin "was really *himself*, and showing himself in the form that suits him best." As the pioneer of a new cultural form, he resembled Molière (though Delluc remarked that some of Molière's later productions were "mighty tedious," unlike Chaplin, who—he predicted—"will never be tedious"). Delluc also found "something of [acerbic nineteenth-century caricaturist Honoré] Daumier in Chaplin's Keystone film *The Fatal Mallet* ('the miming clown, with his cooper's weapon, seems to be standing there like a great figure of civil war, a creature of humor—or tragedy.')." In a comment on *Shoulder Arms*, Delluc mused whether he would "astonish" famous English stage actor Johnston Forbes-Robertson very much "by telling him that Charlie Chaplin is a Shakespearian actor?"[24]

French Critics During the Early 1920s

Essayist, critic, and art historian Élie Faure, writing in the same year Delluc's book was published, compared Chaplin not just to a Shakespearian actor but to Shakespeare himself—judging him to possess the "same bewildering and yet lucid lyricism . . . the same limitless fancy." Like Shakespeare (and, Faure added, Montaigne), Chaplin "never fails to oppose reality to illusion and . . . to play with the contrast between them."[25] "I do not write the name of Shakespeare at random," Faure wrote. "It answers perfectly to the impression of divine intoxication that Charlie Chaplin gives me, for example, in his film *Sunnyside*."[26] In common with Delluc, Faure endeavored to place Chaplin's role in the emergent new art of cinema in the context of other, more traditional art forms. Cinema, he argued, was "the art of movement . . . an immense visual orchestra of which the precursors were the sculptors of the Hindu bas-reliefs and the painters of the drama of lines and masses in action—Michelangelo, Tintoretto, Rubens, Delacroix." This new art, Faure suggested, should be called "cineplastics." It had nothing to do with the theater. Actors ("cinemimics"), of whom Chaplin was the greatest, could not speak at all.[27]

From Faure's perspective, Chaplin was a true pioneer, being the first man to show "that he entirely understands the new art of the cinema . . . the first man to create a drama that is purely cineplastic, in which the action does not illustrate a sentimental fiction or a moralistic intention but creates a monumental whole; projecting from the inner consciousness a personal vision of the object in a form that is actually visible, in a setting that is actually material and perceptible."[28] This seemed to Faure a "very great . . . achievement, comparable with Titian's concentration of all the sound-elements in time, thus creating from them their very soul and sculpting this." He conceded that "most people do not perceive this [being the creator of a new art form] because Chaplin is a clown" and artists are usually expected to be solemn. But to Faure, he was not simply an artist: he was "a poet, even a great poet, a creator of myths, symbols, and ideas, the discoverer of a new and unknown world...[who] reveals to me what is in me, what is truest in me, what is most human."[29]

There was evidence in France during the postwar years of the 1920s of fresh thinking in many areas. "A new cultural ethos was emerging," argues Libby Murray, "—the picaresque—and replacing the traditional, heroic ethos of the Napoleonic legend or the colonial wars. Charlot embodied the spirit of survival—as opposed to self-sacrifice—increasingly associated in popular and literary culture with the *poilu* [the ordinary French soldier of the trenches]." To Murray, Chaplin was a modern *picaro*—a little man surviving despite everything.[30] A precocious Jean-Paul Sartre, only nineteen in 1924, was possibly the first to draw attention to this. The character of the Tramp Chaplin had created and the type of movie in which he appeared ("the film of true misery") could both be compared to the Spanish genre of picaresque novels that had begun with the anonymous *Life of Lazarillo de Tormès and of His Fortunes and Adversities* (1554). In Spanish a *pícaro* is a rascal, a rogue. The heroes of picaresque novels, as Sartre noted, "know true hunger, true misery.... They don't steal, because they have elegance; they cheat with so much shrewdness and cunning that we are always on their side.... They have highs and lows: one evening they will play roulette for a thousand louis, and the next night sleep at a shelter for the poor." Charlot on film is very similar. As Sartre concluded, both Lazarillo de Tormès and Charlot are comparable: both "stand out against a backdrop of black realism. The miseries, the malice, the pettiness of the [lowest possible] world...are not spared."[31]

Élie Faure also articulated the view—shared by other writers, including Dadaists and later surrealists—that Chaplin's movies offered a unique insight into the postwar world. It was, he argued, "the modern spirit" of his time that "guided...and illumined him with the light of dawn: this man, drunk with intelligence, dancing on the summits of despair."[32] To many writers, the figure of Charlot deftly expressed the zeitgeist and pessimism of a time in which France struggled to come to terms with the legacy of an industrialized conflict in which 1.4 million French citizens had died. Belgian-born writer Henri Michaux, who settled in France, saw the figure of Charlot as a "modern soul." He was simple, in many ways primitive, a *bricoleur*—a jack of all trades—in the range of occupations he played on screen. He expressed modernity through his anti-romanticism, his frequent insensitivity, his alienation from the wider society ("he fails in everything, is thrown out from everywhere, has everyone on his back"), and the fact that he appeared either fatalistic or struggling vainly against the absurd.[33] Faure had already singled out several examples of such absurdity in Chaplin's films, including the moment in *A Dog's Life* when, "just as he is settling down to sleep in an open field, he fills up a hole in a fence in order to stop a draught." (Three years later, essayist, novelist, and poet Lucien Fabre would cite this same sequence as a demonstration of Chaplin's "obviously absurd" style of filmmaking.)[34]

Reflecting the growing interest during the 1920s in psychiatry, and the existence of an unconscious as well as conscious mind, a number of writers also linked Chaplin with these developments. Fabre, for example, noted that his performance as a man who is dreadfully drunk in *One A.M.* echoed the psychiatric notion of automatism (the carrying out of actions without conscious thought or intent).[35] To Michaux, he was the "actor of the subconscious." Charlot on-screen could never resist giving in to his subconscious desires. He was driven by them. Michaux wrote that this was "perhaps the key to Charlie. . . . [W]ith a fire hose, [he] sprinkles a theater, the ladies' dressing room, and musicians. We laugh. But he does not laugh. He cannot resist the impulse, the desire to do so, but he does not enjoy it."[36] Although Michaux cited Freud in his article on Chaplin as one of the "essayists" of the subconscious, Jan Goldstein has pointed out that Freudian ideas were comparatively slow to win acceptance in France, in part because of the strength of France's own psychoanalytical tradition, including the work of Jean-Martin Charcot (whose lectures Freud had attended) and Pierre Janet (whose doctoral dissertation launched the term "psychological automatism").[37] The notion of 1920s writers exploring Chaplin's screen performances through the application of psychoanalytical ideas probably had more to do with this Francophone background than Freudian influences. Indeed, Michaux specifically pointed out that Freud conceived the subconscious as "an erotic reservoir" full of "lustful desires" that conscious man normally resisted, whereas the screen Charlot was simply motivated by the impulse "to use things and people and animals" in a highly insensitive way for humorous effect.[38]

In a special issue of French film journal *Positif* on the centennial of Chaplin's first films, Paul Renard observed there were two rival groups of Francophone writers who dominated the French literary landscape after the First World War: the surrealists (often former Dadaists) and those who were linked to the *Nouvelle Revue Française* (*NRF*). The latter, founded in 1909 by a group that included André Gide, Jacques Copeau, Jean Schlumberger, and Michel Drouin, was relaunched in 1919 after a hiatus because of the war. Under editors Jacques Rivière (1919–25) and Jean Paulhan (1925–40) it became the best-known literary magazine for progressive French writers. Both the surrealist and *NRF* groups, Renard declares, "admired Chaplin." The surrealists' views will be discussed in chapter 4. As for the *NRF*, Renard sees one writer and critic, Jean Prévost, as Chaplin's particular champion.[39] Prévost had come to regard cinema as the most potent of the arts based on mimicry, and saw its most perfect expression in the rhythmic gestures and body language of Charlot. Both were very different from those of most ordinary clowns, whose "exaggeration of natural movement" through violent wriggling of hands and buttocks or facial contortions provoked laughter through their very dissonance.[40] In contrast, Prévost argued, Charlot had eliminated "superfluous" gesturing and "mimics emotion without any seemingly controlled play of muscles—by the unstable balance of a forced immobility, by a movement of the soft parts of the face, eyes, cheeks and lips, which recompose at the end of each gesture according to a new unity."[41] What impressed Prévost most about Chaplin was the manner in which he used gestures to develop a narrative in both linear and nonlinear fashion. "To represent by a gesture an object or a simple notion is relatively easy," he wrote, but "the real difficulty is to pass from one gesture to another, to continue a description and a speech." Looking closely at *The Pilgrim* (1922), he discovered that Chaplin's body language made it possible to "not only follow the thread of thought, but go back, recall what he had already expressed." "It is at these moments," Prévost concluded, "that we feel what genius is."[42]

French champions of Charlot in the 1920s, as Richard Schickel has observed, "projected Chaplin into realms of consequence that other movie stars did not achieve."[43] Novelist, biographer, and essayist André Maurois described Chaplin's raison d'être, in 1927, as being "to represent the awkwardness, the melancholy and the resignation of men faced with the absurd unexpected misfortunes that they encounter over and over again in a hostile world."[44] What made Chaplin so crucial in this role was that he was regarded as the foremost practitioner of the new art of cinema—the first truly popular art, Maurois asserted, since medieval cathedrals and the "chansons de geste" (epic poems). Maurois also noted the appeal of Chaplin's films across the entire globe: he was, indeed, a "great worldwide artist."[45] But Maurois, a writer, was concerned to answer the argument that cinema as an art was limited by the fact that it did not use language—that, without words, it would not be possible to preserve contact with "modern man."[46] He posed the issue whether, without using words, cinema "can express, like the novel or the poem, the poetic essence of things and events." In Chaplin's cinema, Maurois believed, it could. Images could be used to put across complicated ideas very simply. (Even a writer of the stature of Marcel Proust, he suggested, would need a very long sentence to make comprehensible what a filmmaker could say with a small number of images.)[47] Maurois frequently compared Chaplin's films to literary fiction; he believed, for example that *The Pilgrim* ended like a story by Prosper Mérimée and that *The Gold Rush* (1925) commenced in a similar way to a novel by Gustave Flaubert. He also saw parallels between the manner in which Chaplin's filmmaking expressed his style and artistic personality and the work of Anatole France and Charles Dickens. Following on from Élie Faure, who regarded Chaplin as the author of "cineplastic poems," Maurois saw him as a true poet of the cinema, musing over a film in the same way as Paul Valéry did over a poem.[48] Yet Charlot's cinematic poetry appealed to a far broader social range than most poetry. *The Gold Rush*, Maurois argued, was "the first illustration since the *Chanson de Roland* of a poem equally accessible to Crainquebille [the character of a poor, victimized street vendor in Anatole France's 1903 play] and Joseph Bédier [a literary scholar who had worked on the *Song of Roland*]."[49]

A Woman of Paris (L'Opinion publique)

After *The Kid* was made in 1921, Chaplin produced six other films during the 1920s. The first three, *The Idle Class* (1921), *Pay Day* (1922), and *The Pilgrim* (1922), were all made for the First National studio. The last trio, *A Woman of Paris* (1923), *The Gold Rush* (1925), and *The Circus* (1928), were produced for United Artists. Whereas *The Idle Class* and *Pay Day* were similar in length to many of Chaplin's earlier films, lasting around half an hour, the remaining four films were much longer, feature-length productions. It was these last four films in particular that would consolidate Chaplin's reputation among French writers and critics as a great cinema artist. The impact of these four on French film writers was all the more apparent since *The Idle Class* (*Charlot et le masque de fer*) and *Pay Day* (*Jour de paye*) were not released immediately in France and, when they were finally screened, received comparatively little critical attention.[50]

Although earlier Charlot films continued to circulate and be popular in France, the first new Chaplin film to be screened there since *The Kid* in 1921 was *A Woman of Paris*, retitled *L'Opinion publique* for French audiences. It is clear that the proprietors of the Aubert-Palace Theater on the boulevard des Italiens, where *A Woman of Paris* was first screened in April 1924, wanted to cash in on Chaplin's reputation while at the same time explaining that the new film differed considerably from his earlier productions. An ad announced that "Charles Chaplin, the popular 'Charlot,'" had now "conceived and directed his first film drama."[51] The new film, remarked René Jeanne in *Le Petit Journal*, was the first in which Chaplin had written the script and directed without himself appearing on-screen. It demonstrated that, more than being simply an actor, he was "an artist of a surprising sensitivity . . . who understands life." Pierre Henry in *Cinéa-Ciné-pour-tous* explained that the idea of a film drama looking at the seamier elements of existence had first occurred to Chaplin while working for the Essanay Studio in 1915, but that movie—titled *Life*—had never been finished.[52] A number of reviewers argued that many of Chaplin's earlier films had combined drama with comedy: Léon Moussinac of *L'Humanité* saw echoes of the downtrodden Charlot of *A Dog's Life* in his new movie, and Pierre Henry called attention to the melancholy scenes in films such as *The Kid*.[53]

Most French critics knew that the original American title had been *A Woman of Paris*. Henry, indeed, published a fairly accurate genealogy of the film's origins, tracing it back to Chaplin's brief affair with socialite Peggy Hopkins Joyce, during which she appears to have shared her memories of her own involvement with wealthy French newspaper owner Henri Letellier (whom Chaplin had met during his visit to Paris in 1921). This, together with his own recollections of Paris night-life, appears to have provided inspiration for the film.[54] It portrayed a story of doomed love: Marie St. Clair (Edna Purviance) and Jean Millet (Carl Miller) plan to escape together to Paris from their provincial town. Jean is prevented from leaving at the last moment by the illness of his father. Marie leaves for Paris alone and eventually becomes the mistress of wealthy Pierre Revel (Adolph Menjou), a character clearly based on Letellier. Marie and Jean meet up again and rekindle their love affair, and Marie plans to leave Pierre. But she overhears Jean talking with his mother (Lydia Knott), who (representing the "public opinion" of the French title) disapproves of his marrying a demimondaine. Marie returns to Pierre, and Jean, after an unsuccessful attempt to win her back, commits suicide. Marie finally abandons Pierre. She and Jean's mother are reconciled and move to the country to remember Jean and spend their lives caring for orphans.

Most reviewers welcomed Chaplin's new film, but some pointed out that *A Woman of Paris* had been greeted in the United States by considerable hostility to its risqué subject matter (Marie's role as Pierre's mistress), and local censors in a number of states had either banned it or insisted on deletions before its screening was permitted.[55] To French critics, all of them male, there seemed nothing remarkable or controversial about the relationship between Pierre and Marie. They were more inclined to find fault with the film's attempts to depict French backgrounds and settings. To Paul Gordeaux in *L'Echo de Paris*, Chaplin's creation of a "Los Angeles France" felt simply too "ersatz" and sham. At many moments, "a small inaccurate detail—that is, insufficiently French or too completely Yankee—reminds us that we are not in France, but in the United States." René Jeanne similarly took Chaplin to task for "having slipped in the reconstruction of the Parisian atmosphere some details that shock us, we French." But he also commented that the movie as a whole was "so general in its humanity that we might not have noticed that the setting was Paris" if French critics had not been so aware of its U.S. title.[56]

Some French reviewers of *A Woman of Paris* located Chaplin's film in the context of current debates in France relating to the increasing use of technological innovation in cinema. Champions of this process included filmmaker Abel Gance as well as critic Léon Moussinac. Moussinac's privileging of "technique," comments Richard Abel, foregrounded "variable speed recording (especially slow motion), various optical devices (superimposition, vignette masks, distorting filters and lenses, 'punctuation' devices (the fade, iris, and dissolve), and accelerating montage." Such technical features, Abel continues, "were unique to the cinema and, therefore, might define its material condition as separate from the other arts and perhaps as even more advanced."[57] Some French critics, Pierre Henry in particular, saw Chaplin's *A Woman of Paris* as a direct challenge to this focus on technique. To Henry, coeditor of *Cinéa-Ciné-pour-tous*, substance was much more important than form. A film that had rhythm, he argued, did not need elaborate staging or special effects. *A Woman of Paris* was able to retain the interest of audiences because it was grounded in a real understanding of psychology and was made up of a "mosaic" of closely observed details. It was an "auteur's" film rather than a "director's" because it was devoid of "sensational effects" and dealt with a simple subject close to life itself. Chaplin's film, Henry predicted, would have more appeal to audiences than productions by "young filmmakers dreaming of 'tricks.'" It demonstrated that the future of cinema did not necessarily depend on "clever lighting, fuzziness, 'memories' [in the form of flashbacks], superimpositions, [and] incessant and sensational close-ups."[58]

The same issue of *Cinéa-Ciné-pour-tous* in which Henry's review was published contained a long article on *A Woman of Paris* by his coeditor, Jean Tedesco. Like Henry, Tedesco argued that Chaplin's film was rooted in human psychology, since "for the author, psychologies alone matter, and acts are less important.") Chaplin himself was an "observer ... first and foremost." His screen characters are allowed to develop in accordance with their individual psychology "without distorting them under the so-called needs of an inept scenario." For these reasons, Tedesco shrewdly argued, Jean is not particularly important as a character. His suicide "does not matter much." What had captured Chaplin's attention when it came to shooting the film was the relationship between Marie and Pierre, the real "subject" of the film. Marie's portrayal, from her "lonely departure" for Paris to her final abandonment of Pierre after Jean's suicide, "seems natural." With open eyes, she becomes the mistress of Pierre, "an intelligent man ... with refined tastes ... who wraps the woman he has chosen in an atmosphere of luxury and pleasure." With open eyes also, she returns to him "without drama, with a mutual smile" after her breakup with Jean. To Tedesco, indeed, the cynical and realistic Pierre was "the hero of the story. He is neither sympathetic to excess nor unfriendly at will. He is himself, true, lived, alive." Chaplin's depiction of him was "no longer cinema—in the ordinary sense of the term," but "cinematic psychology."[59]

There were a number of sequences in *A Woman of Paris* that critics singled out for special praise. Paul Gordeaux of *L'Echo de Paris* declared that the film "abounds in truly original finds, some of which have been warmly applauded: like the arrival of trains at a station at night, simply indicated by the rectangles of light projected as they pass, on the concrete of the platform, by the lighted doors."[60] Saint-Denis, in *Le Courrier Cinématographique*, wrote that "the evening at the bohemian artists" had been treated with "a tact and mastery that was at every point remarkable" and hailed the final scene, in which the former lovers, Marie and Pierre, are traveling in separate vehicles that pass each other and continue on their way, as "beautiful: it is life itself."[61] Several reviewers praised the acting skills of those playing the principal characters: Edna Purviance as Marie and Adolph Menjou as Pierre. Casting Purviance in the role, noted Pierre Henry, fulfilled Chaplin's earlier promise "to make her an independent 'star'" and was also "a reward for the good and loyal service she has given him" during their eight years as screen partners.[62] Paul Gordeaux hailed Menjou as "an excellent French artist" who had created a Pierre Revel who was "elegant, racy, frivolous and disillusioned." Saint-Denis paid tribute to Menjou as "our compatriot" who "delightfully personifies the typical high-liver, skeptical and jaded." Only Henry described Menjou correctly as "an artist of French origin." (Although his father was indeed French, he had been born in Pittsburgh.)[63]

The Pilgrim

It would not have been immediately obvious to French critics and spectators in the 1920s that Chaplin was moving steadily if not straightforwardly toward producing longer feature films. *The Kid*, shown in France for the first time in 1921, was his longest film (1 hour 8 minutes/5,250 feet) up to that point. *A Woman of Paris* raised the bar further when it was screened for the first time in Paris in 1924 (1 hour 22 minutes/7,557 feet). Yet Chaplin's older films from the Keystone, Essanay, Mutual, and First National eras continued to circulate in France, while the films he made in 1921–22 (*The Idle Class*, *Pay Day*) were comparatively short and not released in France until 1924–25, and his first major film after *A Woman of Paris* was *Le Pèlerin* (*The Pilgrim*) which, at 47 minutes/3,647 feet, was little more than half the length of *L'Opinion*.

To French film critics in 1925, Chaplin was already a major cultural influence, especially in France. Paul Achard of *Paris-Midi* hailed him as "the greatest . . . comic force in the world." He had provided the inspiration for "all the young comic literature, all the avant-garde burlesque theatre. . . . he has had a tremendous influence on the postwar generation. Marcel Achard's clowns, Bernard Zimmer's puppets think and act like Charlie Chaplin's characters."[64] Given Charlot's popularity in France, indeed, some critics expressed strong resentment that *The Pilgrim* was released in France only in February 1925, two years after its initial première in New York. Jean Chataigner complained that *The Pilgrim* had been "long announced" and "impatiently awaited," and Paul Gordeaux complained that French spectators had been deprived of a new film featuring Chaplin as Charlot since *The Kid* some four years earlier.[65] Was Charlot as good as he had once been? French critics were uneasily aware that other comedians might now be challenging Chaplin as the world's leading comic. J.P. commented in *Paris-Midi* that it was "currently the fashion for great comedy films" such as Max Linder's *Le roi du cirque*

(*The King of the Circus*, 1924), Chaplin's *The Pilgrim*, and Harold Lloyd's *Voyage de Paradis* (*Never Weaken*, 1921). Chataigner, indeed, reviewed all three of these movies in the same article. Chaplin and Linder, he noted, were already "masters of laughter," with Lloyd improving all the time. He hailed *The Pilgrim* as a "kind sketch" that was "one of the best, if not Chaplin's best movie." Its "flavor and smiling philosophy," he predicted, "would not disappoint those who are able to make out Charlot's genius beneath the humor."[66]

The Pilgrim begins with a shot of a "Wanted" poster for Charlot, a convict who has escaped from prison. (René Jeanne of *Le Petit Journal* pointed out that the film appeared to be something of a sequel to *Charlot s'évade* [*The Adventurer*], first released five years earlier, in which Chaplin had also played a convict.)[67] As J.P. explained in *Paris-Midi*, it is never made clear "what crime has led him to be sentenced to forced labor; but we have an intuition … that our unhappy friend has again fallen victim to one of those monstrous injustices to which he seems resigned." Stealing the clothes of a clergyman bathing in a stream, Charlot takes a train to a small town in Texas that coincidentally is awaiting the arrival of a new minister. The townsfolk escort him to the church, where he is obliged to deliver a sermon, choosing to recount the confrontation of David with Goliath by miming the roles of both. "The sermon scene, in particular," J.P. declared, was "a masterpiece."[68] The hapless new "priest" stays with a respectable middle-class woman (Kitty Bradbury) and her comely daughter (Edna Purviance). But Charlie is recognized by a former cellmate (Charles Reisner), who steals the woman's mortgage money. Charlie manages to get the money back, but his true identity is revealed and he is arrested by a policeman. In the final sequences of the film, the cop realizes Charlot is innocent ("a pilgrim in spite of himself," commented Chataigner) and frees him on the Mexican border.[69]

To many critics, *The Pilgrim* seemed the first "real" Charlot film featuring the character of the Little Tramp since *The Kid*, four years earlier. To Paul Gordeaux of *L'Echo de Paris*, the movie marked the return of "the inspired Chaplin," and to Georges Roche of *Le Matin* he was again as "brilliant and touching" as in his best films.[70] Some French critics endeavored to place the humor of the *The Pilgrim* in a broader cultural perspective. Paul Achard, for example, argued that Charlot's "goodness and apparent candour, as much as his physical appearance, create laughter, but his extreme intelligence always overcomes all obstacles. And from this point of view, Charlot is more Latin than American: there is in his character something of the august Spaniard, the Italian peppino, our own Calino." Yet this intelligence was combined "with the transatlantic humor and precious . . . accessories, carefully chosen, all collaborating together to create the perfection of the film."[71] François-Robert, writing in *Le Gaulois*, hailed Chaplin's new film as "a true masterpiece of humanity, of a truly embarrassing power." Boisyvon in *L'Intransigeant* greeted it as "amazing and beautiful. Amazing because it is based on a vaudeville subject that is not particularly cinematographic, and beautiful because Charlie Chaplin finds once again this prodigious instinct of life which, in all circumstances, shows him acting in a natural, logical way, like a man not particularly bad who has had a lot of trouble in his life, who is still resolved to accept some inconvenience to get by, but who will never forget to take revenge for the tyrannies he is made to bear."[72]

Émile Vuillermoz of *Le Temps* adopted a strategy toward *The Pilgrim* that went back at least as far as 1921: using his own interpretation of Chaplin's work as a means of critiquing French writers and cultural forms with whom he disagreed. The three Fratellini brothers, Paul, François, and Albert, were famous clowns who worked at the Circus Medrano in Montmartre between the First World War and 1924. During these years, they perfected a style of comedy that brought them huge popularity. "They quickly became the talk of Paris," comments Dominique Jando, "as journalists, artists, writers, and Paris literati in general transformed the trio into stars of the first magnitude." On February 21, 1921, for example, the Fratellini brothers took prominent roles in the première of the surrealist ballet *Le Boeuf sur la Toit* (*The Ox on the Roof*), based on a scenario by Jean Cocteau. Cocteau was using them, argues Donald McManus, "as performers to help create a modern theatrical form."[73] Vuillermoz was deeply skeptical of the vogue enjoyed by the three clowns, which he referred to as "fratellinism," and criticized those who encouraged it by "discovering in the somersaults and puns of the most banal clown all the elements of a philosophy, a morality and a metaphysics." Overrating clowns, he argued, had now become a form of snobbery to which Chaplin's new film offered an antidote. In opposition to "the customary, and often pretentious, silliness of most clowns," *The Pilgrim* underlined "the extraordinary psychological penetration, spiritual verve, and classic skill of the acrobatic little genius whose comedy is so true and profound." Even Chaplin's most extravagant on-screen antics, Vuillermoz declared, are always based on his extremely subtle powers of social observation. *The Pilgrim*, he promised his readers, reflected in many ways the characteristic virtues of cartoonist Caran d'Ache (the pseudonym of Emmanuel Poiré, 1858–1909) and novelist and dramatist Courteline (the nom de plume of Georges Victor Marcel Moinaux, 1858–1929), both prominent satirists of modern society.[74]

Many critics besides Vuillermoz also praised Chaplin's skill in observation when writing about *The Pilgrim*. Philippe Sarlat of *Paris-Soir* wrote that "under the humor of his play" he concealed "the most delicate irony and his acute sense of observation, his primordial quality." "Everything, in this being," remarked Paul Achard, "reveals a unique sensibility, in the service of an almost unhealthy acuity of observation." "Observer, that's what Charlot is all about," insisted Georges Roche. "The guys he embodies are the ones we rub shoulders with, with their qualities and weaknesses, but only he knew how to see and copy."[75] Chaplin's sharp powers of observation lay at the root of his skill as a comedian. "The comic details abound in this truly hilarious film," argued Paul Gordeaux, confessing that "it would take three columns of this newspaper to tell them all." Gordeaux himself made no attempt to do so. Others selected particular sequences that demonstrated how Chaplin with "his inimitable talent" exploited "the most unlikely situations." Sarlat, for example, singled out three scenes that demonstrated "the wonderful gifts of this unique artist": his encounter with the sheriff of the small town where he takes refuge, to whom Charlot holds out his wrists for the handcuffs he expects, only to be greeted by the lawman with a handshake as the new pastor; the delicious mime of the story of David and Goliath; and his reluctant liberation at the end of the film, when he is freed by the policeman in order to escape into Mexico, and then attacked by Mexican bandits, so that the Little Tramp exits the screen walking anxiously along the U.S.–Mexican border with feet carefully straddling both sides of the line.[76] Some critics found in *The Pilgrim* proof that Chaplin had lost none of his comic genius after *The Kid*. One, Boisyvon in *L'Intransigeant*, went further, seeing the film as showcasing the continuing development in his work. "Charlie Chaplin," he wrote, "always remains himself and we discover in each scene a new aspect of his genius. He remains the poor devil we have known for ten years, but he expands the picture of his adventures: he imposes himself on us because of our secret sympathy for this character who is never very unhappy, never very honest, but who is always charming."[77]

The Gold Rush

Seven months after *The Pilgrim* was first shown in Paris, *La Ruée vers l'Or* (*The Gold Rush*) had its initial screening there. More than twice the length of *The Pilgrim* (8,555 feet rather than 3,647), *The Gold Rush* was Chaplin's longest and most ambitious film to date. Both Paul Gordeaux and Philippe Sarlat attempted to recount the narrative storyline. The Little Tramp heads north to join in the Klondike gold rush in Alaska in the late 1890s. In his Tramp outfit, he walks painfully through the snow. During a blizzard, he takes refuge in a cabin with successful prospector Big Jim McKay (Mack Swain) and a thief, Black Larson (Tom Murray). The three are soon hungry, and Larsen is chosen to go out in search of food, whereupon he abandons them. McKay and Charlie, left on their own, are very hungry: Charlie cooks one of his own shoes to eat, but McKay is still delirious with hunger and keeps imagining Charlie as a large succulent chicken. In the end, Charlie manages to kill and cook a bear, and once the storm that has trapped them subsides, the two go their separate ways. Charlie ends up in a nearby town, where he falls in love with Georgia (Georgia Hale), a dancer in a saloon. He invites her and her friends for supper on New Year's Eve, but she forgets and stands him up. Left alone at his empty table, Charlie fantasizes about how he would have entertained the women with two bread rolls dancing at the end of forks. Charlie once again meets Big Jim, who has forgotten the location of his claim. Charlie offers to help him find it again, but before setting out, the two men spend the night in a cabin during a snowstorm. The storm moves the cabin to the edge of a precipice and, when both McKay and Charlie escape, they find themselves on McKay's claim. He shares his wealth with Charlie, and the two, both now rich, leave on a boat. Another passenger is Georgia, and she and Charlie end up together.[78]

Interestingly, both Sarlat and Gordeaux, having summarized the storyline of the film, went on to doubt the practicality of what they had done. "It is impossible to recount a film like this," Gordeaux confessed. "It would be necessary to linger on each scene, to narrate it in detail, to show all the humorous features, all the tricks of staging, all the funny ideas which, at every instant, make people laugh." "It is not possible," Sarlat similarly acknowledged, "to summarize in detail the thousand brainwaves Chaplin has enshrined in the magnificent development of his subject." Gaston Thierry in *Paris-Midi* was even blunter in his review of the film, commenting that "the scenario, to tell the truth, is almost non-existent."[79] There was a consensus among reviewers that a Charlot film should be understood and evaluated in a different way from other movies. Again and again, critics listed the "strokes of inspiration" that distinguished *The Gold Rush*. These "inimitable scenes" included the struggle over the rifle between Big Jim McKay and Black Larson (in which the rifle continues to point to Charlot, however he tries to avoid it); the "dinner" of cooked shoe leather for the two starving men; the dance hall sequence in which Charlot first encounters Georgia; and the acrobatics in the cabin poised over a precipice.[80]

Several French reviewers sensed that Chaplin himself was changing. René Jeanne pointed out that the physical appearance of the Little Tramp in *The Gold Rush* was no longer quite the same: he had lost weight, his face had become thinner, and his eyes hollowed out.[81] The on-screen character of the tramp himself had also changed, according to Émile Vuillermoz: he was somehow less active, more passive. Having once mischievously hit back against the police and his toughest enemies, he was now consistently a victim: he relentlessly absorbed the blows fate and society dealt him, a "public slave" condemned to serve what Vuillermoz himself did not hesitate to identify as the "cruelty" of contemporary audiences. Where Vuillermoz saw uncaring cruelty, even sadism, Thierry saw the role of the Little Tramp in *The Gold Rush* as living with an intensity and suffering that suggested the whole of humanity in distress and left it hard for audiences to analyze just what was the spell he cast. To Thierry, this was "great art," representing genius rather than mere talent. (Though he also observed that genius of this kind was often not consistent—he dismissed the ending of *The Gold Rush* as "hastily botched"—revealing itself rather from time to time in "magic sparks.")[82]

Some reviewers reached for historical antecedents (mainly European) to understand Chaplin's appeal. René Jeanne hailed him as a "great artist" who was very reminiscent of Italian comedy of the commedia del'arte type. (He suggested a beautiful essay could be written on "Pierrot and Charlot!")[83] Both Sarlat and G.R. compared him to Molière for his profound understanding that comedy and tragedy, laughter and tears, were often closely linked. To Sarlat, *The Gold Rush* demonstrated the truth of Chaplin's own comment that "a lively comedy can be as moving as a lyrical work" since "the humorous formula disguises a great blast of humanity."[84] Boisyvon in *L'Intransigeant* went even further, seeing Chaplin as a figure with a unique connection to the world of 1925. Chaplin, he argued, "torments our sensibility so strongly" that he is "a great, and perhaps the greatest, figure of the time."[85]

There was a strong sense on the part of some critics that Chaplin's talent as both actor and director was still evolving and that *The Gold Rush* was a major step forward in that evolution. Paul Gordeaux baldly stated that *The Gold Rush* was "the latest of Chaplin's films, and the best." It represented the work of "a brilliant comedian . . . who, year by year, amplified, broadened and refined" his on-screen character, "bringing him closer to perfection." Jean Chataigner argued in *Le Journal* that *The Gold Rush* would disarm any skeptics. Although Chaplin had "perhaps [been originally] inspired by the great comedians of the theatre and the circus," his genius was "so different in its manifestations, that it is permissible to say that it belongs to him alone." In *The Kid*, according to Chataigner, "while keeping the costume of the clown," Chaplin had "freed himself from burlesque . . . a method that seemed to him worn out," to concentrate on developing "feelings that had previously only been sketched out." While *The Kid* had been a "triumphant attempt" to break new ground, *The Gold Rush* had gone considerably further in terms of innovation: it brought together a whole range of elements—"drama, comedy, vaudeville and kind-hearted tomfoolery"— "all . . . tied together in a harmonious manner with no false notes." G.R. in *Le Matin* also discerned a considerable gulf between *The Gold Rush* ("a major work") and Chaplin's most popular earlier films, including *The Kid*, *Woman of Paris*, and *The Pilgrim*. To Thierry, quite simply, *The Gold Rush* was "Chaplin's masterpiece" and a major step forward in the art of cinema. ("It greatly honors," he wrote, "not only American cinema but cinema itself.")[86]

Charlot's "Ignoble Heart"

In the July 3, 1926, issue of the arts newspaper *Comoedia* appeared an article by André Saurès on the lack of female clowns. A byproduct of the book he would publish a year later on clowns generally, it referenced male clowns of the past before segueing into an attack on Charlot, both as a modern clown and as a product of American materialism. "I laugh at that fool and his sentimental grimace only to escape from boredom," Suarès declared. "He is the hero of terrible America. These brutes have a heart, it seems, in a cotton sock stuffed with dollars." He confessed that he would like "to crush . . . like a bug" the "ignoble heart of Charlot."[87] Suarès was a not inconsiderable figure on the French literary scene. Closely associated with the *NRF* in 1912–14, he had been banned from the postwar *Revue* by editor Jacques Rivière, who disliked him, only to be brought back by the new editor Jean Paulhan in 1926. He was a poet and critic who had produced studies of many writers, including Tolstoy, Ibsen, Dostoyevsky, Pascal, and Villon, and had also written about Wagner. A champion of the traditional arts, his brief remarks on Chaplin in this essay on clowns would start to reveal his broader skepticism of cinema's claim to be the newest art.

Just four days later, *Comoedia* published a vigorous riposte from film director Jacques de Baroncelli. Hailing Saurès as a determined polemicist (a "robust writer" with "an aggressive pen"), Baroncelli deconstructed the "misogynistic commentary" that underpinned his wider article with its outlandish claims that women could not be clowns because they lacked self-awareness and were incapable of ridiculing themselves. Baroncelli also dismissed the notion that there were no female clowns: they existed, he insisted, in America, England—and France (where he cited "the Tomboys" of the Alhambra music hall in Paris and "Miss Loulou" of the Medrano circus). But his main purpose in writing was, of course, to defend Chaplin from Suarès's attack. Charlot, he insisted, had "the genius of mimic expression." As a clown, Baroncelli concluded, "although American [*sic*] and dressed in loathsome dollars, [he] remains one of the greatest actors of today." At his best he became "the very figure of humanity. He comes and goes, laughs, suffers, comes up against mystery and fatality, falls, gets up, hopes, begins again, just as we ceaselessly do in life." There had been many moments of real artistry in his films: Baroncelli singled out the sequences in *The Gold Rush* in which the lovestruck Charlot has prepared a New Year's Eve dinner for Georgia, the object of his affections, and the other dance hall girls, but they have forgotten about him. There was, he believed, no cloying sentimentality here: it was not "an artificial grimace, dryness, laughter or pain without nobility; it's life commented on by the beautiful sensitivity of an artist."[88]

The debate inaugurated by the Suarès–Baroncelli articles rumbled on over the summer of 1926. Poet, novelist, and art critic Francis Carco gave an interview in August to *Les Nouvelles Littératures* in which he compared Charlot to fifteenth-century French poet François Villon. (Both Carco and Suarès had published books on Villon.) Carco was asked whether he thought someone who liked Villon could also like Charlot. He replied, "Most certainly not. Charlot is the effect, the grimace, the wink of complicity with the audience or the director, the false pity, the false great art while Villon has nothing calculated to please, to move. He is himself. He is human spontaneously."[89] Carco's assumption that real art could be achieved only through the spontaneity of the artist, whereas Chaplin's screen performances were premeditated, anticipated one line of the argument that would ensue. But for the moment, he simply declared his support for Suarès and claimed that he and his novelist friends Pierre Mac Orlan, Pierre Benoît, and Ronald

Dorgelès all shared Saurès's distaste for Charlot.[90] Writing a few months later, pro-Chaplin film critic Léon Moussinac of *L'Humanité* dismissed the efforts of these writers as "little games of little people of little literary value" and accused them of being intent only on self-promotion. He also praised the work of Henri Poulaille for assembling in *Chroniques du jour* a range of articles "by disinterested writers and critics which testify . . . unanimously" to the originality of Chaplin's artistry.[91]

Moussinac's article itself was provoked by the publication of a second attack on Chaplin by Suarès in *Comoedia* on January 15, 1927. This greatly expanded the arguments of the initial essay on the themes of sentimentality, America, and the weakness of cinema's claim to be regarded as a form of art. Suarès disingenuously claimed to have "nothing against" Chaplin personally (at the same time including two coded references to "American women" and "sex" that demonstrated his awareness of the divorce action launched by Lita Grey five days before his article appeared). But Chaplin was the inventor of a "new type of puppet [the Tramp]" and had founded "a new form of human vulgarity [the cinema]." "What can I do," Suarès asked, "if this art horrifies me and I have disgust for this type?" In his own mind, Suarès was a champion of mind ("esprit") rather than sentimentality ("heart"). Cinema appeared to express a hatred of spirit that he found characteristic of modernity. Based on "gesture alone," it was the very antithesis of poetry for, to Suarès, "an art without words is monkey art." Charlot, he believed, was ignoble because of the "sentimental genius" of his films. Sentimentality to Suarèz was "the soul of the plebs. Charlot is the fiddler playing at this popular wedding." Suarès's own social and cultural elitism was paralleled by a deep-hued anti-Americanism: "the shame and misery" of cinema, he argued, was that "film everywhere is American." Yet "America has only sentimental thoughts," and sentimentality itself was "the grime and garbage of feeling." According to Saurès, Charlot's role was to grease "the pavement of a country without soul" through the sentimentality of his films. Since cinema was "a formidable enterprise against the mind," his work limited the opportunity for real thought. Through his mastery of the "art of the grimace," Suarès bitterly concluded, Charlot "deceives his world and makes it stupid."[92]

The first French writer to launch a critique of Suarès's second article was the multitalented Jean Tedesco, screenwriter, film critic, movie director, and managing director of Paris's Théâtre du Vieux-Colombier. He was also editor of *Cinéa-Ciné-pour-tous*, which published his scathing response. Tedesco began by comparing Chaplin (whom "the whole world knows and admires") to Suarès, whose "brutal polemic" had reached comparatively few. While Suarès had placed his "small pieces of garbage at the feet of the greatest comic genius of our time," he had simultaneously insulted America ("the Atlantic ocean is insufficient to protect it from the virulence of a man of letters") and cinema itself. Tedesco insisted that it was necessary to challenge "the scathing assertions of a Saurès" to defend both Chaplin in particular and the movies in general. "The time is coming," he predicted, "when the world of the artist and the intellectual will recognize in the art of moving images the most powerful mode of expression of the twentieth century."[93]

Suarès's renewed attack spurred several people to spring to Chaplin's defense. Left-wing film reviewer Léon Moussinac praised the artist who had created masterpieces such as *A Dog's Life, Shoulder Arms, Sunnyside, The Kid,* and *The Pilgrim* as immune to all artistic criticism. Chaplin was, literally, "above theories and laws," a filmmaker in a special category all his own. Actor Jean Napoléon Michel made much the same argument: an artist's work speaks for itself, and Chaplin ranked first among the artists of his time. Much of this distinction arose from the growing influence of cinema, but no one else had used that influence as fully as he had done.[94]

Writer Odile Gay directed her comments more personally to Suarès, relating the timing of his attack specifically to Lita Grey's divorce proceedings ("You attack Charlie Chaplin now that he is unhappy, abandoned by an unworthy, venal and frivolous woman.") Gay confessed she had had the courage to read only one of Suarès's books, and tartly remarked "that the pile of unsold books that form your works" would never have the impact on humanity of "a single expression of Charlot." She ridiculed Suarès's assertion that no real art could be produced without words. ("Did Chopin, Mendelssohn, the divine [Attic sculptor] Praxiteles, Corot, use the word?") Probing Suarès's binary opposition between "heart" and "spirit," Gay insisted that "Chaplin has offered his heart to the world." While he "mingles with his fellow men" and "has grasped the often painful side of their lives," Suarès had isolated himself in his contempt for the multitude, locking himself away "between dry, arid formulas." To Gay, Suarès and his supporters were members of a small, arrogant elite that disdained popular tastes. When Suarès wrote of Charlot deceiving and making stupid "his world," Gay demanded to know what made up this world. "Is it," she wrote, "a restricted circle, made up of some 'priests of the spirit' . . . ? So, yes, perhaps Chaplin annoys you, because for members of this narrow 'world,' nothing that is simple, natural, human, is accessible."[95]

Film director Jacques de Baroncelli returned to the fray in a piece for *Comoedia* on February 8, pointing out that Suarès's attacks went far "beyond the contours" of Charlot the filmmaker and screen character: "America and its psychology, the screen and its poetics" had all been questioned and "furiously" denounced. Baroncelli gently criticized Suarès's insistence that cinema was American. ("There is a French film, French style even.") Far from regarding cinema as an enemy of the mind, he defended it (while still in its infancy as an art) as "an awakener and animator" that "gives life and soul to the geography of countries, men and the arts." Like Odile Gay, Baroncelli dismissed Suarès as too elitist: Chaplin and the cinema might appear sentimental to "the intellectual and the cerebral," he declared, but "for us, mixed up with puny realities, in contact . . . with the 'spectacular' [cinemagoing] crowds . . . a certain nobility resides in this humble sentimentality."[96]

The last major contribution in the controversy launched by Suarès in 1926–27 came from novelist, dramatist, and poet Gabriel Trarieux a few days later. Trarieux's article, prompted by his annoyance at Suarès's "furious diatribe" against Chaplin that held him responsible for all the faults of cinema, argued—in common with Baroncelli—that cinema itself was not exclusively American. Yet he praised American moviemakers not merely for the financial success of their films but for their innovation. ("They are afraid of nothing. They are new. . . . They are not prisoners of formulas.") With Chaplin at their head, they appealed to the entire world. "The glory of Charlie Chaplin," Trarieux declared, ". . . is first of all to have found a comedian who always makes people laugh everywhere." Did it matter that Chaplin was only a clown? Trarieux thought not. The modern world was hugely in need of lightness and humor. ("The fact is that since the war, the chorus of Greek tragedy . . . reigns supreme in our dailies.") Moreover, Chaplin was not simply a comic: he directed his own movies, which had succeeded by means of "hard work, patient, ingenious efforts, and sudden happy inventions." Trarieux, indeed, saw Chaplin in auteurist terms as a controlling influence on his films: "He has to combine in himself the multiple qualities of an author, because he sees his work before creating it, of a director [since] he recruits his troupe, of a stage manager . . . and of an editor." Chaplin's artistry consisted of all these things and he had already produced a number of film masterpieces, including *The Gold Rush*. Trarieux regarded this film as "a gift" from Chaplin to his fans and expressed the fervent hope that "puritans" in America did not succeed in banning him from the screen "because he loved several women. . . . It would be an irreparable loss. Because no one compares to him."[97]

The debate launched by Suarès's two articles on Chaplin's "ignoble heart" had effectively petered out by February 1927. Yet occasional skepticism displayed by traditional literary figures toward the cinema in general—and Chaplin in particular—continued. Journalist and war veteran Jean de Pierrefeu noted in *Les Nouvelles Littéraires* in June 1927 that dislike and hostility of this kind had begun to decline. Many serious writers had started to declare their enthusiasm for the movies. Pierrefeu himself believed that the person who had done most to diminish such prejudice was Charlie Chaplin. What had persuaded Pierrefeu to take up his pen, however, was an article by Paul Souday, who wrote the literary column for the daily *Le Temps*. In an article in Toulouse newspaper *La Dépêche* on May 29, 1927, Souday had insisted that "the cinema is not an art" and could not become one. He used the example of Chaplin to underpin his argument. To Souday, Chaplin was "a mediocre clown, crude and puerile." His screen performances consisted only of "gestures and making faces … [a] rudimentary sketch that is of no interest." Rather than being any kind of artist, offering a personal vision, he was in effect "only a model for his operator" (the cameraman). To Pierrefeu, by contrast, Chaplin was far more than the simplistic, wordless actor of Souday's imagination. Screen acting was only one facet of his activity. He was, in fact, "a filmmaker of genius." The scenarios he invented were the result of "intellectual creation, which sometimes touches the highest peaks of spirituality." Cinema was an art still in its infancy, but it was already a "complete art" that in a few seconds could convey an atmosphere or a mood that would take several pages in a novel. Someday it would "have its Homer, its Shakespeare, its Molière." The man who announced this, Pierrefeu contended, was Charlot.[98]

The Circus

In tune with the slower pace of Chaplin's film productions for the rest of his career, his last movie of the 1920s was released almost two and a half years after *The Gold Rush*. As Émile Vuillermoz noted in his review of *The Circus* (1928), the "little genius clown now works slowly and safely. He produces little, but his productions now possess a strength, balance and power of invention that work on everyone." Given Vuillermoz's earlier defense of the quality of Chaplin as an artist in *The Pilgrim*, compared to the banality of then-popular circus clowns ("fratellinism"), it was more than a little ironic that Chaplin's latest film was set against a circus background. The French critic insisted, however, that what distinguished Chaplin was not "his acrobatics, nor his leaps and bounds," and "what galvanizes his art and what makes him so curiously moving is the profound psychology with which he enriches his so-called puppets."[99]

The Circus is constructed around four major characters. The first to be introduced are the circus equestrienne (Merna Kennedy) and her stepfather, the proprietor-ringmaster of the circus (Allan Garcia). The stepfather punishes Merna for making a mistake by assaulting her physically and refusing to let her have food that night. Food is also on the mind of the Tramp (Chaplin), who—hungry and broke—haunts the circus sideshows. Unscrupulously, he eats the hot dog of a small child. A fairground pickpocket, attempting to avoid arrest by the police, hides a wallet he has stolen in the Tramp's pocket, but before the Tramp can profit from this the original owner appears and accuses him of theft and a policeman arrives. In trying to escape, the Tramp first takes refuge in a hall of mirrors and then the circus itself, where the audience—until then bored and listless—is amused by the Tramp's desperate attempts to evade the police. The Tramp is hired by the circus boss as a clown and falls in love with the equestrienne. But it soon becomes clear that the Tramp can amuse audiences only inadvertently, and it is in this way that he becomes indispensable to the circus (and can now insist that the circus owner treat his stepdaughter with greater respect). However, a new high-wire artist, Rex (Harry Crockett), joins the circus and the equestrienne falls in love with him. When Rex misses a performance, the Tramp (having bribed a property man to attach him to a safety wire) goes on in his place. The safety wire breaks and the Tramp is attacked by a group of monkeys while performing but finally returns safely to the ground. After trying to protect the equestrienne from renewed abuse by her stepfather, the Tramp is fired and the young woman runs away. She suggests they go away together, but the Tramp realizes it is Rex she is really in love with. He persuades Rex to marry her, providing him with the ring he has already bought to propose to her himself and scattering confetti over them after their wedding. Rex will now protect her from her stepfather. The Tramp watches the circus leave before setting off on his own for new adventures.

The release of *The Circus* in France in February 1928 climaxed several months in which Chaplin had been the focus of considerable attention from French writers and critics. André Suarès had rekindled the controversy over the "ignoble heart" of Charlot in January 1927, and the argument over this had rumbled on until mid-February. The dispute between Paul Souday and

Jean de Pierrefeu launched by Souday's critique of cinema (with Chaplin as its principal target) took place in May and June. In September, as will be discussed in the next chapter, thirty-two surrealists headed by Louis Aragon signed "Hands Off Love," a manifesto defending Chaplin against the sexual and other allegations made against him by his second wife, Lita Grey, in the divorce proceedings she had initiated. (In his review of *The Circus* in *Le Petit Parisien*, Maurice Huet would liken Chaplin to Molière for a range of reasons, including "his marital difficulties.")[100] Also in 1927, as discussed above, André Maurois compared Chaplin to, among others, Marcel Proust, Gustave Flaubert, Prosper Mérimée, Anatole France, and Charles Dickens. "Much has been said about Charlie Chaplin during the past year," René Jeanne wrote at the start of his review of *The Circus*, yet the arrival of Chaplin's latest film, he insisted, would provoke a new crop of critical commentaries, as was only fair.[101]

A small number of reviewers compared *The Circus* unfavorably with Chaplin's earlier work. Boisyvon of *L'Intransigeant*, although noting that this new work was "above all [other] comedy productions" and better than "many dramatic films," also judged that it was less good than some of Charlot's earlier movies. ("Chaplin is sometimes below Chaplin.")[102] Léon Moussinac of the communist daily *L'Humanité* first noted the arrival of the film on February 18, 1928, with a complaint about the "prohibitive" price for admission at the Marivaux cinema on the boulevard des Italiens, where *The Circus* had begun its Paris run. Chaplin, he reported, had just "banned the bourgeois and snobbish demonstration that was being prepared in Berlin for the première of his film." Did he now "approve of this process of exclusivity . . . towards the ordinary public?" It would not be until three weeks later that Moussinac's review of the film itself was published, and it began critically. "This film," Moussinac observed, "will no doubt disappoint some admirers of Charlie Chaplin, because its unity of composition and expression is less than that of films such as *Shoulder Arms*, *The Kid* and especially *The Pilgrim*, that masterpiece of Charlot's masterpieces. *The Circus* brings us back to the technique of *Charlot machiniste* [*Behind the Screen*, Mutual, 1916], and to its spirit: that is to say this film is more mechanical, that we feel the connections from one scene to another, that its expression is less directly human in the tragi-comic mode than it was in the last films."[103] Yet, having begun on this downbeat note, Moussinac conceded that "this disappointment . . . is quite relative, because joy and emotion are dispensed in *The Circus*, through the sole means of Chaplin's genius, with an intensity which at certain moments cannot be exceeded.... In *The Circus*, as in his other works, Chaplin remains the principal poet of today."[104]

For most French critics, *The Circus* represented a further stage in Chaplin's development as a cinéaste. "How far has the admirable artist travelled," observed Raymond Berner of *Le Matin*, since his "first two-part films [of 1914]."[105] *The Circus*, Raymond Villette insisted in *Le Galois*, had been "eagerly awaited by all those who pay close attention to the constant evolution of the brilliant artist" and "gave us the work we expected." To Paul Gordeaux, writing in *L'Echo de Paris*, the movie represented "the master-piece we hoped for and if there are still people who resist Charlot, they will this time be compelled to recognize that the art of film, at the end of its first quarter-century of existence, has been fortunate enough to find its Molière and Shakespeare in this little man."[106] But if Chaplin's work was still evolving, was *The Circus* actually *better* than the highly successful (and longer) *Gold Rush*? Robert Spa cautiously conceded in *Le Figaro* that it was "at least as good."[107] Vuillermoz, less cautiously, insisted that *The Circus* would challenge the view of "spectators who had admired *The Gold Rush*" and as a result believed Charlot "could not climb higher." Such an assessment, though held "in good faith," misunderstood "this extraordinary fantasist who constantly renews himself because his technique is based on an in-depth knowledge of human nature and on careful observation of the daily comedy" of human life.[108] Comparing the two films, Jeanne pointed out that "*The Circus* does not contain a clearly moving scene like those of the New Year's Eve [when Georgia and the other dancing girls forget Charlie has invited them to dinner]" in *The Gold Rush*. To Jeanne, it was a step forward that there were no such "pauses in the comic action" in *The Circus*, which still managed to move its spectators by means of "a gesture, a look" artfully conveyed through Chapin's own "deep and shivering humanity."[109]

As in many Chaplin films, Raymond Berner commented, *The Circus* was in essence "a series of skits that succeed, overlap, knot and unwind with extraordinary mastery." Some of these, as René Jeanne pointed out, were only "new, improved and purified versions of fantasies that have proved their worth in earlier films." Others were "brand new and unquestionably original."[110] Two of these new sequences had the biggest impact on critics. In the first, Charlot initially discovers and is baffled by the distorting effects of a hall of mirrors that is "so rich in hallucinatory effects." Subsequently, he and the pickpocket and the pursuing police end up in the same hall, creating "the most irresistibly comical scenes," with "all these characters [endlessly] multiplied" and "bumping into the mirrors and not finding the exit."[111] The second, toward the end of the film and demonstrating a new skill on Chaplin's part, sees Charlot as a tightrope walker who, at the climax of his act, is attacked by a group of monkeys in what Jeanne described as a "nightmare situation" (though one with huge potential for comedy).[112] Other scenes that critics found especially funny included Charlot becoming trapped in a lion's cage and, trying to escape into the next cage, being attacked by a panther; Charlot endeavoring to use a tube to blow a large medicinal pill into a horse's mouth, but the animal blows first and Charlot swallows the pill; and Charlot as the incompetent assistant to the circus magician who reduces his act to unpredictable (and hilarious) chaos.[113]

Several reviewers underlined what Raymond Berner called "the impression of melancholy that emerges toward the end" of *The Circus*. (Jacques Vivien used almost exactly the same words, pointing out that "under the gaiety" appeared "a soul in distress.") Charlot, realizing that the woman he loves is in love with someone else, "pushes the lovers into each other's arms."[114] After this generous act of abnegation, Paul Gordeaux noted, he stands sadly and forlornly watching "the cars taking away the one he loved and lost. Ten seconds of melancholy! And then a pirouette! [Actually, a little kick of each foot.] And Charlot, with bowler hat on his head and walking stick in hand, sets off again for new adventures." Robert Spa admired "the profoundly human simplicity with which he pulls himself together and goes away," and even Boisyvon, though he did not regard *The Circus* as being among Chaplin's best films, thought this very last sequence of Charlot's "'inevitable' exit" demonstrated "a luminous, surprising beauty."[115]

Writing about *The Circus* prompted many French critics to focus on what each of them saw as the main features of Chaplin's comedy technique. Vuillermoz emphasized that "what unleashes laughter" was "the astonishing dignity of the puppet [he plays on screen] who does not feel comical and does not suspect the secret causes of the hilarity he provokes." In a similar vein, Vivien remarked that "his great acting strength is to be comic, without seeming to know that he is." But Vivien's own assessment of Chapin's "superior gift" as a laughter-maker focused on his "sensitivity," expressed primarily through gesture and facial expression that moved people's hearts while at the same time making them laugh. Villette's comments were on similar lines, praising the fact that "no gesture is useless" in Chaplin's latest contribution to what the critic hailed as the "silent art."[116] So far as Berner was concerned, what principally characterized Chaplin's films was that they were fantasies that developed according to a "rigorous logic" worked out in stages: first a situation that created "some hilarity" was identified, then it was used as a stepping stone for progressing to new levels, imagining fresh details that would bring the laughter to a climax.[117]

During the 1920s, French critics and intellectuals continued to demonstrate their interest in Chaplin and his films. For the critics, as Louis Delluc demonstrated in his 1921 book, the main issue was what was seen as Chaplin's artistry as a filmmaker. Delluc himself was nothing if not provocative, comparing Chaplin's cinematic art to Beethoven in music, Velázquez in art, Villon in poetry, and Molière and Shakespeare in the theater. Subsequent writers and critics in the 1920s also compared Chaplin's movies to poetry (Élie Faure, André Maurois, Léon Moussinac), novels (Maurois, Jean-Paul Sartre), and plays (Faure, Philippe Sarlat, G.R., and Paul Gordeaux). The weakness of such literary and theatrical analogies, André Suarès and Paul Souday pointed out in their hostile critiques of Chaplin, was that such art forms were dependent on words and no words were actually spoken in Charlot's films.[118] Chaplin's enthusiastic defenders responded by arguing—among other things—that there were many instances of sensitive artistry in his films, that movies themselves could more easily visually convey impressions and moods than a novel, and that music and art were themselves nonverbal cultural forms. To those who championed Chaplin, his films brought humor and lightness to an edgy postwar world, were firmly rooted in human psychology, and were at the forefront of an American movie industry that was increasingly dominant across much of the world. But, as demonstrated in the comments of Gabriel Trarieux, there was also an awareness that Chaplin himself by 1927 was under increasing attack in the United States because of publicity surrounding his private life. The next chapter will show how a group of mainly French surrealists sprang to Chaplin's defense and analyze his relationship—both conscious and unconscious—over several decades with Dadaists and surrealists more generally.

4

Chaplin and the Surrealists

"Hands Off Love"

On January 10, 1927, Lita Grey, Chaplin's second wife, filed a divorce complaint against him, his studio (United Artists), his business manager, and a number of banks holding his assets. Lita, whose real name was Lillita Louise McMurray, had married Chaplin in November 1924. Still only eighteen years of age when she asked for a divorce, she had already borne him two sons. Her divorce complaint, written by her uncle, Edwin T. McMurray, an attorney, rapidly became a sensation. Within two days, it was being sold in mimeographed copies on the streets in Los Angeles. Most divorce petitions run to three or four pages; Lita's had forty-two.[1] Underpinning the stilted legal language lay the mundane and pathetic story of a failed marriage. Lita alleged that her husband had largely ignored her and her children. He had continually insulted and belittled her, insisting he had never wanted to marry her in the first place. At times he had threatened her with a revolver. He had never taken her out but rarely ate with her at home. He had come home late—and drunk. He had resented her entertaining friends in their home, complaining he was unable to work when she and they were around. After she moved out of the family home in November, Chaplin paid nothing for the support of her or their children. Her complaint demanded custody of the children and the payment of "reasonable" alimony.[2]

These things, by themselves, would not have created the enormous public interest they did. It was Lita's sexual allegations that made her complaint sensational. She had become engaged to Chaplin, she claimed, as a "virtuous and inexperienced" sixteen-year-old. Chaplin had then seduced her and made her pregnant. He had tried to persuade her (as he would subsequently do during her second pregnancy) to have an illegal abortion. She claimed that he had married her only to avoid a charge of statutory rape. He had carried on associating with other women throughout their marriage. Most luridly, Lita (or more likely her uncle) described Chaplin's desires in the bedroom as "abnormal, unnatural, perverted, degenerate and indecent."

Charlot. Melvyn Stokes, Oxford University Press. © Oxford University Press 2026.
DOI: 10.1093/9780197839294.003.0005

While refusing what she termed "normal and ordinary...matrimonial inter-course," he had constantly demanded oral sex, graphically referred to in the complaint as "the act of sex perversion defined by Section 288a of the Penal Code of California." So great, indeed, had been Chaplin's craving for oral sex that he had attempted to persuade her to participate by reading her books on the subject and by describing his previous experiences of it with five film actresses.[3] He had also suggested that he and Lita engage in a ménage à trois with another woman.[4]

As Charles J. Maland has commented, the divorce proceedings were "the first serious threat" to Chaplin's star image.[5] In the atmosphere of 1920s America, with its strange combination of moral fervor, puritanism, funda-mentalism, and prohibition, conservatives and traditionalists were deeply critical. The League of Women Voters of DeSalle, Illinois, demanded that Chaplin's films be suppressed. The mayor of Lynn, Massachusetts, prevented his films from being shown in the town during the divorce proceedings. Mrs. R. T. Niles wrote to a film magazine that Chaplin "has the unfortu-nate habit of getting himself mixed up with young women whom he subse-quently marries—probably to keep out of prison or from being deported." Women's clubs around the country tried to embarrass him by raising money "to properly feed and care for Mrs. Chaplin's little boys."[6] But Chaplin had his defenders as well. A spokesperson for the Women's Club of Miami Beach, Florida, condemned the "silly agitation which women's clubs have taken in regard to Chaplin's pictures." Movie theater owners, some journalists, and a number of cinema trade magazines spoke up in Chaplin's defense. Chaplin himself was particularly buoyed by the support of French surrealist writers and artists, thirty-two of whom signed a manifesto in his favor called "Hands Off Love."[7]

"Hands Off Love" was largely written by Louis Aragon in French. It was translated idiosyncratically into English by British writer-heiress Nancy Cunard and first appeared in her magazine *Transition*. It was subsequently republished—this time in French—in the surrealist journal *La Révolution surréaliste*.[8] The manifesto was venomous in its treatment of Lita Grey, whom it depicted as a deadweight cramping Chaplin's genius. She was ac-cused of "a revolting abuse of confidence" and "defamation [that was] so obviously linked to the most sordid self-interest."[9] Lita had embraced mar-riage as "a profession like any other." Far from being an innocent victim of se-duction, she had deliberately slept with Chaplin in order to become his wife ("this was purely business"). If she had really loved Chaplin, she would have agreed to his requests for abortions, since he asked her to do this "for me." "*For me*," Aragon insisted, "means not for social gain, or convenience, but *for love*."[10] He criticized Lita's assertion that she and Chaplin did not have ordinary sexual intercourse "as is customary between man and wife": her two children, he acidly commented, were "doubtless born through her ear." To Aragon, there was "something comic" in Lita's critique of fellatio, a "practice" he described as "so widespread, so utterly pure and defensible." He praised Chaplin's absurdly hyperbolical insistence that "*all married people do it*."[11] Chaplin, according to Aragon, had tried everything to make their marriage "possible" but had run into "a wall of stupidity. Everything seems criminal to this woman who believes or feigns to believe that the procreation of brats is her sole raison d'être." Chaplin had endeavored to open her closed mind with sex books and a suggestion of troilism, hailed in "Hands Off Love" as "a last ditch attempt at acclimatizing the battery hen to the natural proclivities of conjugal love."[12]

Aragon saw Chaplin as a man who sought freedom to follow his desires wherever they might lead. "We recall," he wrote, "an admirable moment in *The Imposter* [*Charlot et le Comte/The Count*, Mutual, 1916] when, of an instant, during a social gathering, Charlot sees an extremely beautiful woman go by, as alluring as can be, and immediately abandons what he's doing to follow her from room to room and out on to the terrace until she disappears from view. At the command of love, he has always been at the command of love, this is what his life and his films constantly proclaim."[13] But Chaplin—or Charlot, Chaplin's screen persona, since the manifesto does not really distinguish between the two—was perpetually frustrated in his search for love. In the case of Chaplin the real-life man, this was the result of his imprisonment in a bourgeois marriage, what Aragon referred to as "the imbecilic codification of love itself."[14] But Chaplin's criticisms of such a type of marriage—as diligently reported by Lita Grey in her divorce complaint— were perceived by Aragon as highly liberating. Had Chaplin told his wife of the example of a couple, unmarried, with five children as "an ideal way for a man and a woman to live together"? "Everybody," the manifesto grandly if inaccurately declared, "... who is not a hypocrite or a whore, thinks like this." Had Chaplin informed his wife that he was in love with another woman and planned to see her whenever he wanted? "This," declared the manifesto, "is the moral foundation of the man's life, this is what he defends: love itself."[15]

The surrealists as a group, argues William S. Rubin, advocated "sexual liberation" as "an important aspect" of "their program for the "total liberation of the individual."[16] Their interest in love/eroticism as a weapon against the hypocrisy and conservatism of existing society was displayed in much of their work. "For me," declared Aragon in his book *The Libertine* (1924), "there is no idea which can't be eclipsed by love. If it were up to me everything which is opposed to love would be abolished."[17] It was mainly for this reason that the Marquis de Sade became a much-admired figure for surrealists. As Paul Éluard observed in an article in 1926, "Sade validated those men who had singular ideas in the realm of love, and stood up to those who saw love only as an indispensable means to perpetuate their filthy race."[18]

Both before and after "Hands Off Love," surrealists continued to probe the issues of desire, love, and sexuality in a series of book-length works, both prose—Aragon's *Paris Peasant* (1926), Robert Desnos's *Liberty or Love!* (1927), André Breton's *Najda* (1928)—and poetry, such as Paul Éluard's *Love, Poetry* (1929). Although surrealists increasingly disagreed about politics in the final years of the 1920s, many continued to share similar views on love and sex. In January 1928, they organized two roundtable discussions at which fifteen of those who had signed "Hands Off Love" openly discussed their own love lives and sexual attitudes.[19] The following year, in the final issue of *La Révolution surréaliste*, twelve of the signatories of the Chaplin manifesto were among the fifty-three replies published in response to the question "What hope do you place in love?"[20] When Luis Buñuel's *L'Âge d'or* (1930) provoked much controversy for its strong sexual themes, the surrealists issued a new manifesto justifying the film on the grounds that it presented love as the best acid to eat away at the chains of convention, prompting a revolution that would sweep away "the social framework" of "a rotting society." Seven of the thirteen who signed the manifesto had also signed "Hands Off Love."[21]

Lita Grey's divorce complaint offered a major opportunity for the surrealists to publicize their belief in the transformative power of love. "Charlie Chaplin has the whole world interested in his divorce," wrote Belgian cinéaste Albert Valentin—soon to be, briefly, a surrealist himself—in 1927.[22] "Hands Off Love" positioned the surrealists as advocates of absolute sexual freedom in opposition to the repressions of bourgeois society. This strategy had a number of flaws. In the first place, as Leon S. Roudiez observed, "submission to erotic desire as a main tenet is rather slim for such an intellectual explosion as surrealism."[23] It was also deeply encrusted with sexism. All thirty-two signatories of the manifesto were men; it advanced what was in essence a fantasy of male freedom to follow sexual desire untrammelled by what were constructed as the stifling constraints of conventional marriage and family life. "Isn't what matters that we be the masters of ourselves, the masters of women, and of love too?" Breton had asked in the first surrealist manifesto of 1924.[24] As Jack L. Spector points out, "The attitude of the Surrealists toward women in large measure reflected the viewpoint of a patriarchal society—for these male writers and artists, women could serve as instruments of the imagination or of pleasure, but could not easily transgress these bounds and make independent contributions."[25]

Since Lita Grey—as acknowledged in her divorce complaint—had neither stimulated Chaplin's imagination nor provided him with the sexual pleasure he sought, she became the butt of Aragon's acid attack. Yet just as he and other surrealists tended to ignore the sexual violence against women at the core of the life and work of their hero Sade,[26] "Hands Off Love" disregarded Lita's allegations that Chaplin had treated her with considerable mental cruelty, that he had abused her verbally and had threatened to kill her with a revolver. It took no account of the huge disparity in wealth, power, and status between the thirty-eight-year-old movie star and his teenage wife. It presented Chaplin not as a bully but as a victim: the misunderstood genius, marked out by "the mysterious ascendancy that an unrivalled power of expression confers on a man," now under threat from traditionalist ideas of marriage and what Aragon termed "the chicanery of the legal profession."[27]

Discovering Charlot

By the time "Hands Off Love" was published, Chaplin had been a favorite of surrealist writers and artists for some time. As discussed in chapter 1, his first comedies arrived in France in March 1915. Baptized and rebranded as "Charlot" by distributor Jacques Haïk, Chaplin was an immediate hit with French popular audiences. His films seemed to many observers, in retrospect, to have been at the heart of the wartime invasion of French screens by American films that were somehow different from—and better than—domestic productions. "With a stroke of his cane," wrote future surrealist Philippe Soupault in 1923, "such a smiling magician was he, Charlie Chaplin was able to give an extraordinary vigor, an incredible superiority, to the American movies." Another future surrealist, Robert Desnos, also writing in 1923, similarly judged that "the era of the American film began with the success of Charlot."[28]

Many of the future surrealists seem to have discovered Charlot fairly quickly. Desnos, for example, claimed in 1929 that he had "liked and admired Chaplin for twelve years," suggesting his appreciation began in 1917.[29] Richard Abel notes that "Indifférence," the first "poème cinématographique" published by Soupault in January 1918, ends its collage of film styles with an allusion to Charlot.[30] In September 1918, while serving with the army at the front, Aragon began to write a novel, *Anicet ou le panorama*, with a major character, Pol, the café waiter, clearly based on Chaplin.[31] In November 1918, three days after the war ended, Jacques Vaché wrote to his friend André Breton, with whom he had visited many cinemas, of a fantasy film that would be a pastiche of contemporary American films, including, "of course, Charlie Chaplin, grinning, with staring eyes."[32]

In spite of their awareness of Chaplin's films, it took some time before the future surrealists began to discuss them in print. For most, this may simply have reflected their youth. In 1915, when Chaplin's first films arrived, many of those who would later sign "Hands Off Love" were not yet twenty-one: Jacques Baron was ten; Pierre Naville and Raymond Queneau twelve; Michel Leiris fourteen; Denos, Jacques Prévert, and Yves Tanguy all fifteen; Maxime Alexandre and Benjamin Péret sixteen; Aragon eighteen; Breton and André Masson nineteen; and Éluard and Paul Nougé twenty. Only in March 1918 did Louis Aragon—then age twenty—publish a poem relating to Chaplin, "Charlot sentimental," in *Le Film*.[33] This referenced sequences from a number of Chaplin films: the man twirling his mustache ("the flirty Mr. Stout" in *Charlot patine* [*The Rink*, Mutual, 1916]), a rooftop chase by the police (as in *The Knockout* [Keystone, 1914], although this was really a Fatty Arbuckle movie), a girl typewriting and an elevator (both in *The Floorwalker* [Mutual, 1916]). It featured a waiter carrying a tray, as Chaplin had done in *Caught in a Cabaret* (Keystone, 1914), *Dough and Dynamite* (Keystone, 1914), and *The Rink*. More interestingly, it explored two crucial gendered aspects of Chaplin's screen persona. First was the hostility displayed toward him ("how bitter their souls are!") by other men: "what is it," Aragon asked, "that they don't like in you?" Second was the sympathy he generated, as in *Tillie's Punctured Romance* (Keystone, 1914), *The Tramp* (Essanay, 1915), and *The Bank* (*Charlot à la banque*, Essanay, 1915), by "giving his heart to some disdainful girl" who then rejects him.[34]

In May 1918, a second Aragon poem, "Charlot Mystique," appeared in the journal *Nord-Sud*.[35] This evokes aspects of *The Floorwalker*. It begins with the store elevator coming down and the escalator going up. As Wolfgang

Babilas has written, "these are, for the young Aragon, incarnations of 'modern magic,' of 'modern beauty.' "[36] The fact that the two pieces of mechanical equipment operate in different directions creates a dynamic for both the film and the poem. The poem uses scenes in the film to establish a series of contrasts based on illusion. It emphasizes that Charlot wishes to make love to a woman who is really an effigy; in contrast, he at first thinks the male shop assistant is just a statue. The "pork-leather briefcase" out of which the corrupt floorwalker gives Charlot twenty dollars actually contains one thousand dollars. (The floorwalker and the manager have been ripping off the store.) But the poem also uses Charlot's filmic world as a basis for Aragon's own imagination: *The Floorwalker* has no "noble foreigner" denying that she is a loose woman (*une femme légère*); nor, for that matter, does Charlot make the shop assistant shriek by tugging on his mustache and eyebrows. Looking back on the jumble of often contradictory ideas and images in his poem, Aragon concluded, "It's always the same system/neither moderation nor logic [*Pas de mesure, Ni de logique*]/a poor theme." Yet, according to Caroline Nataf, this is precisely why Charlot is "mystique": "he isn't governed by the laws of the world, he is entirely a sentient being, deep in an imaginary world."[37]

Poet Philippe Soupault also appropriated Chaplin's movies as a basis for his own creative imaginings. In *Littérature* (June 1919), Soupault published this comment on *A Dog's Life* (First National, 1918):

> At five o'clock in the morning or the evening, the smoke that fills the saloons takes you by the throat, you sleep in the light of the stars.
>
> But time passes. There is no longer a second to lose. Tobacco. At the street corners we cross the shadows; the pushcart peddlers are at the curb. We had better run: hands in pockets we stare at the sign. Café, Bar. At the door we hear the tin mechanical piano. The odour of alcohol sets the couples dancing.
>
> They are here.
>
> At the edge of the tables, at the edge of lips, cigarettes are consumed: a new star sings an old sad song.
>
> You may turn your head.
>
> The sun is laid upon a tree and his reflections in the window panes are bursts of laughter. A story as gay as a French paint shop.[38]

Soupault focused on the cabaret that is the main backdrop to the film's narrative but in fact appears for less than half its running time. The "new star" singing "an old sad song" is the young, innocent cabaret entertainer (Edna Purviance) whom Charlot falls for. But Soupault ignored everything else in the movie—the police, the crooks, Scraps the dog, the stolen wallet that finally allows Charlot and his love to marry and settle in the country—in order to evoke an atmosphere close to that of a Parisian café-concert.[39]

Two months later, Soupault published a similar response (calling it a review would be inaccurate) to *The Immigrant* (Mutual, 1917):

> The tossing of the ship and boredom rock the days to sleep. Enough of these promenades on deck: ever since our departure, the sea is colorless. Neither dice nor cards can make us forget the city we are approaching: life is at stake.
>
> The rain receives us in these deserted streets. Birds and hopes are far off. In every city the inside of restaurants is warm. You think no more; you look at the faces of the diners, or out through the doorway, at the light. Do you realize that you will have to go out and pay the bill? Does not the present moment suffice? There is nothing left to do but laugh at all this anxiety.
>
> And we laugh sadly like hunchbacks.[40]

This time there are more allusions to specific sequences of the film (the rocking ship, the gambling, anxiety over the restaurant bill, the rain), but no reference is made to either characterization or narrative. As Herbert S. Gershman explains, "if this tells us little about the film—who does what, when, and where—it tells us a great deal about the spectator's reaction to *The Immigrant*."[41] As with *A Dog's Life*, Soupault is thinking freely and subjectively about images and issues suggested by Chaplin's films rather than the content of the films themselves. The same could be said of Yvan Goll's *Chaplinade* (1920).

Many of the literary avant-garde in the years immediately after the First World War were searching for new means of writing about and commenting on film. One approach employed by several writers was to write film scenarios as an art form in themselves, without any particular desire—or, at least, urgency—about turning them into films.[42] Goll's *Chaplinade* was part scenario, part poem. It begins whimsically: the image of Chaplin on a poster comes alive and starts to demand that he be left alone. While a bill poster tries to push him back on the wall, Chaplin declaims his loneliness while people pass by talking in clichés. Chaplin escapes again and runs away, followed by all the passersby. Suddenly, vast numbers of Chaplins detach themselves from posters, and the crowd, confused, doesn't know which one to chase. Finally, all "become one: the living Chaplin." He catches a train, passing through many different landscapes. A woman gets on with her daughter (a deer), and Chaplin complains he has been "robbed of my solitude." When the woman starts planning to stay with him at the hotel, Chaplin stabs her with his cane and leaves the train with the deer. At the station restaurant, he joins the restaurateur's family for a (strange) meal. The deer invades the restaurant, and she and Chaplin return to the train. Chaplin asks, "Can a poet ever find peace?" He and the doe wander through a desert, which he finds "so quiet and peaceful," only to suddenly find himself at the center of the Earth, where there is a cacophony of voices.

The scene (Goll says "film") cuts to the harbor of Marseilles, where everyone is working. Newsboys and the police try to attack Chaplin, but he escapes in quick succession to Cairo, Hong Kong, and back to Marseilles. A mob tries to turn him into a revolutionary leader; the mob and a policeman fight until no one is left. Chaplin is alone until a single policeman appears; then Chaplin takes fright and runs away. He is in a wood with the deer, who turns into a pragmatic young woman called Reha, who abandons Chaplin and runs away with a hunter (who shoots her). Chaplin again protests his loneliness ("lonelier than all the others"), but the bill poster reappears, grabs him, and sticks him back on the wall.[43]

Chaplinade is an utterly whimsical piece of work, combining fantasy and absurdity with elements of reality. It demonstrates the strengths and weaknesses of cinema: its power through editing in jump-cutting from place to place and its lack of dialogue. (In the early 1920s, Chaplin's poetic words and the words spoken by others could be reproduced only in intertitles.) In its dreamlike progression of verbally induced images, it anticipates Goll's own later surrealism. But it also offers Chaplin as victim—not of hostile men and indifferent women (as in his films) but of his own stardom and celebrity status. In *Chaplinade*, according to Clinton J. Atkinson and Arthur S. Wensinger, Goll "captured and presented the loneliness of the public hero, the private anguish of the world's buffoon."[44]

Dada

By 1920, Aragon, Breton, Soupault, and Goll were all associated with the Dada movement. Dada had its immediate origins in Switzerland in 1916. It expressed, in many ways, a vast, youthful dissatisfaction with the brutality and carnage of the First World War. The war seemed to call into question the existing values and culture of bourgeois capitalist society. If reason and intelligence had led to such a disaster, then Dadaists would privilege irrationality and intuition. Much of existing art and literature appeared bankrupt in the light of the war, so Dadaists would attack the practices and conventions that sustained them. Their strategy at first was one of iconoclastic, aggressive, sometimes nihilistic protest. At the core of that strategy were the activities of two men: Hugo Ball from Germany and Tristan Tzara from Romania. From early 1916 to the summer of 1917, Ball and Tzara—first apart, then together—organized a series of performances and events in Zurich that crystallized into the Dada movement. In June 1917, Ball abruptly withdrew, and the following month Tzara published the first issue of the *Dada* magazine in which he would develop his ideas of "poetic anti-art."[45]

It is probable that Breton and some of his friends were aware for some time of these activities in Zurich through their friendship with poet Guillaume Apollinaire, who died in November 1918. Tzara had sent copies of Dada publications to Apollinaire.[46] On January 6, 1919, he posted the third issue of *Dada*—containing the "Dada Manifesto 1918"—to Breton. Soupault (and Aragon) were already familiar with the manifesto, since Soupault wrote to Tzara on January 17 that he had "read it aloud to many friends, André Breton, Louis Aragon, and Jacques Vaché." This reading must have occurred *before* January 6, the date of Vaché's suicide.[47] Breton too had heard of Tzara before his letter arrived in Paris. "People besides myself follow you with confidence; I have talked about you at length to . . . Soupault and Aragon," he assured the Dadaist in reply. Responding to Tzara's request for work to publish in *Dada*, Breton sent him a poem he had written, "Pour Lafcadio," and one by Aragon, "Le délire du fantassin." Both were published in issues 4–5 of *Dada* in May.[48] In March 1919, Breton sent Tzara the first issue of the journal *Littérature*, which he, Aragon, and Soupault had just founded. It included a review of Tzara's Dada manifesto and his book *Twenty-Five Poems*. Thereafter, the relationship between the three Frenchmen and Tzara deepened steadily. In July, *Littérature* would publish two of Tzara's poems.[49]

Tzara was an instinctive and highly adept showman, as his career in Zurich proved. In June 1919, he sent Breton a copy of his poster "La seule expression de l'homme moderne" (The only expression of modern man), designed to be used in *Dada*. The poster listed supporters of the Dada movement, one of whom, it claimed, was Charlie Chaplin. In his response, Breton blended elation with skepticism: "That news about Charlie Chaplin is a delightful surprise. But surely it's not true?"[50] Tzara does not appear to have answered Breton's question, but this would not be the last time he would unscrupulously use Chaplin's name as a way of attracting support for Dada.

In early January 1920, Tzara arrived in Paris to stay. His natural skills as a publicist and organizer helped launch Dada in Paris as a militant movement setting out to shock. On the evening of Friday, January 23, 1920, the French Dadaists held their first public event, at which masked participants read a poem by Breton, Tzara read aloud an article from a newspaper "accompanied by an orchestra of rattles and hand-bells," and a bearded version of the *Mona Lisa* by Marcel Duchamp was shown.[51]

On Thursday, February 5, 1920, Dadaists organized a second meeting at the Grand Palais des Champs-Élysées, where an exhibition of over three thousand artworks (many of them Cubist) had been launched eight days earlier in the Salon des Indépendants. Thirty-eight lecturers simultaneously read a series of Dadaist manifestos.[52] Many people were present on this occasion because Tzara, once again exploiting Chaplin's name for publicity purposes, had sent press releases to the newspapers claiming that the comedian would be present. Angry at being taken advantage of, the audience, notes Maurice Nadeau, "left the hall . . . in indescribable disorder, after having cannonaded the readers with coins."[53] Those such as Nadeau who have written about this incident have seen it as an unscrupulous but highly successful means of exploiting the huge popularity of "Charlot" in France to recruit a large crowd to a Dada event. What has escaped comment is the fact that no one at the time seems to have questioned the idea of Charlot's *being* linked to Dada. "Charlie Chaplin, the famous *Charlot*," Émile Duharme reported in the *Journal du Peuple* on February 2, "has just arrived in Paris. We shall have a chance to applaud him; his friends 'the poets of the Dada movement,' invite us to a matinee that they are organizing. . . . The famous American [*sic*] actor will be speaking. . . . We've recently been informed that Charlie Chaplin has just joined the 'Dada' movement."[54] Chaplin was *expected* by many French observers to do the unexpected (as his screen Charlot often did). "Although we denied the rumor [that Chaplin was coming]," Tzara later claimed, "there was one reporter who followed me everywhere. He thought that the celebrated actor was up to some new stunt and was planning a surprise entrance."[55]

American writer Matthew Josephson, who arrived in Paris in 1921, would later recall the passion of Dadaists for American cinema, which had begun during the wartime years. "Though I had come to France with other objects in view," he wrote, "I found myself giving serious study to a lot of old American films in the company of Soupault and Aragon."[56] Josephson was surprised by those involved in the same pursuit: "even the learned André Breton attended the silliest old American films, hoping to discover what Jacques Vaché had seen in them."[57] Chaplin's films were clearly the Dadaists' favorites. "Above all," Josephson wrote, "the American cinema had given Chaplin to the world—the beloved 'Charlot' to the French—who created 'a sublime poetry, a new laughter,' as Soupault wrote in his fine essay on Chaplin."[58]

The importance of Chaplin to Dada was underlined by the appearance in *Littérature* in March 1921 of a survey in which most of the main Dadaists awarded marks to a number of famous names, past and present. The objective was clearly one close to Dadaist hearts: to deconstruct the reputation of many of these, not classifying but declassifying (*non de classer, mais de déclasser*), as was stated in the introduction.[59] The marking system went from –25, expressing the greatest aversion to the name concerned, to +20 as the most positive (0 signified indifference). The participants could vote for their friends but not themselves, which meant that André Breton (with 16.85) and Philippe Soupault (16.30) took the first two places. In third place, with 16.09, was Charlot.[60] Of the eleven "evaluators," it was unsurprising that the names of no fewer than seven appeared in the list of the most favored twenty. (In addition to Breton and Soupault, these were Paul Éluard, 5; Louis Aragon, 7; Tristan Tzara, 8; Jacques Rigaut, 10; and Georges Ribement-Dessaignes, 11). Also on the list were another Dadaist who would later become associated with surrealism, the German-born artist Arp (13), and the late Jacques Vaché, Breton's close friend (14).[61]

The remainder of the "most favored" list consisted—with one exception—of those the Dadaists regarded as their own principal forerunners and cultural reference points.[62] These included poets Arthur Rimbaud (4), Isidore-Lucien Ducasse (6), and Guillaume Apollinaire (12), together with Alfred Jarry (9), whose play *Ubu Roi* (1896) would later come to be perceived as a precursor of both Dada and surrealism. Also listed were Anglo-Irish satirist Jonathan Swift (17), author of *A Modest Proposal* (1729), advising the Irish to eat their own children; two anarchists, Émile-Joseph Duval (18), editor of the journal *Le Bonnet rouge*, who had been shot in 1918, allegedly for taking money from the Germans, and Jules Bonnot (19), involved in a famous gang of criminal anarchists; and two writers associated with sexual libertinage, Donatien Alphonse François, Marquis de Sade (16) and Pierre Choderlos de Laclos (20), author of *Les Liaisons dangereuses* (*Dangerous Liaisons*, 1782).[63]

The fact that, of all the people most favored by the Dadaists, Charlot was the highest rated not to be a member of Dada itself suggests a good deal. Participants in the survey ranked 191 individuals and a few objects, including the Bible and *Mille et une Nuits* (*The Arabian Nights*). Since the main object of the Dadaists was to debunk many reputations (while elevating their own), and some of the participants rated fairly eccentrically (Tzara awarded the lowest rating of –25 to nearly half the names on the list), it is not possible to see the survey as meaningful in any scientific sense. But it does underline the significance of Chaplin to many Dadaists who would later be associated with surrealism. Excluding votes by Dadaists for their fellows, Aragon ranked Charlot twentieth on his list, with the same score (16) as Einstein, Knut Hamsun, Laclos, Shakespeare, and Arthur Young. Breton had him as sixth, equal to Benjamin Constant, Jean-Auguste-Dominique Ingres, Laclos, French revolutionary Jean-Paul Marat, and Swift. Pierre Drieux la Rochelle placed him first with an impressive list of others (Johann Sebastian Bach, Henri Bergson, the Bible, Corneille, Dante, Dostoyevsky, Aeschylus [Eschyle], Goethe, Hegel, Kant, Lenin, *The Arabian Nights*, Napoleon, Nietzsche, Pascal, Racine, Robespierre, Schopenhauer, Shakespeare, and Tolstoy). For Paul Éluard, he shared seventh place with the anarchist Duval and Swift. Théodore Fraenkel had him first with Jarry, Rimbaud, and Igor Stravinsky. He was rated fourth (with Ducasse), after the Bible, Sade, and Swift, by Benjamin Péret. Jacques Rigaut had him at seventh with the Bible and Constant, after Ducasse, Sade, Laclos, *The Arabian Nights*, Francis Picabia, and Rimbaud. For Soupault he came twenty-second, together with Alcibiades (Alcibiade), Bonnot, Chateaubriand, Chirico, Corot, Hamsun, Manet, and Oscar Wilde. Tzara awarded him fourth place, together with Einstein and Dadaist Max Ernst.[64]

One of the interesting features of the survey is that Chaplin was clearly perceived as being in a different league than other actors, including comedian Fatty Arbuckle and western star William S. Hart. Three screen actors (Douglas Fairbanks and French stars Max Linder and Mistinguett) even received negative ratings.[65] In contrast, Chaplin ranked very high in relation to major world philosophers, writers, and artists. His consistent popularity with the eleven evaluators finally guaranteed him his third place.

Dada to Surrealism

The term "surrealism" (*surréalisme*) was first used by Guillaume Apollinaire in a letter of March 1917. It would later be taken up by a group of young men—including André Breton, Paul Éluard, Benjamin Péret, Louis Aragon, and Philippe Soupault—for whom Apollinaire functioned, in Maurice Nadeau's phrase, "as a kind of God."[66] Until 1922, these figures would be the French wing of the international Dada movement. Yet the "semi-failure" of one event in which Breton had taken the lead (the attempt on May 13, 1921, to stage a "trial" of the nationalistic writer Maurice Barrès) and the unquestionable failure of another (the unsuccessful effort between January and April 1922 to organize the Congress of Paris, grandiosely dedicated to "determining the directives and the defense of the modern spirit") exacerbated personal tensions between Dadaists, especially between Breton and Tzara.[67] From the birth of the new series of *Littérature* in March 1922, Nadeau points out, the journal no longer had anything to do with Dada. It had become "the organ of a new current" no longer intent on confining itself "to destructive agitation."[68] In the second issue of the new series, published on April 1, 1922, Breton memorably wrote:

> Let go of everything.
> Let go of Dada.[69]

In the fourth issue (September 1922), he sketched out "Project for Contemporary Literary History," which firmly consigned Dada to the past. His "Project" was divided into five periods: from 1913 to the war; from August 1, 1914, to Apollinaire's death on November 9, 1918; from the Armistice to Dada, November 1918 to January 1920; Dada (January 1920 to October 1921); after Dada (October 1921 to today).[70]

Suggesting the death of Dada occurred in October 1921 could mean that Breton associated it with growing quarrels between Dadaists and ex-Dadaists, notably Tzara and Spanish painter Francis Picabia (who had abandoned Dada at the time of the Barrès trial five months earlier).[71] But it could also mean that he dated the end of Dada from his meeting with Sigmund Freud in Vienna. Although that meeting was a distinct failure—Breton would later make clear his disappointment in a brief report in *Littérature*—he noted in the same article (March 1922) "that the fashion this winter is for psychoanalysis."[72] In his "Manifesto of Surrealism" (October 1924), announcing the official emergence of surrealism, Breton would pay tribute to the influence of Freud on the new movement.[73] His motive, almost certainly, was to give attempts to mobilize the unconscious mind in the cause of literature and art some kind of scientific justification. The reality, indicated by his article "Enter the Mediums" in *Littérature* in November 1922, was very different. Surrealism (Breton used the word in this article) grew, at least in part, from very *unscientific* soil: René Crevel, having been told by a female spiritualist that he had the qualities of a medium, organized the first of a series of séances at which members of the group (starting with Crevel himself) submitted to being hypnotized and questioned. Accessing the unconscious in this way seemed to Breton and the others an appealing way of exploiting its literary/poetic potential.[74] Matthew Josephson, a welcome American guest at many of these events, described psychoanalytical group sessions where people were asked to recite their dreams and have them analyzed by the group, sleep sessions and hypnotic trances, and spiritualist and telepathic séances. "It seemed to me," Josephson later concluded, "that Breton was misusing psychoanalytic methods (essentially a therapy for the mentally ill) and, like a dilettante, was trying to extract literature from the minds of persons in a state of hypnosis or sleep."[75]

Charlot and the Origins of Surrealism

A series of writers have teased out the intellectual antecedents of—and influences upon—surrealism. Chaplin's films certainly were a major attraction to many of those who would become surrealists: Helena Lewis writes of "Chaplin, whom the Surrealists dearly loved."[76] But is it possible that Charlot actually *influenced* the development first of Dada and later of surrealism? At least one contemporary observer *outside* France thought this was indeed the case. Spanish Dadaist Guillermo de Torre, described by Michal Sanouillet as "the most efficient instrument of the Dadaist infiltration in Spain," was already thinking along these lines in 1920, writing to Tristan Tzara, "I am going to read an [*sic*] study of spasmodic erudition on 'the influence of Charlot in the DADA movement.'"[77]

One modern scholar, Richard Abel, has depicted Chaplin as in some respects a precursor of surrealism. His argument is particularly based on an analysis of Louis Aragon's essay "Du Décor," published in *Le Film* in September 1918. Abel sees the depiction of objects in American film, including the machine "Charlot leans against in *The Fireman* [*Charlot pompier*, Mutual, 1916]," as demonstrating how "the common objects of modern life become transformed on the screen, especially in close-ups" that detached them from their context and "isolated them in a newly-defined space. No longer representational and simply part of the story, they became images with a life of their own." To Aragon, the beauty of these "image-objects" lay in what he called their "menacing or enigmatic meanings." Aragon's essay on décor consequently becomes, in Abel's view, "one of the earliest statements of what was to become a central aesthetic principle of the surrealists—true art was enigmatic."[78]

Yet while Chaplin was part of a more general tendency that would influence surrealism, Abel sees his more personal contribution to the movement through the "transformation of reality" in his films. The working out of this process was a focal point of Aragon's article "Du Décor." "The set in which Charlot arranges the elements around his character," he maintains, ". . . is Charlot's vision of the world, and the discovery of its mechanics and laws haunt the hero to the point where, by an inversion of values, any inanimate object for him becomes a living thing and any person a mannequin whose starting crank he must seek." In Abel's view, in writing this Aragon understood that underpinning Chaplin's films was a dramatically different view of the nature of reality: "By having objects participate in the film's action, by relating them intimately to the character, Chaplin had transformed an objective view into a subjective one. In *The Fireman*, for instance, a fire engine boiler became a coffee and cream dispenser, a fire pole reversed the law of gravity, and before a burning house axes turned into props for a musical comedy fire drill."[79] These unexpected shifts—taking place "without assessment nor logic [*pas de mesure/ni de logique*]," as Aragon had written in his poem "Charlot Mystique," published four months earlier—helped prepare the ground for surrealism's attempt to inspire "a revolution against things as we ordinarily see them."[80]

It is also significant that it was the *early* Charlot—the anarchistic, at times brutal Charlot, the Chaplin Charles Maland shows was softened and tamed to satisfy genteel American critics—who appealed to Dadaists and surrealists. The First World War made many writers and artists distrustful of existing social conventions and respectable patterns of behavior. In 1923, Aragon recalled that the first inspiration for *Littérature* had come to Breton, Soupault, and himself during the war as they wandered the streets of Paris "in our sullied uniforms, neglecting to salute the officers, neglecting any sort of manners."[81] Dadaists and later surrealists appreciated Chaplin's "Little Tramp" persona for his asocial portrayal of a man who was indifferent or opposed to society's rules and those charged with enforcing them.[82] Constance Brown Kuriyama has written of this "old quasi-demonic Charlie" of the Keystone and Essanay films that he is "brash, manipulative, unscrupulous. . . . While he is neither precisely malicious nor consistently purposeful, his mission is clearly to subvert order and promote mayhem and destruction. . . . Charlie flouts authority and demolishes his surroundings without a trace of guilt."[83] These tendencies to undermine existing social practices and conventions of behavior, Charles Musser has noted, dated from Chaplin's earliest films. In his first film to be released, *Making a Living* (*Pour gagner sa vie*, Keystone, 1914), he played an "impoverished opportunist," lampooning "the ethic of hard work and honesty—the entire system of values espoused by society." In *Kid Auto Races at Venice* (*Course d'autos pour gosses*, Keystone, 1914), his second film, he was a tramp persistently walking in front of the movie camera attempting to film the event, disrupting "all attempts by the crew to perform its job and to work productively." He was also deeply destructive, demolishing objects he encountered, including the customer's alarm clock in *The Pawnshop* (*Charlot chez l'usurier*, Mutual, 1916), symbolizing his rejection of the strict regulation of time in capitalist workplaces.[84]

For Dadaists and surrealists, the idea of Chaplin transgressing ordinary social bonds and bourgeois morality was appealing. In *Le Film* in 1919, Louis Aragon fantasized about Charlot as an amoral and brutal Darwinian survivor:

Today's man glorifies action, in it he finds his gratification, and laughs at the fruits that it bore. . . . Active life leads him into a state of permanent irritation. He is alien to melancholy. . . . I dream about Charlot choking Carmen. . . . Modern man obeys nothing, neither the established frameworks of life nor that which is allotted to him. You see Lafcadio [a character in André Gide's *Les Caves du Vatican* (1914) who displays an aristocratic contempt for all social conventions and, confronting an elderly, ugly man in a train compartment, kills him without hesitation by throwing him out of the window] on the borderline of morality. . . . Modern man is in need of modern life, a life of free competition, where the weak perish and the strong make their living. Sentimentality is punished with death. . . . Charlot knocks down the elderly.[85]

Imagining a Charlot who, like Lafcadio, is brutal and amoral formed the background to the novel *Anicet, ou la panorama* that Aragon was writing at the time. In this novel, published in 1921, it is Anicet himself who most closely resembles Lafcadio. As Marcel Raval, editor of the literary magazine *Les feuilles libres,* observed, "The moral code of his character is in accordance with the proudest heresies of our era. He unassailably evokes the disturbing and feverish figure of Lafcadio that Mr. Gide, in the *Vatican Caves* [*Les Caves du Vatican*], has endowed with moving life. A similarity of passion, of fortuitous obsessions. The same unwarranted nature of the criminal act."[86] Aragon also, however, included an obvious Charlot figure in *Anicet*: Pol the waiter has a bowler hat and carries a cane. Like Anicet, he is an utterly immoral character. Several years before "Hands off Love," in his article of 1919 and his novel of 1921, Aragon had already created a "Charlot" to whom normal social conventions did not apply.

Aragon's *Anicet* is also significant, however, for directing attention to the movements on screen of Charlot's body. "Everything in his behaviour was mechanical," Aragon wrote of Chaplin's alter ego Pol, "as if there were several distinct personalities with their separate resolutions moving parts of his body so as to bring into relief each one of them." While Anicet was initially inclined to mock "this marionette," he soon was "gripped with a special kind of excitement at the sight of this personality which struggled against [the] material world to the extent that it seemed in dire need to invent . . . even the slightest body movement in order to repeat it. In continuous conflict with things, with all social and natural mechanisms, confounding non-animate objects and living creatures . . . Paul [Pol] is at once a funny prankster and an anxiety-ridden character."[87]

Writing of Anicet's captivation by the "mechanical" movements of Pol was clearly a tactic through which Aragon expressed his own fascination with the jerky movements and actions of Charlot. Such behavior, he suggested, originated in both external and internal conflicts. Charlot, according to Tom Gunning, made use of his body (including representing its "less than genteel functions") to challenge external social conventions and taboos, "breaching the codes of repression that had been imposed with the growth of middle-class propriety in bourgeois culture."[88] In this sense, Chaplin's behavior on-screen was in opposition to existing society, increasing his appeal to Dadaists and later surrealists. At the same time, Aragon's Charlot/Pol is also "anxiety-ridden": a mass of inner conflicts, his bodily movements responding to "several distinct personalities." This reveals itself in his seemingly uncontrolled "mechanical" movements and gestures.

For Aragon, Breton, and Soupault—"the three musketeers of early surrealism"[89]—Chaplin's bodily movements and facial contortions probably had other parallels and associations. All three were former medical students, with extensive experience of psychiatry and psychiatric disorders, including hysteria. Breton had worked for several months in 1917 with Joseph Babinski, the favorite assistant (and subsequent critic) of neurologist Jean-Martin Charcot, who had pioneered the study of hysteria at La Salpêtrière hospital in Paris.[90] In an article in 1928, Aragon and Breton celebrated the fiftieth anniversary of the medical identification of hysteria, characterizing it as "a mental state . . . characterized by the subversion of the relationship established between the subject and the moral world. . . . It can, from every point of view, be considered as a supreme mode of expression."[91]

To Aragon, Breton, Soupault, and others, aspects of the screen Charlot were almost certainly reminiscent of the actions of people suffering from hysteria and other psychiatric conditions. In 1921, film writer Jean Epstein (another former medical student) wrote of the impression conveyed by Charlot's "photogenic neurasthenia," with his film persona a projection "of the reflex actions of a tired, nervous person."[92] The jerky manner in which he moved also paralleled the agitated movements of hysterics. As Rae Beth Gordon points out, "one has only to compare Chaplin's gait [and 'tics, grimaces, gesticulations'] to that of the psychiatric patients filmed at the Salpêtrière between 1910 and 1912 to see that there is but a small step to take from Charcot to Charlot."[93] For surrealists, it seems likely that Charlot's screen performances—like hysteria itself—offered what Joost Haan, Peter J. Koehler, and Julien Bogousslavsky term "a form of psychic release that rejected the rational world."[94] In this way, they may well deserve a place in the genealogy of surrealist thought.

Surrealists regarded cinema (including Chaplin's films) as a means of substituting for dreams. Poet Robert Desnos wrote, "From the desire to dream comes the taste, the love for the cinema. Deprived of the spontaneous adventure that our eyelids let escape on waking, we enter the darkened halls in search of an artificial dream and perhaps the stimulus capable of peopling our empty nights."[95] For some surrealists, the association of cinema with dreams had its roots in moviegoing practices they indulged in during the war. André Breton recalled, "I never began by consulting the amusement pages to find out what film might chance to be the best, nor did I find out the time the film was to begin. I agreed wholeheartedly with Jacques Vaché in appreciating nothing so much as dropping into the cinema when whatever was playing was playing, at any point in the show, and leaving at the first hint of boredom—of surfeit—to rush off to another cinema where we behaved in the same way, and so on."[96] In this way, Breton and Vaché confronted themselves with a succession of visual images liberated from the formal constraints of narration. They juxtaposed these with images assembled by other filmmakers for different purposes. What attracted them to the cinema was above all its "power to disorient,"[97] to transfix and inspire them with dreamlike possibilities. "I have never known anything more *magnetising* [hypnotizing]," Breton would recall. After such an experience, drug-like in its intensity, he and his friend Vaché would emerge "charged" for several days.[98]

A major key to surrealism was its preoccupation with automatism, the idea that material could be accessed and retrieved from the unconscious mind as part of a creative process. Breton, in the first "Manifesto of Surrealism" (1924) defined the surrealist movement as "pure psychic automatism by means of which one intends to express, either verbally, or in writing, or in any other manner, the actual functioning of thought. Dictated by thought, in the absence of any control exercised by reason, free of any aesthetic or moral concern."[99] Automatism as a practice had its origins in the work of neurologist and psychiatrist Jules Baillarger, seemingly the first to employ "psychological automatism" by making his patients write down ideas that came into their heads. The technique was further developed by Charcot and used by a number of psychiatrists during the First World War.[100] "The emphasis on automatic writing" placed by surrealists, observe Haan and colleagues, suggested that they "wanted to parallel aspects of the hysteric's and psychotic's experience in their own processes of artistic production."[101] The founding text in this regard, later regarded as a precursor of surrealism, was *Les Champs magnétiques* (1919), with Breton and Soupault writing very rapidly whatever came into their minds and subsequently completing each other's phrases and sentences, creating unusual, even bizarre associations, juxtapositions, and contradictions.[102]

The underlying rationale for automatism of this kind was to challenge existing language forms, widely regarded by surrealists as an expression of existing social and cultural relations, by appealing from the conscious to the unconscious mind. It may also have been, for some, a means of recovering the sense of intoxication they had earlier derived from moviegoing: when Breton and Soupault wrote *Les Champs magnétiques*, Richard Abel comments, the very title suggests that they "were trying to achieve the same magnetizing power Breton had experienced in the cinema."[103] It is not possible, because of a lack of direct evidence, to prove that Chaplin, despite his vast popularity among surrealists, had any direct influence on their endorsement and use of automatism. But at least one contemporary who was close to surrealism, Henri Michaux, a Belgian writer living in France, suggested that his film-making technique worked in much the same manner: "Conjunction of automatism and the deliberate, the external reality. Surrealist works elaborated diligently, this will probably leave us with some outstanding pieces. In a way, Charlie Chaplin does this sort of thing. From the automatism of a clown, interspersed with fragments of reality, to the actions as defined in the screenplay."[104]

"Hands Off Love": The Aftermath

"Hands Off Love" was the last manifesto many of the surrealists would sign together. Breton, in particular, insisted that the movement must be tightly disciplined and those rebelling against its principles be proscribed. In November 1926, with the aid of Aragon, Éluard, Péret, and surrealist writer/poet Pierre Unik, he effectively expelled Philippe Soupault and theatrical director-writer Antonin Artaud on the grounds that, as Maurice Nadeau would later write, having "acknowledged literary activity as a value, they had no place in a group which had proclaimed its vanity."[105]

Even more serious were the growing political divisions among the surrealists. Surrealist engagement in politics effectively began in 1925, when France helped Spain suppress a major revolt by Berber tribesmen in the Rif Mountains of Morocco. Opposition to the war led surrealists to create a "united front" with communists and left-wing intellectuals, especially the group associated with the journal *Clarté*.[106] In the months before "Hands Off Love" appeared, however, the movement had started to fragment over politics. Among those who signed "Hands Off Love," Pierre Naville was the first to argue that the surrealists could overthrow bourgeois society only if they formed an alliance with the "revolutionary proletariat," in practice represented by the French Communist Party (PCF). For this heresy, he was attacked by Breton and others and effectively exiled from the surrealist movement. This was ironic for two reasons. First, in January 1927, Aragon, Breton,

Éluard, Péret, and Unik all joined the PCF (which, while taking them, held them at arm's length, rightly suspecting that most would not abandon surrealism in favor of Marxist orthodoxy).[107] Second, Naville, having acted as the catalyst for this process, soon reached the conclusion that it was necessary to seek more radical economic and political solutions than the PCF had to offer. After visiting the Soviet Union in 1927, he became a strong critic of Stalin and a supporter of the Trotskyite cause in France.[108]

Other surrealists, including Robert Desnos, declined to submit what they saw as the artistic and spiritual movement that was surrealism to a political agenda and refused to join the PCF. Desnos gradually withdrew to concentrate on poetry—and journalism.[109] It was no accident that "Hands Off Love" was the last time the thirty-two signatories would collaborate. Since the beginning of surrealism, Chaplin's Charlot had been a figure that united them. By 1927, Charlot and a certain conception of erotic love[110] may have been the *only* things that any longer united most surrealists.

Coda: Controversies of the Early 1950s

By the 1950s, some older surrealists still saw Chaplin's earlier films as exemplars of what they hoped would become a new kind of cinema. Benjamin Péret, one of the signatories of "Hands Off Love," wrote in 1951 of his hopes for "the cinema we have craved for since our youth, this cinema whose earliest manifestations—oases in a desert of asphyxiating dust— go by the name of *Nosferatu*, the first Chaplins, *Peter Ibbetson*, *L'Âge d'or*, etcetera."[111] Other writers who had been at the heart of the surrealist movement in the 1920s had abandoned it long before. Aragon, partly under the influence of his mistress, later wife, the Russian-born Elsa Triolet, took seriously his role as a member of the PCF.[112] By the time Aragon had dinner with Chaplin (together with Pablo Picasso and Jean-Paul Sartre) in Paris in October 1952, he was a member of the Central Committee of the PCF.[113]

Chaplin's Paris visit of 1952 saw two politically based attacks on him. One was from a surrealist of a new generation, Jean-Louis Bédouin, who criticized him for behaving in a completely non-surrealist manner and demanded a complete reassessment of his work. Bédouin was outraged by the close relationship Chaplin had apparently forged with the French police, commenting that it had taken "only a few days of social engagements for him to slough off the personification of the legendary tramp and reemerge as the crony of the Prefect of Police." He bitterly condemned Chaplin for thanking the Paris Police "for 'having protected him so well' (against what?)" and accepting both a gold medal and a "presentation truncheon" commemorating the 150th anniversary of the Prefecture of Police. Such acts, he argued, are "marked in infamy in the eyes of all those who had believed in the subversive nature of his work and who had accorded him all their affection." Now that he had revealed himself as nothing but a "copper's nark," Bédouin concluded, "Charlot's world-famous silhouette ceases to be an image of protest to become that of the buffoon capitalism claims for itself at our expense."[114]

The second attack came from a different quarter, not from a surrealist but from those who saw surrealism itself as the enemy (though, curiously, like Bédouin they also associated Chaplin with the police and accused him of "selling out" to capitalism). On October 29, 1952, on the eve of the première of *Limelight* in Paris, Chaplin gave a press conference at the Ritz Hotel on the Place Vendôme. In the midst of the questions and answers, four men started shouting and throwing flyers around the room. Under the headline "NO MORE FLAT FEET," the sheet addressed Chaplin directly:

Sub–Mack Sennett, sub–Max Linder actor, Stravinsky of the tears of unwed mothers and the little orphans of Auteuil, you are Chaplin, emotional blackmailer, master-singer of misfortune.... Because you've identified yourself with the weak and the oppressed, to attack you has been to attack the weak and oppressed—but in the shadow of your rattan cane some could already see the nightstick of the cop. You are "he-who-turns-the-other-cheek"—the other cheek of the buttocks—but for us, the young and beautiful, the only answer to suffering is revolution.... Go to sleep, you fascist insect. Rake in the dough. Make it with high society.... Have a quick death: we promise you a first-class funeral. We pray that your latest film will truly be your last.[115]

The signatures on the flyer were those of the four protestors: Serge Berna, Guy-Ernest Debord, Jean-Louis Brau, and Gil Wolman. In the text, they explained that Chaplin and his film were practicing a form of "emotional blackmail," "compensating" for a tedious human existence but not suggesting any hope "of a new one filled with excitement and adventure." Chaplin, they alleged, now belonged to the past and stood in the way of the creation of a new type of life that would no longer be characterized by "alienation and suffering."[116]

The protest had little impact on Chaplin himself. (He did not, for example, mention it in his autobiography.) Since he had little or no knowledge of French, he could not have understood what the four men were shouting or the point of their flyer. The quartet signed their denunciation on behalf of the Lettrist International, a name that suggested a challenge to the lettrism associated with Romanian artist Isidore Isou. To Isou, all art forms went through what he defined as a "phase amplique," in which "the form developed, became meaningful, [and] created its stylistic vocabulary," and a "phase ciselant," in which it disintegrated, turned in upon itself, and essentially focused only "on the forms and techniques of the medium itself." With Dada, Isou believed, poetry had arrived at the end of the ciselant phase. Poetic language had ended up not meaning anything and, thus, had effectively been destroyed. Consequently, Isou himself had set out to create a new alphabet with new letters as building blocks, hence the name of the movement he created: lettrism. He and his followers set out to apply the lettrist philosophy to poetry and a range of art forms.[117]

The demonstration staged by Berna, Debord, and the other international lettrists at the Chaplin press conference—and their denunciation of Chaplin himself—were intended as a carefully coded critique of Isou and his followers. The latter rose to the bait. Isou and others, angry at this attempt to reformulate lettrism, wrote to the old resistance newspaper *Combat*, criticizing the protest as "outrancier et confus" (extreme and confused). "We," they declared, "join the homage everyone has rendered to Chaplin."[118] The international lettrists replied, insisting "that the most urgent expression of freedom is the destruction of idols, especially when they claim to represent freedom."[119] Both Chaplin—and Isou—were idols out of touch with the times and had to be destroyed to make way for the fresh perspective of a new generation. As Mikkel Bolt Rasmussen points out, the protest at the Ritz Hotel signified "the birth of what later became the International Situationist."[120]

In order to understand how Chaplin became a target for attack, it is important to understand how salient the idea of the failure of the avant-garde was in the outlook first of the international lettrists and later of the Situationists. To Situationists, the period 1850 to 1930 had witnessed a sustained attempt on the part of the avant-garde to alter or destroy traditional artistic forms in order "to create new forms worthy of modernity."[121] This attempt had reached a culmination with Dada and surrealism, two movements that made clear that anti-art was the only true art. To Situationists, surrealism was the more crucial. The surrealists had demonstrated an understanding of the need to transcend art, but their demands had been minimal and they had been unable to expand artistic self-destructiveness into a complete critique of capitalist society because they relied too much on the supposedly liberating qualities of the unconscious. Indeed, far from critiquing capitalist society, surrealists had essentially been assimilated into it: the unusual and irrational objects produced by surreal artists were eventually turned into commodities. Situationists abandoned art as art—they believed that revolutionary self-consciousness was to be created only in the situation, and art should be abolished and realized only in a transformed life. After 1930, they believed, neither Dada nor surrealism nor any other form of art was revolutionary. They stressed the destruction of forms and the impossibility of art only for themselves rather than their consequences. This was where Chaplin came in. The international lettrists/Situationists were well aware of Chaplin's longtime association with the surrealists—especially the "Hands Off Love" manifesto of 1927. When they attacked Chaplin at the Ritz Hotel, they not only gained publicity for their cause but made it clear that they were now prepared to go beyond surrealism in search of what they saw as a true revolution.[122] From being part of the surrealists' inspiration, Chaplin had lived long enough to become associated with what the international lettrists now perceived as an artistic establishment they sought to destroy.[123]

Chaplin as a Cultural Symbol

Chaplin helped shape the cultural and intellectual landscape in which surrealism was born. If the international lettrists' demonstration in Paris in 1952 is understood as signifying at least a symbolic end to the movement, he also witnessed its death. In both cases, he had no comprehension of what was really taking place. From his earliest films to "Hands Off Love," future and actual surrealists manipulated aspects of his films, screen image, or star persona to fit their own ideas and priorities. This showed itself initially in Aragon's poetry, Soupault's film comments, and Goll's *Chaplinade.* Tzara exploited Chaplin's fame in order to draw attention to Dada. In the *Littérature* survey of 1921, Charlot emerged as a clear Dada favorite. As Paris Dada made way for cinema-obsessed surrrealism, it may be that prominent surrealists were influenced by aspects of the screen Charlot in building surrealism itself. In 1927, they sprang to Chaplin's defense at the time of his second divorce, transforming him into a symbol of their own ideas regarding erotic love. ("Hands Off Love" says far more about the surrealists than it does about Chaplin.) Twenty-five years later, international lettrists/Situationists also used him as an unwitting symbol, this time of the decline of surrealism as an intellectual and cultural movement. In many ways, indeed, the engagement of the surrealists and their opponents with Chaplin was as exaggerated and distorted—in the French sense *sur-real*—as surrealism itself.

Plate 1 Advertisement placed by distributor Jacques Haïk in *Ciné-Journal* (March 15, 1915) announcing the arrival of Charlie Chaplin films in France. Haïk renamed Chaplin "Charlot," hailing him as a "dramatic actor" and "irresistible comic."
Source gallica.bnf.fr/Bibliothèque nationale de France.

Plate 2 The first issue of the cinema magazine *Ciné pour tous* featured Charlie Chaplin on its cover (June 15, 1919). The issue included biographical details on Chaplin and a list of his films.

Source gallica.bnf.fr/Bibliothèque nationale de France.

Plate 3 Chaplin's vast popularity encouraged many imitations both in and outside France. Here, American comic actor Billie Ritchie appears in an ad in *Ciné-Journal* (January 22, 1916) dressed like Charlot in a derby hat and ill-fitting jacket and walking with a cane.
Source gallica.bnf.fr/Bibliothèque nationale de France.

Plate 4 French film reviewer, scenario writer, and film director Louis Delluc published the first book on the subject of Chaplin as an artist of cinema in 1921. *Alamy.*

Plate 5 Louis Aragon was a long-term fan of Chaplin who wrote "Hands Off Love," a manifesto defending the comedian against American critics during the divorce proceedings launched against him by Lita Grey in 1927. A passionate defense of "free love," it was signed by thirty-two surrealists.
Alamy.

Plate 6 Philippe Soupault often used Chaplin's films as an inspiration for his own imaginative writings and in 1931 published *Charlot,* a fictional "biography" of the life of Chaplin's character based on his films.
Alamy.

Plate 7 Yvan Goll was the author of *Chaplinade* (1920), a fantasy based on the screen Charlot that was part scenario and part poem. While a whimsical mixture of fantasy and reality, it also suggested the loneliness of Chaplin as a result of his star status.
Alamy.

Plate 8 Marcel Carné, subsequently a distinguished film director, was one of those waiting to welcome Chaplin on his arrival in Paris in 1931. He later attended the press conference at the Hotel Crillon before joining the crowd outside applauding Chaplin's appearance on his balcony.
Alamy.

Plate 9 René Clair refused to support claims in 1936 that Chaplin's *Modern Times* had plagiarized scenes from his own *À Nous la Liberté* (1931) while acknowledging his own debt as a filmmaker to Charlot.
Alamy.

Plate 10 Jean Renoir acknowledged the influence of Chaplin's films in persuading him to become a filmmaker. He wrote strongly supportive reviews of *Modern Times* and *Monsieur Verdoux.*
Alamy.

Plate 11 François Truffaut defended Chaplin's *A King in New York* against its French critics and later (1972) edited a book of his mentor André Bazin's reviews of Chaplin's films.
Alamy.

Plate 12 Distributor Moses (Mo) Rothman with Chaplin and his wife Oona O'Neill arriving at Orly Airport in Paris on November 2, 1971, to attend next day's screening of the reissued *Modern Times*.
Alamy.

Plate 13 Producer Bert Schneider (*Easy Rider*), part of the new syndicate organized by Mo Rothman to reissue Chaplin's films, was also involved in the negotiations that would lead to Chaplin's honorary Oscar in Hollywood.
Alamy.

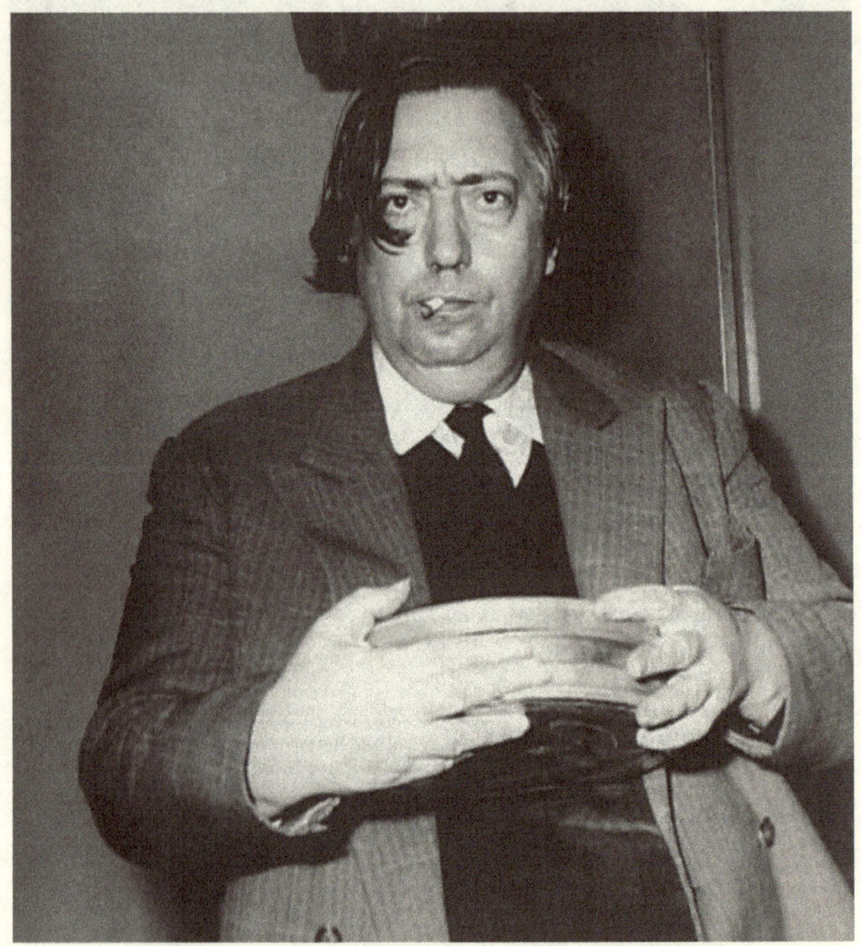

Plate 14 Henri Langlois, cofounder and later director for many years of the Cinémathèque Française and long-term Chaplin fan.
Alamy.

5

Chaplin in France: 1931

On his 1931 visit to Europe—the start of what would turn out to be a world tour lasting sixteen months—Chaplin spent for the first time a considerable period living in France. Arriving in Paris on March 22, he stayed for just over a week in the city, returning there for a few days in August on his way to England for the fall. He spent most of the spring and summer, apart from trips to Algiers and Spain, living on the Côte d'Azur, where his brother Sydney had made his home, and later visiting Biarritz. This chapter will analyze five aspects of Chaplin's French sojourn of 1931. First, the attitudes and behavior of his fans. Second, his recognition by the political world. Third, his growing fascination—which was fully reciprocated—with the international social elite, both moneyed and titled. Fourth, his collaboration with the print media to perpetuate his status as both star and celebrity. Fifth, the French reception of—and debates surrounding—his new film, *City Lights* (*Les lumières de la ville*, UA, 1931), the first since *The Circus* in 1928.

Chaplin's Arrival in Paris

In 1921, Chaplin had arrived in Paris almost unnoticed. His reception in 1931 was very different. Several Paris newspapers on March 22 announced that Chaplin was on his way by express train from Venice and that he would arrive at the Gare de Lyon at 14:25 that day.[1] Since it was a Sunday rather than a working day, large numbers of people—movie fans and those who were simply curious—were free to greet Charlot. Already by midday, large noisy crowds were assembled both inside the station hall and spilling out into the Boulevard Diderot, the Rue de Bercy, and the Rue de Lyon. To contain these crowds and protect Chaplin, Xavier Guichard, head of the Paris municipal police, had arranged for a large squad of officers to be present.[2] The socialist *Le Populaire*, critical of "the cops," commented that so many were present that it was possible "to believe . . . that the City of Light was nothing more than a huge police station."[3] The police strategy was to prevent the crowd

Charlot. Melvyn Stokes, Oxford University Press. © Oxford University Press 2026.
DOI: 10.1093/9780197839294.003.0006

from accessing the platforms, allowing only journalists and photographers onto platform 1, where Guy Croswell Smith, the chief representative of United Artists in Paris, Léon Volterra, the impresario who would shortly exhibit *City Lights* at Paris's Marigny Theater, and Guichard waited to meet Chaplin. Once the train from Venice arrived, it is clear from numerous newspaper accounts that the police lost control of the situation. Men, women, and children broke through the police barriers and rushed toward the train, many endangering themselves by crossing the tracks.[4]

After a short delay, Chaplin appeared on the steps of his carriage dressed all in gray and smiling. Photographers got to work, and there were many shouts of "Long live Charlot!" According to the communist *L'Humanité*, the crowd "was essentially working-class, eager to see in 'flesh and blood' the one who had made them laugh and moved them so many times on the screen."[5] Yet it was so jam-packed that when Chaplin, preceded by a baggage cart, tried to make his way through the station, he was instantly surrounded and hemmed in. With considerable difficulty, the police cleared a passage for him toward the exit, but he was constantly jostled as people tried to touch him. According to the reporter for the Paris edition of the *Herald Tribune*, his clothes were pulled and his hat knocked off. (Chaplin would later confess that "at one point, I was a little frightened.")[6] He finally reached the car that was waiting for him, and the police—"with some vigor," according to *L'Ère Nouvelle*—cleared a path for it to drive off down the Rue de Lyon toward Place de la Concorde. Some of the waiting newsreel cameramen, deprived of the shots of Chaplin they had expected, were reduced to filming the crowd, most of whom did not realize that Chaplin had already left.[7]

A few minutes later, Chaplin's car drew up outside the Hotel Crillon and he was taken to his suite on the first floor, looking out over the Place de la Concorde. Normally reserved for visiting kings and queens, the suite had also been occupied at various times by General John J. Pershing, the commander of the American Expeditionary Forces during the war, President Woodrow Wilson during the peace negotiations of 1919, and Edward, Prince of Wales. Chaplin drank some water and played the piano for a few minutes. Although there had only been around a hundred people awaiting his arrival at the hotel, a large crowd quickly gathered in the Place de la Concorde and there were shouts of "Vive Chaplin! Vive Charlot!" Chaplin went out onto the balcony of his suite, waved at the crowd, and was greeted with an ovation.[8] When he went inside to hold a press conference, the crowd waited patiently until he came out once more on the balcony. He did so, wrote a reporter for *Le Matin*, initially with an air of resignation. But, buoyed by the enthusiastic cheers of the crowd, he "smiled, waved and blew kisses" to those below, for all the world—commented a correspondent for the *Herald Tribune*—"like a king acknowledging the plaudits of his subjects."[9]

There was a strong sense among French journalists and commentators that Chaplin deserved the enthusiastic approval of the crowds. "We may be astonished," wrote a reporter for *Le Petit Journal*, "that such fervent popular delight is not confined only to scientists, great writers, pioneers of all civilization. . . . But Charlot is in his way a benefactor of the poor devils that we can be, all of us, at certain times of our life. Who is there among us who has not found either consolation or a tonic in these wonderful, lively tales he has told us in tender fashion, in a melancholy and moving tone that is very much his own."[10]

Film critic and future director Marcel Carné had watched Chaplin's arrival at the Gare de Lyon, taking with him a photograph of the comedian that, he confessed, he "would have given the world to have signed by the hand that made *The Pilgrim*." Carné was also present at the press conference at the Crillon and, when it was over, hastily made his way to join the crowd on the Place de la Concorde. He saw Chaplin appear for a second time on the balcony and be greeted with a tremendous ovation. To Carné, it seemed not only that his neighbors in the crowd were grateful to Chaplin but also that, long after he had disappeared, they felt uplifted by seeing him and the fact that he had smiled and, in a gesture, pretended to be shaking hands with them. The secret of Chaplin's universal appeal, Carné believed, was that every individual seeing him on the screen could say, "But, that's me! Me with my weaknesses, my good qualities also; me with my permanent desire to escape, my thirst for the ideal, me with my moments of cowardice and of bravery, of sordid avarice and generosity, me with my bumptiousness, my hypocrisy and my occasional appalling crises of misanthropy; but me also with my heart just waiting to love if someone loves me in return."[11]

The cinema magazine *Pour Vous*, impressed by the warmth of Chaplin's public reception at the Gare de Lyon and the Hotel Crillon, asked a number of well-known writers for their views on why Charlot appealed so much to French popular sensibilities. Their responses were printed in its next two issues. While they were in no sense scientific and there is no way of knowing how well their authors understood the basis of Chaplin's popular appeal, they do at least give some insight into what some members of the intelligentsia believed explained the crowd's enthusiasm. Novelist, biographer, and essayist André Maurois argued that Charlot appealed mainly to the popular multitude for two reasons. In the first place, he stirred people's finer feelings "because he is the image of the good sensitivity that we believe each of us to share in." Second, he represented "the infinite difficulty of life: every woman who refuses him, every joy he is deprived of, every job he is unable to get, each of his failures is ours. Since there are on this earth more failures than successful people, he stirs the emotions of most of us."[12] "Charlot," wrote novelist (and sometime film critic) Colette, "stirs popular sensibility by his sadness, because he is one of life's have-nots, and he makes people laugh for the same reason. For it is a law, cruel but rigorous, that to amuse his fellows, man is obliged to use the spectacle of his own distress. The good comic should never laugh. But if he wants to touch the depths of his art, he must not just content himself with provoking laughter, he must also stir people and bring the public, because of him, furtively to wipe away a tear." Playwright, novelist, and screenwriter Henri Duvernois similarly attributed much of Chaplin's popularity with the public to the "bittersweet" qualities of "this comedian bathed in pity," with "his gaiety of which one can say nothing apart from 'after laughing with it, we must also weep.'"[13]

Chaplin at the Quai d'Orsay

Chaplin had arrived in Paris on Sunday for a reason: he was invited to lunch on Monday by Aristide Briand, the French minister for foreign affairs. The possibility of such a lunch had first been aired by French diplomats during a dinner at the British Embassy in Vienna. Chaplin was eager to accept. Briand was well-known in the United States. He led the French delegation in November 1921 at the opening of the Washington Naval Conference to limit the size of navies. In 1928, he had signed, together with U.S. Secretary of State Frank B. Kellogg, the Kellogg-Briand Pact to outlaw war. Eleven times prime minister of France and minister for foreign affairs since 1925, Briand had been awarded the Nobel Peace Prize for his work in negotiating the Locarno Treaties of 1925, an attempt to normalize relations with postwar Germany. In 1929, he had made a pioneering speech promoting the idea of European economic union.

On the Monday of Chaplin's lunch, the crowds that assembled outside the Ministry of Foreign Affairs on the Quai d'Orsay were the biggest since the peace negotiations of 1919. According to *Le Petit Journal*, "well before midday several hundred tenacious onlookers were in front of the entrance to the ministry, waiting for their idol to appear." At 12:45, their patience was rewarded when a "luxurious car" stopped outside the main entrance and Chaplin got out.[14] Wearing a gray overcoat and a black derby hat, he seemed for a moment "surprised and confused" at the sight of the crowd confined behind police barricades. Quickly recovering, he acknowledged them with an "inimitable" gesture: putting on his hat in a way that instantly reminded them that here was the Little Tramp. Chaplin posed briefly for "an army" of photographers and newsreel cameramen before being "snatched" by ushers and taken indoors.[15] He was accompanied to the lunch by Guy Croswell Smith, the representative of United Artists in Paris.

The other guests at this "intimate lunch"[16] were drawn from the world of politics (Briand himself, Minister of Justice Léon Bérard and his wife); diplomacy (Lord Tyrell, the British ambassador in France; Charles de Chambrun, the French ambassador to Turkey; Philippe Berthelot, secretary-general of the Ministry of Foreign Affairs, and his wife); society (Prince Sixte de Bourbon-Parma, Princess Lucien Murat, the Count and Countess of Fels, Mrs. Paul Dupuy, an American woman married to the wealthy owner of *Le Petit Parisien* newspaper);[17] business (Louis Renault); and the world of the arts (poet-novelist Anna, Countess of Noailles, novelist and playwright Tristan Bernard).[18] Mathematician and politician Paul Panlevé—who had twice served as prime minister of France—arrived later for coffee.[19]

According to *Le Journal* and *Le Matin*, both of which somehow managed to obtain copies of the menu, initialed by Briand, Chaplin and the other lunch guests ate their way through a series of courses beginning with Marennes oysters, followed by Loire salmon in a Nantua sauce, saddle of lamb, truffled fatted chicken, asparagus in a mousseline sauce, foie gras from Strasbourg, salad, Ceylonese ice-cream, fruit and desserts. The lunch lasted more than two hours.[20] Although Chaplin spoke no French, the conversation flowed without interruption because everyone there, with the exception of Briand and Bérard, the minister of justice, either spoke or at least understood English.[21] Chaplin himself appears to have been most impressed with Briand and the Countess of Noailles. Briand, he later recalled, was "a small delicate man with round shoulders, his face lined by heavy responsibilities." There was "a hidden humor in his expression and a look of weary resignation." The Countess of Noailles, who informed Chaplin that, like her, he was truly a poet, was "an alert active little lady with a sparkling personality whose gestures resembled those of a bird."[22] When Chaplin came out of the

Quai d'Orsay, he was once again cheered by the crowd and filmed by the cameramen, before leaving—accompanied by the Countess of Noailles, Charles de Chambrun, and Guy Croswell Smith—to go back to the Hotel Crillon.[23]

The only sour notes sounded against Chaplin's lunch at the Quai d'Orsay came from radically different ends of the political spectrum. On the fact that he was to be received by Briand, the communist *L'Humanité* commented that "it is natural that the bourgeoisie try hard to capture completely such a popular man. But if, as we are certain, 'Charlot' puts the best of himself into his films, he must be laughing in the face of official tributes: hasn't he flayed bourgeois hypocrisy in a good number of his best films?"[24] Writing in the right-wing, nationalist *L'Action Française*, André Villeneuve was extremely critical of Briand, whom he regarded as a dreamily impractical internation-alist. But Villeneuve was also antisemitic (he twice referred to Chaplin as "this American Jew") and was clearly using him only as a stick with which to beat Briand. He consequently deplored the fact that Chaplin, whom he described rather curiously as "an acrobat poet," had not "been welcomed onto the soil of France by someone else than M. Briand."[25]

Chaplin and the Légion d'honneur

For some weeks before Chaplin's arrival in Paris, there had been pressure in some quarters for him to receive France's highest decoration, the Légion d'honneur. Chaplin's old friend, the cartoonist Cami, had proposed the award while Chaplin was still in London and launched what film periodical *Mon Ciné* termed "a justifiable campaign in the press."[26] This had stimulated a public debate in which, *Mon Ciné* noted a few weeks later, those hostile to the idea had been more vociferous than its supporters.[27] Yet Cami claimed in a letter to *Ciné-Journal* to have the support of "the majority of French artistes and most of the public," and Briand seems to have "spiritually acquiesced" at a fairly early stage. René Pignères of *Le Journal*—a newspaper that had consistently supported Cami's idea—reported on the morning of Chaplin's lunch at the Quai d'Orsay that Briand would take advantage of their meeting to "present him with the cross of the Légion d'honneur."[28]

Although the decision to give the Légion d'honneur to Chaplin had clearly already been made by the time of the lunch at the Ministry of Foreign Affairs, the honor was not bestowed at that time. This may have been because

Briand and his advisers were intending to decorate Chaplin publicly, as had happened in 1921, at the première of his latest film. (Cami had originally suggested that he be given the Légion d'honneur at the first screening of *City Lights*.)[29] *Hebdo-Film* announced, indeed, that the comedian would be present at the first screening of *City Lights* at the Marigny Theater on April 7 and that it was then he would receive the cross of the Légion d'honneur.[30] On the other hand, since the lunch had been arranged at fairly short notice and took place on a Monday, it may have been—as suggested by *L'Ère Nouvelle*—that there simply had been no time for the Chancellery to prepare the diploma for the ceremony.[31]

When it became clear toward the end of the week that Chaplin would soon leave Paris and might not return for the première of *City Lights*, the Foreign Ministry resorted to subterfuge. Philippe Berthelot, secretary-general of the Ministry, "accidentally" met him at lunch on Thursday and suggested that, before leaving Paris, he stop by at the Quai d'Orsay the next day at 15:30 "to say goodbye to Mr. Briand." On Friday, at the appointed time, when Chaplin arrived with Croswell-Smith, he was escorted directly to Berthelot's office. The secretary-general, waiting there with Pierre de Fouquières, the Foreign Ministry's chief of protocol,[32] in a simple ceremony presented Chaplin with the insignia and diploma of a Knight of the Légion of Honor "on behalf of Mr. Briand with warm expressions of sympathy for a great artiste who had always been a friend of France."[33] Chaplin apparently responded by saying that he was too moved by this honor to find the right words to express his satisfaction and gratitude to the French government.[34] According to a report in *L'Intransigeant*, however, on leaving the Quai d'Orsay he declared, "France is nice."[35]

As *Paris-Midi* pointed out, since Chaplin was of foreign nationality and had no legal address in France, he did not receive the customary embrace involved in the award of the Légion d'honneur, and his nomination to the order did not appear in *L'Officiel*, the government gazette.[36] In the same way that Cami's campaign for Chaplin to receive the decoration had prompted criticism, so too did the news of his admission to France's most coveted fraternity. Some of the criticism was based on nationalistic grounds. For some, Chaplin remained a controversial figure because of lingering resentments from the First World War. Chaplin, an Englishman, not only had not fought on the Allied side in the war; he had become rich by refusing to serve his country. The Association of Members of the Legion of Honor submitted a protest on these lines to the Grand Chancellery of the order: "Combatants of the great war, in particular those whose red ribbon is dyed with their blood, do not understand how an artiste who has gained millions in his occupation of clown can become their colleague in the Grand Order, they themselves having remained poor after shedding their blood for the homeland."[37]

It did not help that there was already a sentiment on the part of some military members of the Order—those awarded it for risking their lives—that the Order was being devalued. Lieutenant-Colonel Léon Faye pointed out, in a letter to the press, that a parliamentary committee of inquiry headed by Louis Marin had shed light on the issue of how members of the National Assembly had sought to secure the award for their friends. Faye suggested the establishment of a system of rankings for civil nominations for the Légion (as already existed for military nominations) and—probably as a criticism of Chaplin's rumored appointment—the removal of the right of the minister for foreign affairs to award the Légion to foreigners without reference to the Council of the Order.[38]

In the cinema trade press, there was also some sense that Chaplin's award of the Légion d'honneur—the first, as *Le Petit Journal* pointed out, to be given to a figure from the cinema[39]—was unfair to the many distinguished *French* pioneers of cinema. Lucie Derain, for example, argued in *Ciné-Journal* "that the French government systematically forgets, in the distribution of awards, French cinematographers who were the founders and propagators of an industry that has revolutionized the world . . . [Georges] Méliès, [Charles] Jourjon, [André] Debrie, [Pierre] Noguès." In Derain's view, the failure to recognize Méliès—"who created the film show and was the first importer of French films into America"—was especially culpable.[40]

Some also believed that honoring a man who was merely a comedian had devalued the Légion d'honneur. *Ciné-Journal*, according to Pierre Ogouz, insisted "that our national decoration was not created for the benefit of clowns."[41] Supporters of Chaplin countered this by arguing, on historical grounds, that comedians had indeed become eligible for the award. Writing in *Le Petit Journal*, Jean Lecoq noted that, under the ancien régime, the monarchy had often awarded the order of Saint-Michel to actors and comedians. Although Napoleon, the founder of the Légion d'honneur, had clearly not intended that it be awarded to theatrical folk (he refused to give it to François-Joseph Talma, a friend and the greatest actor of the day), Louis-Philippe had awarded it to comedians, albeit indirectly, for achievements outside their profession. In 1864, under the Second Empire, the first comedy actor to be decorated as such was Joseph Isidore Samson of the Comédie-Française. Honoring Chaplin as a comedian was thus far from unprecedented.[42]

A second line of defense was the argument that Chaplin had been officially recognized in France not only for his performances as a comedian but also for his major role in developing cinema as an art form. The popular magazine *Mon Ciné* argued that "Charlie Chaplin stands head and shoulders above all other cinematic personalities. He incarnates the cinematic art in which he has been the best and most powerful influence. He is more worthy than anyone to wear the red ribbon."[43]

Chaplin in Society

Chaplin, the comic tramp, by 1931 had developed an irresistible appeal to many members of the European titled and monied elite. A workhouse boy from south London who had become a millionaire through his movies, he seemed to embody both the new cinematic art and, perhaps more important, a new form of wealth. As satirical magazine *Le Canard enchaîné* pointed out, it was not Chaplin the clown ("a gentleman who earns his living by receiving kicks to the backside") who was invited for lunch at the Foreign Ministry, but Chaplin the producer of cinema and part owner of a studio (United Artists).[44] The appointments he kept during his first days in Paris underlined the symbolism of his new international status. Men and women drawn from the international aristocracy—and even royalty—were eager to meet him, and Chaplin himself reciprocated this fascination.

The second invitation Chaplin accepted, after that of Briand to lunch at the Ministry of Foreign Affairs, was from the Duke of Westminster. On the train from Venice, he had met the duke and his wife (whom Chaplin remembered as "grace and beauty personified").[45] A member of the Grosvenor family, the Duke was wealthy by virtue of his landed estates (which included considerable prime land in London). He was traveling with friends in his own railroad car. At some point during the journey, he and his wife were introduced to Chaplin. Chaplin appears to have complained that he had already been in Europe for a month but had found it impossible to rest and relax. The Duke, in response, invited him to his chateau at Saint-Saëns in Normandy, where he was arranging a boar hunt. On the evening of Tuesday, March 24, Chaplin and the Duke took the train to Rouen, where the Duke's car waited to take them twenty miles to the chateau.[46] Chaplin recalled a "bitterly cold drive," but at the chateau (in reality, "a house of about sixteen rooms") he met the rest of the party "in a nice warm room with a cheery fire burning and a table spread invitingly with all sorts of victuals." After supper the Duke finally thought to ask Chaplin whether he could ride, and was visibly concerned when the comedian confessed he had "done practically no riding at all." It was then Chaplin's turn to be disconcerted as the Duke explained how he would have to kill the boar with a knife "if it's your luck to corner him." Far from the boar hunt being a means of rest and relaxation, Chaplin later claimed that he stayed awake all night worrying whether he would be able to avoid falling off the horse and what might happen if he were confronted with the boar.[47]

When he got up on Wednesday, Chaplin also worried that he was wearing the wrong costume. He had riding breeches and boots, hastily bought in Paris, but wore a small borrowed red coat that made breathing difficult. The Duke loaned him a riding hat, waistcoat, and gloves—both of the latter much too large. In addition to feeling inordinately self-conscious about his hunting outfit, Chaplin was also deeply worried that the supposedly quiet horse chosen for him promptly reared up, provoking him—in best Charlot fashion—to take immediate refuge behind a car. At 11:00 a.m., he set off with seven other hunters in the Duke's car toward Envermeu, fifteen miles to the north, where the boar had been scented. It then took an hour for the horses and dogs to arrive before the hunt could commence. To Chaplin's apparent surprise, riding his new horse proved relatively easy, even when galloping through the Hellet wood near Croixdalle, some seven and a half miles from where the chase began. But after two hours, the boar had disappeared and Chaplin was starting to feel tired and experiencing backache and muscle cramps. The Duke, noticing his discomfort, suggested he take the car back to Saint-Saëns. Chaplin was happy to agree. Immediately after dinner that evening, he returned by car to Paris, where he went to a Turkish bath on the Champs-Elysées for a long, restorative massage.[48]

City Lights had premièred in Brussels on Wednesday, March 25. King Albert I of Belgium and his wife, Queen Elisabeth, were in the audience. The following day, the King made an official visit to Paris to have a farewell lunch at the Élysée Palace with French President Gaston Doumergue, whose seven-year term of office would end on June 13. Knowing Chaplin was in Paris, the King asked to meet the filmmaker, and an appointment was made. The King had a very busy schedule: he arrived in Paris at 11:18 after a five-hour journey on an ordinary train. After lunching with the president and members of the government, he went to the Belgian Embassy, where he received the French president and his military aide in the late afternoon, before catching the 18:05 train back to Brussels. Albert still found time, either at 15:00 (Chaplin's recollection) or 15:30 (reported in *L'Intransigeant*), to fit in a half-hour meeting with Charlot.[49]

The King was late returning from his lunch at the Élysée. Chaplin's first glimpse of him was of "a tall stooped figure," with no coat and suspenders dangling, walking past the reception hall on his way to change clothes. When Albert reappeared, the Belgian ambassador, the Baron de Gaiffier d'Hestroy, introduced the two men and left them alone. The King drew up a chair for himself and gestured to Chaplin to sit on another. (Since Albert was extremely tall and his chair much higher than Chaplin's, this was probably the origin of the scene in Hynkel's office in *The Great Dictator* in which Napaloni's chair is much lower than that of Hynkel.) According to Chaplin, talking with the King (in English) was stilted and awkward at first until Albert began to question him about filmmaking. This broke the ice. The King congratulated Chaplin on *City Lights*, which *Paris-Midi* reported he believed to be a "masterpiece," bringing together "comedy and pathos in a combination so far unequaled." Chaplin seems to have been impressed both by Albert's personal simplicity of style and the fact that he was "so well-informed on cinema questions." Their conversation ended with Chaplin extending the King and Queen a quasi-regal invitation of his own: to come and visit him in Hollywood.[50]

Chaplin in the South of France and After

Eight days after his arrival in Paris, Chaplin returned to the Gare de Lyon. In contrast to the scenes that had greeted him earlier, this time he was almost unnoticed. He and his traveling companions, including secretary Carlyle Robinson and personal valet Kono, had reserved three compartments (1, 2, and 3) in the eighth car of the luxurious Train Bleu, the famous overnight express to the Côte d'Azur.[51] Only a few friends, including American film director Rex Ingram, came to see him off. Some journalists and photographers arrived, and just before the train left at 19:50, Chaplin was photographed looking out from the door of his carriage. He arrived in Nice at 12:48 on March 31, to be greeted by a large and enthusiastic crowd. He was met by his brother Sydney, whom he had not seen for several years; Frank Jay Gould, a wealthy American who had invited him to stay at the Majestic Hotel, which he owned; and Edouard Baudoin, who had played a major role in developing Juan-les-Pins as a resort.[52] Chaplin was then driven to his hotel where, following the Paris precedent, he quickly met with the press, declaring that he was "enchanted" by his welcome in Nice.[53]

Frank Gould, son of railroad speculator Jay Gould, had an indirect personal connection with Chaplin: his second wife, Edith, was the sister of Hetty Kelly, the comedian's first real love.[54] He and his third wife, the glamorous Florence La Caze, spent a good deal of time with Chaplin during his first days on the Riviera. Gould was clearly determined to extract as much publicity—and profit—as possible from his famous guest's stay. Shortly after Chaplin's arrival, he invited the star to a late lunch at the Palais de la Mediterranée, the other Nice hotel he owned. Since the terrace of the hotel offered a view of Chaplin, Gould shrewdly charged five francs for people admitted there.[55] The next day saw Chaplin lunch again at the Palais de la Mediterranée, preside at tea over a beauty pageant leading to the crowning of the "queen" of Nice, and attend a gala at the casino in Juan-les-Pins in the evening.[56]

In the days that followed, Chaplin settled easily into the lifestyle of a wealthy visitor to the French Riviera during the winter "season." In the morning, he usually played tennis. He would then be driven to a restaurant for lunch: on Saturday, April 4, for example, he lunched with Mrs. Gould in Juan-les-Pins.[57] In the evenings, there was often a gala dinner or a visit to a casino. Although Chaplin subsequently claimed he found "casino life . . . boring and stupid," he frequented several (including the casino at the Palais de la Mediterannée hotel where, among the baccarat tables, he was introduced to King Gustav V of Sweden).[58]

Chaplin's stardom provided him with an entrée to the different social worlds of the Côte d'Azur. He encountered men active in public affairs, being invited to the villa in Biot of Léon Bailby, the proprietor of the newspaper *L'Intransigeant*, and meeting Sir Oswald Mosley, future leader of the British Union of Fascists, then a Labour Party member of Parliament whom Chaplin impetuously hailed as "one of the most promising young men in English politics."[59] Conscious perhaps of what Kenneth S. Lynn terms his "exceedingly spotty schooling," he sought the validation and company of writers and intellectuals.[60] He met Belgian poet, playwright, and essayist Maurice Maeterlinck at a lunch organized by Florence La Caze Gould, dined with French modernist writer Paul Morand, spent a day with German-born Emil

Ludwig, biographer of Goethe, Napoleon, and Bismarck, and visited H. G. Wells, who was renting a house near Grasse. (Chaplin and Wells planned to visit some of the perfume factories for which Grasse was famous, but Chaplin was recognized as they walked through the town and they were compelled to escape the large crowds that followed them.) Later in the summer, he visited the home in Nice of novelist and biographer Frank Harris, by this stage best known for his sexually explicit four-volume *My Life and Loves* (1922–27).[61]

On vacation, Chaplin was attracted to entertainments put on by "society." He renewed his acquaintance with songwriter and professional party-giver Elsa Maxwell, who, he wrote, had "taken society as her mode of expression and even made an art of it."[62] To aristocrats and the wealthy, Chaplin appeared the embodiment of the "rags to riches" story with the additional glamor of Hollywood stardom. Chaplin in turn was drawn to those who were wealthy or titled, seeing their interest and patronage as a sign that he had "arrived." Never before his 1931 European trip—and never since—was he fêted in quite the same way by the moneyed classes and the aristocracy. Having recently met the kings of Belgium and Sweden and gone hunting with the Duke of Westminster, it must not have seemed unusual to Chaplin when his friend Sir Philip Sassoon, who had once served as Prime Minister David Lloyd George's parliamentary private secretary, took him to tea at the house of the Duke of Connaught at Cap Ferrat. The Duke, the third son of Queen Victoria, was the uncle of the British king George V. He appears to have promised, during tea, to preside over the première of *City Lights* in Monte Carlo on April 7—a decision that would have unexpected results.[63]

If Chaplin had ever intended to go back to Paris for the première of *City Lights* at the Marigny, the few days he spent in the South of France had changed his mind. Instead, he attended the gala screening on the same evening at the Beaux-Arts Cinema in Monte Carlo.[64] Opened only a few weeks earlier, the Beaux-Arts was lavishly decorated with flowers for the occasion, and every other seat was garnished with a spray of flowers for the female spectators. The audience was drawn from international "society." According to the correspondent of *Paris-Midi*, Monaco itself proved too small to house "all the luxurious cars" that arrived with passengers bearing "the most beautiful jewels and the greatest names." From Britain came Lady Cholmondley, Sir Walter and Lady de Frece, Sir Philip Sassoon, Admiral Victor and Lady Stanley, and Captain Clifford Erskine-Bolst, M.P., and his wife. The United States was represented, among others, by Jay Gould and his wife; J. C. Crew, American ambassador to Turkey; and Mr. and Mrs. Vanderbilt-Barton.

French participants included Léon Bailby of *L'Intransigeant*, Philippe Bertholet of the Foreign Ministry, Princesses Murat and Faucigny-Lucinge, and the Duke of Polignac.[65]

Chaplin was invited by Prince Louis II, the ruler of the tiny principality of Monaco of which Monte Carlo formed the largest part, to dine with him before the showing of the film. But urgent business meant that he left Chaplin to have dinner instead with the rest of the Monaco government. It proved a restrained meal since only Chaplin and the British consul spoke English. Although dinner, not surprisingly in the circumstances, finished early, Chaplin's hosts refused to let him leave for the theater until just before 22:00. There had clearly been a misunderstanding over the time the film was supposed to start, since the Duke of Connaught had arrived before 21:00 and both Prince Louis and his daughter were already in their box, waiting for Chaplin to join them so the screening could proceed. The late start does not appear to have influenced the audience's response to the film, which was warmly applauded, and Chaplin was taken after the screening to the Duke's box. But some newspapers and periodicals reported Chaplin's lateness as an affront to the elderly Duke and a danger to his health, since he was driven back to Cap Ferrat an hour later than expected in the chill night air.[66]

Toward the end of April, Chaplin decided to spend some time in Algiers, taking with him May Reeves, a strikingly beautiful woman apparently of Czech origin who may later have influenced the role of Natascha (Sophia Loren) in *A Countess from Hong Kong* (1967).[67] Returning from Algiers in May, Chaplin and his new girlfriend moved to Juan-les-Pins for several more weeks. When he finally quit the Côte d'Azur, it was to drive to Paris via Burgundy with a friend, Harry d'Abbadie d'Arrast, an uncredited researcher on *A Woman of Paris* who later worked on *The Gold Rush* before becoming a film director in his own right. D'Arrast subsequently persuaded Chaplin to drive down to Biarritz, once a fishing village on the Atlantic coast near the Spanish border, now one of the most fashionable resorts in Europe. "In spite of the depression," Chaplin recalled, "life [in Biarritz] is gay and entertaining. Before dinner everybody gathers at Bar Basque." Chaplin was once more part of the international society set: he went to parties given by French fashion designer Jean Patou; was introduced by an old acquaintance, Thelma Morgan Converse, now Lady Furness, to Edward, Prince of Wales, heir to the British throne; and had lunch with Winston Churchill.[68] He made a short visit to Spain and then, in August, journeyed back for a brief visit to Paris on his way to spend the fall in England.

Relations with the Press

In 1931, Chaplin acknowledged—as he perhaps had not in 1921—that the press would have to be dealt with directly. In part, this was because celebrity culture had become more defined in the decade that had passed, and the relations between movie stars and the media more institutionalized. In part, it was because within minutes of his arrival at the Crillon, what one observer termed an "army of journalists and photographers on a war footing" had arrived at the hotel.[69] In part also he needed the journalists for publicity purposes since in Paris—as in London, Berlin, Vienna, and Venice—he had his new film *City Lights* to promote. Consequently, Chaplin seems to have agreed more or less immediately to hold a press conference in the ornate surroundings of the Salon des Aigles, on the first floor close to his suite.

In light of the large number of journalists who had invaded his hotel, Chaplin probably had little choice but to see them en masse. He was probably also aware, as Jean Stelli wrote, that "journalists, all together in a group, are very kind."[70] But the press conference, from the beginning, was characterized by considerable confusion. In the first place, the journalists themselves were a heterogeneous collection drawn from a diverse range of publications— P.G. of *L'Echo de Paris* noted that there were "representatives of daily and weekly newspapers, monthly journals, organs of the cinema trade together with publications devoted to news and politics."[71] Not all of those present were French.[72] There were also a number of photographers in the room, who would continue to take pictures during the proceedings, creating constant flashes of magnesium.[73] Finally, the format of the press conference itself encouraged a diverse range of not particularly searching questions: a "collective interview" of this kind, a reporter from *Le Petit Parisien* realistically remarked, "is always a little disjointed."[74]

The press conference began with Chaplin sitting, one leg crossed over the other, at a small round table. To several of those present, he seemed visibly tired; he had, after all, been traveling overnight on a train, had been caught up in the scrum of his reception at the Gare de Lyon, and—though it was now 15:30—had not yet had lunch.[75] He did not take his friend Cami's advice to start by welcoming those present cheerily in French: "Bonjour, Messieurs." The conference itself consequently started with an awkward silence, which none of the journalists wanted to break. It was the secretary who was there to interpret Chaplin's remarks, Mlle. Lechat, who took the initiative. She asked the journalists to pose their questions in French and informed them that Chaplin would respond individually to the journalist concerned. "We then heard a wonderful combination of stupidities," remarked Lucie Derain of *La Cinématographie Française*, "with even those who would normally have been able to ask something interesting posing ludicrous questions."[76] Chaplin was asked if he found Paris had changed. (He pointed out that, since he had just arrived, he had had the opportunity of seeing nothing yet.) Would he be going to Budapest or to Spain? Would he go to Brussels three days later to attend the Belgian première of *City Lights*? Was he staying long in Paris, and would he attend the later Paris première? What would his next film be? To each of these questions, he replied that he was not sure or did not know.[77] Chaplin, complained novelist and screenwriter Paul Achard, who would publish a critical account of the press conference in *L'Ami du Peuple*, was "vague, always vague."[78]

Until this point, Achard observed, Chaplin had "the air of not being interested."[79] But halfway through the press conference, Jean Tedesco, a journalist from the cinema trade press, intervened to declare that "instead of asking you questions, Mr. Chaplin, it's better to tell you how much we are happy to see you in Paris!" As everyone in the room applauded and Tedesco's words were translated, Chaplin stood up, unbent, and finally smiled.[80] When questioning resumed, however, it proved "more disjointed than ever."[81] Was Chaplin still planning to make a film about Napoleon, a project that had been well-publicized earlier? (He responded that he had abandoned the idea with the coming of the talkies.) Was he about to make a talking film in which he did not appear? (Chaplin said he was thinking about it.)[82] Did he propose, as had been rumored, to make a film about Christ? (Chaplin confessed that this project had been abandoned.)[83] The questions became more and more banal. A journalist from a sports paper asked him what sports he played (tennis) and whether he would be going to the cycling competition known as the Six Days of Paris at the Vél' d'hiv (Vélodrome d'hiver). (He didn't know.) At this point, Mlle. Lechat brought proceedings to an end with a crisp statement: "Enough of sport. Mr. Chaplin is on holiday. Please allow him, gentlemen, a few hours of peace and quiet."[84]

The notion that Chaplin was in Europe on vacation was, at best, only a partial truth. The fact that he was met at the Paris station by the head of United Artists in Paris and the owner of the theater in which *City Lights* would soon open underlined the fact that he also had a new movie to promote. As Jean Pascal commented in *Ciné Magazine*, Chaplin had no intention "of attempting to avoid the necessities of a publicity campaign whose intention was to maintain his supremacy on the screens of the world."[85] United Artists, the French cinema trade press reported, had already driven a hard bargain with the Dominion Theater in London: in return for exclusive rights to show the film for twenty weeks, they had insisted on an unheard-of 60% of the box office (with a minimum of forty thousand pounds sterling guaranteed). At the Marigny Theater in Paris—like the Dominion a "live" theater converted to show *City Lights*—it was rumored that Volterra had agreed to a similar deal, passing on 40 or 50% of receipts to UA.[86] Yet although there were early indications from London that the film would prove commercially successful, a number of doubts remained. It had taken two years to produce and was Chaplin's first film in three years. Had his fans remained loyal? Since *The Circus* had been released in early 1928, the cinema had largely gone over to the production of talking pictures. Would *City Lights*, essentially a silent film with a musical score, now be seen as outmoded? To minimize the threat posed by such uncertainties, United Artists and Chaplin embarked on a major publicity campaign, including personal appearances by Chaplin himself in several countries, to create and maintain popular interest in the movie.[87] This was almost certainly a major influence on why he agreed to meet with the French press so soon after his arrival in Paris.

The press conference at the Crillon itself was one part of a broader strategy aimed at exploiting and protecting Chaplin's star image. His secretary, Carlyle Robinson, frequently joked that "his job was less often that of 'press agent' than of 'sup-press agent.'"[88] There had been little scandal—or even gossip—attached to Chaplin's life since his divorce in 1927.[89] But in Europe in 1931, he would have a succession of romances, with Sari Maritsa in Britain, dancer La Jana in Berlin, concert pianist Jennie Rothenstein in Vienna, and May Reeves (also known as Mizzi Muller) for much of his time in France. Robinson had to work hard to keep Chaplin's girlfriends out of sight of the press. For the most part he succeeded, which meant that French newspapers, in particular, became obsessed with the story of Floriselle Constantinesco. The papers could agree on very little about her: her name (some talked of Florelle Constantine), her hair color (she was variously reported as blonde and brunette), her age (eighteen or nineteen), where she studied political science (Berlin or Paris) or had first met Chaplin (Berlin, Paris, or St. Moritz), and whether or not Chaplin accompanied her to the studio in the Paris suburb of Joinville to make a screen test. There was agreement only on the facts that she was Romanian and beautiful and that Chaplin was apparently intent on making her a star.[90]

Paris-Midi commented rather cynically that there were frequently publicity stunts to announce Chaplin had a new female screen partner and that sometimes this was at Chaplin's initiative, at other times that of the actress herself.[91] Constantinesco claimed that Chaplin told her "you are what I came to look for in Europe for my next films," while Chaplin informed a reporter in Nice that he had never met her. Constantinesco responded by telling the press he was joking and produced a signed photograph of Chaplin she claimed he had given her.[92] Was this another case of Chaplin attempting to seduce, with the offer of fame, a naive young woman? Was Constantinesco (if that was her name) using Chaplin's stardom to propel herself into the public eye? It is impossible to know. Once Chaplin had become romantically involved with May Reeves during his stay on the Côte d'Azur, Constantinesco vanished for good from the pages of the newspapers.

Relatively successful as Chaplin and Robinson were in keeping his private life out of the papers, they could not control everything that was written about him. As in 1921, there were a number of obviously fake interviews in which the tight-lipped Chaplin was quoted as saying things he almost certainly did not say. Jean Berty claimed to have interviewed the star on the eve of his departure from Venice. According to Berty, he welcomed Chaplin in the name of *Paris-Midi* but "he appeared not to understand." When Berty insisted on questioning him, Chaplin declared that he wished to be able to live in peace and demanded, "What do you want to know? I don't smoke and I am rather 'dry.'" Apart from this cryptic reference to his personal habits and, in particular, his view of Prohibition, Berty's "Chaplin" mostly made banal observations: the sky in California was bluer, he admired France, and had a high opinion of French film star Maurice Chevalier. He also supposedly commented that "the talking film is assuredly more alive, and offers more future possibilities than the silent film, but what it gains in being lifelike, it loses in art, at least until the present." Chaplin not only did not speak French in 1931, but the view of the talkies he advanced was clearly Berty's rather than his own.[93]

René Pignères of *Le Journal*, which had campaigned for several weeks for Chaplin to receive the Légion d'honneur, wrote in a slightly proprietorial way of interviewing him in the dining car of his train as he waited for his breakfast (soft-boiled eggs) just after leaving Vallorbe on the French–Swiss border. Chaplin allegedly claimed he had never had time to get to know France, this "beautiful country," since he had first visited it in 1921 at the time of Georges Carpentier's famous prizefight and would not be staying long. Pignères was probably referring to Carpentier's unsuccessful attempt to defeat Jack Dempsey in Jersey City, New Jersey, on July 2, 1921. He does not seem to have been aware that the fight was three months before Chaplin arrived in Paris, that Chaplin and Carpentier were friends, or that Chaplin had visited France before 1921. Toward the end of the interview, according to Pignères, he at last plucked up courage to ask the comedian what he thought of the talkies. Chaplin's supposed response ("What translates most frequently life's emotion is silence, or miming. Silence is so expressive") was much closer to Chaplin's real view than that reported in Berty's article. But it does not at all prove that this "interview" was itself genuine; as Pignères himself acknowledged, Chaplin had been questioned hundreds of times on the subject, and his views had been much reported.[94]

Criticism of Chaplin by some journalists was balanced by attempts to appropriate him politically. In contrast to the situation in 1921, however, the newspapers this time were exclusively from the left. Socialist *Le Populaire* predicted on the day of Chaplin's arrival in the French capital, "Parisians will gather as a crowd to welcome with enthusiasm the artist whose genius expresses with such humanity the life of humble folk and the daily tragedy of common folk."[95] Communist *L'Humanité*, commenting on the prospective award of the Légion d'honneur, observed that "it is natural that the bourgeoisie try hard completely to monopolize a man so popular." Writers for *L'Humanité* seem to have convinced themselves that Chaplin, rather than being what he was, a financially successful producer of films, was an artist sympathizing with the poor who was victimized by a rampantly materialistic industry. One wrote sympathetically of the "official receptions" during his Paris stay during which he "would be obliged to play the role of publicity agent." He would do this, it was implied, solely to meet the needs of "the impresarios and film magnates intent on getting back the millions committed for first-run rentals."[96]

André de Reusse, editor of the film magazine *Hebdo*, adopted the opposite approach. Dismissing the idea that Chaplin had come to Europe, especially France, on holiday in search of rest and recreation, he baldly insisted that his real purpose was to publicize his latest film. Reusse accused Chaplin of not taking his French fans with sufficient seriousness, arguing in somewhat possessive terms:

You are a little our creation, Mr. Charlie Chaplin, for we French have been a major part of your discovery and the construction of your present celebrity.

You have in the past proclaimed yourself the pupil of our famous Max Linder. And if the Agence Générale Cinématographique … had not cast the first "Charlots" onto the Latin market; if my colleagues of the time and myself had not extolled … their irresistible "vis comica"; if our talented writers had not consecrated to you innumerable studies and laudatory books, you would probably have experienced some difficulty in gaining so rapidly the title of "genius" with which we in our day glorify your justifiable celebrity.[97]

In the light of French support for Chaplin, Reusse deplored the fact that the great comedian had not taken the trouble to attend the annual banquet of cinema directors, bringing together managers and reporters for the trade press, which had been held at the Palais d'Orsay in Paris on Wednesday, March 25. At this function, inventor Louis Lumière and filmmaker Georges Méliès had both been honored as the two great French pillars of world cinema. Even if he was on holiday, Reusse insisted, Chaplin could still have put in a brief appearance at the dinner and signed the program for the evening. Not to do so, Reusse argued, showed that Chaplin was ungrateful to his supporters in France and ill-mannered ("you are not a nice guy").

What seems to have motivated Reusse's denunciation of Chaplin was the fact that, two days after the banquet, Chaplin received the Légion d'honneur. Reusse was plainly affronted that the first time this honor was awarded to a figure from the cinema it went to someone who was English by birth and working in the United States, overlooking the claims of French movie pioneers. His article proved the opening shot in a brief and highly successful political campaign for a French cinéaste to receive similar recognition; almost exactly seven months later, Louis Lumière—chosen for his central role, with his brother, in the birth of French cinema—pinned the blue ribbon of the Légion d'honneur to the breast of Georges Méliès at a banquet at Claridge's attended by eight hundred figures drawn from the French film industry.[98]

Writer and sometime actor Paul Achard also emphasized that Chaplin's visit to Paris—and his press conference—was to promote his new film. "He looks sorry when we trail him like a curious beast," Achard declared, "and yet it is absolutely a voyage of propaganda that he is making." Achard emphasized the exorbitant nature of "his financial demands" on exhibitors for *City Lights*, which "have closed to him one part of the English market and worries a little the French market." Yet, Achard pointed out, at his press conference at the Crillon, Chaplin "has the air of not enjoying himself. . . . He hates the mob, and he has been living in the middle of it for weeks. . . . In his whole personality, there is something disturbing, something tense. For someone who communicates so profoundly with the crowd across the screen, he does not communicate at all with men. He gives out a sense of cold, he creates a distance."[99] While Reusse took Chaplin to task more generally for not acknowledging the debt he owed to French cinema, Achard's critique seemed founded on personal pique: when he had spent a week in Hollywood the previous year, Chaplin had refused to see him.[100]

City Lights

The arrival of Chaplin's *City Lights* in France was greeted by critics and commentators with a mixture of anticipation and apprehension. While Chaplin's older films continued to circulate and were popular with audiences, this was his first new film since *The Circus*. Crucially, it was also his first film since the coming of the talkies. (The production of *The Circus* had ended one month after the release of *The Jazz Singer* in October 1927.) Had Chaplin—or his style of filmmaking—changed since 1928? How would Charlot/the Little Tramp fare in he new world of sound—and economic depression? Would he now seem outdated, irrelevant? And how long would Chaplin himself be able to carry on making films without using dialogue?

The fact that *City Lights* was not a talking picture was less anomalous in France than it was in the United States. The French cinema industry generally experienced a low point during the 1920s, and particularly after the onset of economic depression in 1929, there was little money to invest in installing sound systems in studios and theaters. The "first fully sonorised film" to be made in France, Marcel L'Herbier's romantic melodrama *L'Enfant de l'amour* (*The Illegitimate Child*), was not released in Paris until August 1930.[101] For a few years after this, French cinema would undergo something of a revival, since, as Susan Hayward remarks, audiences "did not take to sound films in a foreign language [dubbing would not begin until 1932] or to Paramount's multi-language rehashes."[102] Given the relatively decentralized nature of the French exhibition sector, with many small and independent houses, it took until 1934 to rewire theaters for sound.[103] When *City Lights* arrived in France, conversion to sound was far from complete. A few days before its première, *La Cinématographie Française* reported that only 29% of

Europe's 29,160 cinemas had been equipped for sound (703 of these movie houses for talkies were in France, 256 in Paris).[104]

There was also evidence of resistance from many French cinemagoers to the arrival of the talkies. Writer Hervé Lauwick pointed out that the coming of sound had inspired many women to write to the correspondence columns of women's magazines, and "at least two thirds of these readers regret the passing of silent cinema."[105] Colette, a sometime film critic, echoed such sentiments, deploring the fact that the use of speech had "suppressed the part played by our imagination" and "succeeded in depriving cinemas of their charm, their tranquillity, their mystery."[106] Some spectators obviously protested more actively. Edmond Epardaud, in the April 1931 issue of the journal *Cinéma*, referred to "the sometimes violent demonstrations that for several months have been happening" in many cinemas. Whereas only avant-garde films had provoked anger in the silent era, he argued, the arrival of the talkies had created "a more aggressive atmosphere." Much of this was a consequence of the poor quality of many films. The protests, Epardaud suggested, were rooted in the fact that "a certain number of talkies are not worthy of being shown to the public." Faults included "the poverty of the scenarios, either completely stupid or fabricated in series, the incompetence of the actors and the mediocrity of the recordings."[107] An ad in *La Cinématographie Française* showing a cinema manager showered with objects thrown by an angry mob, suggested a further reason: in some cinemas, the sound system broke down or malfunctioned in other ways.[108]

Marcel Pagnol, playwright and filmmaker, was an early champion of the sound film. "In an article published in *Le Journal* in 1930," he later insisted, "I announced the arrival and triumph of the talkie. I announced the death of the silent [cinema]." Looking back three years later, Pagnol argued that the definitive victory of the talkie over the silent film had come with the release of *City Lights*. In *City Lights*, Chaplin—"the great, invincible Charlot"—had effectively surrendered "since, under the pretext of making fun of the talking film, he had made a talking film." Chaplin had mocked the distortions of the talkie (Pagnol was referring to the incomprehensible voices in the opening sequence) as produced by "primitive equipment." But, Pagnol argued, "his parody derived all its comic force from the soundtrack, even the 'gag' of the whistle which he swallowed so oddly." The "great comic effects" of these two sequences, due to sound effects and the human voice, did the greatest harm to the visual "gags" of *City Lights*: when Charlot was left hanging from the sword of Justice by his trouser leg, or again when he fell into the water five or six times in a row, dragging in his savior with him, we had the impression that this was no longer as funny.... And despite the boundless genius of Charlot, despite the real love of the people for his little character, so intelligent and so touching, despite the memory of *The Pilgrim, The Gold Rush*, and *The Circus*, poor *City Lights* did not twinkle very long on screens all over the world: this was the Waterloo of the silent film.[109]

It is true that *City Lights* did not "twinkle" for very long at the Marigny Theater, where it had its Paris première on April 7. The Marigny was not so much a cinema as a live theater that from time to time showed films. *City Lights* opened there under promising circumstances: the Paris edition of the *New York Herald* reported that there were "more than 1,000 persons" massed outside the theater "three hours before regular performances began" on April 8. It was "probable," the paper reported, that the film would run at the Marigny "throughout the summer."[110] Yet only a few days later, the Marigny was advertising performances of *Moineau*, a romantic operetta in three acts by Henri Duvernois and Pierre Wolff.[111] It may have been that Léon Volterra, who ran numerous Paris theaters, had never planned that the film would have a long run at the Marigny. It may also be that prospective filmgoers were put off by stories of what the first spectators of the film experienced.

According to the satirical *Le Canard enchaîné*, after an early lunch patrons would arrive at 12:45 for a 13:00 screening. They would wait for half an hour for the box office to open, before parting with quite a lot of money for a seat high in the balcony. An usher would then keep them waiting, pestering them to buy opera glasses and a program, before showing them to their places. They would listen for some minutes to prerecorded music. Then the screen finally lit up. Spectators were shown the *Pathé-Journal* news (longer, *Le Canard enchaîné* sardonically observed, at the Marigny than anywhere else), followed by a documentary, *Jeux de fauves*, on parrots and penguins, and an animated cartoon. There was then a long entr'acte, while prerecorded music from a comic opera, *La fille de Paillasse*, was played. Only then, finally, was the eighty-seven-minute *City Lights* screened. The entire performance lasted nearly three hours—much of it taken up with what Jean-Michel Pagès in *CinéMonde* called "badly-chosen hors-d'oeuvres."[112]

To some critics, Chaplin in *City Lights* had managed to defy both time and the talkies. "Impervious to fashion," wrote G.I. in *La Liberté*, Chaplin "does not want sound for himself, which seems to us great proof of intelligence on his part, for his art so full of poetry, sweetness and funniness, made with an exquisite sensitivity and simplicity, would lose its charm and its universality in being translated into words."[113] "We had placed a lot of hopes on this film," declared Marcel Lapierre in *Le Peuple*, "notably because we thought that it was going to prove that a silent film could still triumph.... We have not suffered any deception." Émile Vuillermoz in *Le Temps* wrote that "this work proves to us that a silent film can still impose its law on the screen," while Pierre Desclaux of *Mon Ciné* praised "a work so harmonious that will make us forget so many bad talking productions."[114]

Since Chaplin, according to critic Pierre Henry, was "a convinced partisan of silent film and a declared opponent of the talkie," his first film since the advent of the talkies attracted more attention than it otherwise might have done.[115] Chaplin's dislike of talking in films (Jean le Meur commented that this "vagabond poet of the silent art . . . appears to have the same hatred as Hamlet for words") meant that some critics were inclined to view his film as confirmation that it was still possible to make profitable silent films.[116] Lucie Derain of *La Cinématographie Française* took a different view. Would *City Lights* "convince . . . the public won over to the persuasive power of the talkie?" Derain herself was far from convinced. *City Lights*, as a Chaplin film, she argued, was in a category by itself: it was and would remain an exceptional case, one that would exercise little or no influence on the cinema in general.[117] In this, her first notice of the film, Derain confusingly described it as "fully silent" but also as "almost a satire on talking films." A few days later, in a review in the newspaper *Le Quotidien*, she clarified what she meant: *City Lights* was "a silent film [in the sense that there was no comprehensible dialogue], but there are constantly sound effects, and it must be acknowledged that the music, the noises, the sounds play a big part in this film." In common with many other French critics, Derain understood the opening sequence of *City Lights*, with its sounds of officials making meaningless speeches over the new monument on which Charlot is discovered sleeping, as a conscious parody of the speechifying in many talking films.[118]

The opening monument sequence is largely slapstick, suggesting a traditional Charlot pantomime comedy. But the film is a hybrid: it is also a romantic melodrama. Charlot meets and falls in love with a pretty girl selling flowers (Virginia Cherrill), whom he subsequently realizes is blind. He stops a wealthy man (Harry Myers) from committing suicide by drowning (they both fall repeatedly into the water). Almost all the comedy in *City Lights* arises from Charlot's relationship with this man, who greets him as a bosom friend when drunk but fails to recognize him at all when sober. Persuading his inebriated friend that he should buy some flowers, Charlot purchases two enormous bouquets from the girl and drives her back to her apartment in the rich man's car. When the girl falls ill, he takes a job as a street cleaner to be able to help her. Visiting her during his lunch break, Charlot reads in a newspaper of a cure for her blindness and also discovers that the girl and her grandmother are about to be evicted from their apartment for unpaid rent. He promises to pay the rent but is sacked when he returns late to work. In a desperate attempt to raise money, he agrees to take part in a prizefight, but this effort fails. He meets again the rich man (drunk), who greets him as a long-lost friend and promises to take care of the girl. But when robbers try to steal the money, the rich man is hit over the head and, when the cops arrive, forgets his promise. Charlot runs away with a thousand dollars, which he gives to the girl to cover the cost of rent and an operation on her eyes. He is arrested and spends several months in jail. The girl's operation is a success, and she and her grandmother open a flower shop. She fantasizes that her benefactor is young, rich, and handsome. The Tramp, released from jail and penniless, sees the girl through the window of her shop. She offers him a flower and a coin but, when their hands briefly touch, realizes who he is. The film ends on a note of uncertainty: will the girl reject the Tramp now she has seen him as he is or, as the final shot of a smiling Charlot suggests, will love win out over the social gulf that exists between them?

To some critics, *City Lights*—a non-talking film in the new era of talkies—seemed to suggest what once might have been thought of as lèse-majesté: that the once-great Charlot was now in decline. The cruelest reviewer was André de Reusse, the same Reusse who had already criticized Chaplin for receiving the Légion d'honneur before the great pioneers of French cinema. The founder and proprietor of the journal *Hebdo-Film*, Reusse had already published Jean Pascal's enthusiastic review of *City Lights*. A week later, he himself compared Chaplin's latest film unfavorably with *Easy Street* (*Charlot Policeman*, Mutual, 1917), which he had recently seen revived—to gales of laughter—at the Moulin Rouge cinema. Reusse complained that *City Lights*, by contrast, had been greeted only with shallow laughter and "thin, short, discrete applause" at the end. The Charlot of the early films had been "a great artist"; Chaplin, in *City Lights*, revealed himself as "no more than a hack." In releasing his latest film, launched with "unprecedented publicity" to disguise the thinness of the material, Chaplin, "out of fashion, finished, incapable of renewing himself, had just signed his abdication."[119]

Lucie Derain similarly saw the Chaplin of *City Lights* as past his peak. "We are far from *The Gold Rush*," she wrote, "and this in all sincerity." The art of the comedian consisted of constant renewal, but in *City Lights* "the effects, the gags are those we have been familiar with for ten years (see *The Count* [Mutual, 1916], *The Rink* [Mutual, 1916], *Sunnyside* [First National, 1919], *A Dog's Life* [First National, 1918], etc.)." Only two (the whistle and the cigar) were new and original.[120] In a longer review for *Le Quotidien* newspaper, Derain made her doubts about the film clearer. It displayed at times, she wrote, an exasperating sentimentality. While containing some excellent comic sequences, it also included some that were a little monotonous. Above all, Chaplin himself "seemed to us weakened, tired perhaps by the difficult struggle undertaken against the talky." To Derain, there seemed very little point to this conflict: in *City Lights*, she argued, "several scenes demanded words, brief perhaps, but words all the same."[121]

Like Reusse, Jacques Vivien of *Le Petit Parisien* criticized the loud chorus of publicity accompanying the film's release, which he suggested had raised expectations too high. *City Lights* contained some "of the better Charlot," but at the same time there was "much that had been seen before." Chaplin, the "most famous man in the world," Vivien concluded, in terms very similar to Reusse's, had not attempted to renew himself. Not only did he remain "the eternal vagabond, suffering with resignation the rebuffs of fate," but the story of his love for the blind flower-girl was itself not very new. It stirred vague memories of Charles Dickens while offering what was in essence a rather more clichéd version of *Voile de bonheur*, Georges Clemenceau's play of 1901 revolving around a blind Chinese mandarin who has his sight restored.[122] Yvan Noé pointed out the strong resemblance between *City Lights* and the 1925 play *Les plus beaux yeux du monde* by Jean Sarment (Jean Bellemère), which similarly dealt with the story of a man down on his luck who loves a beautiful blind girl.[123]

Some critics, indeed, treated *City Lights* as Chaplin's swan song. In clinging to the techniques of the past, they believed, he had inevitably announced the end of his long career. There was a near-elegiac tone to some of these notices, as the authors pointedly consigned Chaplin to history. An anonymous writer in *Le Cinéopse* observed philosopically, "Charlot . . . only risks ending more quickly than he expected a glorious career that is already much longer than that of many stars, for the cinema consumes many. After all, it will not be so bad for him to profit from his popular legend by staying in history as the prince of silent cinema, weeping in his own way over his defunct art."[124] To Alexandre Arnoux of *L'Intransigeant*, all Chaplin's lyricism and influence were based on silence. In *City Lights*, he had used sound, but without really understanding its power. The only two sequences that really worked, Arnoux believed, were the successful gag of the swallowed whistle and the "very amusing parody of speaking without words." For the rest, *City Lights* was "a silent film with mechanically recorded music." To Arnoux, the film constituted "an encyclopaedia of Chaplin's art, a kind of general confession and testament, the incomparable monument of a form and a spirit which are obviously in decline, which no longer reflect the current state of the world, but rather apply to the past." *City Lights* seemed to him like "a magnificent symphony . . . incredibly put together and amusing," a work that nonetheless "leaves . . . an aftertaste of melancholy. An admirable symphony, but at the same time a symphony of goodbye."[125]

André de Reusse, while disapproving of Chaplin's film, not only allowed a favorable review by Jean Pascal to appear in the journal he owned and edited; he also permitted Marcel A. Crance to published an article in *Hebdo-Film* summarizing French critical opinion of *City Lights*—an article which made it clear that the balance of opinion was greatly positive. Crance ended his summary quoting approvingly "by way of conclusion" Marcel Lenoir's review in *Le Film Sonore*. Reusse's tolerance here is perhaps surprising, since both Crance and Lenoir were implicitly criticizing the editor's position. Crance made it sardonically plain that Lenoir's article was written "in response to the campaigns more or less sincere and disinterested brought against the Great Clown (we do not say against mankind)."[126] Lenoir himself was quoted arguing that the release of *City Lights* ranked with that of *The Pilgrim* (*Le Pélerin*) and *The Gold Rush* (*La Ruée vers l'Or*): "this deeply moving work . . . shows us the pettiness of spirit and the narrow point of view of all the detractors of Charlot."[127]

Favorable critics offered a range of answers to the accusations that *City Lights* showed Chaplin declining and past his peak, repetitious, and incapable of self-renewal. Jean Proudhomme of *Le Matin* saw no decline in Chaplin's talent. *City Lights*, he argued, was "of the same quality as *The Circus* and *The Gold Rush*." Even more positive, Jacques Bernier of *Ciné-Miroir* declared, "*City Lights* appears, in truth, as the best film of Charlie Chaplin: it represents, we think, an indisputable progress on the earlier ones."[128] *City*

Lights was better than *The Circus*, contended Jorge Felice in *Le Courrier Cinématographique*, because "Chaplin was still broadening and improving his style." Jean Pascal in *Hebdo-Film* assessed it as superior to both *The Gold Rush* and *The Circus*, on the grounds that "Chaplin's art . . . seems still to be refining itself," and Robert Gordeaux of *L'Echo de Paris* similarly commented that "his art is still being refined."[129]

On the question of Chaplin's capacity for renewal, there was a range of views. To Jean Chataigner in *Le Journal*, *City Lights* was Chaplin's "masterpiece" precisely *because* he had understood the need "to resist the desire to renew himself." Chaplin back again on the screen "was like an old friend who . . . makes his return after three years of silence, three years of stubborn work, of struggle against new and abhorrent formulas."[130] Jean Pascal acknowledged that Chaplin had remained true to the tradition of mime established by Jean-Gaspard Deburau and developed by circus clowns and English music-hall performers, but insisted that his screenplay "had evolved to fit the taste of today." Robert de Beauplan of *La Petite Illustration Cinématographique* pointed out that several years had elapsed between each of Chaplin's films since he wanted each one to represent "a step towards perfection." Jorge Felice, at the other extreme from Chataigner, underlined the crucial importance of Chaplin's personal drive for renewal: "Apart from his first films, each of his works—since *Woman of Paris*—marks a new inspiration. The man does not repeat himself."[131]

In reality, of course, there were many references in *City Lights* to sequences in Chaplin's earlier films, including *Tango Tangles* (*Charlot danseur*, Keystone, 1914), *The Knockout* (*Charlot et Fatty dans le ring*, Keystone, 1914), *The Champion* (*Charlot boxeur*, Essanay, 1915), *The Rounders* (*Charlot et Fatty en bombe*, Keystone, 1914), and The *Rink* (*Charlot patine*, Mutual, 1916). The movie itself—as Felice pointed out in *Le Courrier Cinématographique*—was in many ways made up of "a series of 'comic episodes': 'Charlot chez le millionaire,' 'Charlot boxeur,' Charlot en bombe,' etc." To René Pignères of *La République*, who otherwise viewed the film favorably, this made *City Lights* a film without the unity of place and action that had distinguished *The Gold Rush*: it was as if Chaplin had sought to achieve a collection of pieces rather than one really unified work.[132] Felice took a different view. These diverse sequences, he maintained, were tied together by "the principal element of the film . . . I mean the romantic plot, the first that Chaplin has been able thoroughly to follow up. This 'romance'—let us use the English term, almost untranslatable in French—which allows Charlot to demonstrate the qualities of sensitivity and tact that we only just suspected until then, this 'romance,' I say, impossible to introduce in his earlier films, is authorized and legitimated by the device of the young blind girl."[133]

City Lights, according to the critic of *L'Action Française*, was "the first great love film by Charlie Chaplin." The focus on the Tramp's relationship with the young flower seller, the sacrifices he makes out of love for her, created a deeper, more rounded character, with "a more striking humanity," according to Jean Proudhomme, than in earlier films. "The subject," commented Jacques Bernier in *Ciné-Miroir*, "is closer to life, contains a drama more human, a study of characters more profoundly developed. In several films in which he was the protagonist and author, the clowning part took [on] an importance to the detriment of the human document. In *City Lights*, on the contrary, it is the human document that prevails over the rest."[134] "This time," observed Charles Jouvet in *Le Populaire*, "sadness infinitely holds sway over the funniness, primarily because of the subject itself." The Charlot revealed in *City Lights*, commented Marcel Sauvage of *Pour Vous*, was "more simply human, even more moving and more bitter."[135]

Chaplin's role in *City Lights* as the eternal outsider, chivalrously struggling against established society both to save a young woman from losing her home and to cure her blindness, had particular appeal for left-wing critics such as Jouvet of the socialist *Le Populaire*. Léon Moussinac of the communist *L'Humanité* set forth the most detailed political reading of the film. *City Lights*, he wrote, "seems like the most bitter, cruel and hopeless of Chaplin's films, and the one most heavy with loneliness. Never yet has 'Charlot' so completely severed all links with bourgeois life, never has he appeared more naked and alone." The fact that he can have no relationship with established society is demonstrated in the very first sequence, dealing with "one of these imbecilic dedications of symbolic monuments in honor of Peace and Solidarity." "Bourgeois hypocrisy and puritanism," Moussinac wrote, "take a worthy blow with the grotesqueness of the speeches and the salute to the national hymn." Thereafter, Charlot's social conscience forces him to reject the established order of society. To Moussinac, *City Lights* was "a series of cream tarts . . . thrown in the odious face of bourgeois morals. It is the explosion of a secret love, vast, tormented, where a simple man, arising from the anonymous crowd, laughs at his poverty, his distress, his despair, in order to hide his tears and not cry out his hatred."[136]

To several French critics, the story underpinning *City Lights* was tragic rather than funny. "It is clear and strong as a subject for tragedy," observed

Paul Gordeaux in *L'Echo de Paris*. Richard Pierre-Bodin of *Le Figaro* argued that Chaplin had begun to transform himself: he was in the process of becoming "the true Chaplin . . . the greatest tragic actor of modern times." He should no longer be restricted to his comic persona of Charlot. "Dare to reject the little moustache, the little hat, the little Chaplin," he advised the star. "Don't allow the length of your cane to be the measure of your talent."[137]

J.-P. Gelas of *L'Action Française* developed this argument further. *City Lights*, he wrote, "marks, like *A Woman of Paris*, one of the more impressive stages in the evolution of Charlie Chaplin. Schematically, we can say that in his first works he was essentially a comic; that since *The Woman of Paris* all his comedies are constructed on the basis of dramas; and that after *City Lights* the best of his works will doubtless be tragedies. In truth, there is there a change of attitude, but not a change of orientation; it is the real face of Charlie Chaplin that reveals itself little by little."[138] Gelas had his own explanation for this change: Chaplin's evolution was "dominated by a tragedy": his struggle against America. The crucial moment in that struggle, according to Gelas, had been Chaplin's divorce from Lita Grey in 1927. The Little Tramp had been beaten by American society; *City Lights* was the film in which he expressed "the despair of the vanquished." To Gelas, the comic sequences of the film succeeded "because the performer is a virtuoso." But he did not believe Chaplin's heart was any longer in them. He now realized that "laughter is powerless; it does not allow us to escape or stave off anguish." This change revealed itself in Chaplin's physiognomy: "on his face that is now a little marked by age, the lines do not appear those of joy." "The discordance between the man and his screen personality is going to accentuate. We very much hope that they will still give us film comedies, but we will not be surprised to see them develop further the split, until Chaplin makes separately comedies and tragedies."[139]

There were, of course, other speculations on the ways in which Chaplin's career might develop. Paul Gordeaux of *L'Echo de Paris* perceived *City Lights* as "the last masterpiece of a genre that has today come to the end of the road: the silent cinema." But it was far from necessarily the end of the road for Chaplin, "for you will see that Charlot speaks, him also."[140] Whether they thought, like Gordeaux, that Chaplin would adapt to the innovation of sound, or believed, with Alexandre Arnoux, that his career was effectively over, most French critics would have been astonished at the notion that, five years later, the Little Tramp would reappear in another non-talking film that would be phenomenally successful in France, where some would perceive it as particularly relevant to the issues of the day. But, largely hidden behind the coverage of the film star arriving in Paris, the award of the Légion d'honneur, his reception by high society, and the publicity accorded *City Lights* was Chaplin's growing interest in social and economic affairs. Charles Maland traces the beginnings of his left-wing critique of politics to his world trip of 1931–32, when he began seriously to think about the economic depression and possible remedies for it.[141] The only interview Chaplin himself gave dealing with politics during his time in France in 1931 was with the English-language Paris edition of the *New York Herald* immediately after his lunch at the Foreign Ministry. Effectively, he explained his acceptance of Briand's invitation by declaring his approval of the French foreign minister's proposal for a United States of Europe. "Unless some such plan is made a reality," he presciently declared, "the whole of the continent is riding for a fall." But the interview was especially revelatory in terms of Chaplin's thinking about the economic depression. He told the *Herald* reporter that "the standard of living throughout Europe must be raised. It is possible now to produce enough for everyone to have a share; but, at present, the problem seems to be that no one has the money to buy." To cure the depression, it was crucial to raise people's standard of living. It was, he argued, stupid "to preach frugality, thrift and hoarding" at such a time as this—what the world needed was "wholesale spending." Chaplin insisted that he was not speaking of communism but of common sense.[142]

In April 1931, Chaplin was already advocating Keynesian methods of ending the depression—though he probably did not know they were Keynesian. In the same year in which Britain was forced off the gold standard—and two years before the inauguration of Franklin D. Roosevelt's New Deal—Chaplin's economic thinking was already comparatively sophisticated. Yet the impact of the interview in France was highly marginal. Only one French newspaper, *Paris-Midi*, quoted part of it, translated into French. There may have been several reasons for this. French newspapers probably resented the fact that Chaplin had given an "exclusive" to an English-language newspaper. While some may have wished to appropriate the popular figure of Charlot for their own purposes, few were interested in Chaplin's own ideas. *Paris-Midi* minimized the importance of its own report by printing it as an addendum ("Charlot a parlé politique") to a front-page article on his boar hunt in Normandy. The report also ended with the wry comment "Thus spoke Charlie Chaplin, with his disillusioned smile, his inimitable gestures."[143] Emphasizing to readers that the views cited were those of Charlot, the comedian, helped undercut their significance. Five years later, with the release of *Modern Times* (*Les Temps Modernes*), elements of the French press would be considerably more ready to see Chaplin as both comedian and social critic.

In 1931, as in 1921, Chaplin arrived in France with a new film to promote. Just as in 1921, he was awarded an official decoration by the French government, creating a degree of controversy in 1931 that had not been evident a decade earlier. On his 1921 visit, many observers were shocked to learn that Chaplin was markedly different in appearance from the screen Charlot. In the next ten years, the French became far more accustomed to movie fandom and the culture of celebrity: Chaplin was now recognized everywhere he went. "His face," commented the Paris edition of the *New York Herald*, "has become so well-known, even without the familiar moustache, that he cannot go anywhere without being pointed out and stared at."[144] In 1921, members of the French journalistic and intellectual elite sought his company. By 1931, so great was his stardom, it was members of the international aristocracy, including kings and dukes, who were eager to meet him. In the decade he had been away, the relationship between film stars and the press had become more formalized. While a small number of left-wing French newspapers attempted to appropriate Charlot as a symbol, no French journalists— despite the fact he arrived at the nadir of the economic depression—seemed interested in 1931 in his views on politics. In 1921, he had enjoyed the company of French friends, notably boxer Georges Carpentier and cartoonist Cami; in 1931, only the faithful Cami (who had campaigned for his idol to receive the Légion d'honneur) remained to meet him when he arrived in Paris.[145]

For many French, whether writers or ordinary film fans, there was a sense that Charlot belonged to them. Marcel Carné wrote of France as "the country which first knew how to discover the genius behind your farcical clowning-around," and Maurice Huet hailed Chaplin as the "adoptive son of our immortal France."[146] Lucette Benissier, in her imagination writing a letter to Chaplin and assuring the comedian that his old films had now attained a timeless, classic status, reached automatically for a parallel in French culture. Such "charming" works, she asserted, "have not grown old . . . [as] the beautiful verses of [Alfred de] Musset have not grown old."[147]

Looking back from the perspective of 1931, there was a growing tendency to see Charlot as a (perhaps *the*) distinctive figure of the years immediately after the war. "This postwar period," asked Pierre Paraf, ". . . will it be the era of Charlot?"[148] As Edmond Jaloux pointed out in *Le Temps*, this was in many ways ironic: Charlot's screen persona of a poor and humble vagabond was a "systematic negation" of the modern world, with its emphasis on power, vanity, and ostentation. Did his popularity, Jaloux asked, demonstrate that beneath the materialism of modern life lay "an obscure nostalgia for something else, —for liberty, simplicity, poetry, lounging about, daydreaming?" According to Yvan Noé, the influence of Charlot as "a kind of stylization . . . of postwar man" had been particularly marked on Frenchmen who had faced many crises as a result of the war and, "having endured a lot, had turned in on themselves." According to Noé, this was the reason why he and fellow playwrights Marcel Achard, Jean Sarment, and Jacques Natanson "had fallen under the influence of 'Charlot.'" Blasé and ironic after a series of successive blows of fate, they had nonetheless found themselves deeply touched and uplifted by a screen character who, enduring a life of destitution, "remained a man of lofty dreams, great admirations, large enthusiasms, [and] great tenderness."[149] In 1931, many French intellectuals still testified to the influence and appeal of Charlot. But how would he fare as the talkies consolidated their grip on international film production and the economic depression continued?

6
Economic Depression and War

Chaplin's reputation, in France as elsewhere in the world, reached a peak in the 1920s. His world trip of 1931–32, in retrospect, marks the end of the first part of his career. It led to two major changes. The first was a decline in the number of films he produced. In the early 1920s, he had released two films a year—*The Kid* and *The Idle Class* in 1921 and *Pay Day* and *The Pilgrim* in 1922. In 1923, he produced only *A Woman of Paris*. There was then a two-year wait for his next film, *The Gold Rush* (1925) and three-year waits for *The Circus* (1928) and *City Lights* (1931). Chaplin did not release another film for five years: *Modern Times* in 1936. Indeed, after *City Lights* he would make only two films in fifteen years. The second change, to some extent the product of his travels of 1931–32, was his growing interest and involvement in politics. This launched him on a path that would eventually undercut his stardom in the United States and lead to his exile in Europe. This chapter will examine the French reception of Chaplin's two most overtly political films: *Modern Times* and *The Great Dictator*. *Modern Times* (*Les Temps Modernes*) was released very quickly in France: premièred in New York on February 5, 1936, and Los Angeles on February 12, it was first shown in Paris on March 13, a month later. *The Great Dictator* (*Le Dictateur*), by contrast, took a long time to arrive. Premièred in New York City on October 15, 1940, it reached London on December 16. The Second World War, the surrender of France, and the German occupation delayed its arrival in France for over four years: it was not shown in Paris until April 4, 1945.

There had been suspicion as early as 1921 that Chaplin had left-wing political sympathies. Before his departure for Europe in September 1921, he recalled, an American journalist had asked him whether he was a Bolshevik.[1] Yet before his world tour of January 1931 to June 1932, he had rarely commented on politics or economics. Once outside the United States, he seems to have been much more eager to discuss the depression and its effects. Although it is unclear when he first came across them, Chaplin was apparently influenced by Major C. H. Douglas's ideas on social credit—the notion of a credit paid to all citizens to boost demand, with price controls to stop

Charlot. Melvyn Stokes, Oxford University Press. © Oxford University Press 2026.
DOI: 10.1093/9780197839294.003.0007

inflation. After he discussed Douglas with Albert Einstein in Berlin, Einstein famously told him he was an "economist" rather than a comedian.[2] He also talked economics with John Maynard Keynes, British Prime Minister Ramsay MacDonald, and former prime minister David Lloyd George.[3] Yet there were many ambivalences about this trip and what happened after his return to the United States. Whatever his supposed sympathy for the unemployed, Chaplin lived a celebrity lifestyle in Europe, staying in the best hotels. He was drawn to gilded upper-class socialites, including Lady Astor and Lady Cunard in London and the "Riviera set" in France. Biographer David Robinson observes that, after the London première of *City Lights* in February 1931, he amused himself for more than a year by acting as a "playboy."[4] Although he returned to the United States in 1932 with a complicated scheme for ending the depression, and from March 1933 made clear in a number of ways his support as a private individual for Franklin D. Roosevelt's New Deal,[5] he was taken to task by at least one left-wing critic for not responding to the challenge of the times in his work.

In June 1934, the magazine *Living Age* printed a translated article by Mexican Marxist writer Lorenzo Turrent Rozas titled "Charlie Chaplin's Decline." Rozas saw the early Chaplin films as demonstrating "the injustices of a badly-organized society" and "contrast[ing] wealth and excessive poverty." In *The Gold Rush*, Chaplin offered "one of the harshest criticisms ever made of capitalism in its last stages." Yet the onset of the depression had isolated Chaplin, making him appear sentimental, even decadent. The pathos and individualism of the Tramp had nothing to offer in a new situation ("the failure of Yankee capitalism"). Rozas saw no way for Chaplin to move to the left and support the workers ("he would have to throw away the ballast of his millions.")[6] It is possible that Chaplin read Rozas's article, but in any case by the time of its publication he had already been working on his own response to the depression, the film that would become *Modern Times*, for more than a year. As he endeavored to show the Tramp in the new world of factory labor, unions, strikes, and unemployment, he had to cope with many uncertainties. Would his new film be a talkie, or should it remain a "silent"? (He finally compromised with having a sound film in which the Tramp would not speak, though his voice would be heard performing a nonsense song.) Would a more socially and politically conscious Tramp be accepted by Chaplin's existing fans? And how obviously could Chaplin's own left-wing sympathies be expressed in the film? As he was only too aware, Joseph Breen's Production Code Administration, created in 1934, looked with disapproval on matters of social radicalism. It may consequently have been no accident that *Modern Times*, in the end, appealed—though for different reasons—to those on the right as well as the left.

Modern Times in France

The first French advertisement for *Modern Times* appeared in *La Cinématographie Française*, a cinema trade journal, on January 18, 1936. Using the phrase "what has been lost to the world for four years," it foregrounded the fact that a new Chaplin comedy was now something of a rarity.[7] In terms of both the film's popular and critical reception, there was a strong sense of relief in France that—after another long absence—Chaplin had returned so little changed.[8] "The Parisian public," noted one commentator, "has rediscovered the great Charlot in *Modern Times*." "The Charlot of the little comedies before the war has not grown old," observed René Lehmann in *L'Intransigeant*; "he is still . . . the eternal vagabond, the humble and tormented toy of fate, a poor little man delivered into the human jungle . . . clumsy but inspired, a simpleton but without hate."[9] To French critics, Chaplin's new movie evoked many points of comparison with his earlier ones. "This film," insisted Jean Marguet in *Le Petit Parisien*, "takes us back to the magnificent and creative mimer, the Charlot of the first short comedies: *La Partie de campagne* [*The Tramp*, Essanay, 1915] or *Charlot patineur* [*The Rink*, Mutual, 1916]." Others chose later films to compare it to. Henri Jeanson argued in *Le Canard enchaîné* that "the war inspired him [Chaplin] to a sublime film: *Shoulder Arms* [*Charlot soldat*, First National, 1918]. The crisis, the unemployment, the misery, the injustice and the folly have inspired him to this realistic extravaganza: *Modern Times*."[10] To Émile Vuillermoz of *Le Temps*, Chaplin had "only ever treated in his life just a single subject of which all his films are successive chapters. *Modern Times* follows the logic of *The Kid* or *The Circus*. . . . like the other films of Charlie Chaplin [it is] a silent indictment of the egotism of humanity and social injustice."[11]

French critics seem to have been aware that *Modern Times* had been coldly received by a number of American reviewers and accused of disseminating left-wing propaganda. "Certain of our friends in . . . the United States in particular," declared Émile Cerquant in *L'Humanité*, "are thought to have formulated a series of reservations on the social context of *Modern Times*. We will not follow them onto such terrain." In reality, since he was writing in a communist newspaper, Cerquant did bring out to some degree the class implications of the film. On the one hand, there were the workers, spilled out of the subway "like a flock of sheep [and] heading for a large gloomy metal factory," organized on the principles of scientific management. On the other, "the director who spies upon and orders about the whole factory," including Charlot.[12] Many critics pointed out that the film—at least in its opening sequences—was about a worker being broken and driven mad by the stresses of the production line. To Henri Jeanson in *Le Canard enchaîné*, it demonstrated "the horrors of mechanization."[13] To René Lehmann in *L'Intransigeant*, it was "a lively satire on our excessively industrialized epoch."[14] Jean Marguet of *Le Petit Parisian* suggested it was "a satire" that made people think much "more because of his jokes than many authors of so-called social dramas with their insipid and fine-sounding windbags."[15] Some critics, however, were disappointed that the film had not offered a deeper analysis. Charles Jouet, writing in the socialist newspaper *Le Populaire*, warned viewers not to expect "a series of profound or straightforwardly sociological inspirations" and insisted that "the problem of mechanization" was only superficially dealt with. Raymond Lange, in the magazine *Pour Vous*, drily remarked that "those who, on the basis of the [film's] title," expected to see "an accurate reproduction—or even a philosophy—of modern life have not . . . been completely satisfied."[16]

"Some people," noted film fan Roger Karl in the correspondence columns of film magazine *Pour Vous*, "have reproached him [Chaplin] for his too obvious political tendencies."[17] With its critique of American mass production and exposure of the effects of the depression, many assumed that *Modern Times* was sympathetic to the left. *Le Matin*, for example, commented that the film "shows . . . the tumultuous and hard life of the poor."[18] But a few critics pointed out problems in interpreting the film as left-wing. In *L'Echo de Paris*, Paul Gordeaux argued that in spite of the fact that "the Soviets have been able to welcome this work enthusiastically as a propaganda film, *Modern Times* has nothing subversive about it."[19] There were a number of sequences in the movie, indeed, that seemed to suggest Chaplin's Tramp had a fundamentally conservative outlook. For example, as the critic in *La Cinématographie Française* pointed out, when a revolt takes place in the prison where he is incarcerated (for waving a red flag he had in reality only been trying politely to return), Charlot is "instinctively . . . on the side of law and order" and, even if only by chance, helps arrest the ringleaders of the revolt.[20]

François Vinneuil in *L'Action Française* took this argument to an extreme by constructing the film as a critique of communism in the USSR. Vinneuil, the pseudonym of writer and future spokesman of the far right Lucien Rebatet, reinterpreted *Modern Times* as "a satire . . . on a society enslaved by materialism, of which Soviet Russia represents the barbarous apogee." In the incident over the red flag, Charlot had been an unwitting dupe—the symbol, Vinneuil acidly commented, of many real dupes who had embraced communism. Above all, the film was a protest against what he called "social automatisms," the regimented worlds of work (the factory), pleasure (the dancing sequences), rebellion (the "idiotic strike" in the second factory, where Charlot wants only to work), repression (the police pursue the innocent rather than the guilty), and charity (the public assistance workers who continue to try to take the orphan "gamin" into care "even when she has found a job and a home"). To Vinneuil, the society represented in the film was closer to that "of Stalin, of his five million informers and of comrade Stakhanov [the Russian miner who had become famous in 1935 for his productivity]" than it was to the world of Western capitalism.[21]

Reviewers debated the film's structure and aesthetics in addition to its politics. Many thought the film lacked unity—that it was, in reality, little more than a series of disparate sketches. *Modern Times*, commented Jean Laury of *Le Figaro*, "has neither a beginning nor an end; it is a succession of brief images . . . linked up by lengthy effects, jokes that last and which form a pastry that, grey and soft, is unworthy of being amalgamated together." Raymond Lange of *Pour Vous* offered a different culinary analogy: the film was like a collection of hors d'oeuvres, delicious but with nothing to tie them together. To Maurice Bessy in *Cinémonde*, it was simply rambling and disjointed.[22] Gilbert Bernard, writing in *Le Matin*, in contrast rejected the view that the film was a series of unrelated sketches since "there is a line of thought running through the film, a line that drives a poor devil into the twists and turns of mechanization, at the risk of smashing him to pieces between cogs invented by man against man."[23] Chaplin himself seems to have agreed with Laury, Lange, and Bessy rather than Bernard over the film's episodic structure. A few days before the two French critics wrote their reviews, Chaplin sailed to Honolulu on a boat with Jean Cocteau as a fellow passenger. The varied parts of *Modern Times*, he told Cocteau, "existed in their own right. I could show them separately, one by one, like my early one-reelers."[24]

Some critics clearly thought it eccentric for Chaplin to make a film like *Modern Times* several years into the era of talking pictures. "There is hardly a case more curious," wrote Émile Vuillermoz, "than that of Charlie Chaplin, calmly refusing to take account of the technical revolutions of our studios and following his task as a silent film-maker with heroic indomitability. His latest film proves to us that he has abandoned none of the elements of … what we call 'cinema before the war.' We feel very clearly his willingness to die at his post defending a formula he has created."[25] "We know," observed the anonymous critic in *La Cinématographie Française*, "that Chaplin is a powerful mime artist. He has never had to prove it more than in this resolutely silent film." The reviewer in *Le Figaro* was far more perceptive in his assessment that although *Modern Times* was "not a talkie," it was "a sound film from one end to the other, embellished with a musical score that is harmonized with the images, underlining the effects and contributing to giving the whole work a perfect cohesion."[26]

Several writers pointed out, moreover, that although Chaplin did not actually speak in *Modern Times*, his voice could be heard cinematographically for the first time, singing what a preview in *Le Matin* termed "an onomatopeic song which is one of the highlights of the film."[27] More precisely, according to *Le Figaro*, he sang in gibberish to the music originally written for "a song that is well known in France and which was all the rage here a few years ago: *Je cherche après Titine* by Léo Danide[r]ff."[28] First released in 1917, "Je cherche après Titine" had lyrics by Marcel Bertal, Louis Maubon, and Henri Lemonnier. Chaplin's version, commented *La Cinématographie Française*, consisted of "words without sense, without coherence, idiotic to read, but so madly funny in the mouth."[29]

Chaplin and René Clair

There was another, more influential way in which French influence may have helped shape Chaplin's film. The fact that *Modern Times* dealt with the problems created by mass industrialization was not unusual for films made in France. The first film of the Lumière brothers, Louis and Auguste, had been *Workers Leaving a Factory*, shot outside their photographic factory in Lyons apparently at some point in March 1895.[30] French silent cinema in the 1910s and 1920s had shown some interest in the world of industrial relations. Albert Capellani had written and directed *Germinal; Or, The Toll of Labor* (1913), a movie about a miners' strike based on Emile Zola's 1885 novel of the same title. In 1920, Henri Pouctal directed *Travail*, based on another

Zola novel, again revolving around strikes and class conflict. Yet there was no major French film dealing with the tensions caused by industrial mass production to emerge during the depression era until René Clair's *À Nous la Liberté* was released in 1931.

The new film represented a new approach to filmmaking for Clair himself. As Michel Margairaz and Danielle Tartakowsky have noted, his earlier movies—including *Sous les toits de Paris* (1930) and *Le Million* (1931)—had "depicted a popular and fraternal Paris of faubourgs [neighborhoods] . . . a dream Paris where solidarity, friendship and love triumphed over all obstacles and permitted 'little people' to triumph." In *À Nous la Liberté*, they argue, he "abandons this backward-looking vision of Paris like an operetta to show Taylorism and Fordism at work in a factory producing records." Workers on the production line, Clair shows, are "closely subjected to the control of foreman guards, checked off at the entrance to the factory, searched at the exit, working at the same pace, prevented from speaking during working hours, condemned to eat at the production line, dispossessed of all individuality, all autonomy."[31]

Some American reviewers noted that there were strong resemblances between *Modern Times* and *À Nous la Liberté*.[32] A number of French critics also remarked on the similarities. The reviewer for *La Cinématographie Française* commented that *Modern Times* "bears, in two or three places, the light and sketchy influence of René Clair."[33] According to Jean Marguet in *Le Petit Parisien*, the opening sequence of "workers on an assembly line . . . brings back . . . memories of *À Nous la Liberté*."[34] Clair's production company, the Société Française des Films Sonores Tobis, quickly launched a suit for 1.2 million francs in damages against the Chaplin studio and United Artists for plagiarizing *À Nous la Liberté*.[35] In August 1937, the company issued a summons against the Paris office of United Artists alleging:

> The film *Modern Times* is a plagiarism of the film *À Nous la Liberté*. That the idea of Mr. Chaplin's scenario in fact reveals considerable similarities with *À Nous la Liberté*. That the drawbacks, enslavements, and even the ridiculousness of modern life are characterized by a choice of concrete scenes that can be found in both films, as much in general terms (slavery in the factory, the noticeable inactivity of the boss, the constant surveillance in prison, factory and private life, the departure down the road towards adventure) as in specific details (the mechanized meals, the daydreaming interrupted by the police. . .).

That the choice of expressive images (the penal and sinister character of factory life, with the time clock, the similarity between the discipline in prison and in the mass production line of the factory) confirms the plagiarism.

That, in another sense, the presentation, the rhythm of the two films, the scenes that are shot at a certain angle, clearly show the plagiarism.[36]

No one has so far managed to establish the precise motivation of Tobis for the action it took. French film historian Georges Sadoul suggested that the company was a subsidiary of the German studio Universumfilm Aktiengesellschaft, now under fascist control. *Modern Times* itself was banned in Hitler's Germany, and according to Sadoul, it was Minister of Propaganda Joseph Goebbels who "ordered his representative in Paris to bring proceedings against Chaplin."[37] Certainly the Nazis had little love for Chaplin, in part due to their suspicion that he was Jewish and in part for the political content of *Modern Times*. But Clair was angered when it was suggested to him that the prosecution of Chaplin was a Nazi maneuver.[38]

One of the many ironies of the Tobis suit was that Clair regarded Chaplin as his mentor. Many of his own films borrowed heavily from Chaplin's work. *Le Voyage Imaginaire* (*The Imaginary Voyage*, 1925) featured a dream sequence located in the Musée Grévin in Paris during which waxwork models of the Kid (Jackie Coogan) and Chaplin come alive, just in time for Chaplin to prevent the execution of Jean (Jean Borlin) by guillotine.[39] As R. C. Dale comments, the same film has a "Chaplinesque" beginning and end: "a protagonist traveling along the road with a pesky dog at his heels."[40] Celia McGerr sees hints of Chaplin's Tramp in the character of Frémissin (Pierre Batcheff) in *Les deux timides* (*Two Timid Souls*, 1928) and argues that the role of the inebriated millionaire (Paul Olivier) in *Quatorze juillet* (*Bastille Day*, 1933) was plainly "lifted" from *City Lights*. McGerr also argues that Clair's *Sous les toits de Paris* (*Under the Roofs of Paris*, 1930) and *À Nous la Liberté* owed a good deal to Chaplin, particularly—in the case of the latter—the character of Émile (Henri Marchand), "a Chaplinesque type in his romanticism and pathos, and especially his habit of kicking his pursuers in the backside."[41] Conscious of his own debt to Chaplin, Clair refused to associate himself with the Tobis suit. "I sold you the rights to *À Nous la Liberté*," he informed his production company, "and you have the right to protect your property. But I do not wish to have any part of it. The whole world of cinema has learned lessons from Chaplin. We are all in his debt. I admire him very much and if he has been inspired by my film, I consider that a great honor for me."[42]

David Robinson makes a number of points in Chaplin's defense against the charge of plagiarism. He traces critiques of the dehumanizing effects of mass production and the quasi-military aspects of factory life to progressive writers in the United States before the First World War. Neither Clair nor Chaplin was pioneering in this respect. Chaplin had criticized Fordism in an interview as early as 1925. He would later acknowledge in a deposition that he *had* been influenced by one film: Walt Disney's *Santa's Workshop* (1932), a *Silly Symphony* cartoon in which Father Christmas ran his production line at top speed to cope with the demands of Christmas. But Robinson is very skeptical of the testimony of studio technician John D. Palmer that he had screened *À Nous la Liberté* several times for Chaplin in 1934 and 1935 (Chaplin denied having ever seen the film) and argues that many of the gags used in *Modern Times* were closer to those of Chaplin's *The Floorwalker* (*Charlot chef de rayon,* Mutual, 1916) than *À Nous la Liberté*.[43] Pierre Billard, by contrast, cites the evidence of the projectionist that Chaplin had watched *À Nous la Liberté* three times in his screening room while preparing his own film. He finds the resemblances between the two films "striking," even if Chaplin at times inverts the order of particular sequences. (To emphasize that factory work is worse than prison, the factory sequence comes before Charlot goes to prison, which seems more of a vacation for him.) Billard thought two sequences in *Modern Times* were directly inspired by Clair. The transformation of the hunt for Peking duck into the American football match was taken from the rugby game in Clair's *Le Million* (*The Million*, 1931) and the sequences covering factory work and the mechanization of the individual from *À Nous la Liberté*.[44]

Billard judged that the sequences inspired by *À Nous la Liberté* were "more important, more explicit, more spectacular, [and] more varied" in Chaplin's film.[45] At heart, Clair probably felt the same. He regarded his own film as "a typical Chaplin romance, only lacking his genius."[46] In an interview he gave to a Belgian newspaper in October 1936, he respectfully observed of Chaplin that "if he has borrowed some ideas from me, he has paid me great honour." Later, in a letter to Georges Sadoul, he made it clear that he was convinced he had influenced *Modern Times* but remained unassuming about the impact of that influence. "There is no doubt in my mind on that subject [the impact on Chaplin's film]," he wrote, "and I am very happy to be modestly in credit to a man to whom we are all considerably indebted."[47] Possibly because of

Clair's attitude, he and Chaplin remained on good terms for many years despite the Tobis suit. The suit continued, in both France and the United States, for some time. It was undermined by legal delays, Chaplin's near-uncanny skill at avoiding subpoenas, and the Second World War. In 1947, when the complaint was relaunched, United Artists and the Chaplin studio negotiated a deal to have it withdrawn through a one-off payment of 5,000 dollars in the United States and 2.5 million francs in France.[48]

Charlot and the Popular Front

What did seem clear to French critics, as Charles Jouet commented in *Le Populaire*, was that Chaplin's performance in *Modern Times* "amuses and touches the most varied publics."[49] The film's appeal to a broad popular audience was of special significance because its arrival and dissemination in France coincided with a pronounced uprising of the political left: four weeks after the film's release in Paris, left-wing parties gained a "stunning victory "in the national elections of April 26 and May 3. This would lead, on June 4, 1936, to the establishment of the Popular Front government of Léon Blum.[50] Still more interesting in terms of *Modern Times* is the explosion of strikes, especially factory occupations (or "sitdown strikes," as they were commonly known in the United States), beginning in May and spreading across much of France throughout June. Of the twelve thousand strikes in June, three-quarters took the form of occupations. Most of these strikes, as Edward Shorter and Charles Tilly have shown, took place in large industrial establishments and involved primarily assembly-line workers.[51] Or, in other words, exactly the type of factory that was shown in *Modern Times*, where Charlot was driven mad by the repetitive mechanical movements he was obliged endlessly to perform.

If the incidence of strikes by French workers is mapped onto the evidence provided in the cinema trade press of the areas in which Chaplin's film proved most profitable and successful, some interesting facts emerge. It is very striking that many of the cities in which *Modern Times* enjoyed the greatest commercial success—including Lille, Calais, Nancy, Limoges, and Toulouse—were also those with widespread strikes in 1936.[52] But most suggestive of all is the fact pointed out by Shorter and Tilly that the "highest incidences of participation" in the June sit-down strikes occurred in Le Havre and Rouen. In both of these highly industrialized cities, *Modern Times* was screened to large enthusiastic audiences during the June strikes themselves.[53] This suggests that Chaplin's film may have played some part in aiding the expression of—and perhaps encouraging—the June militancy.

In the first place, largely owing to the dominance of commercial cinema in France and the administration of national movie censorship, *Modern Times* was the *only* new major critique of the industrial system—and at least implicit endorsement of the Popular Front—to be shown in mainstream French commercial cinemas in 1936. As Ginette Vincendeau has pointed out, of the fifteen most popular films of 1936—as identified by *La Cinématographie Française* in its first survey of the most profitable films in France—none of the French productions would subsequently be categorized as a classic Popular Front film. While the eighth film on the list was Jean Renoir's *Les Bas-fonds*, this movie—based on a play by Maxim Gorki—was a melodrama belonging to the currently fashionable "Slav" subgenre rather than a movie preoccupied with the plight of workers. The single member of the group (in sixth place) to echo a number of key Popular Front ideas was Chaplin's *Modern Times*.[54] Even outside the list of best-grossing films, there was little competition. Goffredo Fofi noted that "some Paris cinemas" were showing Clair's *À Nous la Liberté* once again after its "unsuccessful first run."[55] *La vie est à nous*, the film Renoir had directed as election propaganda in 1936 for the French Communist Party (PCF), had been banned by the censors.[56] For many of those who went on strike, launching factory occupations, in the summer of 1936, *Modern Times* uniquely offered some degree of understanding—and explanation—for their actions. The film, Fofi argues, was perceived in France as a "revolt" and greeted by "frenetic applause."[57]

In order to understand the popularity the film enjoyed with workers, however, it is necessary to consider the ways in which it touched on issues that resonated for many people in the summer of 1936. As Julian Jackson has noted, the mass unemployment created by the depression of the 1930s handed employers a powerful weapon. They were able to impose much tighter disciplinary regimes—and further rationalization of production— on workers frightened of joining the swelling unemployment queues. Production targets were raised and wages could be reduced or workers sacked if those targets were not reached. There was growing pressure from *chronométreurs* (timekeepers) and supervisors to perform tasks in less time. Workers were encouraged to compete against one another, promoting greater psychological and physical isolation. To an ever greater extent, the factory seemed to those working there to have had its "space . . . controlled and reordered for them by the management."[58] This combination of factors in many ways explains the special character of the strikes in summer 1936. Three-quarters of the strikes in June involved factory occupations. These signified "the reappropriation of an alien space, the domestication of the workplace."[59] Perhaps more than anything else, they account for the atmosphere of gleeful joy that many observers reported among the strikers. It was not just that most strikes were quickly over, making them seem a little like a holiday, but the occupations overthrew what Jackson terms the "traditional hierarchy of authority in factories." They encouraged workers to talk with and get to know one another, now that mutual suspicion—and the managers and supervisors who had encouraged it—were mainly absent.[60]

Many elements of the factory sequences of *Modern Times* may have appealed to French industrial workers as a result of their own experiences during the depression years. Discipline in the factory is tight: supervisors are quick to appear, and the head of the company knows instantaneously when there is a problem on the production line. There is constant pressure to raise the level of production: the section where Charlie works is three times ordered to speed up (and once to check the quality of the work there). The stress caused by the need to work faster and faster at a tedious mechanical task (tightening nuts) finally drives Charlie insane. Everything is ruled by the clock (an emphasis that begins with the face of the clock in the background during the opening credits). Workers clock on and clock off, being paid only for the time they actually work. (Charlot clocks off even to go to the restroom.) The final lunacy in terms of timekeeping is the automatic feeding machine ("it will eliminate the lunch hour, increase your production and decrease your overhead"), carrying Frederick W. Taylor's "scientific management" theories to their absurd if logical conclusion. The workers in the factory, though working together side by side, seem alienated from one another. Reflecting the division of labor, Charlot and the two men next to him are all doing a different task on the production line. They are isolated, too busy to speak except to blame each other (or more commonly Charlot) when problems occur. The boss is remote, checking what is happening in the factory through a panopticon-style system of surveillance cameras. He is an intrusive presence in the most private space, brusquely ordering Charlie back to work when he sees him having a cigarette in the restroom.

Modern Times almost certainly spoke to many of the ideas and values of the strikers in June 1936. By occupying the factories, they overthrew the harsh discipline imposed by owners and managers, liberating the space in which they worked and replacing "the previous atmosphere of [management-induced] mutual suspicion" among workers with a new sense of fraternity. There were attempts to get rid of *chronométreurs*. A mining union in northern France, for example, argued that their abolition would give back to the miner "the love of his job that the bullying has made him lose. . . . The men work better when left in peace."[61] To strikers who had compelled unpopular supervisors (*porions*) in their own factories to carry a red flag at the head of a procession of workers, there was probably wry amusement that Charlot—if only by chance—had done the same.[62]

Jean Renoir and *Modern Times*

While we can attempt to guess the reasons for the commercial success of *Modern Times* in France and the enthusiasm of its audiences, vouched for by journalists and critics, in the Popular Front summer of 1936, we can never know whether such guesses are correct because of the lack of convincing evidence. Like many films, it was subject to interpretation from a number of different political perspectives. Fofi compared it to Clair's *À Nous la Liberté* in embracing what he termed "a subtly irrational, individualistic tendency that encouraged the applause of both the left and of certain sections of the right."[63] It is possible, however, for us to analyze how one prominent cinéaste associated with the Popular Front interpreted it because, on May 20, 1936, director Jean Renoir published a review of *Modern Times*.

Renoir had become a fan of Chaplin during the First World War. He would later remember being recommended to see "a remarkable actor" called Charlot by a friend from the same bomber squadron. When he went to Paris on leave, his elder brother was equally enthusiastic and the two went to see a Chaplin picture in a small cinema close to the Arc de Triomphe. "To say that I was enthusiastic would be inadequate," Renoir subsequently maintained. "I was carried away." Chaplin pushed Renoir toward his ultimate career as a director. An accident ended his flying career and he found himself based in Paris, where he saw every Charlot film that was available again and again. "My love of him," Renoir recalled, "did not grow less. I began to be interested in other films and became a fanatical cinema fan. Charlie Chaplin had converted me. I reached the point of seeing three feature films a day, two in the afternoon and one in the evening. The cinema was beckoning me."[64]

By 1936, Renoir had become a key figure in efforts to mobilize cinema in support of the Popular Front. In 1935, he had made *The Crime of Monsieur Lange*, hailed by Elizabeth Grottle Strebel as "the Popular Front film *par excellence*, full of the exuberance, optimism and confidence in the ability to transform social conditions which characterised that movement."[65] On the strength of *Monsieur Lange*, Renoir was invited by the PCF—at the suggestion of former surrealist Louis Aragon—to produce a propaganda film, *La vie est à nous*, for the forthcoming elections. Since July 1935 when, fearful of fascist aggression, the Comintern had officially endorsed the idea of a united Popular Front, the PCF had been moving toward greater collaboration with socialists and radicals. But earlier it had become wedded to the idea of a united cultural struggle against fascism through the Association des Écrivains et Artistes Révolutionnaires, founded in 1932. In 1935, that organization was expanded into what was hoped would be a national mass organization, the Maison de la Culture. In November 1935, the cinema section of the Paris Maison de la Culture was transformed into the Alliance du Cinéma indépendant, the collective responsible for filming *La vie est à nous* in February and March 1936. Shortly after that, it turned into a new organization, Ciné-Liberté.[66]

The main aims of Ciné-Liberté were to bring together filmmakers and distributors outside the normal profit-making constraints of the movie industry and bring cinema itself closer to working-class people. It produced its own films, principally documentaries, and organized screenings in nontheatrical venues. By November 1936, it would have a total membership of between ten thousand and twenty thousand.[67] In the view of Pascal Ory, it was the only organization during this period to try, even in a minor way, to combine cinema production and political action.[68] Renoir, according to Goffredo Fofi, was "the central figure."[69] He functioned as president of its *ciné* club and was a member of the editorial board of its new magazine. "The importance of Renoir's involvement in the Ciné-liberté project," Christopher Faulkner wrote, "must be judged by the challenge it offered to the existing forces of artistic production. In the context of the other general reforms of the period, it sought to revolutionize those forces. It hoped to effect a change in the social relations between film maker and audience."[70] Given his long admiration for Chaplin and his left-wing political ideals (though he was never a formal member of the PCF), Renoir must have seen the arrival of *Modern Times* in France as extremely well-timed. In May 1936, on the front page of the first issue of the new *Ciné-Liberté* magazine, he published a long and enthusiastic review.

Renoir began his account of the film in a characteristic way. As Elizabeth Strebel comments, "much of his commitment to the left derived from an instinctive predilection for the organic bonding of a small group of *copains* (close-knit friends), like . . . his own team of collaborators."[71] Renoir started his review with a story of how he and his fellow filmmakers, after spending the night "putting the finishing touches to a work we held dear," were sitting round an editing table at the Léopold Maurice factory at Gennevilliers, a northwestern suburb of Paris, as dawn came. In the garden of the factory, they saw a large apple tree in blossom and went into raptures over the lush flowers. As the light grew, however, they were also able to distinguish another world beyond this garden "oasis"—a world of "rundown houses, smoking factories, tragically, all the classic surroundings of the Parisian suburbs, once the most beautiful countryside in the world, today devastated, soiled, disgraced by the greed and the folly of industrialists and landowners." Renoir then segued into Chaplin's film, which he insisted had made him forget not only the difficulties filmmakers faced but also the fact that "imbeciles and moneygrubbers have degraded and trampled on everything like the orchards of the 'L'île de France' [the area around Paris]." To Renoir, *Modern Times* was a major reaffirmation of what cinema could achieve in foregrounding social issues. Yet he recognized that some were slow to accept any new Charlot, constantly harking back to the "true and pure" days of his Essanay films. To appreciate a new work by "a strong personality" such as Chaplin, Renoir argued, needed "some time and effort." He himself saw Chaplin's constant renewal on film as "one of the distinguishing marks of genius." He ended his review by comparing Chaplin's constant "interior renewal" to attempts by directors of commercial cinema to entertain a mass audience through superficial changes. Renoir disliked such directors for political as well as aesthetic reasons: the films they produced hampered the attempt of himself and others to produce movies dealing with the social problems of the working class. In contrast to Chaplin, he wrote with some bitterness, these men were "not to be ranked in the category of real creators . . . and I am waiting impatiently for the moment when this audience that they believe themselves to have conquered will finally find its voice and neatly sweep away all this elegant scum."[72]

Fortunately for Renoir's peace of mind, he can have had no inkling when he wrote these words that the Popular Front he supported would be dissolved by the fall of 1938 and that it would be nine years—which would include the defeat and occupation of France in a world war—before French audiences would have another chance to see evidence of Chaplin's artistic renewal.

The Great Dictator in France

The single most crucial influence on the French reception of *The Great Dictator* (*Le Dictateur*), Chaplin's satire on Hitler (and Mussolini), was the long wait before it could be shown. The war delayed its arrival in Paris for over four years; it was not shown there until April 4, 1945. On the eve of its première in Paris, there was a huge military parade celebrating the liberation from German occupation, and as *Paris-Presse* noted, "for the first time after five years of black-out, Paris came out of the darkness and all the bells rang the resurrection."[73] The war now appeared in its final stages as allied armies pushed on to Berlin and the battle for Vienna raged.

The release of *The Great Dictator* at this particular moment seemed problematic to a number of reviewers. "We have known too closely the horror and the atrocity of the drama," Monique Berger wrote in *Le Populaire*. "Our spirit refuses, for the moment, to see it treated in parody, even if . . . with all the genius of Charlie Chaplin." "There is an incompatibility . . . between the clownishness of this extreme parody," Didier Daix similarly maintained in *Ce Soir*, "and the cruelty of the drama that inspired it. . . . Too often we see the Charlot . . . of his early films and this distracts in a film utterly impregnated with a real-life tragedy in which we ourselves . . . ended up being the sorrowful actors. . . . Where death reigns, irony loses its rights and ridicule no longer hurts."[74] "Without doubt," observed Jean Néry in *Le Monde*, "it is difficult for us, in France, to think abstractly of five years marked by sacrifices and sufferings."[75]

Most French critics seemed aware that *The Great Dictator* had been made in a different world, even if they were a little vague about precisely when. Bernard Zimmer, writing in *Paris-Presse*, asserted that was "produced in the era when the Anschluss [the Nazi takeover of Austria in March 1938] was not yet a reality." Monique Berger bluntly declared that it "was filmed in 1939." In actuality, Chaplin began work on the movie in October 1938, and the main shooting was between September 1939 and March 1940, with some retakes as late as September 1940.[76] To Jean Romeis of *Concorde*, its first service "to the cause of liberty" had been "to shake up the torpors" of Americans still at peace by promoting understanding of "what could cause dictatorship and of what grotesque elements it was made."[77]

In terms of the film's impact on France in 1945, four main critical perspectives can be distinguished. First, some critics believed that *Le Dictateur* had been weakened by its tardy presentation, that it was overtaken by events and outdated by 1945.[78] Second, Chaplin was complimented for his power of prophecy. Jean Romeis pointed out that "all the allusions of Charlot to concentration camps, the storyline [itself] . . . which is the putting into slavery by a single man of thousands of other men . . . are they not a repeated foreshadowing of what would be revealed to us by five years of war and Hitlerism."[79] Third was the recognition that the events of the Second World War had actually underlined the relevance and contemporaneity of the movie. "Far from being dulled by the facts," argued Gabriel Audisio in *Action*, the film "takes all its force from them, precisely because we are well aware of the racial persecution, the Hitlerian folly, the Nazi boot. In 1938, perhaps, we would have been *content* to laugh; in 1945, the tears come to our eyes: we know that while we come to laugh at it, it is [also] necessary to weep." G. Damas wrote on similar lines in *Témoinage Chrétien*: "It is certain that the painful events that have shaken the planet since the production of this film, tragically underline its impact."[80] Fourth was the view best expressed by G. Joly in *L'Aurore* that, rather than arriving too late, the film had in fact come too soon, "for the world, crushed under the iron heel of a Nero-style madman, has perhaps not yet regained enough serenity fully to admire this masterpiece."[81]

The fact that *The Great Dictator* was by far the most profitable film in France in 1945 suggests that many people did not worry too much about the inappropriateness or otherwise of its timing.[82] "Even at times of misery," declared Bernard Zimmer in *Paris-Presse*, "it is good to laugh. Sarcasm, derision, irony have their tonic virtues. We all have need of relief."[83] From the comments of several critics, however, it is evident that *The Great Dictator*'s combination of farce and political message proved disconcerting for some spectators.[84] François Chalais wrote in *Carrefour* of the ambivalence of "a crowd that laughs for an hour and a half in front of the acting of an inspired comedian and that, once the word 'end' disappears from the center of the screen, suddenly finds joy giving place to horror, is embarrassed by its bursts of laughter and applause, leaves on tiptoe, and dives into the entrances of the subway in order to be more quickly exposed to advertisements for less compromising shows."[85] Didier Daix also underlined mixed feelings among audiences: "We laugh, we guffaw unreservedly and good-heartedly. . . . Yet emotion is never very far away."[86]

Writing in *Les Etoiles*, Luc Estang provided an interesting account of how the reactions of audiences shifted throughout the course of the film. *The Great Dictator* revolves around the adventures of a Jewish barber (Chaplin), who fights for his country (Tomania) in the First World War but spends the next twenty years in a hospital with amnesia. He is unaware that a man called Hynkel (also played by Chaplin) has become dictator of Tomania and is persecuting Jews. The barber recovers and returns to the ghetto, but is eventually arrested and imprisoned in a concentration camp. Meanwhile, Hynkel is planning to invade the neighboring country, Osterlich. He invites Napaloni (Jack Oakie), the dictator of Bacteria, to participate but eventually double-crosses him and invades Osterlich alone.

To celebrate his conquest, Hynkel takes a vacation while the barber escapes from the concentration camp. Each is mistaken for the other, and the barber delivers a speech in which he denounces what the dictator has done and praises democracy. Estang saw the film twice, with several weeks between viewings. He thought the film could be divided into three parts in terms of audiences' response. In the first part, there was almost continuous laughter. The wartime sequences had so many gags, it seemed close to being "a new episode of *Charlot soldat* [*Shoulder Arms*, First National, 1918]." Even after the dictator appeared, this laughter continued "thanks to some exaggerated but precisely observed traits, such as the onomatopoeic shouts of rage, the frenetic pace of gestures, or thanks to the ballet sequence—juggling with the balloon globe of the world." In the second part, covering the adventures of the Jewish barber, the audience laughed only intermittently. The third part, covering the meeting of the two "grand-guignolesque [gruesome]" dictators, the invasion of Osterlich, and the barber masquerading as Hynkel, saw the laughter die out almost completely.[87]

When *The Great Dictator* was first shown in France, Adolf Hitler was still alive. He would not finally disappear from the scene until three and a half weeks later, on April 30, 1945, when he committed suicide to avoid capture by Soviet forces. For early reviewers of the film, he was a baleful—if reduced—presence on the international scene. No French critics of 1945 commented that Hitler and Chaplin were probably the most famous small men with mustaches (false, in Chaplin's case) in the world[88]—or that they had been born in April 1889, only four days apart. While Luc Estang observed mordantly after Hitler's death that he "does not remain in the memory of men as a comic character," he insisted "the adjusted perspective" wrought by the events of the war on the spectators of his film was not Chaplin's fault.[89]

Most reviewers agreed that Chaplin, although speaking a mixture of German-sounding words[90] and gibberish, had captured the essential sound of Hitler's voice.[91] To Zimmer, Chaplin re-created "the frenzied language of the tyrant . . . [a] strained voice that reminds us irresistibly of the raucous tone of the Hitlerian harangues." His delivery of Hynkel's speeches, Damas noted, was "a precisely observed satire" of something "that four years of occupation allow us to analyze with too distinctive a knowledge."[92] After the liberation, the widespread distribution in France of Frank Capra's series of seven documentary films, *Why We Fight*, with coverage of Hitler taken from Leni Riefenstahl's *Triumph of the Will* (1934) and newsreel footage, helped—as Badia, Jeanne, and other critics observed—make Chaplin's impersonation of Hitler seem additionally convincing.[93] The images of Hitler "in rages," Joly argued, emphasized that Chaplin had not distorted his model. Zimmer even suggested that Chaplin was "more Hitler than the real one we see, fanatical and vulgar, in front of the microphone throughout *Why We Fight*."[94]

While French critics in general admired Chaplin's impersonation of Hitler, they were more divided by the section of the film in which Hynkel/Hitler and Napaloni/Mussolini meet and attempted childishly to outmaneuver one another. Gabriel Audisio wrote of his astonishment that this fifteen-minute sequence was given so much importance since he found the meeting of the two dictators the least impressive sequence in the film and the only one to appear completely out of date. It was not simply that Mussolini had lost power in July 1943. (He would be executed by partisans coincidentally led by a man with the same surname—Audisio—as the French critic on April 28, 1945, two days before Hitler's suicide.) But the "meeting and rivalry" of the two men before the invasion of Austria/Osterlich seemed to Audisio both absurd and incredible.[95] Other critics, perhaps recalling that Hitler and Mussolini had both invaded France in the summer of 1940 (although Italian troops did not cross the border until two days before the French surrender on June 22), saw Chaplin's satire on the two dictators as a crucial part of *The Great Dictator*. François Chalais, indeed, argued that "all the sequence that presents the dictator and his transalpine competitor has such a strength of evocation that it would be necessary to have lived on a desert island since the assassination of [French] president [Paul] Doumer [in May 1932] not to be affected by it."[96] Critics disagreed not only on the significance of this part of the film but also over Jack Oakie's performance as Napaloni. Badia praised his Mussolini-esque "posturings," while Daix believed Oakie's talent had been frittered away in the production of "a vaudeville-style Mussolini."[97]

Some of the reviews of *The Great Dictator* commented on the changes that had taken place in France in the previous five years. Bernard Zimmer, in a second review, noted that "the welcome for this compelling film" had "everywhere [among newspapers] been a little reserved." He offered two very different theories to explain this phenomenon. "Is it," he speculated, "that what is left of a domestic press after four years, still not entirely purged of friends of Mr. [François] Vinneuil, could not have set the tone." Zimmer was referring to the vast changes that had taken place in the French newspaper world as a result of the war and occupation. Many great papers (including *L'Echo de Paris*, 1884–1942; *Le Matin*, 1884–1944; *Le Petit Journal*, 1863–1944; *Le Petit Parisien*, 1863–1944; *Le Temps*, 1861–1942) had ceased to exist by 1945. Vinneuil (Lucien Rebatet), had reviewed films for the pro-Vichy *L'Action Française* and had also written for the proto-Nazi *Je suis partout*. With the liberation, *Je suis partout* disappeared, *L'Action Française* was banned, and Rebatet fled abroad. Zimmer hinted that some French film critics were still sympathetic to the racial views of Hitler and Vichy, making it unlikely they would approve Chaplin's satirical film, with its critique of Hitler and antisemitism. His second theory was almost the direct opposite of the first. "Is it," he asked, "that the fellow-Jews of Chaplin were not expecting a more vengeful fierceness on his part?"[98] Zimmer's belief that Chaplin, playing the part of a Jewish barber, was himself Jewish fit with earlier rumors of Chaplin's origins.[99] But he offered no evidence to back up either of his theories over the rather mixed reception of *The Great Dictator*.

Monique Berger thought the film "a very labored caricature of Nazism," but other reviewers praised the deft ways in which Chaplin had underlined the barbarity of National Socialism. Gilbert Badia was greatly moved by the "image of Charlot—little Charlot—surrounded on all sides by the great strapping SS." Nothing, he believed, "better evokes the helplessness that one felt in Germany before the war, confronted with the brutality of the regime." Bernard Zimmer similarly praised the subtlety of the romantic scenes between the little Jewish tailor and his ghetto sweetheart, Hannah (Paulette Goddard): "their exquisite sense of decency, their constant delicacy contrasts with the brutality of the Nazis and makes the latter seem more odious."[100] After the French defeat of 1940 and the subsequent German occupation, it was unsurprising that anti-German sentiments often surfaced in reviews. At the end of Chaplin/Hynkel's speech in favor of peace, he is heartened by "an immense clamor of approval, of relief, of support" from the crowd. Zimmer found this a thoroughly false note: Tomania was "certainly" Germany, and the response of the crowd "flatters this incurably obedient people, passive, arrogant in victory and cowardly in defeat." Jean Romeis suggested that *The Great Dictator* even be used in the "political re-education of Germany."

"The day when the Germans . . . will laugh at," he wrote, "that is to say understand the ridicule and the infamy of 'Dictateur,' is when they will be cured [of dreams of war and conquest]." Yet since "that day is without doubt far away," Romeis bitterly concluded, it would be necessary to conserve copies of the film with care.[101]

Film critics inevitably considered *Le Dictateur* in the context of Chaplin's whole career. Didier Daix claimed that it "does not have the exceptional class of Chaplin's earlier films." G. Damas, comparing the opening sequences with *Charlot soldat* (*Shoulder Arms*), confessed that he preferred the latter. "It would be a long article," declared Jean Néry of *Le Monde*, "fairly melancholy to write, that could be entitled: From *Shoulder Arms* to *The Great Dictator*. It would show the graph of the genius of Charlie Chaplin, rising with *The Circus*, *The Gold Rush*, already slightly falling with *City Lights* and *Modern Times*, and showing a very distinct weakening with *The Great Dictator*."[102] Other reviewers were unimpressed by specific sequences of the film—François Chalais described the ghetto scenes as "mediocre," and Jean Sollies disliked the "grandiloquence" of the final speech (which seemed like something "for an agricultural show")[103]—but Néry believed a far more crucial problem with *The Great Dictator* was what he termed "the poverty of thought revealed in its scenario."[104] He also pointed out the dangers in Chaplin's abandonment of his Tramp persona. What this had accomplished, Néry argued, "was to incarnate the qualities and the minor defects of man. Each person . . . [could] see himself in him and laugh at his own reactions." Without the Tramp, Chaplin could no longer hope for such near-universal appeal.[105]

Chaplin, of course, had never lacked admirers in France, and a number of critics sprang to his defense. "No! Charlie Chaplin has not become dated!" insisted René Jeanne in *La France au Combat*. "No! *The Great Dictator* has lost none of its qualities because we have had to wait five years before being able to see it! No! *The Great Dictator* is not inferior to any of the previous films of its author!"[106] Some reviewers suggested Chaplin was reworking in new and creative ways aspects of his earlier work. Jeanne, in particular, said Chaplin was engaging in an adroit negotiation with his past. In the opening sequences of *The Great Dictator*, "he wades about in the trenches of 1918, but this time no longer in an American uniform as in . . . *Shoulder Arms*. This time, he wears a German hat and serves in an artillery battery. And what happens to him parallels almost exactly what happened when he was on the other side of 'no man's land.'" Jeanne also saw *The Great Dictator* as carrying on the protest at increased mechanization and the impact of science on human existence Chaplin had first launched in *Modern Times*.[107]

To some reviewers, the final disappearance of the Little Tramp was a sign of Chaplin's renewal rather than his decline. After the first shots of the film that, with their reference to *Shoulder Arms*, seem to suggest the reassuring continuity of Chaplin's Tramp, Gabriel Audisio remarked, "Chaplin disappears to be replaced by *a man*. See the first reaction of [Chaplin as] the Jewish barber to the first insult of a Nazi: he slaps the man in the face [with a paintbrush]. Certainly, he doesn't yet know the risks he runs, but Charlot would have begun by running away."[108] Another way in which Chaplin's on-screen persona renewed itself was through speech (though some critics complained about the quality of the dubbing of Chaplin's voice into French).[109] From being simply a mime artist, Chaplin metamorphoses into the most articulate of speakers. His final speech, substituting for the dictator, was such an "appeal for a free life, with fertile happiness and fraternal peace," commented Gustav Joly of *L'Aurore*, that it provoked an ovation from the audience.[110]

Chaplin may have proved in *The Great Dictator* that he was comfortable with a speaking role, but the three individual scenes that reviewers commented most favorably upon were all without speech. The one mentioned by nearly all critics—and which both Audisio and Jeanne called "dazzling"—was the sequence in which Chaplin's Hynkel performs a ballet with a balloon that is a globe of the world.[111] The sequence beautifully portrayed the meglomania of Hynkel/Hitler and his madness when the balloon finally bursts. The second scene mentioned by several critics was the one in which the Jewish barber shaves a very worried client to the energetic rhythm of Brahms's Hungarian Dance No. 5. The third was the slapstick sequence in which residents of the ghetto are asked to draw lots in order to decide who will assassinate Hynkel to save Tomania. Schultz (Reginald Gardiner), Hynkel's disgraced assistant and the barber's former protector, has concealed a coin in one of the cakes baked for the men to eat. The one who finds the coin will be the assassin. But Hannah has concealed coins in all the cakes, and the shots of this less-than-heroic group of men, without a word being spoken, transferring the coins to each other's plates (and of the barber swallowing three of them) demonstrated the enduring skill of the man described by Zimmer as "Chaplin, king of the silents."[112]

To many French critics, *The Great Dictator* was a compelling blend of comedy and tragedy.[113] Some compared it artistically to Shakespearian drama;[114] to the literature of the Spanish Golden Age, including Cervantes's

Don Quixote;[115] and, most frequently, what René Jeanne called "the same sad and profound laughter as Molière." "The laughter comes only to save us from a pain that is too close and would otherwise be insupportable," declared Gabriel Audisio, "as happens in the great works of Molière, above all in *Don Juan*." Yet as Audisio also made clear, although the film deals with tragic events, it ends on a note of redemptive optimism. All the great films of Charlot, he argued, save for *The Gold Rush* (and, he might have added, *Modern Times*) "finish pessimistically, with a man defeated by fate." But *The Great Dictator* ends "resolutely optimistic. The man no longer bends his spine before destiny. He straightens himself up."[116]

Chaplin in a Changing World

During the 1930s, Chaplin responded as a filmmaker to two crucial developments: the economic depression and the rise of fascism. Between 1933 and 1940 he produced two films, each dealing with one of these developments. Both movies reflected Chaplin's growing commitment to politics. In each case, they were received by French critics in ways that reflected the contemporary politics and culture of their own society. *Modern Times* arrived in France a few weeks before the elections that resulted in a left-wing Popular Front government, quickly followed by a wave of factory strikes. It repeated, and may have been influenced by, the scenes of industrial mass production in René Clair's earlier film, *À Nous la Liberté*. Yet Chaplin's film reached a much wider audience than Clair's had done. It was being shown in many industrial cities during the strikes in the summer of 1936. The enthusiastic response to it suggests that its critique of industrialism—and the effects of the depression—touched a chord with many. It was also welcomed by director Jean Renoir, a strong supporter of the Popular Front.

The Great Dictator, Chaplin's critique of Hitler and Mussolini, did not arrive in France until the Second World War was almost over. A film conceived in the last months of peace was received and interpreted in the light of six years of war and four of German occupation. Audiences flocked to see it, and in commercial terms it was a huge success. But some critics felt it inappropriate, in the light of the tragedy and destruction of the wartime period, to treat fascism in humorous terms. Others, while conceding that some aspects of the film were now outdated, defending it for its sophisticated blend of tragedy and comedy and its optimistic ending. Cut off from American news at least since the German declaration of war on the United States in December 1941, and understandably preoccupied with their own recent experiences, French critics of 1945 were unaware that Chaplin's antifascist sentiments from the time of *The Great Dictator* had evolved into strong wartime support for the Soviet Union. They were consequently even less prepared than Chaplin himself for the problems this would cause in the postwar period.

7

Chaplin After Charlot

From Cold War to Exile

On September 17, 1952, Charles and Oona Chaplin and their four children sailed from New York on the liner *Queen Elizabeth*. They planned to be in London for the world première of *Limelight* at the Odeon, Leicester Square, on October 23, and then to take a long European vacation. On September 19, when they were in mid-Atlantic, the news broke that U.S. Attorney General James McGranery had revoked Chaplin's reentry permit, given him in July, and ordered that, if he attempted to reenter the country, the Immigration and Naturalization Service would hold him for hearings over "whether he is admissible under the laws of the United States."[1] What had begun as a visit ended up as exile: for the rest of his life, Chaplin made his home in Europe. He would return to the United States for only a short visit two decades later.

Chaplin must have been aware when he left New York that there was a risk he would not be allowed to return. After nearly forty years in the United States, he had never applied for citizenship and remained a British national, vulnerable to being excluded under immigration law.[2] The exact legal justification for McGranery's action was found in the U.S. Code of Laws on Aliens and Citizenship that allowed aliens to be banned on the basis of "morals, health or insanity, or for advocating Communism or associating with Communists or pro-Communist organizations."[3] In the dozen years since the American release of *The Great Dictator* in 1940, many changes had taken place in Chaplin's life and reputation. He had become a controversial figure in the United States, criticized for his private life, his political views, and his art.

The Decline of Chaplin's Reputation and
Star Image in the United States

It was already fairly well-known by the 1920s that Chaplin was sexually attracted to very young women. Both his first wives, Mildred Harris and Lita

Charlot. Melvyn Stokes, Oxford University Press. © Oxford University Press 2026.
DOI: 10.1093/9780197839294.003.0008

Grey, were still teenagers when they married. Chaplin had survived without too much difficulty the scandal launched in 1927 by Grey's divorce petition, which had listed in some detail his sexual demands. A year before his final breakup with Paulette Goddard, he met Joan Barry, a twenty-two-year-old with whom he would have an on-off affair for a year and a half. During this time, it was later alleged, Barry had twice become pregnant and twice been pressured by Chaplin or his representatives into having illegal abortions. In May 1943, Barry was pregnant again. This time, the news became public knowledge. Virulently right-wing Hollywood gossip columnist Hedda Hopper denounced Chaplin on June 3, 1943, for a variety of things, political as well as personal, and accused him of abandoning Barry. A few hours later, Barry's lawyer filed a paternity suit.[4]

The FBI now became interested in a trip Barry and her mother had made to New York in 1942. Since Chaplin had paid for this, FBI agents believed there might be a case for charging him under the Mann Act of 1910 for transporting a woman across state lines for immoral purposes. In March–April 1943, Chaplin was tried on Mann Act charges and acquitted by a jury.[5] Barry's baby was born on October 2, 1943, and four months later blood tests conclusively proved that Chaplin could not be the father. But this did not bring the star's public humiliation to an end: blood tests were inadmissible as evidence in California courts. Chaplin had two more paternity trials, in December 1944 and April 1945. In each case, there was a hung jury. The judge at the conclusion of the second trial finally brought the whole unsavory story to an end by ordering Chaplin to pay child support for Barry's daughter, Carol Anne, until she reached the age of twenty-one.[6] The impression created of Chaplin during the successive trials was deeply damaging to his star image,[7] and the fact that he married eighteen-year-old Oona O'Neill, daughter of playwright Eugene O'Neill, in June 1943 did little to help.

It was almost certainly the fallout of the Joan Barry scandal that was uppermost in Attorney General McGranery's mind when, defending his action in rescinding the reentry permit, he alleged that the press had accused Chaplin of "grave moral charges." In his justification he also pointed out that the actor was accused of being a member of the Communist Party.[8] Chaplin's association with American communists began at least as early as August 14, 1922, when the Los Angeles field office of the Bureau of Investigation, forerunner of the FBI, reported that he had hosted a reception at his home for William Z. Foster, a leader of the American Communist Party.[9] In the late 1930s, a number of his employees—including Dan James, who worked on

The Great Dictator with him—were communists. James was responsible for introducing him to Harry Bridges, a communist who had helped organize and later led the Longshoremen's Union.[10] In the second half of the 1930s, Chaplin clearly sympathized with the Republican side—supported by the Soviet Union—in the Spanish Civil War. He was, in the terminology the FBI would later apply to many left-wingers, "prematurely anti-fascist." At some point—David Robinson suggests during winter 1936–37—he wrote a poem dedicated to a "loyalist soldier" lying dead "on the battlefields of Spain," a victim of "treachery" while playing his part in "freedom's dauntless march." In April 1938, French film magazine *Cinémonde* published a translation of a Chaplin short story called "Rhythme" about the execution of a Loyalist who had once been well-known as a humorous writer.[11] A year later, according to the testimony of Dan James, Chaplin was "horrified" by the Hitler–Stalin pact of August 1939. It was only with difficulty that James and another of Chaplin's employees, Robert Meltzer, persuaded him not to denounce Stalin by name in his final speech in *The Great Dictator*.[12]

The political confusion created by the initial stages of the Second World War disappeared when Hitler's attack on the Soviet Union (June 1941) and the Japanese assault on Pearl Harbor (December 1941) helped turn the Soviet Union and the United States into unlikely allies. In this new situation, Chaplin was among those disturbed by lingering American anti-Soviet sentiment. During the war, for the first time in his life he took on a major role as a public figure, speaking in favor of war relief for Russia and, increasingly, demanding a "second front" in Europe. In the six public speeches he made between May and December 1942, Charles Maland argues, Chaplin "gradually, perhaps imperceptibly to him, moved from a focus on the necessity to oppose the Nazi threat to a tendency to praise the Soviet allies and urge closer ties with them."[13] Although this was not unusual at the time—*Time* magazine, owned by conservative Republican Henry Luce, made Stalin its "Man of the Year" for 1942—the December 1942 denunciation of Chaplin by conservative journalist Westbrook Pegler for being too pro-communist was a straw in the wind.[14] It underlined Chaplin's vulnerability should political circumstances change.

By the time *Monsieur Verdoux*—Chaplin's first film since *The Great Dictator*—had its première in New York in April 1947, American anticommunism was hardening with the advent of the Cold War. At a press conference in New York the day after the première, Chaplin was repeatedly questioned about his political views. While some reviewers liked *Monsieur*

Verdoux, the balance of opinion was hostile and few Americans went to see the movie. When Chaplin withdrew the film from circulation in mid-1949, its gross box office stood at what Kenneth Lynn calls "a paltry $325,000."[15] "In the six and a half years that elapsed between the release of *The Great Dictator* and *Monsieur Verdoux*," writes David Robinson, "Chaplin's troubles over the Joan Barry paternity case and the growth of the McCarthyist spirit had served to effect a reversal in the public's estimation such as few artists since Oscar Wilde had experienced."[16]

It was not only the Joan Barry affair and his reputation for being a communist sympathizer that hurt Chaplin as an artist, however. At the heart of his relationship with his fans, Charles Maland points out, lay an "aesthetic contract": Chaplin provided them with obvious comedy, especially of the slapstick variety, bound up with romance and pathos and clearly representing "two moral universes, one good and one evil."[17] In *Monsieur Verdoux*, he played a character—based on French mass-murderer Henri Landru (1869–1922)—that was about as far from Chaplin's traditional Tramp figure as it was possible to go. The humor this time was macabre and less obvious; there was very little slapstick. Monsieur Verdoux himself is driven to crime by social forces: as a consequence of financial panic and the ensuing depression, he is made redundant from the bank where he has worked for many years. To look after his invalid wife and child, he turns to seducing and murdering a succession of wealthy women. The film had a strong political undertone. It took aim at the capitalist system, which it associated with state violence. At his trial, Verdoux argues that crime pays only when conducted on a large scale—by business. He also arraigns atomic America (if not by name) as a criminal nation. Chaplin had not only broken his "aesthetic contract" with his American fans. He had made a progressive, left-wing film as the Cold War was starting and the House Committee on Un-American Activities (HUAC) was about to launch a major investigation into Hollywood.

Chaplin and Postwar France

In France during the postwar years, however, Charlot remained a popular figure. *Le Dictateur* proved hugely successful after its release on April 4, 1945. Most French commentators (with the exception of the surrealists in 1927) had never revealed much prurient interest in Chaplin's sexual peccadilloes, and the Joan Barry accusations and the subsequent court cases were largely unknown in France as a consequence of the German occupation, the lack of French journalists reporting from the United States, the disappearance of many old newspapers and cinema trade journals, and the distractions of the final stages of the war. It aided Chaplin's reputation in France that his final appearance in court in the paternity suit brought by Barry occurred just a month after the German surrender and two months before the destruction of Hiroshima and Nagasaki by nuclear bombs brought the war finally to an end. Moreover, the isolating influence of the war effectively meant that the French in general had no awareness that Chaplin had moved beyond the mildly left-wing critique of mass production in *Modern Times* or the comical antifascism of *The Great Dictator*. To most French immediately after the war, it was as if Charlot had stayed the same; even the Jewish barber in *The Great Dictator* seemed a first cousin to the Little Tramp.

The allegations concerning Chaplin's closeness to communism and the Soviet Union, even if more had been known about them, would probably not have had the same impact in France, where the political situation was very different from that in the United States. In France, the old right wing had been largely discredited by the war, with many of those who had supported the Germans—or the puppet Vichy regime—imprisoned, executed, or on the run. The PCF, in contrast, emerged strengthened from its role in resisting the German occupation. It was part of President Charles de Gaulle's provisional government, formed in September 1944, and remained in government after de Gaulle's resignation in January 1946. In May 1947, communist ministers were finally dismissed from the ruling coalition for refusing to support continuing efforts to reconquer French Vietnam and the imposition of a wage freeze on workers. Even after their removal from government, the PCF remained the largest party in France's parliament, the National Assembly. In the French legislative elections of November 1946, the PCF won more votes (28.6%) than any other party, and in subsequent elections under the Fourth Republic would regularly win more than 25% of all French votes.[18] The contrast with the situation in the United States could not have been sharper. In the same month, November 1946, the Republican Party won control of both houses of Congress, setting up the context for growing right-wing manipulation of anticommunism—both foreign and domestic—in the early years of the Cold War.

There was one other subtle (and sometimes not so subtle) influence, in addition to the consequences of the German occupation and the political strength of the PCF, that framed the way many audiences and critics in France perceived Chaplin in the years after the end of the war: the phenomenon of French anti-Americanism. Some French could not forgive the American bombing of cities such as Le Havre and Royan (where napalm was first used) during the war. Others minimized the American contribution to the defeat of Nazism. Public opinion polls conducted in France in September 1944 and May 1945 revealed that a majority of the population saw the Soviet Union as more important to the Allies' victory than the United States. Many French people worried that the United States would prove too conciliatory in its treatment of Germany, and some remembered the refusal of the U.S. government after World War I to link the paying off of France's war debt to German reparations.[19] There were also increasing French anxieties about a multifaceted American invasion, both cultural and commercial, once the war ended. There were still approximately 100,000 American armed services personnel stationed in France after 1945—a presence that some on the extreme left equated with the Nazi occupation.[20] The PCF, blaming Washington for being behind its ousting from the government in 1947, thereafter savaged "every feature of the American presence in France." In June 1947, general secretary of the PCF Maurice Thorez attacked the United States as an imperialist power posing a threat to world peace.[21] Also in the 1945–47 period, a number of left-leaning (but not PCF) French intellectuals visited America and disliked much of what they saw. Jean-Paul Sartre hated what he regarded as American conformism, Simone de Beauvoir disapproved of what she perceived as a lack of historical consciousness and skeptical intellectual life, and Albert Camus disliked skyscrapers and what he saw as remorseless American cheerfulness.[22] It is hard to quantify how far such anti-Americanism had grown by early 1948, but the knowledge that *Monsieur Verdoux* had been much criticized in the United States probably made some French more determined to demonstrate their anti-Americanism by liking it.

Chaplin Under Pressure: 1947

Although Chaplin had been found not guilty in April 1945 of the Mann Act charges, it was inevitable that some of the mud produced by the Joan Barry paternity and Mann Act cases would stick. On the eve of anticommunist paranoia emerging on a massive scale in the United States, Chaplin was uniquely vulnerable as a consequence of both his wartime support for the

Soviet Union and his sexual adventures. The fact that he had never bothered to take American citizenship also marked him out for right-wingers as an alien presence—both legally and metaphorically—in the United States.

That Chaplin was now a figure of controversy on a major scale first became evident at the ill-tempered press conference held at the Gotham Hotel in New York the day after the première of *Monsieur Verdoux* on April 11, 1947. He was repeatedly quizzed over his views on communism.[23] On March 7, a month before the release of *Monsieur Verdoux*, Senator William Langer of Missouri had demanded Chaplin's deportation on the grounds of his communist sympathies and his involvement in the debauchery of young American girls. On June 12, Congressman John T. Rankin also demanded Chaplin's deportation in very similar terms. And, as the year continued, it seemed more and more inevitable that Chaplin would be called to testify by that major expression of political paranoia, HUAC.[24]

In early July 1947 rumors began to surface in the United States that Chaplin would shortly be called by HUAC. Chaplin himself refused to be intimidated. On July 21, newspapers reported that he had telegrammed J. Parnell Thomas, chairman of the committee, staking out a combative position. "In order that you may be completely up-to-date on my thinking," the actor informed Thomas, "I suggest you view carefully my latest production, *Monsieur Verdoux*. It is against war and the futile slaughter of our youth. I trust you will not find its humane message distasteful. While you are preparing your engraved subpoena I will give you a hint on where I stand. I am not a Communist. I am a peacemonger." In September 1947, Chaplin did receive a subpoena from HUAC but was never invited to testify. As a congressional committee, HUAC was more about publicity than politics. It was rumored that, if called, Chaplin planned to turn up dressed as the Little Tramp. Thomas and the other HUAC members may have judged they would not come off best in such a confrontation.[25]

On the face of it, Chaplin remained defiant. He supported the presidential campaign of Henry Wallace, the leftish Progressive Party candidate for the presidency, in 1948. In April 1949, he issued a statement in support of a Paris meeting of the communist-fronted World Congress for Peace and, in September 1949, endorsed the Mexico City meeting of the communist front American Continental Congress on World Peace. Yet he had already received a warning shot: in April 1948, the U.S. Immigration and Naturalization Service interviewed him at length in connection with a proposed visit to London. Afterward, Chaplin decided to remain at home in California.[26]

By 1950 there were signs that Chaplin was rowing back from his political commitment to left-wing politics—and also that he was endeavoring to restore his popularity with cinema audiences. One part of this strategy was the re-release of *City Lights* in 1950, reminding people of the glory days of the Little Tramp. Another was the decision to make his next film, *Limelight*, with its incorporation of autobiographical elements from his early career as a music-hall entertainer. All to no avail. Chaplin's dalliance with the left had made him many powerful enemies. Director J. Edgar Hoover harried the FBI—and to a lesser extent the Immigration and Naturalization Service—to produce evidence against him. The FBI itself leaked some of the information it gathered to Hedda Hopper, who had taken Joan Barry's side in her disputes with Chaplin. The Internal Revenue Service was also involved. The whole sorry saga, writes Charles Maland, demonstrates "how various institutions in American culture . . . the press, the FBI, Congress, and other administrative agencies like the IRS and INS . . . can cooperate formally and informally to discredit someone like Chaplin."[27]

French Attitudes to the Persecution of Chaplin

For many French commentators, 1947 was a year in which domestic issues often took prominence over what was happening abroad. Four days after the première of *Monsieur Verdoux* in New York, *L'Humanité*'s front page focused on the shortage of meat in Paris.[28] With the withdrawal of the PCF from government in May 1947,[29] the tempo of industrial protest in France had markedly increased. Strikes formed the background to the municipal elections that took place in October, with *Paris-Presse* reporting that the combination of industrial unrest and the success in the elections of the right-wing Gaullist Rassemblement du peuple français had effectively doomed the government of socialist Paul Ramadier.[30] The PCF, now in opposition, consolidated its position in the elections: *L'Humanité* claimed that the communist vote had been higher than in the municipal elections two years earlier.[31] French newspapers noted that, for some American observers, a worrying feature of the election had been the sharp decline of the "center" parties—the Christian Democratic Mouvement Républicain Populaire and the socialist Section Française de l'Internationale Ouvrière—and the new confrontation between the extreme left and right.[32] In November and early December 1947, France was wracked by a series of industrial and transport strikes.[33]

Despite continuing preoccupation with domestic (and colonial) affairs, some French newspapers nonetheless managed to report on the changes taking place in American attitudes to communism both abroad and at home during the crucial months of 1947 in which the Cold War effectively began. Alarm in Washington at expanding Soviet power and influence led to a new policy of "containment," with the United States offering economic and military assistance to countries resisting communist aggression or subversion. The new policy was launched on March 12, 1947, when president Harry S. Truman asked Congress for 400 million dollars in aid to Greece and Turkey.[34]

The political struggle to secure congressional agreement was covered by several French newspapers: the initial approval by the Senate Foreign Relations Committee, the adoption by the Senate itself, the final approval by Congress, and Truman's signing the bill into law.[35] By the summer of 1947, however, American policymakers were increasingly concerned by the possibility that much of Europe, economically devastated by the war, might fall victim to communism. In June, Secretary of State George C. Marshall announced that the United States would offer financial aid to help European economies recover. After several months battling congressional opposition, what would become known as the Marshall Plan was signed into law in April 1948. Yet, faced earlier with the possible collapse of the French and other economies, on December 17, 1947 the United States had already agreed to give emergency aid of 40 million dollars to France and three other countries.[36] Eleven days earlier, *France-Soir* reported that such American aid would be conditional: it quoted the assurance of Undersecretary of State Robert A. Lovell to the Senate Committee on Emergency Aid that no such assistance would go to France if communists were part of the government.[37]

There was also coverage in France of the growing American campaign against internal communist subversion—coverage revealing awareness from the very beginning that this campaign was an attempt by Republican rightwingers to discredit their opponents. As early as January 1947, Henri Pierre wrote in *Le Monde* that HUAC had "an unfortunate tendency to describe as 'red' all liberal, 'progressive' or pro-Soviet elements."[38] French newspapers mapped various strands of the anticommunist movement. One was the unsuccessful attempt to formulate and pass legislation to ban the Communist Party USA.[39] A second was the political struggle over the enactment in June 1947 of the Labor Management Relations Act (otherwise known as Taft-Hartley), with its antiunion and anticommunist provisions.[40] A third was the public hearings held by HUAC in the fall to investigate communist subversion in Hollywood. During the first week of these hearings, a series of "friendly" witnesses appeared. Jack Warner of Warner Bros. and Louis B. Mayer of MGM were questioned about—among other things—the pro-Soviet films produced by their studios during the war, *Mission to Moscow* (1943) and *Song of Russia* (1944), respectively.[41] Walt Disney insisted that all the members of his studio were "100% Americans."[42] Right-wing actors Robert Taylor (who had starred in *Song of Russia*) and Adolphe Menjou also testified. Menjou (who had once starred in *A Woman of Paris*) singled out Charlie Chaplin in particular for criticism, attacking him for his "communist sympathies" and his support for "those who wish to use film as a means of overthrowing the government of the United States."[43]

Since in the end, despite receiving a subpoena from HUAC, Chaplin was never called to give testimony, French commentators—while noting Menjou's attack—did not develop the story further. There were, in fact, only three periods during 1947 when the press covered Chaplin stories in any detail. The first came with the première of *Monsieur Verdoux* in New York. French critics and writers emphasized that the film reflected the final disappearance of the Little Tramp.[44] All that physically remained of Charlot, according to *Le Canard enchaîné*, was the mustache on the face of Verdoux.[45] To *Ce Soir*, *Monsieur Verdoux* was "the most original film that Chaplin has ever made." Its subject, a reworking of the story of wife-murderer Henri Landru, would—according to *Paris-Presse*—have put off all other filmmakers.[46] Stylistically, commentators observed, there was little in common with Chaplin's earlier pictures: *Monsieur Verdoux* offered no sweetness or hope, its humor was black and bitter, and it moved quickly from comedy to drama.[47] French reporters and critics, broadly favorable to Chaplin, showed themselves apprehensive about the film's reception in the United States. A writer in *Le Canard enchaîné* cautiously pointed out that, although reviewers had been "very harsh" in their initial treatment of *The Great Dictator*, the film had subsequently been recognized as a classic.[48] *Paris-Presse* wisely commented that the applause at the end of the première "does not mean very much. It's necessary to await the reaction of the critics and the real public . . . to judge the probable fortunes of this new production." The same article noted that the publicity campaign preceding the film's release had provoked a parallel campaign by "some local journalists" who had accused Chaplin of being sympathetic to communism. "It is," remarked *Paris-Presse* of such anti-Chaplin allegations, "the fashion of the times."[49]

A writer for *Le Canard enchaîné* saw the character of Monsieur Verdoux as very much a reflection of Chaplin's growing isolation in the United States. "Why," he asked, "is Verdoux so alone, so antisocial, so very moving in his cynicism? Because this is what Charlie Chaplin has become." The reason for the change in Chaplin's outlook was easy to identify, he argued:

> You have only to open it doesn't matter which American newspaper. Chaplin is the man who, for many years, has been mercilessly pursued by all the bigots, all the chauvinists, all the imbeciles without talent from all over the country.
>
> Columnists who have nothing to write, for the good reason that their heads are empty, can always attack Chaplin, covering with mud one of the greatest artists of our time. Chaplin is sensitive, creative, independent. He will never howl with the wolves. So, Chaplin is the enemy![50]

At his press conference the day after the première, the same writer noted, Chaplin had confronted a barrage of questions: whether he was a communist, what he had done in the war, why he did not participate in American political life or become a U.S. citizen, and what his views were of the USSR. "The press conference," the commentator concluded, "had become a veritable court of justice with Chaplin as the accused." Abandoning *Le Canard enchaîné*'s traditional house style, based on satire and cynical detachment, the columnist came down warmly on Chaplin's side, tartly dismissing his tormenters as "a pack of dogs" whose attacks "knew no respite."[51]

The second period with Chaplin much in the news in France came in June. On May 20, 1947, *Le Figaro* reported that the chair of HUAC had alleged—based on the testimony in secret session of actor Adolphe Menjou and studio boss Jack L. Warner—"that several eminent Hollywood filmmakers were notorious communists."[52] Just over three weeks later, it was made clear that Chaplin in particular was under suspicion. Several French newspapers covered the June 12 speech by Mississippi Democratic congressman John Rankin, a leading member of HUAC, in which he demanded Chaplin's expulsion from the United States. Rankin was quoted complaining that Chaplin had refused to become an American citizen and insisting that his very life was an "attack on the American social structure." Expelling him from the United States, Rankin argued, "would make it possible for us to distance him from American screens and avoid having our young people influenced by his degrading films."[53] This news, remarked the left-leaning *L'Aurore*, was "more surprising than it might appear (Chaplin really leads, in his Beverley Hills villa in Hollywood, a thoroughly bourgeois existence with no taint of political Machiavellianism)." The newspaper also found it very strange that, with all of Chaplin's films making a profit for those who financed them, "America should seriously be thinking of expelling the man who remains its greatest comedian." But the reporter for *L'Aurore* at the same time made it clear that the move to oust Chaplin was "the logical consequence of a campaign, waged for several years, against the maker of *Modern Times*. His repeated refusal to swap British for American nationality, the paternity proceedings . . . which he lost, the humanitarian speeches with which his last film, *Monsieur Verdoux*, was peppered, had only increased the contempt in which he was held by a small section, to tell the truth very limited, of American opinion."[54]

Chaplin's own immediate riposte to Rankin's call for his expulsion from the United States was approvingly quoted in several French newspapers: "This kind of procedure . . . is a traditional method used by fascists. It consists of an attempt to suppress the liberty of speech and of expression, above all in what concerns cinema."[55] "Experience has shown where this intellectual ostracism ends up," commented *Le Monde*, expanding Chaplin's criticism into a more general indictment of totalitarianism of both left and right. "It begins by condemning someone's work as 'degrading' and 'pernicious,' then it ends by reducing the author to silence. A totalitarian technique tried and tested in Berlin and Moscow."[56] In the statement he issued, reported *Ce Soir*, Chaplin implied that it was his critique of warmongers that had prompted Rankin's action: "My film *Monsieur Verdoux* is essentially pacifist and this seems the major reason for the anxieties of Mr. Rankin." *L'Humanité* similarly explained the demand for Chaplin's expulsion in terms of "the violent campaign recently launched in the United States" against *Monsieur Verdoux*, with the film attacked "for building up a subtle critique of those who are thinking about leading the world into a new war."[57] Coincidentally, the same issue of *Ce Soir* that covered Rankin's speech also broke the news of the first success of this "Boycott Chaplin" campaign: the banning of *Monsieur Verdoux* in Memphis, Tennessee.[58]

In *Le Monde*, Henri Pierre emphasized the seedy ambivalence of Chaplin's attacker: "Mr. Rankin is of his kind certainly a unique case. . . . he has given proof of a complicit indulgence towards the terrorists of the [Ku Klux] Klan and other professional persecutors of blacks. His harshness is uniquely practiced against communists, and above all against a good number of liberals labeled circumstantially as 'reds.'"[59] Pierre plainly disagreed with the view expressed in *L'Aurore* that Chaplin's critics were only a small minority. He located Rankin's diatribe within a much wider context in which right-wingers sought to restrict freedom of expression among those on the left. Citing an attempt to prevent left-winger Henry A. Wallace, vice president of the United States from 1941 to 1945, from speaking in Washington, Pierre declared, "Democratic liberties are decidedly in bad shape. Never before has the world boasted so many volunteers ready to kill in order to cure. But there are certain remedies that kill the patient more surely than the illness itself."[60]

While they were covered far less in the French press, in the last weeks of 1947 Chaplin made two gestures that had significant implications. The first grew out of the arrival of German composer Hanns Eisler in Hollywood in April 1942. Eisler and his wife became close personal friends of Chaplin, and together with a group of other emigré left-wingers, including Bertolt Brecht, they supported him during the Joan Barry trials. Both Charles Maland and Kenneth S. Lynn suggest that Eisler and Brecht may have influenced the politicized humor of *Monsieur Verdoux*.[61] In early February 1947, Eisler's brother Gerhard was arrested in the United States and charged with passport fraud. A few days later, accused by his sister, Ruth Fischer, of being a Soviet agent, he was called to testify by HUAC.[62] At his confrontational press conference at the Hotel Gotham in New York on April 14, Chaplin was asked if he was "a personal friend of Hanns Eisler, the composer." He responded that he was and was "very proud of the fact." This exchange then followed:

Question: Are you aware of the fact that his brother is a Soviet agent, so attested by—
Chaplin: I know nothing about his brother!
Question: Do you think Mr. Eisler is a Communist?
Chaplin: I don't know anything about that. I don't know whether he is a Communist or not. I know he is a fine artist and a great musician and a very sympathetic friend.[63]

Chaplin was disingenuous in denying knowledge of Eisler's political beliefs. Like Brecht, Eisler had been a Marxist since the 1920s. In common with Gerhard Eisler, he was accused by his sister of being a Soviet agent.[64] Also like Gerhard, he was subpoenaed to give testimony to HUAC and appeared before the committee in both May and September 1947.[65]

Chaplin must have realized, in part at least because of his close relationship with Hanns Eisler, that he was likely to be called in by HUAC. When it was reported in the papers in July that Chairman Thomas had said as much, Chaplin fired off his "I am not a Communist. I am a peacemonger" telegram to Thomas. A few weeks earlier, he had joined a group demanding that the trial of Gerhard Eisler and others for contempt of Congress be delayed, according to the U.S. Communist Party newspaper *The Daily Worker*, "in order that they may have proper time to prepare their case and in order to avoid undue prejudice against them at a time when red-baiting hysteria is so violent."[66]

In late November 1947, when it seemed increasingly probable that deportation proceedings would be launched against Hanns Eisler and his wife, Chaplin cabled artist Pablo Picasso in France asking if he "could bring together a committee of French artists with the aim of protesting to the American Ambassador in Paris about the criminal deportation facing Hans [*sic*] Eisler, and send me a copy of the protest for use over here."[67] Chaplin did not know Picasso other than by reputation. It would not be until he was in Paris in 1952 for the première of *Limelight* that the two met.[68] But he was clearly aware of Picasso's importance in artistic and cultural terms and may also have remembered the way surrealist intellectuals and artists in France had rallied to his own cause in 1927. "I doubt," Chaplin's son Charles subsequently commented, "if the incongruity of asking a confirmed Communist [Picasso at that point in his life] to intercede for a man accused of Communism in a non-Communist country ever even entered my father's head. He was an artist appealing to another artist to come to the aid of a third artist."[69]

The protest letter finally delivered to the ambassador was signed (whether because of the prestige of Chaplin, of Picasso, or more likely of the two combined) by a large cross-section of the Parisian intellectual and cultural elite, some of them—in common with Picasso—members of the Communist Party. It was made up of artists (Christian Bérard, Henri Matisse, Picasso), writers (Louis Aragon, Francis Carco, Jean Cassou, André Chamson, Louis-Martin Chauffier, Paul Éluard, Henri Malherbe, Léon Moussinac, Elsa Triolet), two composers (Georges Auric and Claude Delvincourt), a conductor (Roger Désormières), two actor-directors (Jean-Louis Barrault and Louis Jouvet), several actors (Pierre Brasseur, André Luguet, Françoise Rosay, Madeleine Renard), and screenwriter and film director Jacques Feyder.[70] The episode of the Picasso telegram demonstrated both Chaplin's courage and his loyalty to his friends, on whom he came increasingly to rely as his own isolation in Hollywood intensified.[71] But it also encouraged his enemies. The New York branch of the Catholic War Veterans responded to the Picasso telegram by sending telegrams of its own, to the secretary of state and attorney general, demanding an investigation into the affair. The Los Angeles branch of the FBI later showed a similar interest, and in 1949 Republican senator Harry P. Cain cited it as a reason for Chaplin's own deportation.[72]

The year 1947 ended dramatically with the publication in France of a controversial article in which Chaplin criticized Hollywood, attacked his critics, and effectively predicted his own exile from the United States. It was published in the weekly *L'Action* under the title "I've Had Enough of Hollywood."[73] According to Chaplin, Hollywood was "dying." It no longer had "anything to do with cinema, which is supposed to be an art." All that mattered any longer was mass-producing "kilometers and kilometers of film" according to the same old formulas. There was no longer the prospect "for anyone to gain any cinematographical success if he refuses to conform his behavior to that of all the others, if he presents himself as a pioneer who dares to defy the rules produced by the big business of film." As an example of what he had in mind, Chaplin cited Orson Welles, the director of *Citizen Kane* (1941) and the man who had first come up with the idea for what became *Monsieur Verdoux*. Welles had "dared to say 'no' to the men of big business. And now he is finished in Hollywood." According to Chaplin, Hollywood was "fighting its last battle and it will lose it, unless it stops mass-producing films, unless it finally understands that cinematic masterpieces cannot be born from assembly-line production, like tractors in a factory."[74]

Chaplin saw American movies as declining in artistry and creativity because studio bosses ("big-shots") were interested only in guaranteed profits from formulaic productions and were intent on squeezing out original filmmakers like Welles and, by implication, himself. In reality, of course, his argument that money should "no longer [be] the all-powerful god of a decaying community" was very much a response to the financial failure of *Monsieur Verdoux*. He himself had been a major figure in Hollywood for a generation because of his success in producing over seventy very profitable films between 1914 and 1940, most of them dealing—in a formulaic, if often highly inventive fashion—with the adventures of Charlot, the Little Tramp. Ignoring the fact, moreover, that *Modern Times*, *The Great Dictator*, and *Monsieur Verdoux* had all in their different ways been "political" films, Chaplin also pleaded that art should not become mixed up "with the dubious political intrigues that are spreading across the world." What he had in mind, of course, was the reception of *Monsieur Verdoux*, especially in New York, where—he noted resentfully—he had been accused of being "communist" and "anti-American." He also denied that he was a "revolutionary, a fire-brand," as a journalist from Boston had alleged. Chaplin had been deeply wounded by the many attacks he had suffered, both personally and as an artist. While he would not be forced out for nearly five more years, by the end of 1947 he was apparently already beginning to think that, to preserve his artistic independence and faith in himself, his days in Hollywood—and America itself—were drawing to a close. "I will certainly before long leave the United States," he wrote prophetically in *L'Action*. "And in the country where I go to finish my life, I will try to remember that I am a man like all the rest and that I have the right, in consequence, to the same respect as other men."[75]

Differing American and French Reactions to *Monsieur Verdoux*

Although some American critics liked *Monsieur Verdoux*, the weight of critical opinion in the United States was hostile.[76] "A very large part of those who wrote about *Monsieur Verdoux*," comments David Robinson, ". . . felt a positive duty and determination to execrate *any* work" by Chaplin, and many reviews in the "more popular press" were characterized by "hysterical anger."[77] Reviewers often looked back nostalgically to the early Chaplin films. They felt his choice of subject matter this time was unfortunate: the life of a murderer was not an appropriate theme for comedy. Some critics even suggested that comedians in general should not take on serious roles. Others, including John McCarten in the *New Yorker* and Philip Hartung in *Commonweal*, praised the film's comedy sequences but asserted that attempts to put across what Hartung called a "spurious social philosophy" distracted attention and undermined the film as a whole. To some American critics, the film perfectly expressed what Chaplin had now become. Its "broadsides of indictment against society (particularly the ruthlessness of business)," argued the reviewer in the *Christian Science Monitor*, "become merely petty and meaningless expressions of hatred, contempt, and personal bitterness."[78]

If *Monsieur Verdoux*—as Tino Balio pointed out—grossed only 325,000 dollars in the United States in the two years after its release, it made over 1.5 million dollars *outside* the United States. In France, where it premièred in January 1948, the film's reception was particularly warm. It did very well at the Paris box office.[79] It also proved popular—according to the cinema trade press—in the Midi (the South of France), especially in Marseilles, where it played simultaneously in three houses, but also in Avignon, Toulon, Nice, and Cannes; in the southwest, including Bordeaux, Tarbes, Béziers, and Montpellier; in Nantes in the west and Dijon, Strasbourg, and Metz in the east.[80] Its commercial success in France can be explained in a number of ways. It was a Chaplin film, and both *Modern Times* and *The Great Dictator* had demonstrated his continuing ability to appeal to French audiences. Like *L'Opinion Publique* (*A Woman of Paris*), it had a French theme and French characters, set this time in 1930s Paris. Most French spectators saw a version of the film dubbed into French. There was an initial series of complaints from reviewers that this version was greatly inferior to the original one in English,[81] but ordinary spectators seem to have demonstrated little concern over this. According to Jean Antoine in *Paris-Presse*, "they unreservedly applaud Charlie Chaplin 'speaking French' and because they understand, they approve what he has said in full knowledge of the facts."[82] In many ways, indeed, French cinemagoers seem to have responded more warmly and positively to the film than a number of reviewers.

Jean Renoir and André Bazin

The first French commentator seriously to engage with *Monsieur Verdoux* did so three months after its American release. In July 1947, writing from Hollywood, director Jean Renoir greeted it as an example of Chaplin's artistic spirit that would one day locate him "alongside . . . the paintings of the French Impressionists, between a tale by Mark Twain and a minuet by Lully." "I don't believe," Renoir insisted, rather disingenuously, "that the people who attacked Chaplin so sharply over his latest film did so for personal or political reasons." In essence, they had panicked when confronted with a "particularly long step forward" in Chaplin's evolution as an artist. Comparing Chaplin to Molière, Renoir made a spirited defense of an artist's right to change. He specifically defended Chaplin for abandoning his Tramp persona in order to enter "a world that is more dangerous, because it is closer to the one we live in." The Little Tramp belonged exclusively to the fairy-tale world of the movies. *Monsieur Verdoux* "really takes place in our own time, and the problems faced on the screen are really our own."[83]

A second writer, who was to become one of Chaplin's greatest champions in France, also published an essay on *Monsieur Verdoux* before the film's

Paris première. André Bazin, who had written amusingly in 1945 about the mustache of Chaplin/Hitler/Hynkel in *The Great Dictator*,[84] was also responding to criticism of the film in the United States. "We understand," Bazin wrote, "that Mr. [Eric] Johns[t]on [president of the Motion Picture Association of America, the association of film studios], the spokesman for the Legion of Decency, and all the American women's clubs, found the last of Chaplin's films smacked of heresy."[85] Bazin, who had seen *Monsieur Verdoux* in Czechoslovakia before its French release, argued that the film was an artistic masterpiece, susceptible to interpretation in an "inexhaustible" variety of ways. Chaplin's own opinions, whatever he may or may not have intended, "have no more importance than those of Mr. Homer or Mr. Shakespeare because their works reveal just as many." What the film had done, according to Bazin, was to transform the traditionally passive Charlot-as-victim into "his complete opposite . . . a Charlot who would dare to challenge the world." But the new Charlot-as-Bluebeard proved almost as likable as his predecessor: "If it is so easy for Verdoux to turn us against society, it is because we do not stop—even for an instant—being on his side." In the end, Bazin suggested, the earlier Charlot and Verdoux became fused together: when Verdoux has his hands tied and is taken off to be executed, it is Charlot's face and customary "bouncy walk" that are shown, allowing "hundreds of millions of people . . . to witness the death of the greatest hero of modern mythology."[86]

Bazin expanded considerably some of the ideas contained in this essay in response to a critical article about the film from French writer Nathalie Moffat. Born Nathalie Sorokine, Moffat now lived with her screenwriter husband Ivan in Los Angeles. A former lover of both Simone de Beauvoir and Jean-Paul Sartre, she had already published an account of the making of *Monsieur Verdoux*, based on visits to the Chaplin studios, in Sartre's journal *Les Temp Modernes* (itself named after the French title of Chaplin's *Modern Times*).[87] Moffat published her critique of *Monsieur Verdoux* in July 1947, also in *Les Temps Modernes*.[88] According to Bazin, she identified two major faults in Chaplin's film: first, that it was devoid of psychological realism; second, in sharp contrast to his American critics, that it *lacked* a political message. "Marxists," Bazin wrote, "condemn Chaplin for his pessimism and for not clearly formulating the message they felt he owed them since . . . *Modern Times*. Thus literary and political distortion join hands. Those in favor of a classical art with a psychological foundation find themselves in agreement with the politically minded."[89]

Bazin's answer to Moffat was first published in *Les Temps Modernes* in December 1947; a final version appeared in *Revue du Cinéma* in January 1948.[90] He argued that Moffat dismissed the work as "ideologically, psychologically, and aesthetically incoherent" for the most part because she—as well as other critics—failed to see it as part of what he termed "the Chaplin myth."[91]

This myth, in Bazin's eyes, had begun with "a person called Charlie," a "black-and-white form printed on the silver nitrate of film." The form "had proved human enough to grip us and encourage our interest and sympathy." Over time, it developed "enough continuity of appearance and behavior . . . to attain to the autonomous existence of what is called . . . 'a character.'" Other screen characters had emerged at the time, "but there was an exceptional depth [to Charlie] . . . the appeal of a special kind of credibility, a consistency of behavior . . . a magical radiance in his glance" that somehow differentiated him. In less than fifteen years, Bazin observed, "the little fellow with the ridiculous cut-away coat, the little trapezoid moustache, the cane, and the bowler hat, had become part of the consciousness of mankind. Never since the world began had a myth been so universally accepted."[92] In Bazin's eyes, this myth of "Charlie" had grown across many films with different narratives and settings. The structure and story of these films was less important than the presence of Charlie and how he responds to the situations in which he finds himself. Charlie's own character evolves: at first, he is "rather naughty" but later transforms into "Saint Charlie of *The Kid, The Circus* and *Gold Rush*."[93] The character of Verdoux is the dialectical opposite to this but (and this was Bazin's principal point) is still recognizable as Charlie: "Charlie is always there as if superimposed on Verdoux, because Verdoux *is* Charlie."[94] This distracts attention from Verdoux's "qualities or his defects," since "the audience's sympathy for Verdoux is focused on the myth, not on what he stands for morally."[95]

Bazin's essential argument was that "the moment one includes Monsieur Verdoux in the Chaplin myth everything becomes clear, ordered, crystallized."[96] He found the basis of the film's psychological realism in Charlot's preference for women modeled after "the tender and gentle Edna Purviance." The only difference is that, in *Monsieur Verdoux*, Charlie is married and attempting to care for an invalid woman of this type.[97] At this point, in attempting to contextualize Charlie/Verdoux's misogynistic "assault on women"—the killing of the "wives" he marries for their money—Bazin considerably extended the "Charlie" myth. Chaplin, he suggested, had first been interpreted as a "Bluebeard" figure by "public opinion . . . even before he created *Monsieur Verdoux*."[98] Although he did not mention Chaplin's divorces, numerous affairs, and the Joan Scott imbroglio, these were clearly what he had in mind. But Chaplin, Bazin believed, had substantially vindicated Verdoux "in the viewer's mind" by choosing for the part of Annabella Bonheur, the one woman he tries and fails to kill, "the unspeakably comic termagant, . . . Hollywood's number-one pain in the neck, the nagging Martha Raye, who could . . . justify the acquittal of a dozen Bluebeards." At this point, Bazin blended the psychology of the mythical Charlie he was writing about as a screen character with that of the real Chaplin who, he wrote, "symbolically recoups, through Monsieur Verdoux, the alimony extorted from him with the complicity of American society and the law by various 'Edna Purviances' who turned into 'Martha Rayes' after divorcing him."[99] In his attempt to explain—possibly even excuse—Verdoux's misogyny, Bazin's "Charlie" myth is expanded to include Chaplin's image as the Tramp, the characters he and Martha Raye have previously played on screen and his decision to cast her in *Monsieur Verdoux*, extrafilmic public knowledge of his personal life, and even a theorization of his psychological motivation in making this particular movie.

From an aesthetic point of view, Bazin held that "the only serious formal criticisms that can be leveled against a Chaplin film concern its unity of style, the unfortunate variations in tone, the conflicts in the symbolism implicit in the situations." He conceded that from this perspective, "the quality of Chaplin's films since *The Gold Rush* has definitely fallen off. . . . even *Modern Times* suffers from an evident lack of unity between gags."[100] Ordinarily "this falling off in quality in Chaplin's next to last films" was explained by the influence of "a parasitic ideology." Chaplin "has some pretensions to being a social philosopher," and whereas his earlier films did "not set out to prove anything . . . there is no mistaking the purpose or theses of *Modern Times*, *The Great Dictator*, and *Monsieur Verdoux*." Bazin made abundantly clear his own hostility to this change: Chaplin's attempted politicization of his movies was "an encumbrance," something "we could willingly do without." To whatever extent a film character was animated by a "message," he noted, this "displaces the myth and tends to displace the character too." Yet this process was by no means automatic. "Thank God," Bazin fervently declared, "this destruction does not follow as inevitably as one might suppose. The myth resists; harassed and constrained by Chaplin's ideas, it finds in the genius of Chaplin himself a way to escape from them."[101] *Monsieur Verdoux* might suggest the final abandonment of the Little Tramp character (Bazin endorsed Chaplin's right to evolve in his screen roles), but the broader Charlie myth survived, ensuring the movie would remain a work of art rather than a political critique.

"It is difficult to know what Chaplin's ideological intentions were in conceiving this film," Bazin concluded, "but they have in no sense interfered with the character [of Verdoux himself] since his behavior in the situations in which he finds himself is thoroughly autonomous, coherent, and meaningful."[102]

French Critics and *Monsieur Verdoux*

When *Monsieur Verdoux* had its French première in January 1948,[103] some critics adopted Renoir's line that the film was a further step in Chaplin's artistic development. "*Monsieur Verdoux* was necessary," insisted Robert Pilati in *Ce Soir*. "It was a stage in the evolution . . . of Charlot." Pilati believed that "since the first Charlots, Chaplin has become more and more serious" while remaining "just as funny."[104] P.R. similarly argued in *La Cinématographie Française* that the Charlot of *Monsieur Verdoux* was much changed: there was now "a Charlot who was urbane, distinguished, broad-minded, transformed in spirit. The comic expressions of Chaplin are still the same, but this mask, between bouts of craziness, is sometimes somber, bleak, and resolute in adversity."[105] Aware that the film had been much criticized by American reviewers, some French reviewers sought to preempt attacks of this kind in France. *Monsieur Verdoux*, declared Gustave Joly, "will doubtless arouse the same polemics as on the other side of the herring pond [Atlantic], where his non-conformism and his anarchistic tendencies were vehemently denounced." Joly himself hailed it as "a very great film made with impeccable technique. The mastery of Charlie Chaplin is dazzlingly confirmed; never has his restraint been more moving and his humor more direct." But that humor, he cautioned, was now "mixed up with a bitterness that will not be to the taste of the whole world."[106]

In many of the reviews, Chaplin had clearly moved from being a marginal, mythical figure (the Tramp) into a political symbol of the late 1940s. "The little man of earlier times," observed *Le Canarde enchaîné*, "has become, in 1948, laden with the weight of the dark years, of all the experiences, of all the crimes of a mad humanity."[107] In the socialist *Le Populaire*, Monique Berger hailed the emergence of a new Charlot—one who was "in revolt against injustice, against misery" and made people laugh "through the strength of cruelty and lucidity."[108] In *Jeunesse ouvrière*, a fortnightly Catholic publication for young workers, Jean Thevenot interpreted *Monsieur Verdoux* as a direct outcome of the personal travails Chaplin himself had recently encountered. This had given a "passionate sincerity" to his new critique of social injustice.[109]

In the United States, the social message of *Monsieur Verdoux* made the film unpopular because it seemed to challenge essential American values revolving around capitalism, individualism, and the search for wealth. As Pierre Kast shrewdly commented in *L'Action*, Chaplin's Henri Verdoux shed light on "the fundamental relations of man with society," but this was "not society in general, but very precisely capitalist American society." To Kast, "the France of the film" did "not resemble the real one."[110] In France, there appeared to be much more understanding of the more fixed nature of social hierarchies. Robert Pilati wrote of the character of Verdoux in *Ce Soir*: "A bank employee over twenty years, he had seen how the important people of the world acted. He had come to understand that there was only one place in the world for the strong and that to have scruples no longer made sense."[111] To Pilati, the character of Verdoux was "exactly contrary" to the earlier character of the Tramp. Where the Tramp had been "timorous, he has become cynical; formerly hesitant, he is now powerful and determined. His clothes are well-cut, his step assured." Yet, for all the changes, "Verdoux is still Charlot. The poor man clipping the feathers of the rich," and at the same time taking "revenge, in passing, on his old enemies: the police and women, whom he poisons with great panache."[112]

Inevitably, perhaps, *L'Humanité*, the official organ of the French Communist Party, offered the most detailed and favorable view of *Monsieur Verdoux*. Chaplin, wrote Guy Leclerc, "is the man who has always denounced with courage the abuses of capitalist society: the power of money, the Taylorism [of the mass-production line] which reduces the worker to the level of a pitiable automaton, the social injustice of all kinds, the warlike imperialism and fascism." *L'Humanité*'s critic admired Chaplin for the courage he had shown in daring to criticize capitalism in its most important bastion. For this, Leclerc maintained, he had been subject to "slanders, threats and most refined persecutions" by "the Hearst Press, [Eric] Johnston [of the Motion Picture Association of America], the Legion of Decency, and the Ku Klux Klan." To *L'Humanité*'s film critic, Chaplin's troubles all derived from his interest in the Soviet Union and critique of American capitalism. He had "tried to push to their most absurd consequences the fundamental principles of 'this jungle that is society.'" Leclerc admired Chaplin's courage, fighting "alone or almost alone, in the most powerful bastion of international capitalism." But he believed that "the revolt of individuals can offer glimpses of new truths. It cannot lead to anything definitive." In order to be able to fight capitalism "with solidarity and confidence," Leclerc argued, Chaplin needed to join the communist-led "world struggle against the malignity of current society."[113]

Other French reviewers were alienated by the political and social attitudes set forth in *Monsieur Verdoux*. Perhaps the most outspoken was humorist Hervé Lauwick in *Noir et Blanc* magazine. Lauwick originally discounted the hostile views of American critics for whom Chaplin was a "red," but after viewing the film he confessed he now agreed with them. Chaplin had become serious and lost his sense of humor: "the greatest comic of the world, when he takes up philosophy, bores us." Worse, some of the political points in the film were "naive enough to make one weep": Lauwick cited Verdoux's claim to the judge that "when a man kills one person, he is a murderer; when he kills thousands, he is a hero." This simply was untrue: "neither Hitler nor Himmler were heroes." To Lauwick, the few gags in the film were insipid and it ended up no better than "the middling sort of little French comedies." Formerly a huge fan of Charlot, the screening left him completely disillusioned.[114]

Henri Michel, writing in *Education nationale*, declared that the new film "obliges us to say goodbye to Charlot. Not only because of the decline of his comic imagination, already clear in *The Great Dictator*, and the disappearance of the cane and moustache—these were only accessories." Chaplin's silent films had often ended with his heading off in hopeful anticipation of "roads without end and space without limit"; the last scene of *Monsieur Verdoux* showed him led away at dawn to the guillotine. Like Lauwick, Michel criticized Chaplin's unconvincing references to morality and politics and dismissed Verdoux's philosophizing as "puerile." In contrast to Renoir and Bazin, he saw *Monsieur Verdoux* not as a step forward in Chaplin's development as an artist but as confirmation of his "difficulty in renewing himself." Cinema was an art based on continual reinvention; Chaplin evoked now only "retrospective" interest.[115]

In *Le Figaro*, Louis Chavet criticized Chaplin's attempt to combine humor with an attempt "to make this modern Bluebeard a public accuser who, towards the end, preaches like the Charlot of *The Great Dictator* against political and social iniquities." It had been, he wrote, "a serious error . . . to entrust the grapes of wrath to a monster such as Landru." Treating Verdoux as a serious commentator reduced the character's comic potential, while the fact he was a mass-murderer gravely undercut his social message. Chavet insisted that Chaplin's now-abandoned Tramp figure, "with his clumpy shoes, his shabby stick, his despondent walk . . . transmitted to us his movements of revolt against the world that was badly made much more efficaciously than M. Verdoux with his glossy paradoxes" while "entertain[ing] us much more at the same time." Chavet judged *Monsieur Verdoux* "in terms of humor . . . [as] an almost total failure. We don't laugh any longer. The film's rare funny moments have a diminished effect."[116]

To Claude Hervin of *Paris-Presse*, the making of *Monsieur Verdoux* was essentially an attempt by "a man of genius, whose destiny has been bound up with that of the cinema," to escape that destiny. Yet the attempt had failed: "under the disguise of Monsieur Verdoux and in spite of all the efforts of his creator, Charlot remains Charlot." But Chaplin himself was now too politicized: "when he sets himself up as a social critic," Hervin insisted, "when he tries to show his hero as a victim of the cruelty of men, when he calls upon the universe to witness the misfortunes of Verdoux and his family—while serving up a facile sentimentality and the demagogy of the public meeting— then we cannot follow him any more."[117]

For Henry Magnan of *Le Monde*, the principal weakness of the film was the mismatch he discerned "between the murderer, who is scarcely more able to repulse us than Charlot [himself], and the reality of his crimes—that are not actually shown on the screen—[creating] a sense of absurdity that will shock. This, together with the preachiness we are coming to deplore that has in part caused this incongruity, is the most serious reproach that I will level against *Monsieur Verdoux*."[118] Magnan also dismissed the political message of the film, writing ironically of the "joy of learning—following [philosopher Jean-Jacques] Rousseau and [left-wing singer-songwriter Gaston] Montéhus—that society perverts man, that it manufactures weapons and has people who are unemployed." At the same time, however, he confessed that it was "impossible to describe the funniness of some scenes . . . the boating scene is pure classic Charlot; the sudden bursts of energy that agitate him at the least sound of bells—and God knows there are plenty of these!" Magnan recognized that Chaplin was changing his style of filmmaking, but hoped he would always keep his ability "to convey the bitter-sweet flavor of daily life." He cited, by way of example, Verdoux's response to the offer of a glass of rum before his execution: "He makes a vague gesture of turning it down then changes his mind: 'Yes, give me this glass. I have never tasted rum.' He inhales it, savors it, tastes it, fills his lungs with air and his eyes with light, then marches towards the scaffold, joyous until the very end in taking all from the life he is about to leave."[119]

Henri Queffelec, in the syndicalist newspaper *La Bataille*, similarly praised the film's last moments as "magnificent." *Monsieur Verdoux* had its comic aspects (Queffelec singled out the scene in which Verdoux believes he himself has been poisoned) but succeeded as a mélange of "tragedy, vaudeville, sentimental drama, farce and pantomime." Certain passages were overlong, Queffelec believed, and "two or three" scenes seemed lacking in taste. As a critic, he was far from certain that "those who love cinema" would like *Monsieur Verdoux* ("a bizarre and uneven film"). Queffelec was nevertheless struck by the engaged and enthusiastic response of the audience when he viewed the film: phrases such as "crime doesn't pay for ordinary people" and "a single murder makes a criminal, millions make a hero" were greeted with loud applause.[120]

Although Chaplin's political views were under attack in the United States, French critics and intellectuals rallied to his defense. In the same year that *Monsieur Verdoux* arrived in France, the French Association of Cinema Critics unanimously—across all political viewpoints—demanded that Chaplin be awarded a Nobel Peace Prize. In a letter to the Norwegian parliament, the Association declared, "The nature of Chaplin's films is shown by their pacifist character, by the love of humanity shown in them. . . . This nature . . . becomes especially more marked in his two last films, *The Great Dictator* and *Monsieur Verdoux*, which contain, in their last parts, statements that have most certainly contributed powerfully to diffusing Mr. Alfred Nobel's dearest ideas."[121] The Association seemed unaware of the irony of asking the Nobel Prize for a filmmaker who, in *Monsieur Verdoux*, had comprehensively indicted armaments manufacturers such as Nobel himself.

Chaplin's Reception in France: September 1952

The liner *Queen Elizabeth*, carrying the Chaplin family, docked at Cherbourg in the early afternoon of Monday, September 22, 1952. At 14:30, sixty journalists were allowed onboard for a press conference with Chaplin. Most of them knew that Chaplin had declared, in a mid-Atlantic radio interview with news agency Reuters, that he was not "worried" by suggestions that the U.S. Department of State had gathered a dossier accusing him of "moral turpitude" to prevent his returning to the United States after his European trip. They had also been told that at the press conference he would respond to the various allegations made against him by Attorney General McGranery.[122] French newspapers had already covered the remarkable turnaround in Chaplin's fortunes: on September 19, Léo Sauvage pointed out in *Le Figaro* that he had obtained his reentry permit without any difficulty. Later that same day, Attorney General McGranery announced both the revocation of the permit and an inquiry into whether he should be allowed back into the United States.[123]

Journalists and photographers from France, Britain, and the United States were shown into the Winter Garden on the liner's promenade deck. Full of wicker chairs, it was decorated with geraniums, chrysanthemums, and orchids. When Chaplin entered the room, he was greeted by a storm of applause and cries of "Bravo!" Wearing a navy blue suit, he looked pale—a paleness accentuated by the whiteness of his hair. The only splash of color was a red ribbon worn under his suit. One French journalist, Henry Neel of *Le Figaro*, thought he was wearing the sash of the Légion d'honneur; another, Christine de Rivoyre of *Le Monde*, perhaps more familiar with clothing and fashions, believed he had made an imitation sash out of the hair ribbon of one of his daughters.[124]

Chaplin began by posing with "extraordinary amiability" for the photographers. He moved on to answering journalists' many questions with patience and good humor—even if, at times, it seemed to some that he was sad, perhaps even bitter.[125] At this point in time, Chaplin knew he had to choose his words with care. He had not yet accepted the inevitability of exile from the country where he had lived for almost forty years and was uneasily aware that "everything I possessed was in the States."[126] He said he hoped to go back but could not be sure precisely when. He expressed surprise at what had happened. Chaplin insisted that the immigration service had issued him a valid reentry permit three months earlier (allowing ample time for any necessary inquiry before his departure) and that the immigration service official he had dealt with in New York had expressed best wishes for a good journey and a speedy return. Claiming, disingenuously, that he was ignorant of the reasons for the actions of the U.S. government, Chaplin insisted that he was apolitical: he was not a politician, had never belonged to any political party, and his only political conviction was "I believe in liberty."[127]

Now under intense pressure, Chaplin retreated to the position he had advanced on the eve of his departure for Europe in 1921: that he was an artist, not a politician. At Cherbourg, he presented the two as being in conflict, with art threatened by politics. "I'm afraid for the future," Rivoyre of *Le Monde* quoted him as declaring. "Ours is no longer the world of the great artists. It's a world of froth, turmoil and bitterness. A world overrun, drowned by politics."[128] Most French journalists, sympathetic to Chaplin, did not challenge his construction of himself as a misunderstood artist who knew nothing of politics. Yet one newspaper, the communist *L'Humanité*, in an article published after the news of the revocation of the reentry permit but before the press conference in Cherbourg, broke ranks by clearly listing the political reasons for his exile:

> In reality, what people have reproached Chaplin for is that all of his work—from *Shoulder Arms* to *Modern Times* and *Limelight* [*Les Feux de la rampe*]—takes on, as he himself has said, "the defense of the little man"; that he ridiculed fascism in *The Great Dictator*; that from June 1942 he demanded the opening of a second front in the war; that he declared himself [in his telegram of July 1947 to HUAC chairman J. Parnell Thomas] a "peacemonger" [*un fauteur de paix*]; that he welcomed the [Soviet-backed] World Peace Conference [in Paris in April 1949]; that he supported the Progressive Party candidate [Henry Wallace, who campaigned calling for better relations with the USSR] in the American presidential election of 1948; [and] that he protested against the expulsion [from the United States] of composer Hanns Eisler.[129]

Chaplin's Reception in France: October–November 1952

After the press conference was over, Chaplin with his family (and twenty of the British journalists) sailed to Southampton on the *Queen Elizabeth*. On October 16, he attended the world première of *Limelight* in London. A few days later, leaving their children with a British friend, Chaplin and his wife Oona, together with his secretary-publicist Harry Crocker, traveled to Paris for the French opening of *Limelight*. Their Air France DC-3 landed at Orly Airport on the afternoon of Wednesday, October 29, to be greeted "with enthusiasm" by "a dense crowd of photographers, journalists, and bystanders."[130] The Chaplins were welcomed by film directors Louis

Daquin and Jean Benoit-Lévy, Marxist cinema writer (and former surrealist) Georges Sadoul, director-screenwriter-actor Carlo Rim, representing the Society of Playwrights and Composers (Société des auteurs et compositeurs dramatiques), and André Lang, president of the French Union of Cinema Critics (Syndicat français de la critique de cinéma).[131] They were taken to a room in the airport where, surrounded by "a battalion of air hostesses," Chaplin made a few remarks into a microphone, mainly recalling his first visit to Paris, in 1909. Scarcely had he finished when a customs and immigration officer asked to see the passports of the three visitors, which he pronounced "perfectly in order."[132] Getting from this room to the large gray limousine waiting to take the Chaplin party to the Ritz Hotel proved difficult. The crush in the terminal was still so great that the French luminaries who had come to greet Chaplin, together with the police, acted as a phalanx surrounding the three new arrivals to get them through the mass of enthusiastic fans. So complete was the confusion that many in the crowd (including reporter Pierre Macaigne of *Le Figaro*) failed to get any clear sight of Chaplin at all.[133]

By the time the little party reached the Ritz, a crowd was gathering in front of the hotel on the Place Vendôme. One young girl carrying a bouquet of flowers arrived ten minutes after Chaplin and refused to believe that he was already inside. The Chaplins and Harry Crocker occupied a five-room suite looking out over the hotel gardens. At 19:00, Chaplin gave a press conference attended by around three hundred people, both French and non-French.[134] The conference itself was chaotic. Although United Artists had tried to restrict admission to "specialist journalists" by issuing invitation cards, many others gained entrance, including the international lettrists who were attacking the lettrism of Isidore Isou (see chapter 4), adding to the confusion created by the constant popping of photographers' flashbulbs.[135] Christine de Rivoyre of *Le Monde* commented that Chaplin appeared to know only two phrases in French: he said he would be going away for the weekend from the Gare Saint-Lazaire (he pronounced it "Sainte-Lézard") and he loved "beautiful Paris" (though he got the gender of Paris wrong). After this, what Chaplin said at the conference was translated by the press attaché of United Artists. Since this man's knowledge of English was barely that of a fifth-grade lycée student, Rivoyre sardonically commented, "the sharp and sparkling spirit of the maker of *Limelight*" was passed on in French "watered down to the point of anemia."[136]

Chaplin was asked if he would ever return to the character of Charlot, the Little Tramp. He responded negatively, arguing that "since [Franklin D.]

Roosevelt and the advent of the 'common man,' this character had lost his importance. Who does he resemble these days?" Some journalists raised the perennial subject of Chaplin's projected film about Napoleon. Chaplin confessed that he had originally intended to create a Napoleon who was "childish" and "conceited," "quick-tempered and poetic," but the actions of Hitler had made him forget about Napoleon in order to put all of his energies into *The Great Dictator*. Asked which of his own films he preferred, Chaplin "naturally" chose his latest: *Monsieur Verdoux* and *Limelight*. Yet he also expressed some anxiety over the welcome French spectators would give to *Limelight*. "It isn't a silent film," he pointed out, "consequently not as universal as the ones you have loved." He even speculated that *Limelight* might be *too* much a talkie and expressed hope "that the sub-titles are well-made, so that you can understand me." Ignoring both the personal problems created by the revocation of his reentry permit and the fact that he had come to Europe to publicize a new film, he asserted—improbably after nine years of marriage and four children—that the trip was "above all a delayed honeymoon."[137]

From the very start of Chaplin's visit, French politicians showed their support for him, put off neither by the past indiscretions of his private life (Attorney General McGranery's "moral turpitude") nor his supposed association with communism. Vincent Auriol, a socialist, had been president of France since January 1947. He invited Chaplin to the Elysées Palace at 20:30 on the day of his arrival in Paris. There, fresh from the press conference at the Ritz, he was present at a private screening of *Limelight* for Auriol, his cabinet, and some of his personal friends.[138] On Friday, October 31, Chaplin and his work were again officially honored (as in 1921 and 1931) by the French state. At a 17:00 ceremony at the headquarters of the Society of Playwrights and Composers on rue Ballu, he received a promotion within the Legion of Honor, being elevated from knight (*chevalier*) to officer (*officier*). The presentation was made by André Marie, the minister of national education. By tradition, three speakers then paid tribute to Chaplin's achievement: Roger Ferdinand, president of the Society of Playwrights and Composers; director, screenwriter, and actor Carlo Rim; and Marie himself. In his autobiography, first published twelve years later, Chaplin reprinted a long letter from Ferdinand, praising Chaplin's "fidelity" to his "earliest memories" (as expressed in *Limelight*) and his record as an author of filmic stories and music.[139] He probably said much the same at the Society of Playwrights and Composers. (One critic commented that he spoke "like a monotonous chant.") Rim, with humorous hyperbole, argued that Chaplin's glory "surpassed that of Joan of Arc, Louis XIV, and Clemenceau," with Jesus Christ and Napoleon as his only real equals. Marie hailed him as a "man of substance." Chaplin listened to the speeches, wrote a tactful commentator, "in a language that he admires but doesn't understand." In his own remarks, he claimed that he had recognized the names of the "great men" to whom he had been compared, that he had "never been more proud of my life," and that all the praise had gone to his head.[140]

On Thursday, October 30, the day before Chaplin became an officer of the Legion of Honor, a second private screening of *Limelight* was held at the Biarritz cinema on the Champs-Elysées. The cinema was packed with journalists, critics, and people involved in the movie industry.[141] Since Chaplin was present, the performance—effectively if not in name—became a gala première.[142] The screening was preceded by the showing of an animated cartoon (*Woody Woodpecker*), which satisfied none of those waiting impatiently to see *Limelight*. Then Chaplin suddenly appeared on the first-floor balcony. André Lang, president of the French Union of Film Critics, greeted him with some pompous words. ("I award you the much-envied title of number one friend of the public.") Film director Jean Delannoy, speaking "in an English that was shaky but touching," offered a similar panegyric to the uniqueness of Charlot. Chaplin himself, leaning on the handrail of the balcony, asked everyone to sit down and declared that, since he was too nervous about how the audience would respond to *Limelight*, he would creep outside once the cinema had gone dark. He reappeared at the end of the film, to the crowd's cheers, "his eyes bright with joy and tears."[143]

After the performance was over, Chaplin was the guest at a reception organized jointly in his honor by the Society of Playwrights and Composers and the French Union of Film Critics at the Crichton Club on the rue François I. Because of the enormous crush of people there, Christine de Rivoyre of *Le Monde* commented, the buffet was as unreachable as the summit of the Himalayas. Chaplin had asked that a piano be installed on a platform, perhaps intending to demonstrate that he was a composer as well as an actor-director, but quickly disappeared in the crowd.[144]

The next day, straight after the Legion of Honor ceremony, *Limelight* opened to the public simultaneously at four large Paris cinemas: the Marignan, the Marivaux, the Normandie, and the Rex. Chaplin, together with his friend Jean Renoir, attended the first performance, at the Marignan. Associated Artists had also invited to the Marignan for this first performance Prime Minister Antoine Pinay, Minister André Marie, and—among other guests—the American and British ambassadors.[145] This time Chaplin seems to have stayed and watched the movie. Afterward he rounded off an eventful day (which had included a trip to the Louvre Museum and a walk in the Bois de Boulogne, the park to the west of Paris) by taking Oona to supper at Maxim's on the Champs-Elysées.[146]

In general, Chaplin later wrote, he and Oona were "received like conquering heroes." They were invited by President Auriol to lunch at the Elysées and also went to lunch at the British Embassy on the rue du Faubourg St. Honoré. On Wednesday, November 5, they were the guests of honor at a special gala performance of Molière's *Don Juan* at the Comédie Française. "That night," Chaplin recalled, "the fountains of the Palais Royale were lit up and flowing and Oona and I were met by students of the Comédie Française, dressed in eighteenth-century liveries and holding lighted candelabras." The students escorted them to the Grand Circle, filled, noted Chaplin—always susceptible to attractive females—"with the most beautiful women in all Europe." That evening, he met President Auriol for the third time in little more than a week.[147]

Two days earlier, Chaplin had been the guest of playwright Henri Bernstein and the stage and screen actors of Paris at the Théâtre des Ambassadeurs. Many of the best-known French stars of the time were present, including Pierre Blanchar, Fernand Gravey, André Luguet, Jean Marais, Gaby Morlay, and Valentine Tessier. Bernstein, as the master of ceremonies, welcomed Chaplin from a box in the stalls. There followed a moment of pure farce: Chaplin, on the stage, in moving closer to hear him, fell into the prompt box. He recovered quickly with a throwaway line: "This is what I do every day." Actor and stage director Jean Darcante, after a short speech, presented him with an 1860 edition of the "Registre de La Grange," the record kept by Molière's troupe of traveling actors between 1659 and 1685. With the audience now warmed up, he read an account of the death of Molière. After much applause, Chaplin made a short speech of thanks. "You French," he declared through an interpreter, "are gifted with eloquence. I'm not. I will tell you that I love you and that I feel myself at ease with you, my brothers, for we have the same mission: to entertain people."[148]

During a busy few days in Paris, Chaplin also managed to see his old acquaintance from the surrealist movement, Louis Aragon, together with Pablo Picasso and Jean-Paul Sartre, neither of whom—despite his telegram to Picasso on behalf of Hanns Eisler in 1947—he had previously met. When Aragon telephoned to say that Sartre and Picasso would like to meet him, Chaplin invited all three to dinner. Since they preferred to meet "somewhere private," Chaplin asked them to dine in his suite at the Ritz. His publicity agent, Harry Crocker, was concerned at the whole idea: Aragon was now a member of the Central Committee of the French Communist Party, Picasso had joined the Party in 1944, and Sartre had embraced Marxism even if he had not become a Party member. Crocker was worried that, if the news of the meeting leaked out, Chaplin's chance of returning to the United States would be considerably reduced. (In his autobiography, Chaplin joked that Crocker was not invited to dinner because "we expected Stalin to arrive later and did not want any publicity about it.")[149] The dinner itself was not a great success. Chaplin later wrote that he was "not too sure about the evening. Only Aragon could speak English, and conversation through an interpreter is like shooting at a distant target and waiting for the result of your aim." Later that evening, after Aragon and Sartre had left, Picasso took Chaplin and his wife to his Left Bank studio, which Chaplin remembered as "the most deplorable, barnlike garret," with dusty old masterpieces scattered around it. According to Picasso's later account, the two finally managed to communicate with each other without interpreters when Picasso took the comedian up to his painting studio and showed Chaplin the pictures he had recently being working on. Chaplin "understood at once" and pantomimed hilariously some of the actions from his earlier films.[150]

There was some feeling in parts of the press that, given Chaplin's reception by President Auriol, his "sumptuous" lunch at the Ministry of Industry and Commerce on November 6, the tributes paid him by the smart set of diplomats, filmmakers, and entertainers known as "Tout-Paris," he had now all but completely abandoned his persona as Charlot, the Little Tramp. "We can only state," declared a writer for *La Cinématographie Française*, "that Charlie Chaplin has truly become a very officially-recognized personality, something that would have made the 'Charlot' of 1914 smile." A cartoon in *Le Canard enchaîné* even suggested that the old Charlot would have found it impossible to break through the welcoming crowds and police line at Orly Airport to greet international star Charlie Chaplin when he arrived on October 29.[151] Christine de Rivoyre of *Le Monde*, one of the journalists who had seen Chaplin onboard the *Queen Elizabeth*, asserted:

Since *Monsieur Verdoux* we have known that the "Underdog" with the walk of a hunted penguin had, in a supreme flourish, relegated his walking stick to the museum of his accessories. His walking stick, his giant clumpy shoes, the flour with which he coated his face of a modern Pierrot, capped with a bowler hat. Yes—sunny Cherbourg relentlessly confirmed for us—Charlie Chaplin from now on is the precise opposite of Charlot. A white so striking, there where in spite of oneself one looked for black: this smile of ceruse [a cosmetic containing white lead as a pigment], this hair like moonlight, these eyes colored like wet slate, could we ever get used to them?[152]

In ways similar to previous visits, Chaplin was used by journalists and commentators to shed light on French politics and contemporary concerns. *Le Canard enchaîné* published an ironic series of cartoons on its front page, supposedly introducing Chaplin to "our clowns": conservative prime minister Antoine Pinay and his Christian Democrat foreign minister Robert Schuman. It speculated that Pinay's government was about to fall (it survived until early January 1953) by satirizing the National Assembly as being like the cabin balanced on the cliff edge in *The Gold Rush*.[153] There was also an attempt (as in 1921) to appropriate Chaplin's name and fame by the Communist Party. Writing in the right-wing *Le Figaro*, Georges Raven took to task communist publications—the newspaper *L'Humanité* and magazine *Les Lettres Françaises*—for endeavoring "to annex Charlie Chaplin." Raven argued that Chaplin was too much an individualist to commit himself to any particular political philosophy and that, while in France, "he has abstained . . . from all political declarations." As for the suggestion in *Les Lettres Françaises* that he would now prefer to live in Europe or "elsewhere" (a coded reference to the USSR), Raven insisted that he "has never, so far as we know, renounced the cinematic virtues of the sun of California, nor demonstrated any intention of going to work in Moscow, even"—in a sardonic allusion to Stalin—"to make a second version of *The Great Dictator*."[154]

The French Reception of *Limelight*

Weeks before its first performances in Paris, French newspapers and magazines had begun to publicize *Limelight*. The first articles appeared while Chaplin was still working in the United States on the final version. They summarized the narrative of the film: that Chaplin played Calvero, a once successful comedian who saves Theresa (Claire Bloom), a young dancer who is paralyzed and believes she will never dance again, from a suicide attempt.

He nurses her back to health and watches as she achieves new success as a dancer. Calvero's own career declines, but Theresa organizes a benefit performance at which he once again succeeds in making people laugh. But he dies after falling into the orchestra—initially perceived by the audience as part of the act. French commentators, even at this early stage, noted that the film was autobiographical, with Chaplin drawing on his memories from the English music halls, but also—as in a burlesque sequence with Buster Keaton—referencing the early days of silent comedy as well.[155]

A number of French journalists also covered the screening of *Limelight* for the British and foreign press in advance of the film's première in London on October 16. Chaplin himself was present—*Les Lettres Françaises* reported that he slipped into the room as the lights dimmed at the beginning, *L'Aurore* that he appeared "to a new and interminable ovation" only after the audience had already applauded at the end of the screening.[156] According to *Combat*'s correspondent, Chaplin's presence in the room "released . . . an indescribable emotion." The same writer noted, however, that this "unanimous" admiration was sometimes tinged with surprise; *Limelight*, like all Chaplin films, had been "passionately awaited" but turned out to be "a grave and melancholy film" that—since it dealt with an ageing comedian—some regarded as his testament. These points would be taken up and expanded by later French critics.[157] "The general impression," wrote the correspondent of *Libération*, summarizing the reaction of British reviewers to *Limelight*, "is that this excellent film is not Chaplin's best and critics deplore that comedy has been sacrificed to drama." The same writer noted the comment in the *Daily Mail*, for example, that "in the autumn of his great career, the man who is not only a clown but *the* clown, has wanted to make us cry rather than laugh."[158] Other newspapers, including *The Times*, the *Daily Express*, and the *Daily Herald*, criticized the melodramatic character of the film—an accusation rejected by Henry Magnan of *Le Monde*. Magnan observed that the members of the French press present at the preview—in contrast to British critics—had greeted the film with "almost unanimous enthusiasm."[159]

Whereas the first screening of *Limelight* in London had been solely for the press, the first showing in Paris—on the afternoon of October 30 at the Biarritz cinema—had an audience making up a cross-section of the French cinema community, with directors and screenwriters as well as critics. (No wives were allowed.) For those present, Chaplin in many ways *was* the cinema. Many had grown up with his films. "It is difficult to write that *Limelight* is the best film we have ever seen," wrote the critic of *Paris Presse/*

L'Intransigeant, "since *Limelight* is not a film, it is a man. And . . . that man is Charlie Chaplin." Chaplin, declared R.-M. Arlaud of *Combat*, "floats in another world."[160] Chaplin's appearance at the theater and his crowd-pleasing comment that the French would understand him heightened the emotional atmosphere at the screening. According to Monique Berger, there seemed to be a "collective delirium" in the room. "I wept, we all wept," wrote Georges Sadoul. The ovation for Chaplin, according to Simone Dubreuilh, "was an ovation based on joy, tenderness, I would like to write love."[161] In the first of three articles he would devote to *Limelight* over the next six months, André Bazin pointed out that there was something "sublime" about this first Parisian performance: "the selectness of the spectators, and above all the presence of Chaplin, made of it a complex affair of which the film itself was just one component. The audience was at once the most alert and the most receptive ever assembled. Its predisposition to be favorable was conjoined with the greatest lucidity."[162]

Critics who had attended this performance placed Chaplin's film in a number of contexts. Some made the now traditional comparison between Chaplin and Molière (though Monique Berger observed that "more than Molière, who could express himself only in French," Chaplin could amuse and move an array of people from many different national backgrounds). In *Limelight*, indeed, as Janine Bouissounouse and Bazin pointed out, Chaplin's Calvero—like Molière himself—died on stage.[163] Other writers compared Chaplin to Shakespeare—a comparison first suggested, Georges Sadoul pointed out, by Élie Faure in 1920. "Never has this comparison been more appropriate than today," Sadoul declared à propos of *Limelight*. "This drama involving two people is profoundly Shakespearian and Chaplin here attains once again the summit of tragic greatness."[164] But the main point of comparison was between Chaplin's earlier career and the Chaplin of *Limelight*. There was a sense of time passing and some recognition that—in physical terms— he no longer resembled the Little Tramp: Kléber Haedens commented that for the first time in *Limelight* Chaplin showed his own face, that of a sixty-three-year-old man, bare on the screen.[165] But some reviewers also claimed a strong element of continuity between Charlot and Chaplin's performance in *Limelight*. Just as before, Bouissounouse wrote, Chaplin "made people weep and laugh, above all love life." "All Chaplin is there," observed Claude Garson of *L'Aurore* in very similar terms, "we laugh, we weep, we hope." There was one change from the classic narrative of many earlier Chaplin films: as Claude Mauriac would later point out, "for once it is not Charlot who will be abandoned." When Theresa shows she loves Calvero, he sacrifices his own love for her to encourage her relationship with a considerably younger man.[166] For many of those present at this first French screening, however, Chaplin's Calvero was only another expression of his Charlot persona. Those who saw *Limelight* that afternoon, commented Christine de Rivoyre in *Le Monde*, "had laughed at Charlot imitating a Japanese tree, a thought, a sardine; at Charlot eating a rose like a choux bun and murmuring words of love to Phyllis, the learned flea; had wept over Charlot sad, or Charlot sympathetic, loving; or Charlot dead on a large crate."[167]

In the essay he wrote after attending this special screening, André Bazin again insisted on the importance of the Chaplin myth in interpreting his latest film. The story of Calvero, he argued, was inseparable from the Chaplin myth. This had little to do with the "obvious autobiographical elements" (Calvero, like Chaplin, was a comedian on the London stage before World War I) but with what Bazin saw as "a self-criticism of the myth by its author." *Limelight*'s "direct evocation of Chaplin's childhood" was "subordinated to the theme of the actor's relation with the character he plays." From this perspective, "the true subject of the film" is "Can Charlie die? Can Charlie grow old?" Rather than answering this question, Bazin argued that Chaplin exorcized it in *Limelight* "through a story of the lost fame and old age of a man who resembles him like a brother." Chaplin thus "reached that supreme and paradoxical position in his art of being in himself the object of his tragedy." When he died on-screen, the audience of cinéastes was even more emotionally involved "because we knew he was present and alive." Chaplin's appearance once the movie was over demonstrated that "the film was just a sublime bad dream, but a dream . . . that allowed us to measure our love for him in his most beautiful role: the death of a clown called Charlie."[168]

Bazin continued his analysis of *Limelight* as a means by which Chaplin had finally liberated himself as a filmmaker in an article in *Cahiers du cinéma*, the new film journal he had help launch in April 1951. Essentially, Bazin argued, Chaplin had been hobbled by a "double myth: his everlasting youth and Charlot." Charlot had already "died, guillotined under the false identity of Verdoux; Chaplin's old age died at the end of *Limelight* with Calvero." To Bazin, the creation of Calvero was "sheer genius. It forces us to evoke Charlot [by echoing Chaplin's own career as a comedian on the London stage] and at the same time deprives us of all resemblance because nothing in his silhouette and even less in his comic genre allows any confusion." Chaplin was himself "the complete opposite of Calvero because the world has not forgotten his name or that he is married to a very young woman who has given him three children."[169] Indeed, he had everything that Calvero lacked: "glory, wealth, love and health." At this point, Bazin was exaggerating Chaplin's advantages over his own creation: Chaplin may not have wrecked his health through drink like Calvero and did apparently have a happy family life, but he had not made a financially successful film since 1940, his reputation had declined in the United States through scandal and his association with left-wing politics, and—by the time *Limelight* was shown in Paris—he was an exile from his adopted homeland. But Bazin maintained that what he termed the "double assassination" of Charlot in *Monsieur Verdoux* and of Calvero in *Limelight* had opened the door to the birth of a "new" Chaplin, "a fabulous actor who obtained the right to have his own old face and the relief of being able to wear new masks."[170]

In contrast to Bazin, some critics emphasized the degree to which the spirit of Charlot survived in *Limelight*. According to Eugêne Mannoni of *Combat*, "Chaplin wants at all costs to cast off the skin of the character he created and who he was. But the character resists the creator."[171] Consequently, argued the reviewer for *La Cinématographie Française*, "the public that waits for 'Charlot' will not be completely deceived. . . . The spirit of the 'little vagabond' and the psychological atmosphere of his adventures are found again." In part, this was a product of the film's narrative that recalled Chaplin's earlier career: "an unhappy man who forgets his misery at last by creating the happiness of a desperate young girl and who sacrifices himself in order to protect her (cf. the first 'Charlots': *The Circus, City Lights, Modern Times*, etc.)." What Calvero offered, like Charlot, according to Pierre Laroche of *Le Canard enchaîné*, was "a melancholy kindness grappling with the difficulties of a malicious world."[172] Chaplin, declared Monique Berger, "has retained the same vision of the world, a vision at the same time pessimistic, saddened and amused."[173]

In *Limelight*, indeed, as the critic of *La Cinématographie Française* noted, the public also rediscovered Charlot the comedian. Michel de Saint-Pierre, who had seen the film in London, wrote in *Temoignage Chrétien* that the Chaplin of *Limelight* "finds the means of dazzling us with wonderful clown numbers . . . the sketch of the flea, description of the boulder, the rose and the Japanese garden, the musical parody with Buster Keaton."[174] Over and over again, French reviewers drew attention to two of these sequences in particular. "I love that he amuses himself, in the taming of the fleas, in order to remind us that he is the most extraordinary mime in the world," remarked

André Lang. "I have never laughed so much," confessed Claude Garson. Janine Bouissounouse compared the sequence to the "dance of the dinner rolls" in *The Gold Rush* and hailed it as "a classic of the cinema."[175] Monique Berger bracketed this scene with that featuring Buster Keaton toward the end of the film as ones "that will reintroduce you to the Charlot of your youth." The critic of *La Cinématographie Française* similarly commented on rediscovering Charlot and "his joy from . . . times past when Chaplin and Buster Keaton, on the stage of a music-hall, improvise a very 'Mack Sennett' sketch"—a sequence greeted, according to Bouissounouse, "with thunderous applause and a tempest of laughter."[176]

In another review of *Limelight*, published six months after the film's release in France, Bazin referred to what he termed the "critical terrorism" that had accompanied the first screening of the film to French reviewers and filmmakers. "To have reservations about it," he observed, "was to set a limit to one's admiration for its maker." The presence of Chaplin himself in the auditorium reinforced feelings of this kind.[177] Every reviewer was aware of Chaplin's reputation. As Pierre Laroche remarked in *Le Canard enchaîné*, Chaplin was "the only genius cinema has produced up to this point." To Claude Garson, he was "the real cinema personified." "Chaplin—because of his earlier work—is not a filmmaker like the others," wrote Jean-Pierre Guyo. "He has been for a long time part of the history of the seventh art. At the top, together with Eisenstein, Griffith and Jacques Feyder."[178] There was a strong sense, on the part of some reviewers, that—rather than being subject to ordinary film criticism—Chaplin's work could be evaluated only as part of his oeuvre. "We cannot 'explain in detail' *Limelight*," insisted Jean-José Richer. "It is too immense to fit usual norms, unclassifiable among recognized genres."[179]

Richer explicitly rejected the notion that *Limelight*, as proposed by some British critics, was simply a melodrama.[180] "Rather than a work neatly defined," he argued, it was "the summit of an age, of a moment in the evolution of a man and his artistic experience."[181] The pressure on critics to write favorably of the film was increased by their awareness of the autobiographical aspects of *Limelight* and the fact that Chaplin himself was now a white-haired man in his sixties. "It's no longer just a film," declared Guyo, "it's already a 'testament.' The author says once more all the things closest to his heart: he speaks there of love, friendship, of death and of that which he loves most, his craft."[182] This feature of the film seemed to disarm the (few) critics who were natural iconoclasts. "I hate idols," confessed Michel de Saint-Pierre. "I went to the new film of Mr. Chaplin without joy, with a certain bias towards denigration. But he 'had' me. This testament stirred in me the deepest fibers."[183]

In what was effectively his third essay on the film, Bazin observed that *Limelight* had enjoyed an "exceptional run" since its first screening in France six months earlier but had not been "a resounding success" with the public. He conceded, in fact, that if it had not been for the favorable publicity generated by Chaplin's presence in Paris it would probably "have been a resounding flop, even allowing for its importance."[184] Bazin and other reviewers resisted the notion that this relative lack of commercial success might have been caused by problems with the film itself. "Is *Limelight* an imperfect work?" asked Georges Rouquier. "Are there some longueurs? Some imperfections? . . . I do not know. I don't see them." Even Bazin confessed that, having seen *Limelight* three times, he had three times been bored (even if not always in the same place) and conceded that "many deplore the *longueurs* and the talkiness" of the film's first half.[185] Yet, like most French critics, he was reluctant to criticize a Chaplin film. In part, this was a product of the realization that particular films had grown in reputation over time. "I believe," commented André Michel, "that since *The Gold Rush* reviewers have always been a little more hesitant with each of his productions. It is always the one before that one prefers. Distance alone gives them their true grandeur."[186] Bazin, in particular, refused to acknowledge that there were flaws in a masterpiece he compared to Molière's *Don Juan*, whose "perfection in its dramatic structure" had been revealed only in the speeded-up version played without an intermission Jean Meyer had recently directed at the Comédie Française. (Symbolically, Chaplin had been present at one performance.) To Bazin, *Don Juan* and *Limelight* were both "deeply pondered" works that had finally been quickly executed. (Chaplin had shot his film in only fifty days.) The speed with which they had been made created the impression of "blemishes and weaknesses." Bazin believed that the genius of Chaplin's latest film would someday be recognized; like *Don* Juan, there were no "faults" in *Limelight*, only "qualities. . . whose secret we have not so far been able to fathom."[187]

Aftermath

At the end of what had been a tumultuous year for Chaplin, setting the scene for his final quarter-century, spent living outside the United States, an event took place in Paris that recognized his place in the pantheon of cinéastes. On

Tuesday, December 16, the Cercle du Cinéma Français organized the Festival Charles Chaplin in the Great Amphitheater of the Sorbonne University. Many representatives of French cinema and students (the Amphitheater can accommodate almost a thousand people) came to view or review extracts from Chaplin's best films, as selected by Chaplin himself and made available through United Artists and Henri Langlois's Cinematheque Française. The program, presented by film writer Roger Régent, included *Making a Living* (Keystone, 1914), *Mabel's Married Life* (Keystone, 1914), *A Woman* (Essanay, 1915), *A Night in the Show* (Essanay, 1915), *Police* (Essanay, 1916), *The Rink* (Mutual, 1916), *The Adventurer* (Mutual, 1917), *A Day's Pleasure* (First National, 1919), *City Lights* (UA, 1931), *Modern Times* (UA, 1936), *The Great Dictator* (UA, 1940), and *Monsieur Verdoux* (UA, 1947).[*] The film extracts were shown in chronological order, with the exception of *City Lights*, which was introduced by director and longtime Chaplin fan René Clair, who, "speaking in measured but precise tones," compared it with *Limelight*.[188] By December 1952, Chaplin had been exiled from the country in which all his films had been produced, but tribute was being paid to his art in a great European university more than six centuries old, and, in general, his reputation as a great filmmaker was still secure within France's vibrant film culture.

---

[*] *Pour Ganger Sa Vie, Charlot et Mabel en Ménage, Mam'zelle Charlot, Charlot au Music-Hall, Charlot cambrioleur, Charlot patine, Charlot s'évade, Une journée de plaisir, Les Lumières de la Ville, Les Temps Modernes, Le Dictateur,* and *Monsieur Verdoux.*

8

Europe and Renaissance

For the last twenty-five years of his life, Chaplin lived as an exile in Europe. He made his home at the Manoir du Ban in Corsier-sur-Vevey, a municipality close to Lausanne and Lake Geneva in the French-speaking Vaud district of Switzerland. For the first time in his career, he was obliged to produce and direct films not in the United States but in Europe. He had abandoned the Little Tramp figure that had made him the most famous comedian (and possibly the most famous man) in the world with the release of *Modern Times* in 1936 (though echoes of the Tramp character would reemerge in *The Great Dictator* [1940], his political satire on Hitler and Mussolini). His last two films produced in the United States were very different from what he had done before: a movie loosely based on the career of French mass-murderer Henri Landru (*Monsieur Verdoux*, 1947) and a bittersweet reflection on his youthful years as a stage performer (*Limelight*, 1952). Although Chaplin considered a number of film projects during his first years of exile in Europe, it would not be until 1957 that he released his first film there: *A King in New York* (1957).

A King in New York

Chaplin began work on this film at the start of 1954. It was shot at the Shepperton Studios in England between May and July 1956, after which he took a two-week vacation on the Côte d'Azur. On August 19, he arrived in the French capital to supervise the editing of the film and the addition of the soundtrack at the studios of Laboratoires Franay Tirages Cinématographiques in Saint-Cloud, a western suburb of Paris. Unhappy with the final version, he spent the period January to April 1957 shuttling between Paris and London, reediting the film and its soundtrack. During this period, he also wrote the musical score. On June 24, he arrived in Paris to record the score with a thirty-seven-piece orchestra. (A short film exists of him conducting this recording.) In early July, Chaplin left for a long summer

Charlot. Melvyn Stokes, Oxford University Press. © Oxford University Press 2026.
DOI: 10.1093/9780197839294.003.0009

vacation at the Villa Scoglietto at Cap Ferrat on the Côte d'Azur. During this period, he was subjected to pressure from Hollywood to stop or delay the distribution of the film in France and other countries. On September 2, he returned to Paris for a few days, during which he selected the actors to dub the French-language version of the film.[1]

In essence, *A King in New York* was a story of exile. King Shahdov (Chaplin), ruler of a fictional European country called Estrovia, has been overthrown in a revolution and flees to the United States. He thinks he has brought much of the wealth of his country with him, but it turns out that he has been double-crossed by his prime minister (Jerry Desmonde), who has put all the bonds and securities in his own name and promptly disappears. Encouraged by Ann Kay (Dawn Addams), a dynamic young American TV producer, he begins to make television commercials to earn some money. On a visit to a progressive school, he meets a young boy, Rupert Macabee (Chaplin's son, Michael), who spouts all kinds of left-wing propaganda. Shahdov takes Rupert under his wing, but when Rupert's father (a former communist) is cited for contempt of Congress for not naming names to HUAC, Shahdov himself is subpoenaed to testify to the committee. In the elevator on the way to the hearings, he gets his finger caught in a fire hose. The hose opens up and drenches all the members of the committee with water. Shahdov is cleared by HUAC of any political involvement, but Rupert, to save his parents from jail, "names names." On his way back to Europe, Shahdov visits Rupert at his school and the camera lingers on the boy's anguished, tearful face.

Because the new film was "a satire on American life," noted the London correspondent of the socialist-leaning newspaper *L'Aurore*, "no distribution agreement has as yet been signed for the United States. Its release is announced only for Great Britain, France . . . Scandinavia, Italy and Japan."[2] *A King in New York* was previewed to the British press on September 10, followed that same evening by a press conference at the Savoy Hotel. Both at the press conference and, the following day, at a meeting with the Association of Foreign Journalists in London, Chaplin was criticized by American reporters for producing a movie that was "tendentious and anti-American." He responded that he had not attacked the United States itself but only the influence of a harmful minority. Accused by another journalist of ingratitude toward the country where he had made his fortune, Chaplin declared that he could truthfully claim to have been a "good guest," insisting that 75% of the income from his films had always come from *outside* the United States, while American taxes on his income had at times come close to 100%.[3]

On the whole, the initial London reception of *A King in New York* was muted. (Georges Sadoul would later point out that no British newspaper mentioned the arrival of Chaplin's latest film on its front page and there was in general less coverage of the London première in English than in French newspapers.)[4] There was also criticism by British—as well as American— reviewers of the quality of the film itself.[5] The accusation most wounding to Chaplin himself, commented Marthe Louis-Lévy, London correspondent of *Populaire-Dimanche*, was that his new movie lacked humor. In a review published only thirteen days before the Paris première of *A King in New York*, Lévy consciously tried to reassure French filmgoers that she herself had found the film funny. Only the serious "soap box" diatribes of Rupert, she explained, prevented it from achieving complete perfection.[6]

On October 23, 1957, Chaplin and his wife Oona arrived in Paris. The French première of the film took place the next day, at the Gaumont-Palace, with the proceeds going to a charity for retired journalists.[7] It was difficult that evening to access Place Clichy, where the cinema was located, in part because of the crowds gathered there for the première, in part because Paris itself was in the grip of a general strike. But Chapin himself—wearing, Jean de Baroncelli of *Le Monde* noted, the rosette of the Legion of Honor—arrived punctually at 19:00 in the foyer of the theater to answer questions from reporters.[8] Most of these were fairly anodyne. (After his experience a few weeks earlier in London, Chaplin had banned the American press from the première.)[9] He rejected the idea that he had made a "political" movie: "I have wanted solely to make people laugh, so don't look for a message in this film." Politics itself, he argued, was "justly criticized" in *A King in New York*. Was it anti-American? Chaplin insisted that the movie was not "against America, but against a certain vision of America." French film writer Jean Mitry (described in *Combat* as "a truly sentimental old cinéaste") asked whether the Tramp figure had really gone for good. Chaplin laughed and explained that the Tramp was young and agile; audiences would no longer laugh at him played by an actor of Chaplin's age. He also flattered those present by insisting on his love for France "because one finds there the art of living amongst civilized people."[10]

There was a brief interlude after the press conference, then Chaplin and his costar Dawn Addams appeared in the stalls of the 4,500-seat Caumont-Palace to a long ovation. (It was reported that singer Charles Trenet was one of those shouting "Long live Charlot.") Chaplin responded "with a debonair gesture" to this outburst of enthusiasm, passing through the orchestral bay to join Oona in the dress circle "to the popping of flashbulbs and enthusi-astic cheering."[11] Jean de Baroncelli, covering the première for *Le Monde*, summarized what happened next: "An hour and a half of laughter and ap-plause. And, in spite of a light sense of disappointment towards the end, the warmest of welcomes." The anonymous reporter for *L'Aurore* went consider-ably further, suggesting that "when the lights came on again after the perfor-mance, the response [in contrast to the adulation shown earlier] was more difficult to determine. 'A masterpiece,' some enthused. But on the faces of many spectators there was a sense of being deceived, of not having seen the Charlot of yesteryear." Among the audience itself, according to this reporter, "it was possible to hear people saying laudatory things: 'Marvelous, extraor-dinary, what a man!' But equally one could hear acute criticisms." In view of the nature of the event, many journalists were also present, and they too divided into two camps—those who liked the film and those who found it "very stilted."[12]

The French Reception of *A King in New York*

In the days after the première, divisions of this kind appeared in reviews. In some cases, even admirers of Chaplin tried to balance initial feelings of disap-pointment against what they perceived as the countervailing strengths of the film. This was true even of André Bazin, long a champion of Chaplin's work. Bazin published two reviews of the film, the first in *France-Observateur* on October 31, the second in *Education Nationale* a day later. In poor health (he would die just over a year later), Bazin—as Jean Bodon has pointed out—was narrowing down his work to focus on the two filmmakers who inter-ested him the most, both now exiles from Hollywood: Chaplin and Orson Welles.[13] Bazin began his review in *France-Observateur* with the unprom-ising comment that his job as a critic sometimes made him suffer. Despite his admiration for Chaplin's work in general, he confessed that he didn't re-ally like *A King in New York* very much. If it were to be judged only on its screenplay (or what might be termed its "message"), Bazin thought that only Chaplin's prestige saved it from ridicule. Its satirical anti-Americanism—and especially its assault on the anticommunist witch-hunt that had helped drive Chaplin himself out of the United States—seemed to Bazin too sub-jective. He wondered whether Chaplin's attempt at revenge did not come at too great a price in terms of his own reputation. He also pointed out that it had been five years since Chaplin himself had lived in America. Time had moved on: HUAC itself was no longer the force it once had been, and it had already been "more or less indirectly denounced" in twenty Hollywood films. By contrast with such films, Chaplin was now an outsider when it came to criticizing the United States, his anti-Americanism—as Bazin commented in *Education Nationale*—"scarcely more convincing than that of [French writers] Georges Duhamel or Marcel Aymé."[14]

It must not have been easy for Bazin to criticize Chaplin in this—or indeed any—way. But having voiced his personal and political reservations, he turned to analyzing more positively the film itself. Bazin confessed that he had "laughed heartily" during the first part of the film, "a satire on contemporary American life" that had been "entirely burlesque" with "everything made up of comic brainwaves in the style of the Charlot of old." The second part of the film, with its critiques of American politics (President Eisenhower's golf, the HUAC hearings) was, he believed, much less impressive.[15] Nevertheless, he argued that the film as a whole was redeemed by the genius of Chaplin as director: the very weakness of the storyline, indeed, necessitated that he excel in this area. Never, Bazin argued, had Chaplin demonstrated so much control over a film's aesthetics: "The neatness and vigor of the acting, the sharpness of the rhythm, the science of breaks in tone and time within a sequence, the prodigious intelligence of ellipses, and other qualities (including the beauty of [cinematographer Georges] Périnal's images and that of the music [by Chaplin himself]) make this show, for those who know how to see a little beyond the plot, an enchantment of the eye and even more of the spirit."[16] On this basis, Bazin concluded, there was "more to admire and learn from in *A King in New York* than in a year of world cinema."[17]

Like Bazin, many French critics also divided *A King in New York* into two parts. The first part offered a satire on modern American life and culture. "For 30 wildly cheerful minutes," observed Claude Brulé of *Paris Presse/ L'Intransigeant*, "the little man smashes into pieces the civilization of 1957." Most commentators liked this section—Jean de Baroncelli termed it "absolutely irresistible." The gags begin with King Shahdov's arrival in New York. While the king is praising the warmth of American hospitality in a "little speech," an immigration officer takes his fingerprints.[18] Shahdov claims he wants to experience the vitality of New York but, walking the streets of the city with his former ambassador Jaume (Oliver Johnstone), is put off by the noise and crowds of people. The two seek (as they think) a more peaceful environment by going to a cinema. But this is now the era of Elvis and rock 'n' roll: they arrive during the intermission to be confronted by a band playing and what Armand Monjo of *L'Humanité* described as "hysterical young people swaying their hips to the bestial rhythm of rock and roll."[19] Having taken a swipe at rock 'n' roll, Chaplin moved on to target contemporary Hollywood. Shahdov and his companion sit through spoof previews of a noir-ish film, *A Killer With a Soul—You'll Love Him*; a gender-bending "problem" movie, *Man or Woman?*; followed by a western in which two cowboys alternately shoot at each other for no obvious reason while the audience follows the action like spectators at a tennis match. With these brief clips, observed Claude Garson in *L'Aurore*, "Chaplin definitively buries Hollywood by showing us its stupidity."[20] Abandoning the cinema, Shahdov and his aide go to a restaurant whose peace is immediately disturbed by the arrival of a loud band. This place is so noisy that Shahdov attempts to order food by miming a sturgeon being cut up for caviar and using a plate covering his wriggling hand to suggest turtle soup.[21]

Much of the first part of *A King in New York* was concerned with the impact of commercial television on American life. One sequence in particular spoke to the ubiquity of television and its advertisements encouraging consumption: Shahdov finds a TV installed above the bathtub in his hotel (with wiper blades to remove the steam!); he is shown watching a seductive ad for a brand of beer while taking a bath. Jean Dutourd, writing in the periodical *Carrefour*, described this sequence as "low-key but delicious."[22] Shahdov is invited by Ann Kay to a society dinner, which is in reality a secretly filmed TV program. At two points, Ann breaks off her conversation with the king to deliver advertising pitches for brands of deodorant and toothpaste. She also encourages Shahdov to make a fool of himself by declaiming a highly bombastic version of Hamlet's soliloquy and inserting cutlery into the mouth of his hostess (Joan Ingram) to mimic a visit to the dentist.[23] Humiliated, Shahdov doesn't immediately realize that the program has made him a celebrity, and when a businessman offers him ten thousand dollars to make an ad for cheese (all he has to do is spread it and say "Yum, yum") he initially refuses.[24] But the king's financial position is now so precarious that he changes his mind and, with the aid of Ann Kay, starts to earn a good living from making TV ads. At her suggestion, he even agrees to plastic surgery to make him look younger and more appealing to clients. J. P. Vivet in *L'Express* considered it "the most beautiful, comical and pathetic moment" in the film when Shahdov learns from the surgeon that, to protect his new features, he is not able to laugh. The situation is resolved when the king goes to a nightclub in which two slapstick clowns are performing. Although he tries hard to follow the surgeon's advice, Simone Dubreuilh of *Libération* observed, "their cream pie act is really so funny that Shahdov bursts out laughing," initiating the return to his old appearance.[25]

In the main, French critics approved of the gags in the first part of *A King in New York* and liked the sequences devoted to satirizing American television in particular. Louis Chauvet of *Le Figaro* was an exception, dismissing Chaplin's treatment of commercial television as "a comparatively timid indictment." To Chauvet, recent American treatments of the subject were far better: Frank Tashlin's *The Girl Can't Help It* (1956) offered "an irresistible caricature of the fake advertising and abuses of television," and Elia Kazan's *A Face in the Crowd* (1957), which had just arrived in France, "ranted and raved" against some of U.S. TV's "monstrous features."[26] The second part of the movie focused its attention on politics. It is politics that has driven King Shahdov into exile: several reviewers pointed out that the main reason for the revolution against him had been his policy of using nuclear power only for energy needs and refusing to acquire atomic bombs that might make his country a target for destruction.[27] But it was *American* politics that provided the background for this part of the film, essentially a critique of American anticommunism. "McCarthyism and the 'witch-hunts' are the main targets of *A King in New York*," suggested the correspondent of *Le franc-tireur*. To Robert Benayoun of *Demain*, it was clear that Chaplin—whatever his protestations—was now "settling accounts" with the anticommunist crusade that had driven him into European exile.[28]

Shahdov's visit to a "progressive" school begins the process that will see him brought to testify before HUAC. The school, variously described by French commentators as "bedlam," "a moral void," and "destructive anarchy," encourages young boys to follow their own interests.[29] Its star pupil, Rupert, is reading Karl Marx when introduced to Shahdov and immediately launches into a series of left-wing diatribes. (Armond Monjo of the communist *L'Humanité* archly described them as "sound political messages.")[30] For some critics, however, Rupert seemed "unsympathetic" or "ridiculous," unlike the appealing Jackie Coogan of *The Kid* (1921).[31] To Marthe Louis-Lévy of *Populaire-Dimanche*, his tirades were "never funny," while Jeander in *Le Canard enchaîné* dismissed him as "a little 11 year-old monster" who "vomits his politics" in much the same way as contemporary French child poet Minou Drouet her verses.[32]

The sequence in which Shahdov is summoned to testify before HUAC attracted considerable criticism. Even Baroncelli of *Le Monde*, who liked the film in general, thought it brought the movie "to the edge of failure." Chaplin, he argued, had taken the members of the committee seriously, not mocking them as he did Hitler and Mussolini in *The Great Dictator*. Shahdov throughout "remains on the defensive," and the only laugh in this part of the film is the fire-hose incident, which is "too late" to bring life to the whole subject.[33] Roger Fressoz remarked in *Témoignage chrétien* that the whole anticommunist crusade itself had in any case become "somewhat anachronistic" by 1957—HUAC's second major investigation into communist subversion in Hollywood had ended in 1952 and Joseph R. McCarthy, whose name with the suffix "-ism" had become virtually synonymous with American anticommunism, died on May 2, 1957.[34]

As the Cold War developed, moreover, other voices had begun to argue that McCarthyism—however vile it may have been—did not necessarily represent the principal threat to human freedom. Claude Garson suggested in *L'Aurore* that "McCarthyism lasted two years," whereas Stalinism, its "much more cruel" repressive equivalent in the USSR, "has lasted much longer."[35] Claude Brulé in *Paris-Presse/L'Intransigeant*, went further, alleging that *A King in New York*—with its critical view of America—had now become "part of the Soviet [propaganda] arsenal." He finished his review with the savage comment that, if Chaplin really wanted to rediscover the spirit of *The Kid*, it was to be found not with Rupert but among the small boys of Budapest now commemorating "in silence" the forcible Soviet suppression of the popular Hungarian uprising of 1956.[36]

There was a general consensus among French critics that the first part of the film was better than what came afterward. According to J. P. Vivet, the "whole first part of *A King in New-York* is remarkable, but you have to make an effort to remember the pleasure you took in it, since the sequel annoys, irritates, bores so much." More mildly, Jean Dutourd observed, "we experience less pleasure in the second part . . . than in the first."[37] A variety of reasons were suggested why this was the case. Claude Garson thought it too diffuse to meet the anticipation for a new Chaplin film: "we expected more . . . [but *A King in New York*] disappoints not only because we are too demanding with Mr. Chaplin, but also because Chaplin wanted to embrace too much and did not choose a single subject." François Gault confessed that the movie "filled me with a melancholy bitterness. And a large part of the audience will react in the same way—I think." To Gault, the principal problem was that earlier

American films had "pulled the rug out from under it," making it now seem stale and passé. There was also some suspicion that the film was a means through which the director and star had endeavored to take his revenge on the persecutions he had suffered in the United States: Roger Fressoz suggested that the once "warm and tender, human and generous" Chaplin had now revealed himself as "marked by the stigmata of resentment."[38]

Some critics expressed concern that Chaplin was now less interested in comedy than in putting across a political point of view. (It was very noticeable that in the final part of the film, the only really important gag was the drenching of the members of HUAC.) Claude Brulé confessed that he left "this film with a broken heart and a bitter taste in the mouth. As if I had drunk sour wine. Yet there are millions of us in the world who love Charlot like a brother. He gave us so much. But *A King in New York* brings overwhelming disillusion: Chaplin once made films of genius; now he makes political films."[39] And, as a number of writers made clear, *A King in New York* was not even a *good* political film. The manner in which the movie treated the "witch-hunting" of HUAC, Louis Chauvet argued, was "weak, outdated." Arthur Miller had gone "further, more courageously" in his 1953 play *The Crucible*. Chaplin had been less outspoken than Miller and other Americans either because he "did not dare or was not touched by inspiration." (Chauvet himself favored the second explanation.)[40] André Lang, by and large, had a much higher opinion of *A King in New York* than Chauvet, arguing that "two-thirds" of the film was "the best of Chaplin—irresistibly satirical and full of comic richness." Yet even Lang also concluded that the movie had been gravely weakened by a "firecracker" (the HUAC issue) thrown into the film which, when it detonated, annoyed and disconcerted the public because of its "complete ineffectiveness." Chaplin, Lang sadly but realistically concluded, had "missed the target."[41]

The reviews by Chauvet and Lang in particular provoked a strong response from Bazin's protégé François Truffaut, who had just launched his own career as a movie director by shooting a short film, *Les Mistons*. Truffaut took both critics to task for their insistence on the weakness of the film's storyline. "You might as well blame the 'New Testament' for lacking suspense," he argued. Pursuing the analogy further, Truffaut puckishly suggested that much of the film was really based on the life of Jesus. The fact that Shahdov's prime minister steals all "his" money was drawn from the Parable of the Talents (Matthew 25:14–30), which deals with a rich man who entrusts his fortune to a faithless servant. At the society dinner, the king is betrayed by a "Judas" (the camera hidden in the wall). When he buys clothes for a shivering Rupert, this was based upon the parable of the Healed Possessed (Mark 5:1–20), about a man possessed by demons who is clothed and returns to sanity. The sequence in which Chaplin is summoned by members of HUAC, whom he douses with a fire hose, echoes the story of Christ's expulsion of the moneylenders from the Temple (Matthew 21:12), with their tables and chairs also overturned. "I don't claim that my interpretation of the script is the only one," Truffaut mischievously conceded, before going on to offer a spirited defense of *A King in New York*. The film was not, he argued, a comedy. Instead, Chaplin was reflecting on his own "misfortunes with Uncle Sam"; this produced "the saddest of his movies and the most personal." As an "autobiographical film," it offered "a slice of life more painful than others because Chaplin understood that the most agonizing problem of the time" was "this organized destruction of freedom across the whole world, soon to be driven to the brink."[42]

Jean Mitry and the "Myth" of Charlot

In 1957, French film writer and filmmaker Jean Mitry published two major studies of Chaplin and his work. The second was a sustained analysis of all of Chaplin's films to date, detailing the plots and commenting on the aesthetics, which appeared in April in a special edition of the journal *Images et Son*.[43] It followed closely after the appearance in bookstores of *Charlot et la "Fabulation" Chaplinesque*, in which Mitry endeavored to shed light on the parallels and differences between what he saw as the "character" and "myth" of Charlot.[44]

Mitry was by no means the first French writer to interpret Chaplin's on-screen persona as embodying a myth. In 1935, Pierre Leprohon had published the first edition of his biography of Chaplin under the title *Charlot ou la naissance d'un mythe*. The same year witnessed the appearance of an essay by Jean Epstein, similarly entitled "Le Mythe de Charlot." In 1950–51, Barthelémy Amengual published two works on the Charlot myth.[45] Mitry, however, was perhaps the best prepared of anyone to treat the subject. According to William Gilcher, one of his students when he lectured for a time at the University of Iowa, he had "an encylopedic knowledge of film—and he remained eager to add to his knowledge. . . . To this end, Mitry took on Herculean tasks: he compiled endless files, analyzed all of Chaplin's gags."

Far more than Bazin, as J. Dudley Andrew noted, Mitry was qualified to be a historian of cinema: "Bazin had to rely on his memory of screenings at *ciné*-clubs, whereas Mitry had the films at his fingertips, the documentation in his files."[46] Ironically, Bazin himself played a role in persuading Mitry to write a book about Chaplin/Charlot and his myth. In April 1947, Mitry had delivered three lectures at events organized by "Travail et Culture," a communist-supported program offering popular education to the working class for which Bazin was secretary-general. A year later, Mitry noticed that Bazin had appropriated some of his ideas on Chaplin in a review of *Monsieur Verdoux*. Diplomatically, Mitry observed that Bazin himself had acted perfectly properly, but the ideas he expressed with regard to Chaplin had subsequently been taken up by others, including Barthelémy Amengual and Portuguese writer José Augusto França. In part at least, *Charlot et la "Fabulation" Chaplinesque* was Mitry's attempt to reassert ownership of his own ideas.[47]

To Mitry, the development of the character of Charlot had not been the result of a conscious strategy consistently pursued by Charlie Chaplin. It was something that had evolved over time. Even the archetype of Charlot the Tramp or vagabond figure did not appear immediately. In most of his first films for Keystone, Chaplin was simply Mabel Normand's sidekick. In *Making a Living* and *Cruel, Cruel Love* (both from 1914), he was dressed in a long fitted coat and top hat and wore a monocle—a dandy with a drooping moustache who, according to Mitry, bore a marked resemblance to the way French symbolist poet Henri de Régnier had looked around 1900. In *Mabel at the Wheel* (1914), he also had a little pointed goatee.[48] Even after the Tramp figure had fully emerged, moreover, Mitry argued, there were movies in which Charlot was essentially either an aristocrat down on his luck or a man-about-town observing society.[49] What he never was, Mitry insisted, was a professional vagabond. Rather, his character was that of someone who had been obliged to adopt the itinerant vagabond lifestyle only through force of circumstances.[50]

Mitry's perception of the social origins of the character of Charlot differed from that of film historian Georges Sadoul, who had published a book on Chaplin's life and films in 1952.[51] Sadoul, like Louis Aragon a surrealist who later embraced communism, regarded the Charlot figure on-screen as socially marginal, according to Amengual, "an unemployed person" rather than Mitry's "deposed member of the middle class."[52] But Mitry's own insistence on the social origins of Charlot was in some ways a blind alley: his analysis of the development of the Charlot myth was more psychological than so-cial. The myth itself, Mitry explained, was the product of a series of opposing influences. Charlot's instinct was to assert himself—in a Nietzschean-style Will to Power—against a world that seems determined to marginalize and frustrate him. When he inevitably encounters resistance to what he is de-termined to achieve, he responds with child-like rage since he is unable to understand why his needs and wishes have been denied. Since he can beat stronger opponents only through cunning and trickery, he delights in de-grading them by unfair means. (Mitry singled out *Mabel at the Wheel* as an example of Charlot's rejoicing in his own vindictiveness.) He also displayed such joy, Mitry noted, when pursuing women in nearly all his Keystone films, many of his Essanays, and even some Mutuals. Yet such pursuits, he argued, were motivated more by sexual attraction than love: if Charlot, while chasing one woman, met a prettier one, he would abandon the first and run after the second.[53]

Nevertheless, Mitry insisted, Charlot would not always act in these ways. He would gradually realize that he had a heart and a soul. To Mitry, Charlot's evolution along these lines was the product of a continuous and complicated dialectical struggle within himself between a series of impulses that simulta-neously pushed him in different directions.[54] Charlot also learned from ex-perience. His failures made him more aware of the existence of others. And he found out what it means to love—a sentiment that would become even deeper and purer as the woman he loves distances herself or unexpected problems arise between them. In the end, there will be impossible obstacles between them and the romance will end, leaving Charlot free to take the road to somewhere else, as the cycle of hope and disappointment starts all over again.[55]

In a perceptive review of Mitry's book in *Cahiers du cinéma*, Luc Moullet compared it to the thirteen existing French books about Charlie Chaplin. Such "abundance," he observed, "often hides a considerable mediocrity." Whereas his predecessors had usually contributed "a poetic dissertation" on each of Chaplin's films, Mitry's approach was to analyze them all together in the context of the development over time of the Charlot myth.[56] Charlot, Mitry argued, was fundamentally a living human being who evolves as he grows older. His films recount a series of events experienced by a man who, in common with other humans, is altered and shaped by what happens in his life.[57] Ultimately, a new Charlot, transformed by love, would appear, having thrown off the cruel instincts he had earlier displayed. The first hints that

Charlot was capable of sacrificing himself for love, Mitry argued, had already appeared in *The Tramp* (1915), *Police* (1916), and *The Vagabond* (1916). The idea became explicit in *The Circus* (1928) when Charlot, in love with the horsewoman who prefers the handsome tightrope walker, organizes their marriage and sees them happily depart, leaving him with his lonely heartache. In *City Lights* (1931), Charlot's sacrifice was even greater: he destroys his own happiness by helping to restore the sight of the blind woman he loves.[58]

Mitry emphasized that Charlot was far from being an antisocial loner. He thirsted for love and fraternity but always remained on the fringe—a romantic voyager in revolt against outside pressures and social conventions but still searching for some kind of vanished paradise of purity and innocence he is unable to rediscover. He was perpetually on the lookout for someone who understood him and could see beyond his ragged clothes to the warmth of his heart. Although he is frequently shown in a temporary job or following a particular occupation—and demonstrates he can work in a very zealous and committed way—in the end there is always some problem that leads to his being sacked. His dream of happiness, Mitry noted, was to have a cottage and someone to love him.[59] But in articulating this dream in *The Vagabond* and at the end of *A Dog's Life* (1918) and in the dream sequence of *Modern Times* (1936), he simultaneously managed to caricature and ridicule such hopes. A number of Charlot films, Mitry conceded, did show him married and ostensibly conforming to a middle-class lifestyle. But some of the wives in these films were so impossible or shrewish that he was compelled to run away. Other films appear to end in a marriage that promises happiness. But this happiness is not displayed in the film itself, and, Mitry concluded, so potent is the Charlot myth that there is little surprise when Charlot appears as lonely as ever at the start of his next film.[60]

One aspect of the myth identified by Mitry was the ambiguous nature of sexuality in some of the earlier Charlot films. In *Behind the Screen* (1916) he is mocked by his boss for apparently kissing a man (actually Edna Purviance dressed as a male carpenter). In *The Cure* (1917), he responds to what he sees as the advances of the large gouty man (Eric Campbell)—who is really addressing himself to the woman (Purviance again)—in a decidedly coquettish manner. Mitry also pointed to the number of films in which Charlot appeared dressed as a woman. These included *A Busy Day* (1914), *The Masquerader* (1914), and—most crucially—*A Woman* (1915), in which the looks and attitudes of the character he was playing seemed to Mitry truly emblematic of femininity itself. In other movies featuring Purviance, Mitry pointed out, Charlot managed to undermine and triumph over a (male) adversary by pretending to be beaten and victimized, even almost child-like, thereby attracting the female support and consolation that would enable him to turn the tables on his opponent.[61]

In Chaplin's later films, from 1936 to 1952, Mitry traced the continuing evolution and eventual destruction of the Charlot myth. *Modern Times* (1936) ended with an optimistic image of hope renewed: Charlot sets out once again on the open road, but this time he is accompanied by the young woman (Paulette Goddard) who, being even weaker and more wretched than he is, offers him her naive trust.[62] In his next two movies, Mitry argued, Chaplin effectively repressed the darker side of Charlot's character, his more brutish instincts and will to power, by identifying them with other characters. His role as Hynkel/Hitler in *The Great Dictator* (1940) expresses the vindictiveness and desire for domination that Charlot had once shown but had long ago abandoned. As the eponymous *Monsieur Verdoux* (1947), he was also an "anti-Charlot" in the sense that Verdoux himself expressed the tendencies toward destruction that the earlier Charlot had often displayed. The victory of the little Jewish barber (also played by Chaplin) over Hynkel and Verdoux's eventual execution, by eliminating the anti-Charlot, set the scene for the disappearance of the character of Charlot itself. In *Limelight* (1952), playing Calvero, a music hall comedian in his declining years, Chaplin revealed for the first time on-screen his own unadorned and ageing face. In discarding his traditional mask, he had finally repudiated the myth of Charlot. Chaplin himself might make other films, Mitry commented, but he would no longer play Charlot.[63]

A Countess from Hong Kong

After the release of *A King in New York*, Georges Sadoul observes, Chaplin for several years hardly left his home in Switzerland.[64] During this period, much of his focus was on family life. Between May 1957 and July 1962, his wife Oona gave birth to three more children to add to the five born between 1944 and 1953. Chaplin also worked for several years on his autobiography, published in 1964.[65] While the book sold well in France, it proved disappointing to many readers—especially cinéastes—because of its focus on his travels, the financial side of his life, and the fellow celebrities he had met rather than his filmmaking career.[66] Once the book was published, Chaplin turned his attention to a film project that would see him, for the first time since *A Woman of Paris* in 1923, not take on a major role in a film he was directing.

A Countess from Hong Kong (Universal, 1967) had its roots in the 1930s. Chaplin himself claimed in a highly fictionalized publicity piece that it had been inspired by a visit he had made in 1931 to Shanghai, where he was introduced to a group of impoverished aristocratic Russian émigrés. After World War II, many of their children found themselves in Hong Kong in even worse plight as refugees. It was the existence of such refugees that provided the background (in the form of the character Natascha) for *A Countess from Hong Kong*.[67] In reality, Chaplin did not visit the Far East until 1932, and China was not on his itinerary.[68] He would see both Shanghai and Hong Kong for the first time in the spring of 1936, accompanied by his lover and costar from *Modern Times*, Paulette Goddard.[69] David Robinson suggests that it was a visit to a Shanghai nightclub, and the sight of American sailors dancing with "taxi-girls," that gave Chaplin the idea for *Stowaway*, the story of a former Russian countess (Goddard) who, reduced to the role of nightclub hostess, tries to escape by hiding herself in the cabin of a wealthy American diplomat on a liner sailing from Hong Kong. Chaplin worked hard on the script for several months before abandoning it in favor of another project.[70]

When he returned to the *Stowaway* story as the basis for a new film, it was almost three decades later. Superficially, what now became *A Countess from Hong Kong* was made in auspicious circumstances. It would be Chaplin's first film in color and the first time he was able to use and direct two major international stars, Marlon Brando (as the American diplomat) and Sophia Loren (as the "taxi-girl"). Chaplin himself appeared only briefly on-screen as an elderly steward who suffers from seasickness. The film itself was generously financed by Universal Studios, and for the first time in fifty years, Chaplin was not his own producer. Shooting took just fourteen weeks at the Pinewood Studios in England. The film premièred at the Carlton Theatre on the Haymarket in London in the presence of the Duchess of Kent. Yet the reviews it received in the British press were almost unanimously hostile.[71] This, in itself, posed problems for French film critics who, well aware of the response to the screening by their London colleagues, had to deliver their own judgments a few days later.

Both Universal Studios and Chaplin himself made strenuous efforts to influence the reception of the film in France. On Wednesday, January 11,

1967, accompanied by his wife and two youngest daughters, Josephine and Victoria (both with minor roles in the film), he held a press conference on the Champs-Elysées ("with champagne," observed one critic). Dressed in a dark blue suit, wearing the colorful red sash of the Légion d'honneur, and seated behind a green desk, he answered questions from a large group of journalists and film critics.[72] The conference itself was rather stilted. With the London disaster in mind, Universal Studios had arranged for two interpreters: one from the studio who translated French journalists' questions to Chaplin—apparently watering down anything that might prove embarrassing—and another who translated Chaplin's answers verbatim. The fact that none of the French journalists present had yet seen the film ensured that their questions would in any case be fairly general.[73] Chaplin himself was clearly on the defensive and at the same time very much focused on "selling" his film. He conceded that he had dismissed the British critics as "stupid" and lacking humor, mainly because he claimed they had come to the film expecting to see a traditional "Charlot" movie. He insisted that ordinary British cinemagoers had been amused by *A Countess from Hong Kong* since he had gone incognito to watch the reactions of the audience at one London screening.[74] Asked why he had waited more than a quarter of a century to make the film, he gallantly claimed that he had been waiting for the perfect "Countess" to appear, in the form of Sophia Loren.[75] Was his new film a "masterpiece"? Chaplin agreed with the suggestion, going on to make even wilder claims that it was "my best film" and "very brilliant."[76]

Next evening, *A Countess from Hong Kong* had its French première at the Garnier Opera House in Paris. This was a gala performance aiming to raise money for a worthy cause: the French Foundation for Medical Research. Tickets cost 350 francs including dinner, and the audience consisted primarily of the social and cultural elite, including Madame Pompidou, wife of the French prime minister, several cabinet ministers and their wives, members of the Rothschild family, and couturiers such as Marc Bohan and Pierre Cardin. One anonymous writer in the newspaper *France Soir* commented that as spectators arrived and were greeted on the main staircase by a fanfare of trumpets from the Republican Guards, they seemed unsure—in the light of the disaster in London—of what to expect. But when the first applause and laughter was heard a few minutes into the screening, it seemed that French moviegoers were reacting differently from the London critics. Chaplin's new movie, doctor and writer André Soubiron was quoted as saying, had "won over" the audience.[77] It seemed to the reporter for *Le Nouvel Observateur* that the Paris public wanted to avenge Chaplin for all the vitriol directed at him in London.[78] Canvassing opinion during supper, Odile Grand of *L'Aurore* found that most people liked the film, though she conceded that some of the less well-known members of the audience appeared more critical.[79] Michèle Fabron, writing in the weekly *Minute*, went much further, arguing that the opinions offered by the kind of people who regularly attended premières were no real guide to what Parisians generally would think. Discovering what the public reaction really was would be established only when the film was on general release.[80]

In the days after the première, as the first French reviews of the film appeared, it began to become clear that many critics were unable to see *A Countess from Hong Kong* as just another movie. It had been conceived and directed by one of the great pioneers of cinema itself—a man who had now been making movies for more than half a century. Consequently, Jean de Baroncelli insisted in *Le Monde*, a Chaplin film could not be approached in the same way as films by other directors. Spectators who "loved cinema and loved Chaplin" brought with them "a stock of memories that creates in us an exceptionally receptive state." To Baroncelli, *A Countess from Hong Kong* was neither the "disaster" announced by British critics nor, as Chaplin had claimed, his "best" film. The only question really was whether the movie was simply a "trivial boulevard comedy" or if, "behind the seeming banality of the characters and situations," Chaplin "once again makes his voice heard." Baroncelli, a longtime admirer of Chaplin, admitted he could answer this question only "in a personal capacity." He confessed he had watched the film "with emotion" and believed it "possible to rediscover" in it "the fleeting shadow of the one we have so much admired and applauded."[81]

Louis Chauvet, writing in *Le Figaro*, adopted exactly the opposite approach from that of Baroncelli. He confessed he found writing his review a "painful" experience since Chaplin was the man who effectively invented cinema and he was sad not to be able to write more positively about a film Chaplin himself "cares so much about." Yet, he argued, it would be an insult to Chaplin's genius to be too tolerant of his lesser works. *A Countess from Hong Kong* began "like a mediocre American comedy" with several minutes of futile conversation. It then followed closely the plot of French writer and director Jacques Deval's comic stage play *La Prétentaine* (1957), including the ideas of a stowaway on a luxury liner and a cabin door that is constantly opening and closing.[82] The only real gag in the film, Chauvet believed, was the panic inside the cabin each time the doorbell rings—and this became monotonous through overuse. There were also scenes of seasickness that he dismissed as "vulgar" and "not very funny." Chauvet did concede that there were some amusing moments in the movie: a scene with the "inimitable" veteran actress Margaret Rutherford playing with teddy bears and ribbons, for example, and the appearances of the "ribald" servant Hudson (Patrick Cargill). But these were few and far between. When looking back on his viewing of the film, Chauvet could remember very few real comic moments. Chaplin's latest film, he gloomily concluded, was a failure as a comedy.[83]

To many French critics, *A Countess from Hong Kong* seemed like a throwback to classic American films of the 1930s. For Michel Aubriant, Chaplin was inviting moviegoers to pretend that "thirty years have not gone by" and cinema had not moved beyond *Love Affair* (*Elle et lui*), an RKO production of 1939 in which Charles Boyer and Irene Dunne fell in love aboard an ocean liner. Some reviewers commended this return to the style and preoccupations of the past. Samuel Lachize argued in *L'Humanité* that cinema, as the "Seventh Art," had reached a peak in the 1930s and expressed a hope for "many more films of this quality." Henry Chapier commented in *Combat* that "not to feel Chaplin's nostalgia for a faded past is to turn our backs on a whole cinematic era."[84] But for many others, the film appeared very old-fashioned. Many of its features were formulaic: a writer in *Carrefour* judged that the same tropes had already been used a hundred times by Hollywood, "with more sparkling results." Even Claude Brulé, a French correspondent in London who generally liked the film, conceded that "in the modern world . . . of [directors Jean-Luc] Godard, [Michelangelo] Antonioni, [Roger] Vadim and [Joseph] Losey, the art of *The Countess of Hong-Kong* [sic] seems to arise from an era as far away as the later years" of French poet and essayist Charles Baudelaire (1821–1867). Writing in the satirical *Le Canard enchaîné*, Michel Duran dismissed this film by "Grandpa Chaplin" as passé, a relic of the early 1930s, "when billionaire diplomats took luxury boats to go from Hong Kong to the USA. Chaplin's mistake is to have located the action in our own epoch, at a time of jet planes and a cinema that has evolved."[85]

A Countess of Hong Kong begins with Ogden Mears (Brando), American diplomat and son of the richest oilman in the world, on a luxury liner about to sail from Hong Kong to the United States via Honolulu. Estranged from his wife Martha (Tippi Hedren)—his friend Carruthers (Chaplin's son Sydney) predicts the couple will be divorced in six weeks—he spends the night partying. Waking up with a hangover, he finds that Natascha (Loren), one of the women he has been partying with, has stowed away in his cabin. An émigrée Russian countess, Natascha is intent on escaping her empty existence as a dance-hall girl and, it is hinted, prostitute by starting a new life in the United States. Ogden discovers Natascha only after the ship has left Hong Kong and, after first attempting to get rid of her, finally comes to accept that he will have to hide her until the boat reaches Honolulu. As a result, there is panic in the cabin each time the doorbell rings. Having brought only the clothes she was wearing, Natascha spends much of the film in oversized pyjamas, heightening the atmosphere of farce. Over time, Ogden—encouraged by Harvey—grows more sympathetic to Natascha, to the extent that he orders his valet Hudson (Patrick Cargill), who has American citizenship, to marry her so that she can legally enter the United States. But when the legality of the marriage (performed by the ship's captain) is challenged by a U.S. immigration official, Natascha leaps from the boat as it arrives in Honolulu and swims ashore. She thumbs a lift to Waikiki Beach. Harvey, sent by Ogden, finds her on the beach and books her into the Waikiki Hotel. In the meantime, Martha—who has arrived unexpectedly in Hawaii—meets with Ogden in his cabin and they decide to stay together for the sake of his career. Seated at a window in the Waikiki Hotel, Natascha watches sadly as the liner sails past en route to the mainland. But Ogden suddenly appears, having decided to abandon both career and wife for love of Natascha, and the two of them dance happily together.

To Claude Mauriac, writing in *Figaro Littéraire*, the main problem with the film was that, while there were some gags that were worthy of Chaplin, there were just too few of them.[86] If he had really spent a quarter of a century developing the film, another reviewer remarked, "he would have come up with more than the ten or so [gags] that, like refreshing oases in a desert, punctuate the two hours of screening."[87] Louis Chauvet was far from being the only writer to complain that the panic of the characters each time the cabin doorbell rings becomes too hackneyed as a humorous device: after the twentieth time, Henry Rabine succinctly remarked in *La Croix*, "we scream."[88] One writer thought that Chaplin's own two brief appearances (as a steward announcing the imminence of a storm and subsequently as himself suffering from seasickness) was "beautiful"; another, on the basis of these sequences, regretted that he had not taken on a more important role in the film. But Robert Chazal of *France-Soir* dismissed Chaplin's appearance as "more a resignation than a gag" in what he termed this "dizzyingly empty film."[89]

Part of the problem, it seemed to some writers, was the stars Chaplin had selected for his film. V. Volmarez argued in a letter to *Aux Ecoutes* that Loren and Brando could never really be anything other than Loren and Brando.[90] When it came to actually evaluating their respective performances, however, most reviewers seemed to prefer Loren. The anonymous critic in *Nouvelles littéraires* sarcastically commented that Brando, with the look of a middle-weight boxer who had suffered too many knockouts, seemed bored and dragged himself through the film without ever changing his expression. Loren was much better at handling the film's gags. The critic for *Carrefour* argued that Loren played her role "brilliantly," whereas Brando lacked the "lightness and charm" needed for his character. In *Le Figaro*, Louis Chauvet similarly judged that Brando's "puffy mask of tragedy" did not really lend itself to comedy, while Loren excelled in "touching or poignant" sequences (though he conceded there were very few of these).[91] With the exceptions of Michèle Fabron, writing in *Minute*, who suggested that if *A Countess from Hong Kong* did become a success much of the credit would be due to Brando, and Claude Mauriac, who maintained in *Figaro littéraire* that he had been "thoughtful and good" in a role not designed for him, there were very few positive comments by French critics on his performance.[92]

The release of *A Countess from Hong Kong* launched a debate between French critics over how completely Chaplin had abandoned the behavior, outlook, and values of the Tramp figure who had gained iconic status in France as Charlot. According to some, Chaplin had lost or abandoned "a large part of his virulence and generous fighting spirit" and "renounced his violent satirical ferocity."[93] In focusing on the luxury class aboard a liner, lamented Pierre Billard, he was far removed from the "vengeful laughter" of *The Immigrant* (1917). Régine, in contrast, suggested in the magazine *Arts* that the film represented the revenge of Charlot, transposing the role of the sad little immigrant in the Mutual film into a billionaire.[94] Brando's character, the wealthy Ogden, according to Chazal in *France-Soir*, represented the world "poor Charlot had always attacked."[95] Chaplin's defenders countered such accusations with two main arguments. First, as Claude Brulé pointed out in *Candide*, the first title card of the film drew attention to the overpopulation of refugees in Hong Kong after two world wars, reflecting "Chaplin's eternal sympathy for those who live in a hopeless situation, in fear, in solitude." In *Countess from Hong Kong*, it was Natascha—the orphaned outsider and "taxi-girl"—who came to represent this world of the dispossessed. To Brulé, she clearly evoked "the silhouette of the little man in the bowler hat, with the worn cane and the oversized shoes." In this film, he insisted, Sophia Loren "plays Charlot."[96] Second, Claude Garson suggested in *L'Aurore*, the film dealt with a very Chaplinian theme: having hope in humans. It showed a cold billionaire rediscovering human dignity through the love of a disinherited person.[97]

At his press conference on January 11, Chaplin himself claimed his new film was "a comedy mixed with romance . . . without a message or cream pie."[98] Some journalists took him to task for not using his reputation and talents to denounce injustices in the world. Chaplin's self-deprecating response was that he didn't take himself seriously enough and what the world needed was "relaxation, harmless laughter and romance" since there was already too much realism in contemporary cinema. Pressed on whether he could now identify sufficient material to write a new *Great Dictator*, Chaplin contented himself with what seemed at the time a bland general comment: "There is revolt in the air; it is very healthy."[99] Little over a year later, as the student protests at Nanterre signaled the opening stage of what would become "les evénéments" of 1968 in France, his analysis would perhaps come to seem more prescient. And, as Robert Chazal in *France-Soir* and Louis Chauvet in *Le Figaro* would point out in their reviews, there was at least one political element in the film: the difficulties faced by Natascha in attempting to reach America—including the sham marriage to Hudson—offered a jaundiced view of U.S. immigration services that may have had its first expression in *The Immigrant* (1917) but now echoed Chaplin's own continuing resentment at the cancellation of his reentry permit in 1952 that had led to his European exile.[100] Gérard Guegan in *Cahiers du cinéma* suggested there was another aspect of Chaplin's personal history evidenced in the film: Tippi Hedren, reduced to little more than platitudes in a cameo role as Ogden's soon-to-be-divorced wife, "implicitly [evokes] the memory of the public humiliations of a Chaplin hated by so many [former] wives."[101]

In insisting that there would be no "cream pies" in *A Countess from Hong Kong*, Chaplin was consciously turning his back on the type of highly physical comedy that had its roots in the music hall tradition and, before that, in the *commedia dell'arte*. There would be no slapstick comedy of the "pie in the face" variety that Chaplin himself was still using a decade earlier in *A King in New York*. Instead, an anonymous writer perceptively argued in *Nouvelles littéraires*, it was a farce of the type made popular in France before the First World War by George Feydeau (1862–1921). But, the writer tellingly added, it was "a Feydeau-style farce without Feydeau, consequently without precision, without rigor, without dramatic progression." Worse, it embraced at times a cloying sentimentality and simply went on too long. ("An old hand" such as Chaplin ought to have realized "that the film was over when Natascha dives from the top of the boat.")[102] So monotonous was the movie—and so dependent on the single gag of the lovers being surprised—that Pierre Billard of *L'Express* even fantasized about the film's characters "praying to heaven that a single cream pie might explode to liven up this mess."[103]

There was a strong conviction on the part of many reviewers that, by the 1960s, cinema itself had changed while Chaplin himself had not. Some writers defended him for this. Claude Brulé wrote in *Candide* that Chaplin "remains faithful to his own universe, to the magic and dust of his own circus." He could not be blamed "for not bringing us [comedies such as] *The Knack* [Richard Lester, 1965], *Help!* [Richard Lester, 1965] or *Morgan* [Karel Reisz, 1966]." Henry Chapier of *Combat* advised that "if one does not expect from *The* [sic] *Countess from Hong Kong* a philosophical thesis or a demonstration of writing in the style of the 'new cinema,' Chaplin still has a sensitivity and charm that will not fail to move."[104] But many critics compared Chaplin's *Countess* to other films of the time and found it wanting. The movie's paucity of gags and repetitive sequences, commented Henry Rabine in *La Croix*, were "all weaknesses we can no longer bear since *Breakfast at Tiffany's* [Blake Edwards, 1961], *Charade* [Stanley Donen, 1963] or *Designing Woman* [Vincente Minnelli, 1957]." Jean-Louis Bory in *Le Nouvel Observateur* even refused to discuss Chaplin's *Countess* in order to review Alain Robbe-Grillet's enigmatic *Trans-Europ-Express* (1966), which he described as "madly clever, funny . . . and of sparkling intelligence."[105] One commentator pleaded with Chaplin to "make another film quickly to make us forget this luxury liner that sails on an ocean of boredom." More realistically, others recognized that, at almost seventy-seven, this was probably his last movie. Pierre Billard, indeed, cautiously suggested that although Chaplin himself seemed to want to achieve the impossible by adding further to his fame, "after fifty years of triumph and nine years of inaction" the only thing most people now wanted was to leave untarnished the "precious image he has given us of himself." More nostalgic still, Claude Brulé hailed what he termed the last "goodbye of the old magician to his two magic spells, his two mirrors: love and comedy."[106]

From Disaster to "Renaissance"

While Chaplin was deeply depressed by the failure of *A Countess of Hong Kong*, he still carried on working—on another film project that would never be produced, called *The Freak*, in which he planned to star his daughter Victoria, and on composing/reworking musical accompaniments to several of his movies.[107] Yet following his greatest failure, the last decade of his life would see a marked revival of his reputation—to the point where, in 1972 during his first visit to the United States in two decades, he would speak of "being born again" and "my renaissance."[108] This improvement in his fortunes came about mainly as a result of two factors: the growing availability of his films and increasing institutional and public recognition.

As François Truffaut explained, Chaplin—frustrated by "countless pirate re-editions" of his films—had banned their distribution as the exploitation rights expired. He then adopted a policy of reissuing them every few years through United Artists.[109] While this proved profitable to Chaplin himself, it had the serious drawback of limiting the opportunities for moviegoers to watch and compare the films. As a result, Truffaut argued, new generations of spectators had appeared who knew of films such as *The Kid*, *The Circus*, *City Lights*, *Monsieur Verdoux*, and *Limelight* only by reputation rather than by actually watching them on-screen. In 1970, according to Georges Sadoul, the French Society of Writers for Cinema and Television even published an open letter to Chaplin asking him to make his films freely available in cinemas once again.[110]

By this stage, as David Robinson points out, Chaplin himself was moving toward the idea of "leasing out the distribution rights" to his films and giving "someone else" the task of making as much money as possible from them. In the 1950s, Chaplin had become acquainted with Moses "Mo'" Rothman, the Paris-based European manager for United Artists, who subsequently moved to Columbia Studios where he would rise to the position of vice president for worldwide marketing.[111] Chaplin's assistant, Rachel Ford, suggested Rothman as someone who would be able to put together a group of investors to handle the distribution of his films, and Rothman took on the job with enthusiasm. Rothman organized a syndicate that included producers Bert Schneider (*Easy Rider*, 1969 and *Five Easy Pieces*, 1970) and Oliver A. Ungar. After several months of negotiations in 1970–71—some of which, according to Charles Maland, took place at Cap d'Antibes on the French Riviera, where the Chaplins were on holiday—Rothman offered a deal giving Chaplin an advance of six million dollars on half the profits for the next fifteen years, renewable for a further five. Chaplin accepted the offer, which covered the distribution of ten of the feature films he had made for First National and United Artists. (Robinson comments that he was so pleased with the way the deal was working by November 1971 that he also added *The Kid* and *The Idle Class* to the package of available movies.)[112] Part of the deal was that Chaplin would also make a number of "undemanding personal appearances" to help publicize the re-releases. Consequently, when the first of the re-issues, *Modern Times*, was shown on November 3, 1971, in Paris, Charlie and Oona Chaplin were in attendance.[113]

Chaplin's decision to farm out the distribution of his films—which made them increasingly available to wider audiences—suggested to Truffaut that interest in Chaplin and his work was likely only to increase. Accordingly, in 1971 he proposed to Paris-based Éditions de Cerf that they republish—as one book—the articles by André Bazin on Chaplin "with an emphasis on the 'revivals.'" The publisher accepted the idea in principle—but, curiously, only on condition that "someone well-known writes a piece on *A Countess from Hong Kong*" as part of the volume. Truffaut immediately contacted fellow director Eric Rohmer, writing, "I know how much you adore the film," and Rohmer's essay—together with the text of Chaplin's final speech from *The Great Dictator* and Jean Renoir's article on *Monsieur Verdoux*—appeared in the final volume published by Cerf in 1972.[114]

Cannes 1971

When it came to public recognition of Chaplin's significance as a filmmaker, France led the way. The organizers of the Cannes Film Festival of 1971—celebrating a quarter-century since the first festival was held in 1946—planned an opening ceremony with a difference. It began on May 12 at 20:45 with a short speech by Minister of Culture Jacques Duhamel, reflecting on the festival and how it had developed. This was followed by a twenty-five-minute film showing highlights of earlier festivals, a montage constructed from television reports over the years by François Chalais.[115] At this point the gala transformed into something much closer to Oscar night in Hollywood. Nine directors who had received awards at Cannes over the past twenty-five years were introduced.[116] Clips from their films were shown, and each was successively invited onto the podium by the director

of ceremonies, French actor Jean-Pierre Cassel, to receive a golden stat-
uette from the hands of Hollywood star Mia Farrow. The nine came from
seven different countries: Réne Clément and Robert Bresson from France,
Michelangelo Antonioni and Federico Fellini from Italy, Luis Buñuel from
Spain, Lindsay Anderson from Britain, Vojtech Jasny from Czechoslovakia,
Masaki Kobayashi from Japan, and William Wyler from the United States.[117]
Considerable cinematic figures in their own right, the nine proved to be only
the hors-d'oeuvre to the evening's main course. When the presentations had
come to an end, the lights dimmed. Through a translucent curtain, the audience could see a large shadowy figure doing a jerky "Chaplin" walk. Then the
curtain was drawn back and three men stood in the middle of the stage, the
stocky white-haired Chaplin in the center. The festival hall exploded into applause that lasted for almost three-quarters of a minute.[118]

Jacques Duhamel, standing beside Chaplin, paid a graceful tribute to
the comedian as "one of the great directors of this [cinematic] art and the
greatest actor it has produced." The popularity of the character of Charlot, he
suggested, lay in the fact that it reflected both the eternal nature of mankind
and the plight of humans in the modern world. Was the laughter Chaplin
created bitter, at times melancholic? Duhamel insisted there was a particular
understanding in France (Molière's birthplace) of the fact that laughter came
in many forms and could express a whole range of sentiments, effectively
functioning as "a reaction against the stupidities of men and the defects of
the societies they have built." He found the bitterness in Chaplin's films to be
at its most obvious in films in which the Charlot persona was absent, notably
L'Opinion Publique (*A Woman of Paris*, 1923) and *Monsieur Verdoux* (1947).
Pointing out that both of these were set in France, Duhamel moved on to a
summary of Chaplin's links with France. Chaplin, he claimed, had "often"
spoken of the French origins of his family, but Duhamel did not belabor this
point. Instead, he emphasized that the comedian had acknowledged that he
had learned a lot from some French filmmakers, above all Max Linder, and
that he had paid tribute generally to the art of mime in France. According
to Duhamel, Chaplin had advised French moviemakers that they should always "remain faithful to the principle of artistic courage and integrity that
have won you such high prestige in the world." In broader terms, the minister
complimented the "tenacious courage" Chaplin had shown between 1940
and 1952, a period in which he had been the object of deep-seated grudges
held by many Americans. Duhamel quoted with much pride Chaplin's comment at the very end of this period: "Civilized men of all nations have a debt

to France for her spirit of liberty, intelligence and art." The affection shown by Chaplin for France, insisted the minister of culture, was equaled by that for Chaplin in France where "we all . . . admire your genius but we love your heart." At the end of his speech, Duhamel "in the name of the president of the republic" tied the blue ribbon of Commander of the Legion of Honor—France's highest award—around Chaplin's neck and ceremonially kissed him on both cheeks.

Visibly moved, Chaplin began to respond in French ("Mesdames, Messieurs") but immediately switched to English ("I don't speak that very well either"). He told the audience he had been spoiled living in Switzerland, where he would ask for something in French and shopkeepers would invariably respond in English. A few people laughed at this. But otherwise he had little to say: everything was "nice" or "wonderful," and he expressed his gratitude for the fact that people in the audience "have appreciated me . . . not only in the past, but also in the present." At this point, he turned and shook hands with the minister before looking back a little uncertainly at the audience, which was dutifully applauding. But Chaplin, the old music-hall entertainer, seemed to recognize that his spectators expected something more. He started to do a "Chaplin" walk. Jacques Duhamel, afflicted with multiple sclerosis, had brought with him a cane to lean on during the ceremony. He offered it to Chaplin, who walked along the stage twirling it, to tremendous applause. According to René Rousseau of *Le Figaro*, he made the cane "flutter about in the best style of Charlot, once again conquering his admirers with his kindness and simplicity." To some in the room, this was a truly magical moment in which the years fell away and, in the words of Robert Chazal of *France-Soir*, Chaplin had "suddenly rediscovered his youth and his legendary character [of the Little Tramp]."[119] It was an illusion that would last for only a few seconds. Chaplin handed back Duhamel's cane, and the minister offered it one more time. Chaplin started twirling it again, but the old skill had plainly gone and twice he came close to hitting himself on the cheek. Chastened, he handed it back, applauded the still-cheering audience, and walked stiffly off the stage.[120] On the following night, with Chaplin again in attendance, there was a special screening of *City Lights* (1931). While this showing does not appear to have been covered by the French press, Jonathan Rosenbaum commented in *The Village Voice* that it "re-affirmed, in startling contrast to the rest of the festival, how fresh and contemporary Chaplin's art remains."[121]

The deal to distribute a range of Chaplin's films more widely and the tribute to him and his work at the Cannes Festival set the scene for the final stage of what Chaplin himself would claim to be his "renaissance": his return to the United States to receive an honorary Oscar in April 1972. In an interview with Jeffrey Vance many years later, Mo Rothman claimed that "Chaplin needed to be rehabilitated in America, and we got all sorts of offers. I negotiated with the Lincoln Center tribute in New York with Martin Segal and Bert Schneider arranged Chaplin's Academy Award."[122] There was truth in both these claims, but the second ignored the role played by screenwriter Daniel Taradash, who had been president of the Academy of Motion Picture Arts and Sciences in Los Angeles since 1970. Taradash had been particularly critical of McCarthyism—as critiqued in *Storm Center* (1956), a film he directed—and had come to see the revocation of Chaplin's entry permit in 1952 as a particularly egregious example of the excesses of the anticommunist inquisition. Taradash developed a plan to counter what he saw as political persecution by persuading the governors of the Academy to agree to award an honorary Oscar to Chaplin at the 1972 Academic Awards. Moreover, he also secured agreement that—in contrast to the several directors recognized at Cannes a year earlier—Chaplin alone would receive such an award. Taradash then wrote a letter to Chaplin asking if he was prepared to accept the award and be present at the ceremony to receive it. He asked Bert Schneider to take the invitation personally to Chaplin.[123]

The first of the worldwide re-releases of films under the deal agreed by Chaplin and Rothman was scheduled to be screened in Paris on November 3, 1971, with Chaplin in attendance. Schneider and his current girlfriend, actress and photographer Candice Bergen, met Charlie and Oona in their suite at the Ritz the evening before. They were joined by Chaplin's daughter Geraldine and her husband, and the three couples went out to dinner at Le Grand Véfour. Bergen, who was seated next to Chaplin, would later recall that "his sight was not all it once was but surprisingly sharp when his eyes fell on pretty girls." It was during this dinner in Paris that Schneider broached Taradash's suggestion of Chaplin's returning to America to accept a special Oscar. Chaplin would take two months to consider the invitation—"making up and changing his mind many times," according to Bergen—before finally deciding to accept in January 1972.[124]

Chaplin himself had never been a fan of the Academy Awards. At the very first Oscars, in 1929, he had initially been ignored, but the Academy later had second thoughts and gave him an honorary Oscar for his "versatility and genius" in making *The Circus*. Three years later, when Walt Disney was also awarded an honorary Oscar ("for the creation of Mickey Mouse"), Chaplin was supposed to present it but failed to turn up.[125] While he would later be nominated for *The Great Dictator* and *Monsieur Verdoux*, he would never win an Oscar in his own right for his acting, directing, writing, or producing,[126] remaining—in Anthony Holden's words—"a Hollywood giant whom his peers were too small-minded to honour."[127]

By 1972, Chaplin was in his eighties (the Oscars ceremony took place shortly before his eighty-second birthday), reluctant to leave his home in Vevey, and nursing bitter memories of the persecutions he had endured in America in the 1940s and early 1950s. After meeting with Chaplin in Paris, Schneider told Taradash that his interest in the invitation had been "tempered by fear of the long trip and even more by the possibility of outraged editorials, pickets at the airport, even catcalls at the Awards ceremonies."[128] But in the end, a combination of persuasion from Oona Chaplin together with pressure from Rothman and Schneider overcame his doubts. By January 1972 they had arranged for the series of re-released Chaplin movies to be shown in twenty-eight American cities. According to Chaplin's son Sydney, his decision to return to America was "purely financial," a means of publicizing his films once again to a mass audience.[129]

Rothman and Schneider planned Chaplin's return to America as effectively an advertising campaign designed to restore his reputation. Schneider arranged for Candice Bergen to join the "crazed crush of photographers and news teams" that greeted the Chaplins on their arrival at New York's Kennedy Airport on April 3 as a photographer for *Life* magazine. (She can be seen on the TV footage snapping away.)[130] Rothman had negotiated with Martin E. Segal, the founding president and chief executive of the Lincoln Center Film Society, to arrange a tribute to Chaplin in Philharmonic Hall on April 4 that would include screenings of *The Idle Class* and *The Kid*.[131] The evening went well, the 2,800-strong audience applauding him as he arrived, "repeatedly" cheering the films themselves, and giving him an ovation at the end. Once he could make himself heard, Chaplin tearfully thanked those present for making "him feel as if he were the object of a complete 'renaissance,' as if he were being 'reborn.'" To McCandlish Phillips, who reported what happened for the *New York Times*, the whole evening "suggested the triumphal final flourish of a motion picture script—reconciliation and rejoicing after long estrangement, with the hero having it all his own way."[132] The day after the event, an equally emotional Chaplin was ceremonially presented with the Handel Medallion, New York's highest cultural award, by Mayor John V. Lindsay.[133]

In spite of the warmth of his welcome in New York, however, Bergen—who was with him and Oona on the flight to Los Angeles a few days later—recalled that Chaplin "boarded the plane with great ambivalence . . . the memories of what he had been put through there were too painful." There had been some threats and talk of protests to the point that Schneider had arranged additional security.[134] Chaplin himself worried either that no one would come or that he might be booed.[135] Yet the Awards ceremony on April 10, 1972, ultimately went off without a hitch. In a departure from Academy tradition, the presentation of the honorary Oscar to Chaplin replaced the Best Picture award as the final act of the evening. Taradash appeared on the stage to deliver an eloquent tribute, a series of clips from Chaplin's films was shown, and Chaplin himself appeared on the stage. He was greeted by the longest standing ovation, at twelve minutes, in the history of the Academy Awards. Chaplin himself seemed overcome: in a very brief speech he confessed, "this is a very emotional moment for me and words seem so futile," and contented himself with simply thanking members of the Academy ("dear sweet people") for inviting him. At this point, Jack Lemmon appeared and offered him two of the principal artifacts of his Little Tramp persona: a derby hat and a cane. Chaplin stood for a moment leaning against the cane and holding the hat, before laying the stick on the stand in front of him and attempting to put on the hat. But the brief illusion of timelessness he had created at the Cannes Festival eleven months earlier could not be repeated: he fumbled trying on the hat, which slipped out of his hands and fell to the floor.[136]

Outside the ceremonies in New York and Los Angeles, Chaplin managed to meet up again with many of those he had known and worked with during his long career. They included Paulette Goddard, Claire Bloom, Georgia Hale (who he pretended to reproach for looking so young), and Jackie Coogan (now a stout, bald, middle-aged man Chaplin nevertheless greeted as "little boy").[137] When he returned to Switzerland in April 1972 he must have known—given his age and declining health—that it was unlikely they would meet again. Honors still lay ahead—a Golden Lion at the Venice Film Festival in September 1972 and his knighthood by Queen Elizabeth II in March 1975—but the impetus from the Cannes Film Festival and the distribution deal he had signed with Mo Rothman had ultimately brought him back one last time to America while rehabilitating his reputation and encouraging new focus on the movies he had made over more than half a century.

Chaplin, Henri Langlois, and the Cinémathèque Française

The gesture of approval by the French government in making Chaplin a Commander of the Legion of Honor at Cannes in 1971 was all the more remarkable because, three years earlier, he had taken a position that was hostile to that adopted by one of Jacques Duhamel's immediate predecessors. On February 9, 1968, at the instigation of President de Gaulle's minister of culture André Malraux, Henri Langlois was dismissed as director of the Cinémathèque, the organization to preserve and screen films he had founded with Georges Franju and Jean Mitry in 1936. For many French cinéastes, the gifted and energetic (if often eccentric and disorganized) Langlois and the Cinémathèque were at the heart of French film culture. Led by François Truffaut and other well-known French film directors and based in the offices of film magazine *Cahiers du cinéma*, where Truffaut and many of his colleagues had formerly worked, a campaign to reinstate Langlois sprang vigorously to life. Older French filmmakers, including Jean Renoir and Marcel Pagnol, refused to permit further screenings of their films at the Cinémathèque unless Langlois was restored to his position. Campaign workers also sent telegrams to many well-known cinema personalities abroad. Chaplin was one of those who replied, in a telegram of support that similarly banned the screening of his films at the Cinémathèque until Langlois was reinstated as director.[138] Filmmaker and anthropologist Jean Rouch claimed that he persuaded *Le Monde* newspaper to report that "Chaplin had wired to inquire whether the Cinémathèque was planning to return his films by plane or by boat." Although there had been no such telegram, it was later sent to Chaplin, "who obliged by immediately returning it, properly endorsed."[139] Finally, on April 22, 1968, a special meeting of several hundred members of the Cinémathèque Française met to ratify the campaign's success and Malraux's defeat: Langlois was unanimously reelected as artistic and technical director of the institution.[140]

Ten days later, the old screening room on the rue d'Ulm was the first part of the Cinémathèque to reopen, with a program that included "by special permission of Charlie Chaplin . . . the complete version of *The Kid*."[141] On July 31, the screening room at the Palais de Chaillot reopened with a homage to Chaplin and a showing of *Monsieur Verdoux*—a film not seen in Paris since its original commercial release in 1948.[142] Langlois appeared before the screening ("always a little untidy, his hair casually tossed back, his tie crooked," according to one observer) and was warmly applauded. Chaplin, he explained, had personally approved this screening, for one evening, of his movie.[143]

While Chaplin's role in the campaign to reinstate Langlois was comparatively small and mainly symbolic, Langlois himself over the years had played a major part in nurturing Chaplin's reputation with the French cinemagoing public. Born in 1914, Langlois had grown up during the silent era, with Chaplin as his favorite cinéaste. As a high school (*lycée*) student in Paris, he failed his *baccalauréate*, according to his brother Georges, because his dissertation, "The Comic and Comedy," compared Chaplin and Molière. Once asked about the ten best films in the world, he reportedly answered, "Easy: ten films of Chaplin!"[144] Langlois remained entranced by silent cinema: from 1932 to 1934, he continued to attend "two forgotten theaters … on the *grands boulevards*," showing silent films by Chaplin and others and "squeaking by thanks to their low prices and the opportunity they afforded certain women to rest awhile without altogether eliminating the prospects of finding a customer."[145]

In 1936, still in his early twenties, Langlois founded the Cercle du Cinéma, a club for Friday evening screenings that showed films unavailable anywhere else in Paris. Once he had discovered the club, recalled Jean Rouch, "there was no question of doing anything else on Friday night."[146] Screenings continued at the Cercle du Cinéma even after the founding of the Cinémathèque. In 1936, one evening was devoted to a Chaplin festival.[147] The program for the last April screening of 1937, titled "Humor on the Screen," was supposed to begin with Chaplin's *Shoulder Arms*. But since prints of films sometimes did not arrive on time, *Shoulder Arms* was not, apparently, screened on this evening. Conversely, when a planned program on German avant-garde films (May 7, 1937) had to be abandoned because they could not be brought out of Nazi Germany, Langlois replaced them with a Charlie Chaplin Festival.[148]

After German forces occupied Paris and the north and west of France in the summer of 1940, Langlois found himself fighting a long and complex campaign to defend the stocks of film he had acquired for the Cinémathèque.[149] At one point, the German head of the regional bureau of propaganda (the Propaganda staffel de Paris) accused the Cinémathèque of being "pro-American and pro-Jewish" and "concealing poisoned treasures." After a bibulous dinner with Langlois and filmmaker Marcel L'Herbier, then president of the Cinémathèque, at a restaurant on the Champs-Elysees, the same official changed his tune markedly—to the amusement of Langlois and L'Herbier—"by loudly singing the praises of the American cinema, and particularly Charlie Chaplin, Jew among Jews [*sic*]."[150] Nazi dislike of Chaplin—in part because of his left-wing politics, in part because he was erroneously identified as Jewish—had led to the suppression of *Modern Times* in Germany in 1936.[151] The release in 1940 of *The Great Dictator*, with its parody of Hitler/Hynkel, made him even less appealing to the Nazis. It would have been dangerous for Langlois to screen Chaplin movies during the German occupation. But after the Cercle du Cinéma reopened on December 7, 1944, just over three months after the Liberation of Paris, he would make sure Chaplin films were again on the program.[152]

It is not clear when Langlois and Chaplin first became personally acquainted. It may have been in December 1952, at the beginning of Chaplin's long exile from the United States, when the Cercle du Cinéma put together its festival devoted to Chaplin's work. The films for this, chosen by Chaplin himself, were provided by the Cinémathèque and United Artists.[153] It is inconceivable that Langlois was not involved in these arrangements. Certainly, after Langlois in 1960 walked out of the Fédération Internationale des Archives des Film, the organization he had cofounded in 1938, Chaplin maintained "complete trust" in him. Richard Roud, later cofounder of the New York Film Festival, knew both men and—in his biography of Langlois—told a revealing story about Chaplin's request "to store all his nitrate prints and negatives with the Cinémathèque." Langlois offered Chaplin "a whole bunker" on condition that Chaplin put his films there, put his own lock on it, and took away the key. "There were so many Chaplin films floating around the archive world," Roud observed, "that Langlois wouldn't run the risk of Chaplin's even suspecting that they came from him."[154]

Over the years, Langlois paid tribute to Chaplin in a variety of ways. In 1955, he was offered the opportunity to organize a large exhibition on cinema ("300 Years of Cinematography, 60 Years of Cinema") at the Musée d'art moderne in the Palais de Tokyo, Paris. Determined to make Chaplin a major focus of the exhibition, he put enormous effort into gathering posters, documents, scripts, sketches for sets, and a few costumes. Despite his best efforts, however, Truffaut recalled, "the most famous costume in movie history . . . a pair of boots, a cane, and a bowler hat," had not yet arrived when he [Chaplin] visited the exhibition.[155] Eight years later, in June 1963, when Malraux as minister of culture provided additional funding, a small new movie theater attached to the Cinémathèque at the Palais de Chaillot opened with a homage to Charlie Chaplin.[156]

On September 12, 1973, exactly two years and four months after the warm tribute paid him at the Cannes Film Festival, Chaplin arrived at the Cinémathèque Française to introduce a screening of *Monsieur Verdoux* before its re-release to commercial cinemas in France. Langlois waited on the avenue Albert de Mun, next to the Palais de Chaillot, to welcome Chaplin, his wife Oona, daughter Josephine, and business manager Rachel Ford. When the black car carrying them arrived at 20:30, Chaplin got out only with difficulty. He was now eighty-three years old and in increasingly poor health.[157] A photograph taken at the time shows him unsteady on his feet and carrying a cane, supported by Oona to his left and Langlois to his right as he descended the stairs to the Cinémathèque. Arriving in the crowded screening room, he was given a standing ovation by the audience. Chaplin waved to them and stammered a few words of thanks. Langlois then delivered a more formal introduction, explaining "in his breathless voice" that "in spite of the very old bonds between the Cinémathèque and Chaplin," this was his first actual visit to the institution. While he was speaking, Chaplin sat on the edge of his seat in the balcony to watch what was going on below, occasionally murmuring "Wonderful, wonderful." When the lights dimmed and *Monsieur Verdoux* started, the Chaplin party slipped out of the room to see the exhibition "75 Years of Cinema" launched a few months earlier at the Cinémathèque. (There, Langlois and Chaplin paused for a long time in front of a series of "Charlot" posters.)[158] At the end of the screening, Chaplin returned to the auditorium and tried to express his feelings in English, but no one had thought to provide a microphone and, "understanding that people could not hear him, Charlot blew kisses and waved his hand as a way of saying goodbye."[159]

As Glenn Myrent and Georges Langlois later noted, "Chaplin's insistence on showing the confidence and esteem in which he held the Cinémathèque by attending in person lent a very emotional tone to the screening."[160] The warmth of the applause for the white-haired comedian as he entered the screening room was a final fitting personal tribute to the very special bond Chaplin had enjoyed with France and French audiences since his first Keystone comedies had arrived in Paris in the grim wartime winter of 1915, almost sixty years earlier. It is worth pointing out, though, that the audience that crowded into the Cinémathèque that evening (Langlois mentioned in his introduction the tradition of sitting on the floor) was primarily made up of young people. As Samuel Lachize pointed out in *L'Humanité*, they "had not been born when the film had been shot and first shown in France."[161]

Yet Chaplin's film touched a chord with young French men and women; Langlois perceptively pointed out in his introduction the "modernity" of Verdoux himself, "a character very close to a [post–May 1968] generation that the revolt against the hypocrisy of the system sometimes pushes beyond leftism and anarchism."[162]

Many of the journalists and critics who wrote about the event at the Cinémathèque were themselves too young to remember the first screening of *Monsieur Verdoux* in France twenty-five years earlier. (The correspondent of the Catholic newspaper *La Croix* observed that he had then been "sous les drapeaux" [doing his military service].)[163] They knew that French reviews of 1948 had been positive for the most part (the names of Chaplin's supporters André Bazin, Jean Mitry, and Pierre Leprohon were mentioned), but also that *Monsieur Verdoux* had not been very profitable. "Even in France," Jean de Baroncelli remarked in *Le Monde*, "in spite of press support, the film's success was in doubt."[164] They were aware, of course, of Chaplin's later films: *Limelight* and the two he had produced in European exile, *A King in New York* and *A Countess from Hong Kong*. They must have realized, seeing his frailty at the Cinémathèque, that he was unlikely to make another film. Yet Chaplin's earlier policy of retiring his films from circulation for long periods and re-releasing them with much publicity as rarities had, as Albert Cervoni explained in *France Nouvelle*, a major drawback: it made it possible to study and assess only fragments of Chaplin's complete oeuvre.[165] In September 1973, the only opportunity a few French film critics had enjoyed to do more than this was to attend the Venice Film Festival a year earlier, as had Samuel Lachize of *L'Humanité* and G.T. of *L'Aurore*. For Venice, while giving Chaplin a Golden Lion for lifetime achievement, had also put on what Lachize called "a significant retrospective" of his films.[166]

To critics who had been in Venice, the screening of *Monsieur Verdoux* at the Cinémathèque underlined even more strongly its pivotal position in the development of Chaplin's career as a filmmaker. With this movie, commented G.T., he "definitively abandoned his old cast-offs as 'Charlot' in order to create a new character, at once funny and disturbing." Lachize made much the same point: the film marked "the very moment when Chaplin finally decides to appear on screen bare-faced. He is no longer the 'Little Guy,' with bowler hat, acrobatic playfulness, and down-at-heel shoes."[167] Other reviewers in 1973 were not so convinced. Charlot had not vanished into thin air, argued the critic of *Le Nouvel Observateur*, "he is still there [in *Monsieur Verdoux*] as a watermark." Albert Cervoni in *France Nouvelle* acknowledged that Chaplin was still a marvelous mime artist (as in the sequence in which Verdoux thinks he has poisoned himself). The gags in the film, both Cervoni and Henry Chapier of *Combat* commented, were as impressively inventive as ever.[168] Jean de Baroncelli in *Le Monde* even pointed out that, in playing Verdoux as "vindictive and pitiless," Chaplin had returned to the "maliciousness and aggressiveness" of the very first Charlot films.[169] Yet while they disagreed about how much of a break *Monsieur Verdoux* represented from Chaplin's earlier persona as Charlot, the critics of 1973 were united in their view of its status. The reviewer for *La Croix*, musing on *Monsieur Verdoux*'s arrival in France a quarter of a century earlier, declared that it was "truly difficult to understand that this film did not appear, at once, as a masterpiece." Yet, as Michel Duran pointed out in *Le Canard enchaîné*, opinion had been divided in 1948: "the film astonished, enthusing some, disappointing others who regretted [the loss of the character of] Charlot." Duran explained philosophically that "it is always like that for masterpieces; the first time, they are invariably not easily accepted." Nevertheless, Lachize of *L'Humanité* advised contemporaries, "the summit had been reached with *Monsieur Verdoux*. Go and watch or re-watch this film. . . . It is one of the greatest delights for a film enthusiast, a monument to the cinematic art."[170]

The meeting at the Cinémathèque in September 1973 poignantly was the last time Chaplin and Langlois would see one another. Langlois died on January 13, 1977, at the age of only sixty-two. Chaplin himself died peacefully only eleven months later, age eighty-eight, during Christmas night 1977.

Afterword

As a study of the reception of Charlot in France, this book has analyzed the varying interpretations offered by French movie critics and intellectuals of Charlie Chaplin and his films from 1915 to 1973. When the first Charlot films arrived in Paris, France was beginning to adjust to the dismal reality of a deadlocked, bloody war, and Chaplin's comedies—what Louis Delluc called his "comic frenzy"—offered much-needed relief and distraction.[1] He quickly became a favorite with both audiences and critics. In the postwar period and the 1920s, he reached his peak as a film star in France. As his movies became longer and more complex, some avant-garde writers began to argue that they were not just brilliant comedies, that they reflected and spoke to the historical moment. Élie Faure saw Chaplin as the embodiment of the spirit of the postwar era ("dancing on the summits of despair") in which the French, though on the winning side in the war, were so traumatized by the loss of life, injuries, and destruction it had wrought that they could do little more than celebrate in a brittle way their own survival.[2]

For many French cinéastes and intellectuals, Chaplin became a crucial influence on their lives. Watching Charlot movies (and DeMille's *The Cheat*) during World War I convinced Louis Delluc of the emerging significance of cinema. He went on to become a film critic, scenarist, and movie director. Jean Renoir remembered being "carried away" by watching these new comedies while on leave from his duties as a pilot in the war. Chaplin films, he later wrote, had "converted" him into "a fanatical cinema fan" who would also in time become a film director. Jean Mitry recalled that he had seen his first Chaplin film, *Charlot s'évade* (*The Adventurer*, Mutual, 1917) as a young boy in 1918 and had been so impressed that he immediately began to search for other Charlot movies.[3] Looking back on the first Chaplin films he had seen in Nantes during the First World War at the age of three or four, journalist Morvan Lebesque paid tribute to "our friend, the one we realize with a kind of astonishment that he has accompanied us all our lives and that if he were suddenly to disappear it would be a little as if our own death had begun."[4] Henri Langlois, cofounder and for many years director of the

Charlot. Melvyn Stokes, Oxford University Press. © Oxford University Press 2026.
DOI: 10.1093/9780197839294.003.0010

Cinémathèque in Paris, failed his *baccalauréat* in 1933 because his assigned dissertation on the subject of comedy was given a zero for focusing on Charlot. (Forty years later, Langlois would proudly welcome Chaplin himself to the Cinémathèque.)[5] In the years after the Second World War, new enthusiasts for and supporters of Chaplin appeared, including influential film critic and theorist André Bazin and his protégé François Truffaut, who would later (1972) publish Bazin's articles on Chaplin as an edited volume. At times, indeed, enthusiasm for Chaplin in France seemed to pass from generation to generation. Film director Jacques de Baroncelli was a fan of his earlier work. His son Jean, longtime movie critic for *Le Monde* newspaper, would carry on the family tradition, writing supportive reviews of Chaplin's final films, *A King in New York* and *A Countess from Hong Kong*.

Chaplin's visits to France in 1921 demonstrated both his new status as probably the greatest movie star in the world and the fact he was now important enough for people to claim his support for their opinions. The attempts by the right-wing newspaper *Le Journal* and the left-wing *L'Humanité* to suggest that Chaplin shared their very different views of the Bolshevik Revolution of 1917 underlined the fact that his views seemed to *matter* even if no one was able to define precisely what they were. The point was underlined still further by the fact that a whole range of other French newspapers and periodicals not normally noted for their great interest in film—the right-wing Catholic *La Libre Parole*, the Republican radical *L'Homme Libre*, the communist *Le Journal du Peuple*, the anarchist *La Libertaire*, and the syndicalist *Le Peuple*—also became engaged in the ensuing controversy. Chaplin's star status could be used by many groups to further their own ideas. Moreover, it was not simply that Chaplin/Charlot became a symbol that could be interpreted differently. His actual films—particularly after he began to make more "political" movies during the 1930s—were at times understood and written about in vastly different ways. To left-wingers such as Jean Renoir, for example, *Modern Times* seemed an indictment of the capitalist system and, especially, of the regimentation and depersonalization of American factory workers. But to right-wing François Vinneuil (the pseudonym of future Nazi collaborator Lucien Rebatet) it was an indictment of the materialism and emphasis on productivity that characterized Stalin's Russia.

French politicians were also keen to take advantage of Chaplin's popularity and star status. On a 1921 visit to Paris he was decorated by André Bérard, minister of beaux-arts, as an "officer of public instruction" for allowing his new film *The Kid* to be shown—and appear himself—at a glossy charitable gala in aid of rebuilding areas of northeastern France devastated by the First World War. Chaplin himself had probably expected to receive the Legion of Honor, France's highest distinction, which he did on his next visit to France, in 1931. Invited to lunch at the French Foreign Office by the Minister for Foreign Affairs Aristide Briand, a few days later he became a knight of the Legion of Honor in a private ceremony at the Quai d'Orsay. In 1952, after his permit to reenter the United States had been withdrawn, he was invited for lunch by socialist president Vincent Auriol. Shortly afterward, he attended a ceremony in which André Marie, the minister of education, promoted him from knight to officer in the Legion of Honor. In 1971, at the Cannes Film Festival, he was further elevated by Minister of Culture Jacques Duhamel to commander, the highest rank in the Legion of Honor available for someone not a French citizen. French politicians were apparently completely uninterested in American allegations concerning Chaplin's private life or his political views, preferring to focus on his vast and enduring popularity in France. They honored him long before he gained recognition in the land of his birth; in spite of a long acquaintance with British politician Winston Churchill, he would have to wait until 1975 to receive a knighthood from Queen Elizabeth II.

One issue much discussed in the period after World War I was whether cinema could be regarded as a new art form. In his 1921 book on Chaplin, Delluc compared him to Beethoven in music, Velázquez and Dürer in painting, Villon in poetry, and—among others—Duncan, Pavlova, and Nijinsky in dance. In presenting Chaplin as a "creative artist" on a par with great figures in four major existing arts, Delluc was controversially suggesting that cinema—as epitomized in Chaplin's films—was now recognizably an art form.[6] This was contested by, among others, literary critic Paul Souday, who argued in a newspaper article in 1927 that Chaplin's films demonstrated that film was not and could never be an art because it was not based on words. Souday had already made this argument in *Le Temps* in 1916.[7] The difference in 1927 was that Chaplin's reputation had grown enough for Souday to make Charlot the principal target for his critique. To Souday, Chaplin was simply a "clown" who pulled faces and made gestures. Souday's focus on language ignored the use of words in movie intertitles—and the fact that several traditional arts were not language-based. But journalist Jean de Pierrefeu countered Souday's attack by arguing that—inspired by Chaplin's films—many French writers increasingly were embracing the cinema with enthusiasm. Chaplin himself, he argued, was not simply a nonspeaking actor but the inventor of brilliant scenarios and shots that in only a few seconds could communicate a mood or feeling that would take pages for a novelist to create. André Maurois, also writing in 1927, similarly hailed Chaplin's skill in communicating complicated ideas quickly and simply while arguing that even a major literary figure such as Marcel Proust would need many words to convey a similar impression.[8]

As the controversies launched by Paul Souday and André Suarès suggested, both Chaplin and his films were at times the subjects of vigorous criticism in France. Yet when such attacks were launched, noted Georges Sadoul, "the majority of public opinion and the cinematic press took Chaplin's side."[9] French writers and cinéastes also frequently found themselves defending Chaplin against his American critics. When Lita Grey, Chaplin's second wife, filed for divorce in 1927, her accusations provoked a moral backlash, especially from women's organizations, with demands that his films be banned. In France, Louis Aragon wrote a spirited (if highly sexist) defense of Chaplin's right to sexual freedom that was signed by thirty-one other (male) surrealists. According to his biographer David Robinson, Chaplin was "greatly heartened" when he learned of this French protest.[10]

After the Second World War, there was considerable sympathy in France for Chaplin when he was pursued by right-wing American anticommunists. In November 1947, when he asked Pablo Picasso to organize a protest to the American Embassy in Paris over the threatened deportation from the United States of Chaplin's friend, composer and sometime member of the Communist Party Hanns Eisler, many French actors, artists, and intellectuals lent their names to it.[11] By the time *Monsieur Verdoux* was premièred in France two months later, most French intellectuals and cinéastes were well aware that Chaplin was under increasing pressure in the United States for his alleged moral failings and suspected pro-communist outlook. This, together with the fact that the film itself was set in France and grew out of the experiences of a French Bluebeard figure, ensured an enthusiastic reception. In 1952, when Chaplin and his wife—now exiled from the United States— arrived in Paris for the release of *Limelight*, they were initially greeted with great warmth and sympathy by writers, cinéastes, and members of the public alike. Yet, at the same time, *Limelight* itself can be seen—at least in France— as the start of the decline of Chaplin's reputation as a filmmaker. Had it not been for the publicity generated by Chaplin's presence in Paris, even André Bazin conceded, the film would probably have been a miserable failure at the box office. With *A King in New York* (1957), most French reviewers were either critical or of two minds. Even Chaplin supporter Jean de Baroncelli left the première with a feeling of mild disappointment, and Bazin liked only the first half (the satire on modern American culture) and not the mainly humorless and political second part. The movie did not do well at the box office. *A Countess from Hong Kong* (1967), which Chaplin directed rather than starred in, was a critical and financial disaster.

At the same time, however, it was in the years between 1952 and 1973 that Chaplin's star image and reputation began to change, preparing the ground for what he himself referred to as his "renaissance." By the time *Limelight* was released, some French commentators were arguing that he could not be perceived—and critiqued—in the same way as other filmmakers. As a major influence on the creation of cinema itself, he was in a category of his own and should be judged on this basis. And during the 1950s and 1960s, as new movies made by Chaplin began to suggest his decline, French critics and cinéastes increasingly turned their attention to defining and securing his legacy as an outstanding filmmaker. This underpinned François Truffaut's plans to bring together all Bazin's essays on Chaplin's films in book form. It also motivated the request from the French Society of Writers for Cinema and Television that Chaplin re-release more of his films. Chaplin himself was probably already thinking along these lines. At least some of the negotiations for the distribution deal with Mo Rothman and Bert Schneider that began such a program of re-releases took place in France with the very first such screening—of *Modern Times*—in Paris with Chaplin himself present in November 1971.

Just under six months earlier, he had been honored at the Cannes Film Festival, where French Minister of Culture Jacques Duhamel praised him as the greatest actor the cinema had produced. In 1973, Henri Langlois's screening of *Monsieur Verdoux* at the Cinémathèque in Chaplin's presence demonstrated two things. First, earlier Chaplin films could grow in stature over time: *Monsieur Verdoux* had been well enough received by French critics in 1948, but with the benefit of hindsight, a number of critics noted, it was now clearly recognizable as a masterpiece. Second, since the bulk of the audience consisted of young people who had not yet been born when Chaplin was at the peak of his career, their appreciation for the film suggested that his work was ripe to appeal to new generations. The French love affair with Charlie Chaplin was not over. In many ways, indeed, it still continues.

Note on Sources

In a thoughtful book on Charlie Chaplin and politics, Richard Carr observed that the filmmaker and comedian "lived a global life and has thus left behind an internationally scattered collection of material that numerous accounts of his work have overlooked."[1] This book is based on materials relating to the reception of Chaplin and his films in France, a country with a good claim to having invented cinema itself that also witnessed the early emergence of a vibrant film culture. While this was hampered by the outbreak of the First World War—many writers were called up, and paper and printing materials were in short supply—what Richard Abel terms a "rich, insightful, and combative" collection of writings on cinema nonetheless emerged even in these straitened circumstances.[2] By a happy coincidence, the fortnightly magazine *Ciné-Journal* resumed publication in March 1915—the same month the first Chaplin films arrived in France. It was joined a year later by the relaunched weekly *Le Film*, perhaps the main vehicle until 1919 for discussions relating to cinema.[3]

With the war ending in November 1918, other movie periodicals either resumed publication (*Filma*, founded in 1908) or appeared for the first time (*La Cinématographie française* [1918], *Le Cinéopse* [1919], and *Ciné pour tous* [1919]). Some French newspapers, while operating on a reduced scale during the war, had also responded to the growing public interest in cinema that coincided with the appearance of Charlot and a rising tide of other imported American films. In 1916, the daily newspaper *Le Temps* introduced a biweekly series of movie reviews by Émile Vuillermoz and *Paris-Midi* followed in 1918 by Louis Delluc's weekly column. Soon after the war's end, film reviews were being published in a range of other newspapers, including *Comoedia*, *Le Figaro*, *L'Humanité*, *L'Intransigeant*, *Le Journal*, *Le Matin*, *Le Petit Journal*, *Le Petit Parisien*, and *Paris-Soir*. By the early 1920s, Abel writes, the number of French periodicals devoted to cinema was experiencing an "explosive expansion."[4] In addition, the first serious books on cinema began to be published—including Delluc's *Charlot* (1921).

The 1920s also witnessed a major change in broader French culture. A perceptive American journalist who lived in Paris at various times in the

1920s and 1930s later recalled his experience of the city as "a world capital … bursting with an artistic and intellectual vitality unmatchable anywhere else."[5] One of the major symptoms of that vitality was the vast range of literary, artistic, and intellectual journals that existed. In the postwar period, as Abel points out, many of these periodicals, demonstrating "cinema's acceptance as a legitimate art form … began, on a consistent basis, to open their pages to essays on the cinema as well as to film reviews."[6] They were often written by enthusiasts for film who came from other intellectual backgrounds and disciplines. Thus, for example, as noted earlier, art historian Élie Faure contributed an article titled "Charlot" for the avant-garde *L'Esprit Nouveau* in 1921, novelist and poet Lucien Fabre published an article with the same title in *La Revue hebdomadaire* in 1925, and writer-critic Jean Prévost wrote "Essai sur Charlot" for the literary review *Le Navire d'argent* in 1926. Among other journals, the satirical magazine *Le Canard enchaîné* merits attention for its frequent references to Chaplin and his films.

The main sources for this book between the First and Second World Wars have been newspapers and periodicals that have focused on cinema. Among newspapers, Gallica, the digitized library of the Bibliothèque national de France (BNF), has an excellent range for this period available online. These include *Ce Soir, Comoedia, La Croix, L'Echo de Paris, Le Ère Nouvelle, Le Figaro, Le Gaulois, L'Homme libre, L'Humanité, L'Intransigeant, Le Journal, Le Libertaire, La liberté, Le Matin, Paris-Midi, Paris-Soir, Le Petit Journal, Petit Parisien, Le Populaire, Le Quotidien, Le Radical,* and *Le Temps.* The BNF–François Mitterrand has microfilm copies of *L'Éclair, Le Journal du Peuple, Le Libre Parole, Le Peuple, La Republique française,* and *La Victoire.* For cinema periodicals during this period, Gallica has online versions of *Ciné-Journal, Cinéa, Ciné-Miroir, Cinémagazine, La Cinématographie française, Le Cinéopse, Le Film, Hebdo-Film,* and *Mon Ciné.* The BNF has a range of microfilm copies that includes *Ciné pour tous* (which in 1923 amalgamated with *Cinéa* to become *Cinéa-Ciné-Pour-Tous*), *Le Cinéma et l'Echo du Cinéma Réunis, Ciné-Monde, Le Courrier Cinématographique, Filma,* and *Pour Vous.* The Bibliothèque du Film (BiFi) in Paris, part of the Cinémathèque, has a vast collection of film journals from the period available on microfilm. Of these journals, *Ciné pour tous, Cinéa, La cinématographie française, Cinémonde, Le courrier cinématographique, Le Film,* and *Pour Vous* are currently also available in digital form.

The Second World War created great changes in the world of French newspapers and periodicals. The right-wing *Le Figaro* and communist

L'Humanité were fairly unusual in their survival. Many daily titles, often tracing their lineage back to the Second Empire or Third Republic, simply disappeared during or soon after the war. These included *Le Journal, La Liberté, Le Matin, Le Petit Journal, Le Petit Parisien,* and *Le Temps.* More recently established papers—*L'Action française, Comoedia, Paris-Midi,* and *Paris Soir*—also ceased publication. In their place emerged newspapers that had their origin in the resistance movement (*L'Aurore, Combat, Le Franc-tireur,* and *Défense de La France,* which changed its name to *France-Soir*) or, in the case of *Le Monde* (1944), at the request of General Charles de Gaulle. Most of these, apart from *Le Monde,* are available on Gallica. The same period saw the founding of two major periodicals devoted to cinema: *Cahiers du cinéma* (1951) and *Positif* (1952). For anyone wishing to consult French newspaper and periodical reviews of Chaplin's films (or any others) in the postwar period, the BiFi has created an extremely helpful archive of post–World War II movie reviews drawn from a huge range of publications. This source is referenced in chapters 6, 7, and 8 as the "BiFi Collection."

Finally, I would like to offer a personal thanks to the select group of people who have run bookshops in Paris focusing primarily on cinema. I have spent many happy hours browsing in these shops, the source of cherished personal copies of, for example, Philippe Soupault's *Charlot* (1931), Jean Mitry's *Charlot et la "Fabulation" Chaplinesque* (1957), and Georges Sadoul's *Vie de Charlot* (1978). Sadly, none of the shops I knew survives, but hopefully their successors are—or soon will be—open for business in one of the most cinematically conscious of modern cities.

Filmography

Keystone Films (1914)

1. *Making a Living* (French title: *Charlot journaliste*. Other titles: *Pour gagner sa vie*; *Charlot reporter*)
2. *Kid Auto Races at Venice* (French title: *Charlot est content de lui*. Other title: *Course d'auto pour gosses*)
3. *Mabel's Strange Predicament* (French title: *L'Etrange aventure de Mabel*. Other title: *Charlot à l'hôtel*)
4. *Between Showers* (French title: *Charlot et la parapluie*. Other titles: *Charlot sous l'averse*; *Charlot flirte*)
5. *A Film Johnnie* (French titles: *Charlot fait du cinéma*; *Piqué du cinéma*)
6. *Tango Tangles* (French title: *Charlot au bal*. Other title: *Charlot danseur*)
7. *His Favorite Pastime* (French title: *Charlot entre le bar et l'amour*. Other title: *Charlot est trop galant*)
8. *Cruel, Cruel Love* (French title: *Charlot Marquis*. Other titles: *Charlot fou d'amour*; *Charlot veut en finir*)
9. *The Star Boarder* (French title: *Charlot pensionnaire*. Other titles: *Charlot aime la patronne*; *Agathe cherche un mari*)
10. *Mabel at the Wheel* (French title: *Charlot et Mabel au volant*. Other titles: *Charlot contre Mabel*; *Charlot et Mabel au courses*; *Charlot coureur automobile*)
11. *Twenty Minutes of Love* (French title: *Charlot et le chronomètre*)
12. *Caught in a Cabaret* (French title: *Charlot garçon de café*. Other title: *Charlot l'imposteur*)
13. *Caught in the Rain* (French title: *Charlot et la somnambule*. Other titles: *Un béguin de Charlot*; *Charlot est encombrant*)
14. *A Busy Day* (French title: *La jalousie de Charlot*. Other title: *Madame Charlot*)
15. *The Fatal Mallet* (French title: *Le maillet de Charlot*. Other title: *Charlot briseur de crânes*)

16. *Her Friend the Bandit* (French title: *Le flirt de Mabel*)

17. *The Knockout* (French title: *Charlot et Fatty dans le ring*. Other title: *Charlot arbitre*)

18. *Mabel's Busy Day* (French title: *Charlot et les saucisses*. Other titles: *Mabel marchand ambulante*; *Le Flirt de Mabel*)

19. *Mabel's Married Life* (French title: *Charlot et Mabel en ménage*. Other titles: *Charlot et le mannequin*; *Charlot marié*)

20. *Laughing Gas* (French title: *Charlot dentiste*. Other title: *Charlot opère lui-même*)

21. *The Property Man* (French title: *Charlot garçon de théâtre*. Other titles: *Charlot accessoiriste*; *Charlot dans les coulisses*; *Charlot monte sur le planches*)

22. *The Face on the Bar Room Floor* (French title: *Charlot artiste-peintre*. Other titles: *Charlot fou*; *Charlot cabotin*)

23. *Recreation* (French title: *Fièvre printanière*. Other title: *Charlot s'amuse*)

24. *The Masquerader* (French title: *Charlot acteur dramatique*. Other titles: *Charlot grande coquette*; *Charlot et l'étoile*)

25. *His New Profession* (French title: *La nouvelle profession de Charlot*. Other titles: *Charlot garde-malade*; *Charlot bon à rien*)

26. *The Rounders* (French title: *Charlot et Fatty en bombe*. Other title: *Charlot et Fatty au café*)

27. *The New Janitor* (French title: *Charlot concierge*. Other title: *Charlot portier*)

28. *Those Love Pangs* (French title: *Charlot rival d'amour*. Other titles: *Charlot supplanté par Joseph*; *Charlot et Joseph rivaux d'amour*)

29. *Dough and Dynamite* (French title: *Charlot mitron*. Other title: *Charlot pâtissier*)

30. *Gentlemen of Nerve* (French title: *Charlot et Mabel aux courses*. Other title: *Charlot et Mabel à l'autodrome*)

31. *His Musical Career* (French title: *Charlot livreur de pianos*. Other title: *Charlot déménageur*)

32. *His Trysting Place* (French title: *Charlot en famille*. Other title: *Charlot papa*)

33. *Tillie's Punctured Romance* (French title: *Le roman comique de Charlot et Lolotte*. Other title: *L'extravagante aventure de Charlot*)

34. *Getting Acquainted* (French title: *Charlot et Mabel en promenade*. Other title: *Charlot marié*)

35. *His Prehistoric Past* (French title: *Le Rêve de Charlot*. Other titles: *Charlot roi; Charlot nudiste; Le Passé préhistorique de Charlot*)

Essanay Films (1915–16)

36. *His New Job* (French title: *Charlot dans les coulisses*. Other titles: *Charlot débute au cinéma; Charlot acteur dramatique*)
37. *A Night Out* (French title: *Charlot fait la noce*. Other title: *Charlot en bombe*)
38. *The Champion* (French title: *Charlot boxeur*. Other title: *Charlot champion de boxe*)
39. *In the Park* (French title: *Charlot dans le parc*. Other titles: *Charlot se promène; Charlot fait des siennes*)
40. *A Jitney Elopement* (French title: *Charlot veut se marier*. Oher title: *Charlot enlève sa fiancée*)
41. *The Tramp* (French title: *Charlot vagabond*. Other titles: *Charlot à la campagne; Charlot à la ferme; Charlot chemineau*)
42. *By the Sea* (French title: *Charlot à la plage*. Oher title: *Charlot sur le sable*)
43. *Work* (French title: *Charlot apprenti*. Other titles: *Charlot travaille; Charlot plombier; Charlot trimardeur*)
44. *A Woman* (French title: *Mam'zelle Charlot*. Other titles: *Charlot travesti; Charlot fait des siennes; Charlot demoiselle*)
45. *The Bank* (French title: *Charlot à la banque*. Other titles: *Charlie détective; Charlot garçon de banque*)
46. *Shanghaied* (French title: *Charlot marin*. Other title: *Charlot matelot*)
47. *A Night in the Show* (French title: *Charlot au Music-Hall*. Other title: *Charlot au spectacle*)
48. *Charlie Chaplin's Burlesque on Carmen* (French title: *Charlot joue Carmen*)
49. *Police* (French title: *Charlot cambrioleur*)

Mutual Films (1916–17)

50. *The Floorwalker* (French title: *Charlot chef de rayon*)
51. *The Fireman* (French title: *Charlot pompier*)

52. *The Vagabond* (French title: *Charlot musicien*. Other title: *Charlot violoniste*)
53. *One A.M.* (French title: *Charlot rentre tard*. Other title: *Le Noctambule*)
54. *The Count* (French title: *Charlot et le Comte*. Other titles: *Charlot tailleur; L'imposteur*)
55. *The Pawnshop* (French title: *Charlot chez l'usurier*. Other title: *Charlot brocanteur*)
56. *Behind the Screen* (French title: *Charlot fait du ciné*. Other title: *Le Machiniste*)
57. *The Rink* (French title: *Charlot patine*. Other title: *Patinage*)
58. *Easy Street* (French title: *Charlot policeman*. Other titles: *Charlot ne s'en fait pas; Le Policeman*)
59. *The Cure* (French title: *Charlot fait une cure*. Other title: *La Cure*)
60. *The Immigrant* (French title: *Charlot voyage*. Other title: *L'émigrant*)
61. *The Adventurer* (French title: *Charlot s'évade*. Other titles: *L'évadé; L'aventurier*)

First National Films (1918–22)

62. *A Dog's Life* (French title: *Une vie de chien*)
63. *Shoulder Arms* (French title: *Charlot soldat*)
64. *Sunnyside* (French title: *Une Idylle aux champs*)
65. *A Day's Pleasure* (French title: *Une journée de plaisir*)
66. *The Kid* (French title: *Le Gosse*)
67. *The Idle Class* (French title: *Charlot et le masque de fer*)
68. *Pay Day* (French title: *Jour de paye*)
69. *The Pilgrim* (French title: *Le pèlerin*)

United Artists Films

70. *A Woman of Paris* (1923) (French title: *L'Opinion publique*)
71. *The Gold Rush* (1925) (French title: *La Ruée vers l'or*)
72. *The Circus* (1928) (French title: *Le Cirque*)
73. *City Lights* (1931) (French title: *Les Lumières de la Ville*)
74. *Modern Times* (1936) (French title: *Les Temps Modernes*)

75. *The Great Dictator* (1940) (French title: *Le Dictateur*)
76. *Monsieur Verdoux* (1947) (French title: same)
77. *Limelight* (1952) (French title: *Les feux de la rampe*)

Other Productions

78. *A King in New York* (1957) (French title: *Un Roi à New York*)
79. *A Countess from Hong Kong* (1967) (French title: *La Comtesse de Hong-Kong*)

Notes

Introduction

1. Charles Chaplin, *My Autobiography* (Bodley Head, 1964), 187–90, quotation from 190.
2. Ibid., 169. On August 9, 1914, Chaplin wrote to his brother Sydney, "Well, Sid, I have made good. All the theatres feature my name in big letters. . . . in this country I am a big box office attraction . . . . It is wonderful how popular I am in such a short time." David Robinson, *Chaplin: His Life and Art* (Grafton, 1985), 131–32.
3. Robinson, *Chaplin*, 152.
4. Charles J. McGuirk, "Chaplinitis," *Motion Picture Magazine* 10 (August 1915): 87.
5. Richard deCordova, *Picture Personalities: The Emergence of the Star System in America* (University of Illinois Press, 2001), 113–14.
6. Charles J. McGuirk, "Chaplinitis," *Motion Picture Magazine* 9 (July 1915): 121.
7. Robinson, *Chaplin*, 142, 152–53; McGuirk, "Chaplinitis" (August 1915): 87–89, quotation from 89; David Robinson, *Chaplin: The Mirror of Opinion* (Secker and Warburg, 1984), 35, 37; Charles J. Maland, *Chaplin and American Culture: The Evolution of a Star Image* (Princeton University Press, 1989), 10–11.
8. Tom Gunning, *D. W. Griffith and the Origins of American Narrative Film: The Early Years at Biograph* (University of Illinois Press, 1991), 6–7, 41–42.
9. deCordova, *Picture Personalities*, 25.
10. Paul McDonald, *The Star System: Hollywood's Production of Popular Identities* (Wallflower, 2000), 22, 27–28.
11. Ibid., 22.
12. The available statistics for the total number of nickelodeons can only be regarded as approximate since, as Eileen Bowser observes, "they were constantly going out of business and springing up anew." Bowser cites estimates that there were 2,500 by the start of 1907, 8,000 by 1907–8, and 10,000 by 1910. Eileen Bowser, *The Transformation of Cinema, 1907–1915* (Scribner's, 1990), 4, 6.
13. Charles Musser, *The Emergence of Cinema: The American Screen to 1907* (Scribner's, 1990), 417, 433; McDonald, *The Star System*, 25–26.
14. deCordova, *Picture Personalities*, 27–28; McDonald, *The Star System*, 27; Robert C. Allen, *Vaudeville and Film 1895–1915: A Study in Media Interaction* (University Microfilms International, 1977), 212.
15. See, for example, Terry Ramsaye, *A Million and One Nights: A History of the Motion Picture* (Simon and Schuster, 1926), 1:523–25; Lewis Jacobs, *The Rise of the American Film: A Critical History* (Harcourt, Brace, 1939), 86–88, quote from *Moving Picture World*, 87; Alexander Walker, *Stardom: The Hollywood Phenomenon* (Stein and Day, 1970), 19–39; Richard Dyer, *Stars* (BFI, 1979), 9–10; David A. Cook, *A History of Narrative Film* (Norton, 1981), 40.
16. Janet Staiger, "Seeing Stars," *Velvet Light Trap* 20 (Summer 1983): 11–12; Richard deCordova, "The Emergence of the Star System in America," *Wide Angle* 6, no. 4 (1985): 9–10; deCordova, *Picture Personalities*, 41–44, 52–53, 55–58; Bowser, *The Transformation of Cinema*, 108; McDonald, *The Star System*, 30.
17. See Janet Staiger, "The Eyes Are Really the Focus: Photoplay Acting and Film Form and Style," *Wide Angle* 6, no. 4 (1985): 21.
18. Kathryn H. Fuller, *At the Picture Show: Small-Town Audiences and the Creation of Movie Fan Culture* (Smithsonian Institution, 1996), 136, 145–46.
19. Jane Gaines refers to competing claims that the first press books were for the imported Italian film *Quo Vadis* (1913) or Jesse Lasky's *The Squaw Man* (1913). Jane Gaines, "From Elephants to Lux Soap: The Programming and 'Flow' of Early Motion Picture Exploitation," *Velvet Light Trap*, no. 25 (Spring 1990): 42n16.
20. deCordova, *Picture Personalities*, 86–91.

21. *Photoplay*, March 1912, 72, quoted in deCordova, *Picture Personalities*, 105–6.

22. deCordova, *Picture Personalities*, 98–102, 105.

23. Ibid., 3, 70–71, 82, 89; McDonald, *The Star System*, 34.

24. Robinson, *Chaplin*, 121–22.

25. Richard Koszarski, *An Evening's Entertainment: The Age of the Silent Feature Picture 1915–1928* (University of California Press, 1990), 263.

26. Maland, *Chaplin and American Culture*, 197.

27. Richard Dyer, *Stars* (BFI, 1979), 1, 68; Maland, *Chaplin and American Culture*, xv.

28. Maland, *Chaplin and American Culture*, xvi.

29. Ibid., xiv–xv.

30. Ibid., 6.

31. Ibid., 14–16.

32. Ibid., 20–23.

33. Ibid., 26–29.

34. Ibid., 41, 43–49.

35. Ibid., 55–59.

36. Ibid., 70–76.

37. Ibid., 55, 59, 62–68, 80–82, 84–93.

38. Ibid., 95–98, 110–15, 27–31.

39. Ibid., 94–99.

40. Ibid., 99–105, quotation from 105.

41. Ibid., 110.

42. Ibid., 127–28.

43. Ibid., 149–57, quotation from 157.

44. Ibid., 165.

45. Ibid., 170–72.

46. Ibid., 178–79, 186–87.

47. Ibid., 187–94.

48. Ibid., 197–206, 213–18.

49. Ibid., 230–32, 234–35, quotation from 234.

50. Ibid., 247, 253–64.

51. Ibid., 264–73.

52. Ibid., 273–77, 279.

53. Ibid., 280, 282–83, quotation from 283.

54. Ibid., 326–47, quotation from 337. In 2016, Lisa Stein Haven published a fine book that supplemented Maland's work by analyzing the groups and forces inside the United States—including Bohemian writers, Beat poets, screenings both legal and illegal, filmmakers and collectors—who helped keep Chaplin's reputation alive in the United States between 1947 and 1977. Lisa Stein Haven, *Charlie Chaplin's Little Tramp in America, 1947–1977* (Palgrave Macmillan, 2016).

55. Maland did, however, suggest that his research had convinced him "that it would be interesting and worthwhile to examine the evolution of Chaplin's star image in a number of countries, especially Great Britain, France, and the Soviet Union" (*Chaplin and American Culture*, 375n2).

56. See Richard Abel, *The Red Rooster Scare: Making Cinema American, 1900–1910* (University of California Press, 1999); Richard Abel, *Americanizing the Movies and "Movie-Mad" Audiences, 1910–1914* (University of California Press, 2006).

57. Colette, "Cinéma," *Excelsior*, August 7, 1916, reprinted in Colette, *Colette at the Movies: Criticism and Screenplays*, ed. Alain and Odette Virmaux, trans. Sarah W. R. Smith (Frederick Ungar, 1980), 19; Louis Delluc, "Beauty in the Cinema," *Le Film* 73 (August 6, 1917): 4–5, translated in Richard Abel, *French Film Theory and Criticism: A History/Anthology 1907–1939*, vol. 1: *1909–1929* (Princeton University Press, 1988), 138–39.

58. Julian Johnson, "The Girl on the Cover," *Photoplay*, April 1920, 57, quoted in Koszarski, *An Evening's Entertainment*, 273. For more on the influence of Pearl White and other "serial queens" on French, Swedish, Czechoslovak, Indian, and Chinese audiences, see Marina Dahlquist, ed., *Exporting Perilous Pauline: Pearl White and the Serial Film Craze* (University of Illinois Press, 2013).

59. Robinson, *Chaplin: The Mirror of Opinion*, 61.

60. Maland, *Chaplin and American Culture*, 59; Béla Balázs, "Mr. Chaplin, kommen Sie nach Europa" (1927), cited in Sabine Hake, "Chaplin Reception in Weimar Germany," in "Weimar Mass Culture," special issue, *New German Critique*, no. 51 (Autumn 1990): 87.

61. Maland, *Chaplin and American Culture*, 113.

62. Of the five names cited above, three were born outside the United States: Chaplin (London), Pickford (Toronto), and Hayakawa (Minamibosō, Japan).

63. Helen Taylor, *Scarlett's Women: "Gone With the Wind" and Its Female Fans* (Virago, 1989); Jackie Stacey, *Star Gazing: Hollywood Cinema and Female Spectatorship* (Routledge, 1994); Annette Kuhn, *Dreaming of Fred and Ginger: Cinema and Cultural Memory* (New York University Press, 2002).

64. Miyao argues that Hayakawa's enthusiastic reception in Germany, Russia, and, especially, France was not at first matched by that in Japan, his home country, where audiences could not see *The Cheat* for many years and the initial Japanese response to Hayakawa was heavily conditioned by the California Japanese American community's criticism of him for playing so unfavorable a character. Daisuke Miyao, *Sessue Hayakawa: Silent Cinema and International Stardom* (Duke University Press, 2007), 3–5, 26–29.

65. Russell Meeuf, *John Wayne's World: Traditional Masculinity in the Fifties* (University of Texas Press, 2013); Russell Meeuf and Raphael Raphael, eds., *Transnational Stardom: International Celebrity in Film and Popular Culture* (Palgrave Macmillan, 2013).

66. C. Brian Morris, "Charles Chaplin's Tryst with Spain," *Journal of Contemporary History* 18 (1983): 517–31; David Selbourne, "Charlie Chaplin in Calcutta," *History Workshop*, no. 5 (Spring 1978): 237–38.

67. Hake, "Chaplin Reception in Weimar Germany"; Joseph Garncarz, "'Films That Are Applauded All over the World': Questioning Chaplin's Popularity in Weimar Germany," *Early Popular Visual Culture* 8, no. 3 (2010): 285–96.

68. Nobert Aping, *Charlie Chaplin and the Nazis: The Long German Campaign Against the Artist* (McFarland, 2024).

69. Ibid., 33. Aping covers this period in more detail in Nobert Aping, *Charlie Chaplin in Deutschland 1915–1925: Der Tramp kommt ins Kino* (Schüren Verlag, 2014).

70. Aping, *Charlie Chaplin and the Nazis*, 38–39, 42–43.

71. Ibid., 48–55, 66–67, 77.

72. See, for example, ibid., 83–85.

73. Ibid., 97–98, quotation from 98.

74. Ibid., 120–73.

75. Ibid., 187.

76. Ibid., 226–27, 255–56, 260–63. *The Great Dictator* would not be shown for the first time in West Germany until 1958 and East Germany until 1980 (362).

77. Ibid., 249.

78. Dyer discerned limits to how stars could be read or interpreted. He defined "structured polysemy" as "the finite multiplicity of meanings and affects they embody and the attempt so to structure them that some meanings and affects are foregrounded and others are masked or displaced" (*Stars*, 3). "Audiences," he subsequently wrote, "cannot make media images mean anything they want to, but they can select from the complexity of the image the meanings and feelings, the variations, inflections and contradictions, that work for them." Richard Dyer, *Heavenly Bodies: Film Stars and Society* (BFI/Macmillan, 1986), 5.

79. Groucho, given an Armenian name, "was so well-liked that some Armenians . . . even claimed to be relatives." Ahmet Gürata, "Hollywood in Vernacular: Translation and Cross-Cultural Reception of American Film in Turkey," in *Going to the Movies: Hollywood and the Social Experience of Cinema*, ed. Richard Maltby, Melvyn Stokes, and Robert C. Allen (Exeter University Press, 2007), 341.

80. While no birth certificate has ever been found, most Chaplin biographers accept that he was born on April 16, 1889. He died in the early hours of December 25, 1977.

81. Harvey O'Higgins, "Charlie Chaplin's Art," *New Republic* 10 (February 3, 1917), quoted in Maland, *Chaplin and American Culture*, 28.

82. Kenneth S. Lynn, *Charlie Chaplin and His Times* (Aurum, 2002), 261; Robinson, *Chaplin: His Life and Art*, 431.

83. Simon Simsi, *Ciné-Passions: 7e art et industrie de 1945 à 2000* (Éditions Dixit, 2000), 2, 16; Georges Sadoul, *Vie de Charlot: Charles Spencer Chaplin, ses films et son temps* (1952; Lherminier, 1978), 251; Maland, *Chaplin and American Culture*, 226, 251, 280, 307–10.

84. Tom Whitehead, "MI5 Files: Was Chaplin Really a Frenchman and Called Thornstein?," *The Telegraph* (London), February 17, 2012.

85. Louis Delluc, *Charlot* (Maurice de Brunhoff, 1921); English edition, *Charlie Chaplin*, trans. Hamish Miles (Bodley Head, 1922).

86. French caricaturist Cami admired Chaplin, and the two exchanged drawings and photographs. When they met for the first time in 1921, they discovered they had no language in common and were unable to communicate, which may partly explain why the friendship later ended. Robinson, *Chaplin: His Life and Art*, 288, 431–32.

87. Jean Cocteau, *My Voyage Round the World*, quoted in Robinson, *Chaplin: His Life and Art*, 480; Chaplin, *My Autobiography*, 418–20.

88. Florey, who published a laudatory study of Chaplin and his work in French in 1927, came to know him quite well while working in Hollywood as an assistant to directors such as Josef von Sternberg and King Vidor, and served as associate director for *Monsieur Verdoux*. Robert Florey, *Charlie Chaplin* (Jean Pascal, 1927).

89. The first all-talking movie was not made in France until 1930. Susan Hayward, *French National Cinema* (Routledge, 1993), 135.

90. *Cinéa* and *Ciné-pour-tous* amalgamated in 1923 as *Cinéa-Ciné-pour-tous*.

91. Lynn, *Charlie Chaplin and His Times*, 98–100; Robinson, *Chaplin: The Mirror of Opinion*, 84–85.

92. Tim, "Max Linder: The Overlooked Silent Movie Star from Saint-Loubès," *Invisible Bordeaux*, December 19, 2012, https://invisiblebordeaux.blogspot.com/2012/12/max-linder-overlooked-silent-movie-star.html.

93. See, for example, "Le Cinéma: Les Films que nous verrons—A propos des *Temps Modernes*," *Le Figaro*, March 12, 1936, 5; X, "*Les Temps Modernes*—Tragi-comédie sonore," *La Cinématographie Française*, no. 907, March 21, 1936, 12.

94. Most accounts of the origins of a film based on the life of Landru emphasize the role of Orson Welles. See Robinson, *Chaplin: His Life and Art*, 519–20; Lynn, *Charlie Chaplin and His Times*, 424; Chaplin, *My Autobiography*, 454–55. Landru, whose trial began in November 1921, had been much in the headlines a few weeks earlier, during Chaplin's visits to Paris. Although hard evidence is lacking, Chaplin may have come across the story at that point.

95. Louis Aragon, "Charlot Sentimental," *Le Film*, March 1, 1918; Robert Phelps, ed., *Professional Secrets: An Autobiography of Jean Cocteau*, trans. Richard Howard (Farrar, Straus and Giroux, 1970), 81.

96. Maland, *Chaplin and American Culture*, 94–95.

97. Although *The Pilgrim* had been released in the United States in 1922 and *A Woman of Paris* in 1923, they were screened for the first time in France in reverse order: *A Woman of Paris* in April 1924 and *The Pilgrim* in February 1925. *The Gold Rush* was released in France in the same month as *The Pilgrim*, and *The Circus* in February 1928.

Chapter 1

1. Hew Strachan, *The First World War*, vol. 1: *To Arms* (Oxford University Press, 2001), 242–80; Robert A. Doughty, *Pyrrhic Victory: French Strategy and Operations in the Great War* (Harvard University Press, 2005), 91–104.

2. Strachan, *The First World War*, 278.

3. See, for example, "Notre entrée à Vauquois," *Le Figaro*, March 15, 1915, 1; "Communiqués officiels," *L'Humanité*, March 15, 1915, 1; "Nouvelles du Front," *Le Gaulois*, March 15, 1915, 1; "Communiqués officiels," *Le Petit Parisien*, March 15, 1915, 1. The assault on Vauquois formed the background to a disastrous French attack on the St.-Mihiel salient that would cause sixty-five thousand casualties. Doughty, *Pyrrhic Victory*, 144–48.

4. Ad, *Ciné-Journal*, no. 308/wartime no. 4 (March 15, 1915), 8.

5. "Jacques Haïk," *Les Indépendants du premier siècle*, accessed November 9, 2024, https://www.lips.org/bio_Haik_GB.html; "Biographie—Jacques Haïk, de Charlot au Grand Rex," *Le Petit Journal*, February 20, 2023, https://lepetitjournal.com/tunis/actualites/jacques-haik-de-charlot-au-grand-rex-52493.

6. See "The Early Silent Comedians: France," *European Film Star Postcards*, January 22, 2022, https://filmstarpostcards.blogspot.com/2022/01/the-early-silent-comedians-france.html.

7. Ad, *Ciné-Journal*, no. 308/wartime no. 4 (March 15, 1915), 10–11.

8. Ad, *Ciné-Journal*, no. 309/wartime no. 5 (April 1, 1915), 7.

9. Ad, *Ciné-Journal*, no. 309/wartime no. 5 (April 1, 1915), 37; ad, *Ciné-Journal*, no. 312/wartime no. 8 (May 15, 1915), 33.

10. Ad, *Ciné-Journal*, no. 313/wartime no. 9 (June 1, 1915), 37.

11. Société Adam et Cie, "Liste des 'Charlot,'" ad, *Ciné-Journal*, no. 334/wartime no. 30 (January 8, 1916), 26.

12. George Sadoul, *Vie de Charlot: Charles Spencer Chaplin, ses films et son temps* (Lherminier, 1978), 229.

13. Louis Delluc, "*Le Gosse* (*The Kid*)," *Paris-Midi*, September 9, 1921, reprinted in Louis Delluc, *Écrits cinématographiques*, vol. 2: *Le Cinéma au quotidien*, ed. Pierre Lherminier (Paris: Cinémathèque Française, 1990), 251. Delluc listed some of these "useless pearls": "J'ai la dent"; "Ce boxeur est le champion du droit"; "Les poi ... ssards et les poi ... vrois"; "Hé! là-haut, voulez-vous ... des cendres."

14. Some movies, moreover, had very sophisticated French intertitles: *Charlot joue Carmen* (*Charlie Chaplin's Burlesque on Carmen*), an Essanay production from 1916, according to the critic for *Ciné-Journal*, had "humoristic titles and sub-titles rhymed by the excellent song-writers Dominique Bonnaud and Mévisto the Older, adding a Montmartre-style spirit to the somersaults of Essanay's irresistible comic." "A Majestic," *Ciné-Journal*, no. 425/wartime no.121 (October 6, 1917), 34; cf. "Paris—Pour Prendre Date," *Le Film*, n.s. no. 76 (August 27, 1917), 11. Dominique Bonnaud (1864–1943) was a songwriter and poet, Jules Mévisto (Mévisto Aîné; 1857–1918) a songwriter, actor, and café-concert singer.

15. Susan Hayward, *French National Cinema* (Routledge, 1991), 101.

16. Richard Abel, *French Cinema: The First Wave, 1915–1929* (Princeton University Press, 1984), 9; Gilles Delluc, *Louis Delluc, 1890–1924: L'éveilleur du cinéma français au temps des années folles* (Éditions Pilote 24, 2002), 55–56.

17. Abel, *French Cinema*, 9–10; Interim [H.C.], "Des Chiffres," *Ciné-Journal*, no. 334/wartime no. 30 (January 8, 1916), 3.

18. "Charlot (Charles Chaplin)," *Ciné-Journal*, no. 331/wartime no. 27 (December 18, 1915), 13.

19. Nyctalope, "Productions Hebdomadaires," *La Cinématographie Française*, no. 4 (November 30, 1918), 56.

20. Louis Delluc, *Cinéma et Cie* (Grasset, 1919), 11, 13; Eve Francis, *Temps Héroïques* (Gand, 1949), 309–11, 328–31; Eugene C. McCreary, "Louis Delluc, Film Theorist, Critic and Prophet," *Cinema Journal* 16, no. 12 (1976): 29.

21. Guillaume Danvers, "La présentation hebdomadaire," *Le Film*, n.s. no. 69 (July 9, 1917), 13.

22. See, for example, Monte-Cristo, "Échos—Les faux Charlot," *Ciné-Journal*, no. 433, n.s. 129 (December 1, 1917), 5; "Un procès," *Le Film*, n.s. no. 119 (June 24, 1918), 16; "Le *Ciné-Journal* à L'Etranger," *Ciné-Journal*, no. 490 (January 4, 1919), 29.

23. "Mary Pickford et Charlie Chaplin," *Ciné-Journal*, no. 495 (February 8, 1919), 10; "Une Constellation," *La Cinématographie Française*, no. 18 (March 8, 1919), 23.

24. "Brins de film—Charlot se marie," *Le Film*, n.s. no. 143 (December 10, 1918), 7; "Par Film Spécial—Charlot," *Filma*, no. 39 (January 1–15, 1919), 2.

25. "Par Film Spécial—Charlot," *Filma*, no. 46 (April 15–30, 1919), 2.

26. "Charlot en deuil," *Ciné-Journal*, no. 518 (July 19, 1920), 34; A. Martel, "Charlot divorce ... ," *La Cinematographie Francaise*, no. 57 (December 6, 1919), 44.

27. "Charles Chaplin," *La Cinématographie Française*, no. 7 (December 21, 1918), 1; "Echos et Informations—Charlot se remarie," *Ciné-Journal*, no. 609 (April 16, 1921), 22. A few weeks later, it was reported that, while Charlot was shortly to marry Collins, his first wife had been awarded alimony of five million dollars (sixty million francs). "Echos et Informations—Mme Charlot et son ex-mari," *Ciné-Journal*, no. 617 (June 11, 1921), 17.

28. In September 1915, an advertisement by the Western Import Company claimed that Mack Sennett's latest "find" for Keystone Comedies was Syd Chaplin, the brother of Charlot, whom it dubbed "Julot." *Ciné-Journal*, no. 319/wartime no. 15 (September 1, 1915), 10; also see "Le frère de Charlot," *Ciné-Journal*, no. 523 (August 23, 1919), 29; "Sid Chaplin," *Le Cinéma et L'Echo du Cinéma Réunis*, no. 370 (July 11, 1919), 2; "Par Film Spécial—Sydney Chaplin," *Filma*, no. 53 (September 1–30, 1919), 3; "Le lama Charlot," *Ciné-Journal*, no. 442/wartime no. 138 (February 2, 1918), 20; "Par Film Spécial—Le Lama Charlot," *Filma*, no. 19 (March 1–15, 1918), 3.

29. "Echos," *Le Cinéma et l'Echo du Cinéma Réunis*, no. 264 (June 29, 1917), 1; "Par Film Spécial—Petits Cachets," *Filma* no. 58 (December 15–31, 1919), 5; "Maurice Maeterlink, Douglas Fairbanks ... et Charlot," *Filma*, no. 72 (September 1–30, 1920), 11.

30. H[enri] C[outant], "A Propos de Charlot," *Ciné-Journal*, no. 547 (February 7, 1920), 17–18.

31. Charles Chaplin (Charlot), "Charlot N'est Pas Mort," ad, *Ciné-Journal*, no. 320/wartime no. 16 (September 15, 1915), 38–39.

32. Ad, *Ciné-Journal*, no. 316/wartime no. 11 (July 1, 1915), 29.

33. Ad, *Ciné-Journal*, no. 317/wartime no. 12 (July 15, 1915), 26–27. The same issue contained an ad from Haïk's Western Import Company criticizing the circulation of fake Keystones. "It is not by imitating the moustache or the shoes of the Keystone actors," declared the ad, with Chaplin clearly very much in mind, "that one can succeed in making comics who . . . conquer all the cinematic markets of the world" (31). Six weeks later, another front-page ad by the AGC in *Ciné-Journal* observed that Chaplin was "more and more imitated" yet "less and less equaled." *Ciné-Journal*, no. 326/wartime no. 22 (November 13, 1915).

34. *Ciné-Journal*, no. 321/wartime no. 17 (October 1, 1915), front cover.

35. "Exclusivités Ch. Roy," ad, *Ciné-Journal*, no. 382/wartime no. 78 (December 9, 1916), 6.

36. See advertisements in *Ciné-Journal*, no. 337/wartime no. 33 (January 29, 1916), 20 and no. 339/wartime no. 35 (February 12, 1916), 9.

37. L. Aubert, ad, *Ciné-Journal*, no. 541 (December 27, 1919), 12; ad, *Ciné-Journal*, no. 603 (March 5, 1921), 18. A review of *Billy chez les Peintres* in 1919 commented that West, "not without talent, plagiarizes the mannerisms of Charlot." The writer suggested that West was a good enough performer to make films in his own right, without needing to imitate Chaplin. "Productions Hebdomadaires," *La Cinématographie Française*, no. 32 (June 14, 1919), 82.

38. *Ciné-Journal*, no. 340/wartime no. 36 (February 19, 1916), 29.

39. "L'Eclipse," ad, *Ciné-Journal*, no. 561 (May 15, 1920), 30.

40. "The Mysterious Man of the Foot that Grips is Charlot, admirably mimed by Biscot," ad, *Ciné-Journal*, no. 354/wartime no. 50 (May 27, 1916), 44.

41. "Le *Ciné-Journal* à l'Etranger," *Ciné-Journal*, no. 490 (January 4, 1919), 29.

42. Ad, *La Cinématographie Française*, no. 34 (June 28, 1919), 29.

43. Teddy, "Nice," in Échos—Informations—Communiques," *Le Film*, n.s. no. 5 (April 15, 1916), 24; "Échos—Informations—Communiques," *Le Film*, n.s. no. 10 (May 20, 1916), 24.

44. A. Dolbois, "Province-Nantes," *Le Film*, n.s. no. 74 (August 13, 1917), 12.

45. E. Meignen, "Echos—Faux 'Charlot,'" *Le Cinéma et l'Echo du Cinéma Réunis*, no. 276 (September 21, 1917), 1.

46. "Il y a Charlot et Charlot," *Ciné-Journal*, no. 398/wartime no. 94 (March 24, 1917), 49; cf. Les Tréteaux, "Charlot," in "Le Carnot de Glaneur," *Le Cinéma et L'Echo du Cinéma Réunis*, no. 255 (April 27, 1917), 1. It was gleefully later reported that the "fake Charlot" had been banned from appearing in Nantes because he had been judged "suspicious" by the military authorities. "Charlot fumiste," *Le Cinéma et L'Echo du Cinéma Réunis*, no. 270 (August 10, 1917), 1.

47. "Le seul Charlot," *Le Film*, n.s. no. 81 (October 1, 1917), 4; Georges Dureau, "Respectons le Public!," *Ciné-Journal*, no. 426/wartime no. 122 (October 18, 1917), 3–4; also see "Par Film Spécial—Charlot," *Filma*, no. 14 (December 16–31, 1917), 2.

48. "Un procès," *Le Film*, no. 119 (June 24, 1918), 16.

49. Georges Baille, "Le 'Courrier' à Marseille," *Le Courrier Cinématographie*, 9th year no. 49 (December 6, 1919), 22.

50. Guillaume Danvers, "La Présentation hebdomadaire," *Le Film*, n.s. no. 13 (June 10, 1916), 16; ad, *Ciné-Journal*, no. 359/wartime no. 55 (July 1, 1916), 57.

51. Ad, *Ciné-Journal*, no. 360/wartime no. 56 (July 8, 1916), 45.

52. Ad, *Ciné-Journal*, no. 362/wartime no. 58 (July 22, 1916), 33; "Avis aux Exploitants," *Ciné-Journal*, no. 362/wartime no. 58 (July 22, 1916), 5. Haïk's ad was also published in *Le Film*, n.s. no. 19 (July 22, 1916), n.p.

53. "*Charles Chaplin et l'Éléphant Blanc*," *Ciné-Journal*, no. 363/wartime no. 59 (July 29, 1916), 29. Later publicity for the series spoke only of "Charlie Chaplin" and not of "Charlot." See ad, *Le Film*, n.s. no 22 (August 12, 1916), 17.

54. Guillaume Danvers, "La Présentation hebdomadaire," *Le Film*, n.s. no. 25 (September 2, 1916), 31; ad, *La Cinématographie Française*, no. 1 (November 9, 1918), 12. A reviewer found the cartoons an agreeable interlude: they were "fairly amusing" if also somewhat "monotonous." Nyctalope, "Production Hebdomadaire," *La Cinématographie Française*, no. 2 (November 16, 1918), 52.

55. Ad, *Ciné-Journal*, no. 496 (February 15, 1919), 3. It may be that legal pressure was brought to bear to prevent this misuse of Charlot's name. The next but one edition of *Ciné-Journal* featured another ad by the same company, Raoultfilm Location, in which no mention was made of the Charlot cartoons. *Ciné-Journal*, no. 498 (March 1, 1919), 43.

56. "Autour de l'écran—La biographie de Charlot," *Filma*, no. 42 (February 15–28, 1919), 6; "Par Film Spécial—La nationalité de Charlot," *Filma*, no. 24 (May 15–31, 1918), 3.

57. Les Tréteaux, "Le Carnot de Glaneur—Charlot," *Le Cinéma et L'Echo du Cinéma Réunis*, no. 255 (April 27, 1917), 1.

58. "Le Carnet du Glaneur—Debuts de Charlot," *Le Cinéma et l'Echo du Cinéma Réunis*, no. 280 (October 19, 1917), 1; cf. "Par Film Spécial—Les débuts de Charlot," *Filma*, no. 20 (March 15–31, 1918), 2.

59. Nemo, "Échos," *Le Cinéma et L'Echo du Cinéma Réunis*, no. 436 (October 15, 1920), 1.

60. See, for example, Agence Générale Cinématographique, "Charlot en famille," ad, *Ciné-Journal*, no. 387/wartime no. 83 (January 13, 1917), 38. A profile of Chaplin for a cinema journal in 1918 began with the statement that he was "born in 1889 in Walworth (England)." "Charles Chaplin," *La Cinématographie Française*, no. 7 (December 21, 1918), 1.

61. "Le Représentant d''Essanay' à Paris," *Ciné-Journal*, no. 500 (March 15, 1919), 33; "Charlot parisien?," *Ciné-Journal*, no. 573 (August 7, 1920), 18; "Autour de l'écran—La biographie de Charlot," *Filma*, no. 42 (February 15–28, 1919), 6; "Biographie—Brins de Films," *Le Film*, n.s. no. 145 (December 24, 1918), 7.

62. Le Souffleur du Cinéma, "Bavardages et Potins," *Le Cinéma et l'Echo du Cinéma Réunis*, no. 306 (April 19, 1918), 1.

63. "Aux Etats-Unis," *Ciné-Journal*, no. 413/wartime no. 109 (July 14, 1917), 37.

64. "Par Film Spécial—La Popularité," *Filma*, no. 7 (August 15–31, 1917), 6.

65. "Par Film Spécial—Le Cinéma à bord," *Filma*, no. 7 (August 15–31, 1917), 6.

66. See "Charlot," *Le Courrier Cinématographique*, 7th year no. 45 (November 17, 1917), 16.

67. Fred Nelvo, "Le Ciné au Front," *Le Courrier Cinématographique*, 8th year no. 36 (September 7, 1918), 4, 6.

68. On the U.S. army, see, for example, "Charlot soldat," *Le Film*, n.s. 112 (May 6, 1918), 17; "Par Film Spécial—La Nationalité de Charlot," *Filma*, no. 24 (May 15–31, 1918), 3 and "Par Film Spécial—Charlot Soldat," *Filma*, no. 26 (June 15–30, 1918), 3; Le Souffleur du Cinéma, "Bavardages et Potins," *Le Cinéma et l'Echo du Cinéma Réunis*, no. 307 (April 26, 1918), 1; Nemo, "Echos," *Le Cinéma et L'Echo du Cinéma Réunis*, no. 309 (May 10, 1918), 1.

69. "La Propagande," *Le Film*, n.s. no. 125 (August 5, 1918), 8.

70. See, for example, "Propagande," *Le Film*, n.s. no. 126 (August 12, 1918), 7; "Par film spécial—L'emprunt américain," *Filma*, no. 33 (October 1–15, 1918), 3.

71. "Nouvelles et Autres," *Le Cinéma et l'Echo du Cinéma Réunis*, no. 330 (October 4, 1918), 2. *The Bond*, a short propaganda film intended to raise money to help the American war effort, was never released in France.

72. "Etats-Unis," *Ciné-Journal*, no. 449/wartime no. 145 (March 23, 1918), 37; *Le Film*, n.s. no. 130 (September 9, 1918), 14.

73. "Par Film Spécial," *Filma*, n.s. no. 5 (July 1–15, 1917), 2. Nearly three years later, Max Linder put a different spin on Chaplin's First National contract, pointing out that his "salary" included the costs of producing the eight pictures, and passing on Chaplin's claim that rising costs meant he was making no money from them. "Max Linder chez Charlot," *Le Cinéma et L'Echo du Cinéma Réunis*, no. 409 (April 9, 1920), 2.

74. "Le *Ciné-Journal* à l'Etranger," *Ciné-Journal*, no. 418/wartime no. 114 (August 18, 1917), 42. This correspondent actually underestimated how much Chaplin's salary of $1,075,000 represented in French francs. In 1917, the conversion rate was 5.7640 francs to the U.S. dollar. This gave a total salary of 6,196,300 in French francs, or 16,976 a day. Robinson, *Chaplin: His Life and Art*, 656; Lawrence H. Officer, "Exchange Rates Between the United States Dollar and Forty-One Currencies," *Measuring Worth*, 2025,http://www.measuringworth.com/exchangeglobal/.

75. Jay Winter and Jean-Louis Robert, *Capital Cities at War: Paris, London, Berlin 1914–1919* (Cambridge University Press, 1997), 260, 263, 271, 275; Jean-Jacques Becker, *The Great War and the French People*, trans. Arnold Pomerans (Berg, 1985), 205–16. According to Edward Shorter and Charles Tilly, there were more French strikes in 1917 than in any other year of the war (686 involving 28,100 workers). Edward Shorter and Charles Tilly, *Strikes in France, 1830–1968* (Cambridge University Press, 1974), Appendix B, 362.

76. "Un homme économe," *Filma*, no. 7 (August 15–21, 1917), 6; AGC, "Charlot Chef de Rayon," ad, *Ciné-Journal*, no. 430/wartime no. 126 (November 10, 1917), 23.

77. "Où sont les Vedettes?," *Ciné-Journal*, no. 506 (April 26, 1919), 42.

78. Patati et Patata, "Propos Cinématographiques," *La Cinématographie Française*, no. 23 (April 12, 1919), 84.

79. See, for example, Maxime Denniel, "Charlot," *Le Cinéma et l'Echo du Cinéma Réunis*, no. 229 (October 27, 1916), 6; "*Charlot Noctambule*" [*One A.M.*], *Le Cinéma et L'Echo du Cinéma Réunis*, no. 382 (October 3, 1919), 3.

80. "Intérim," "Les Nouveautés de la Semaine—Critique Cinématographique," *Le Cinéma et L'Echo du Cinéma Réunis*, no. 228 (October 20, 1916), 5; Guillaume Danvers, "La Présentation de la Semaine," *Le Film*, n.s. no. 68 (July 2, 1917), 15.

81. Edouard Debain, "Lorient," in "Echoes—Informations—Communiques," *Le Film*, n.s. no. 7 (April 29, 1916), 24; "Echos—Informations—Communiques: Province," *Le Film*, n.s. no. 26 (September 9, 1916), 20; A. Dolbois, "Province," *Le Film*, n.s. no. 59 (April 30, 1917), 16; A. Fournol, "Le Courrier à Nantes," *Le Courrier Cinématographique*, 8th year no. 25 (June 22, 1918), 13.

82. "Charles Chaplin," *La Cinématographie Française*, no. 7 (December 21, 1918), 1.

83. Abel, *French Cinema*, 11; Henri Coutant, "Mise au Point," *Ciné-Journal*, no. 419/wartime no. 115 (August 25, 1917), 3–5; "De l'importation des films," *Ciné-Journal*, no. 420/wartime no. 116 (September 1, 1917), 9.

84. Jean Noely, "Marseille," in "Echos—Informations—Communiques," *Le Film*, n.s. no. 5 (April 15, 1916), 24.

85. F. Camoin, "Les Soirées Cinématographiques Parisiennes—Omnio-Pathé," *Le Courrier Cinématographique*, 8th year no. 49 (December 7, 1918), 12.

86. Guillaume Danvers, "La Présentation hebdomadaire," *Le Film*, n.s. no. 50 (February 26, 1917), 16.

87. Guillaume Danvers, "La Présentation hebdomadaire," *Le Film*, n.s. no. 11 (May 27, 1916), 16, 18. For Louis Delluc's very similar reflections on *Charlot au music hall* and what may have been *Pied qui Etreint*, see Louis Delluc, "Accessoires," *Le Film*, n.s. no. 69 (July 9, 1917), 9.

88. Philippe Soupault, "Charlot voyage" [*The Immigrant*], *Littérature*, no. 6 (August 1919), reprinted in Odette Virmaux and Alain Virmaux, eds., *Philippe Soupault, Ecrits de cinéma, 1918–1931* (Librairie Plon, 1979), 45.

89. Eugene C. McCreary, "Louis Delluc, Film Theorist, Critic, and Prophet," *Cinema Journal* 16, no 1 (1976), 15; Louis Delluc, "Cinema: *The Outlaw and His Wife*," in Abel, *French Film Theory and Criticism*, 188.

90. "Charlot (Charles Chaplin)," *Ciné-Journal*, no. 331/wartime no. 27 (December 18, 1915), 13; Max Linder, "L'Homme qui fait rire le Monde—Charlot vu par Max Linder," *Le Film*, n.s. nos. 133–34 (October 14, 1918), 40; Boisyvon, "Le Public n'aime pas ça," *Le Film*, n.s. no. 174 (September 1920), n.p.

91. Edmond Floury, "Charlot cambrioleur," *Le Courrier Cinématographique*, 7th year no. 26 (July 7, 1917), vi. Also see, for example, Maxime Denniel, "Charlot," *Le Cinéma et l'Echo du Cinéma Réunis*, no. 229 (October 27, 1916), 6; "Charlot joue Carmen," *Le Courrier Cinématographique*, 7th year no. 36 (September 15, 1917), viii; Nyctalope, "Production Hebdomadaire," *La Cinématographie Française*, no. 4 (November 30, 1918), 56; "Présentations de la Semaine," *Ciné-Journal*, no. 588 (November 20, 1920), 55.

92. See, for example, "L'Ouvreuse de Lutetia," "Production Hebdomadaires," *La Cinématographie Française*, no. 49 (October 11, 1919), 102; "Max est revenue," *Le Film*, n.s. no. 81 (October 1, 1917), 8.

93. "Présentations," *Le Courrier Cinématographique*, 7th year no. 13 (April 7, 1917), 21.

94. Guillaume Danvers, "La Présentation hebdomadaire," *Le Film*, n.s. no. 10 (May 20, 1916), 11; Guillaume Danvers, "La Présentation hebdomadaire," *Le Film*, n.s. no. 16 (July 1, 1916), 16; Guillaume Danvers, "La Présentation hebdomadaire," *Le Film*, n.s. no. 46 (January 29, 1917), 15; Abel, *French Film Theory and Criticism*, 102.

95. Guillaume Danvers, "La Présentation hebdomadaire," *Le Film*, n.s. no. 64 (June 4, 1917), 20; Guillaume Danvers, "La Présentation hebdomadaire," *Le Film*, n.s. no. 46 (January 29, 1917), 15; Guillaume Danvers, "Les Présentations de la Semaine," *Le Film*, n.s. no. 37 (November 25, 1916), 15. *Tillie's Punctured Romance*, at six thousand feet, was far longer than Chaplin's typical one- or two-reel films. Danvers's comment suggests that the French exhibitor had decided to release it in several installments.

96. On this point, see Henri Diamant-Berger, "Le Scènario," in *Le Cinéma* (Renaissance du livre, 1919), translated in Abel, *French Film Theory and Criticism*, 183–85.

97. Simounet, "Les Nouveautés de la Semaine—Critique Cinématographique," *Le Cinéma et L'Echo du Cinéma Réunis*, no. 237 (December 22, 1916), 3; Simounet, "Les Nouveautés de la

Semaine," *Le Cinéma et l'Echo du Cinéma Réunis*, no. 253 (April 13, 1917), 3; Simounet, "Les Nouveautés de la Semaine," *Le Cinéma et l'Echo du Cinéma Réunis*, no. 260 (June 1, 1917), 3.

98. Paul Barrière, "La Semaine Niçoise," *Le Courrier Cinématographique*, 9th year no. 44 (November 1, 1919), 26, 28.

99. Voittout, "Critique Cinématographique," *Le Courrier Cinématographique*, 7th year no. 3 (January 27, 1917), 16; "Intérim," "Les Nouveautés de la Semaine—Critique Cinématographique," *Le Cinéma et L'Echo du Cinéma Réunis*, no. 215 (July 21, 1916), 1; Edmond Floury, "Critique Cinématographique," *Le Courrier Cinématographique*, 7th year no. 17 (May 5, 1917), 22–23.

100. Louis Delluc, "Abel Gance après *La Zone de la mort*," *Le Film*, no. 85 (October 22, 1917), cited in Abel, *French Film Theory and Criticism*, 101.

101. Louis Delluc, "La Foule," *Paris-Midi*, August 24, 1918, reprinted in Abel, *French Film Theory and Criticism*, 159–60, 163; Louis Delluc, "La Beauté au cinéma," *Le Film*, no. 73 (August 6, 1917), reprinted in Abel, *French Film Theory and Criticism*, 139.

102. Ad, *La Cinématographie Française*, no. 30 (May 31, 1919), 83.

103. Hans Robert Jauss, *Toward an Aesthetic of Reception*, trans. Timothy Bahti (University of Minnesota Press, 1982), 23. On the processes used by audiences to create meaning from films and mass media specifically, see two books by Janet Staiger: *Perverse Spectators: The Practices of Film Reception* (New York University Press, 2000) and *Media Reception Studies* (New York University Press, 2005).

104. F. Camoin, "Les Soirées Cinématographique—Aubert-Palace," *Le Courrier Cinématographique*, 9th year no. 26 (June 28, 1919), 16; Jean Epstein, "Magnification" (1921), in Abel, *French Film Theory and Criticism*, 238.

105. Rae Beth Gordon, "From Charcot to Charlot: Unconscious Imitation and Spectatorship in French Cabaret and Early Cinema," *Critical Inquiry* 27, no. 3 (Spring 2001): 524, 534.

106. For an account of the friendship between the two comedians, see Tim, "Max Linder: The Overlooked Silent Movie Star from Saint-Loubès," *Invisible Bordeaux*, December 19, 2012, https://invisiblebordeaux.blogspot.com/2012/12/max-linder-overlooked-silent-movie-star.html. The same website has a fascinating picture of Chaplin and Linder together. Chaplin is dressed as the Tramp, but without his mustache. Linder is affecting the same posture, leaning on his cane. But Linder is wearing a more stylish trilby hat than Chaplin's bowler, together with a carefully knotted small tie, a well-fitting waistcoat, and a handkerchief in the breast pocket of his suit. Linder's shoes are polished and of normal size.

107. "L'Art de Charlie Chaplin," *Ciné-Journal*, no. 503 (April 5, 1919), 18–19.

108. Ibid., 19.

109. "Comparaison," *Ciné-Journal*, no. 448/wartime no. 144 (March 16, 1918), 4.

110. Vanessa Schwartz, *Spectacular Realities: Early Mass Culture in Fin-de-siècle Paris* (University of California Press, 1999).

111. Edmond Floury, "Les Nouveautés de la Semaine—Critique cinématographique," *Le Cinéma et l'Echo du Cinéma Réunis*, no. 383 (October 10, 1919), 3.

112. In 2010, a thirty-sixth film made by Keystone and including Chaplin in a minor role as a policeman was discovered. It does not seem to have been shown in France.

113. Cinémargus, "Programme de Jeudi," *Le Courrier Cinématographique*, 8th year no. 13 (March 30, 1918), 4.

114. Robert Desnos, "Cinéma d'avant garde," *Documents 7* (December 1929), reprinted and translated in Paul Hammond, ed., *The Shadow and Its Shadow: Surrealist Writings on the Cinema* (BFI, 1978), 37.

115. Richard Abel, "The Contribution of the French Literary Avant-Garde to Film Theory and Criticism (1907–1924)," *Cinema Journal* 14, no. 3 (Spring, 1975): 23.

116. Jane C. Desmond, *Dancing Desires: Choreographing Sexualities on and off the Stage* (University of Wisconsin Press, 2001), 69n57. Also see Tracy A. Doyle, "Erik Satie's Ballet *Parade*: An Arrangement for Woodwind and Percussion with Historical Summary" (DMA diss., Louisiana State University, 2005), 12, 44, 45; Jennifer Wild, "The Automatic Chance of the Modern Tramp: Chaplin and the Parisian Avant-Garde," *Early Popular Visual Culture* 8, no. 3 (2010): 273.

117. Cendrars's poem "Le Musickissme" (dated November 1916), with its brief reference to Charlot, for example, was not published until 1923. See Richard Abel, "American Film and the French Literary Avant-Garde (1914–1924)," *Contemporary Literature* 17, no. 1 (Winter 1976): 90.

118. Louis Aragon, "Charlot Sentimental," *Le Film*, no. 105 (March 1, 1918), 5.

119. Louis Aragon, "On Décor," *Le Film*, n.s. no. 131 (September 16, 1918), 9, here as translated by Paul Hammond in Abel, *French Film Theory*, 167; Jean Cocteau, "Carte Blanche," *Paris-Midi*, April 28, 1919, 2.

120. Louis Delluc, "Notes pour moi," *Le Film*, no. 112 (May 6, 1918), 15.

121. "Présentations de la semaine," *Ciné-Journal*, no. 530 (October 11, 1919), 64.

122. Philippe Soupault, "À l'abri des lois," *Littérature*, February 1920, reprinted in Virmaux and Virmaux, *Philippe Soupault*, 44; Élie Faure, "Charlot," *L'Esprit Nouveau*, no. 6 (March 15, 1921), translated and reprinted as "The Art of Charlie Chaplin," *New England Review* 19, no. 2 (Spring 1998): 147.

123. Ibid., 151.

124. Louis Aragon, "Du Décor," *Le Film*, n.s. no. 131 (September 16, 1918), 9.

125. Robert Phelps, ed., *Professional Secrets: An Autobiography of Jean Cocteau, Drawn from His Lifetime Writings*, trans. Richard Howard (Farrar, Straus and Giroux, 1970), 81.

126. Margaret Crosland, ed., *Cocteau's World: An Anthology of Writings* (Peter Owen, 1972), 393.

127. Voittout, "Critique Cinématographique," *Le Courrier Cinématographique*, 7th year no. 3 (January 27, 1917), 18. These French "re-editions" of Chaplin films were most probably simply "re-releases," probably with new intertitles. Not until 1920 would a firm of distributors (AGC) claim both that fresh intertitles had been added and that the re-released films themselves were new copies from the original negatives.

128. Edmund Floury, "Critique Cinématographique," *Le Courrier Cinématographique*, 7th year no. 14 (April 14, 1917), 18.

129. "Les Nouveautés," *Le Courrier Cinématographique*, 7th year no. 20 (May 26, 1917), 24; AGC, ad, *Le Courrier Cinématographique*, 7th year no. 25 (June 20, 1917), back page.

130. Ad, *Le Courrier Cinématographique*, 8th year no. 31 (August 3, 1918); Ad, *Ciné-Journal*, no. 474/wartime no. 170 (September 14, 1918), 29; cf. *Le Film*, n.s. no. 130 (September 9, 1918), 21.

131. Ad, *Le Courrier Cinématographique*, 8th year no. 42 (October 19, 1918), 3.

132. For a time there were competing pressures. In November 1918, Pathé was showing *Une vie de chien* (*A Dog's Life*) and AGC *Charlot patine* (*The Rink*) ("the big success of the moment"). But this was also the peak of the Spanish influenza pandemic, and in a number of French cities, including Bordeaux, the local prefect attempted to reduce the spread of infection by closing all cinemas, theaters, and cafés. "Le Cinéma en Province—Bordeaux," *Le Cinéma et l'Echo du Cinéma Réunis*, no. 334 (November 1, 1918), 2.

133. "Présentations de la Semaine—AGC," *Ciné-Journal*, no. 491 (January 11, 1919), 35.

134. AGC, ad, *Ciné-Journal*, no. 512 (June 7, 1919), 26; AGC, ad, *Ciné-Journal*, no. 534 (November 8, 1919), 9; AGC, ad, *La Cinématographie Francaise*, no. 54 (November 15, 1919), 101.

135. Ad, *Ciné-Journal*, no. 513 (June 14, 1919), 42; ad, *Le Courrier Cinématographique*, 9th year no. 24 (June 14, 1919), 21.

136. Ad, *Ciné-Journal*, no. 519 (July 26, 1919), 22; ad, *Le Cinéma et l'Echo du Cinéma Réunis*, no. 371 (July 18, 1919), 3; L'Operateur, "Sur l'Écran—Les présentations sensationnelles," *Le Courrier Cinématographique*, 9th year no. 45, (November 8, 1919), 50.

137. AGC, ad, *Ciné-Journal*, no. 568 (July 3, 1920), 6–7.

138. Louis Delluc, "Notes pour moi," *Le Film*, n.s. no. 115 (May 27, 1918), 14; cf. the very similar comment on *Charlot dans le parc* (*In the Park*) in Nyctalope, "Production Hebdomadaire," *La Cinématographie Française*, no. 1 (November 9, 1918), 54.

139. O. Réol, "Les Nouveautés de la Semaine," *Le Cinéma et l'Echo du Cinéma Réunis*, no. 437 (October 22, 1920), n.p.; O. Réol, "Les Nouveautés de la Semaine," *Le Cinéma et l'Echo du Cinéma Réunis*, no. 441 (November 19, 1920), 4; O. Réol, "Les Nouveautés de la Semaine," *Le Cinéma et l'Echo du Cinéma Réunis*, no. 447 (December 31, 1920), 4; cf. the comment of a reviewer on a re-edition of *Charlot mitron* (*Dough and Dynamite*) as "quite amusing" if "a little old." "Présentations de la Semaine," *Ciné-Journal*, no. 604 (March 12, 1921), 40.

140. "Production Hebdomadaires," *La Cinématographie Française*, no. 50 (October 18, 1919), 116.

141. Maland, *Chaplin and American Culture*, 20–23.

142. Des Angles, "Les Avant-Premières," *Le Courrier Cinématographique*, 9th year no. 42 (October 18, 1919), 52; Edmond Floury, "Les Nouveautés de la Semaine—Critique Cinématographique," *Le Cinéma et L'Echo du Cinéma Réunis*, no. 376 (August 22, 1919), 2.

143. "Production Hebdomadaires—*Charlot va dans le Monde*," *La Cinématographie Française*, no. 52 (November 1, 1919), 80; "Production Hebdomadaires—*Charlot brocanteur*," *La Cinématographie Française*, no. 59 (December 20, 1919), 87.

144. "Les Nouveautes de la Semaine," *Le Cinéma et l'Echo du Cinéma Réunis*, no. 453 (February 11, 1921), 3. Normand had been replaced as Chaplin's leading lady by Edna Purviance when he moved from Keystone to Essanay.

145. "Présentations de la Semaine," *Ciné-Journal*, no. 606 (March 26, 1921), 40.

146. Edmond Floury, "Les Nouveautés de la Semaine—Critique Cinématographique," *Le Cinéma et L'Echo du Cinéma Réunis*, no. 372 (July 25, 1919), 3.

147. "Présentations de la Semaine," *Ciné-Journal*, no. 592 (December 18, 1920), 21; "Présentations de la Semaine," *Ciné-Journal*, no. 596 (January 15, 1921), 36; Nyctalope, "Production Hebdomadaire," *La Cinématographie Française*, no. 4 (November 30, 1918), 56; Nyctalope, "Production Hebdomadaire," *La Cinématographie Française*, no. 16 (February 22, 1919), 46; "Présentations de la Semaine," *Ciné-Journal*, no. 594 (January 1, 1920), 52.

148. Maland, *Chaplin and American Culture*, 17–18, 27–29.

149. "Présentations de la Semaine," *Ciné-Journal*, no. 588 (November 20, 1920), 55; "Les Nouveautés de la Semaine," *Le Cinéma et l'Echo du Cinéma Réunis*, no. 449 (January 14, 1921), 4.

150. P[ierre] H[enri], "Rééditez," *Ciné Pour Tous*, no. 3 (July 15, 1919), 2.

151. AGC, ad, *Ciné-Journal*, no. 479/wartime no. 175 (October 19, 1918), 23.

152. Pathé Frères, ad, *Ciné-Journal*, no. 476/wartime no. 172 (September 28, 1918), 2.

153. One reason for the relative chaos of the distribution of the movies Chaplin made for his first three studios—Keystone, Essanay, and Mutual—was that he himself never owned the rights to them. Only with his move to First National in 1917 did he negotiate a contract specifying that rights to the films he made would revert to him after five years. See Jeffrey Vance, *Chaplin: Genius of the Cinema* (Harry N. Abrams, 2003), 85.

Chapter 2

1. Robinson, *Chaplin: His Life and Art*, 273; Charlie Chaplin, *My Trip Abroad* (Harper and Brothers, 1922), 2–3.

2. "Propos Cinématographiques," *La Cinématographie Française*, no. 42 (August 23, 1919), 114.

3. Luigia Rezzonico della Torre, "Pearl White en Europe," *Le Cinéma et L'Echo du Cinéma Réunis*, no. 410 (April 16, 1920), 1; "Pearl White à Paris," *Le Courrier Cinématographique*, tenth year no. 16 (April 17, 1920), 32; Filmus, "Pearl White à Paris," *Filma*, no. 87 (May 1–15, 1921), 4; "Les fantaisies de Pearl White," *Le Courrier Cinématographique*, eleventh year no. 19 (May 7, 1921), 18.

4. "Fatty arrive à Paris," *Le Cinéma et l'Echo du Cinéma Réunis*, no. 442 (November 26, 1920), 1; Nemo, "Echos—Fatty est à Paris," *Le Cinéma et l'Echo du Cinéma Réunis*, no. 443 (December 3, 1920), 1.

5. "Le Banquet de 'Comoedia' en l'honneur de Mary Pickford et Douglas Fairbanks," *Le Cinéma et l'Echo du Cinéma Réunis*, no. 424 (July 23, 1920), 1.

6. Robinson, *Chaplin: His Life and Art*, 269.

7. Les Artistes Associés, ad, *Ciné-Journal*, no. 620 (July 9, 1921), 35; Les Artistes Associés, ad, *Le Cinéma et l'Echo du Cinéma Réunis*, no. 474 (July 8, 1921), 4; Les Artistes Associés, ad, *Le Cinéma et L'Echo du Cinéma Réunis*, no. 474 (July 8, 1921), 4. Five years earlier, Smith was the man who opened up the South American market for U.S. films with D. W. Griffith's spectacular but highly racist *The Birth of a Nation*. Kristin Thompson, *Exporting Entertainment: America in the World Film Market 1907–34* (BFI, 1985), 79.

8. United Artists, ad, *Le Cinéma et l'Echo du Cinéma Réunis*, no. 478 (August 12, 1921), 5; ad, *Le Courrier Cinématographique*, eleventh year no. 33 (August 13, 1921), 58; ad, *Le Courrier Cinématographique*, eleventh year no. 35 (August 27, 1921), 43; United Artists, ad, *Ciné-Journal*, no. 628 (August 27, 1921), 2.

9. Robinson, *Chaplin: His Life and Art*, 277–78; "Échos et Informations—Fairbanks et Mary Pickford en Europe," *Ciné-Journal*, no. 631 (September 17, 1921), 34; "Douglas Fairbanks et Mary Pickford à Paris," *Ciné-Journal*, no. 633 (October 1, 1921), 27.

10. Robinson, *Chaplin: His Life and Art*, 274–76, 281.

11. Arbuckle was tried three times (November–December 1921, January–February 1922, and March–April 1922). The juries in the first two trials failed to agree; the jury in the third trial acquitted him. Arbuckle's career as a film actor, however, never recovered.

12. On September 24, 1921, a re-edition of the unfortunately titled *Charlot a debauché Fatty* (probably *The Rounders*, Keystone, 1914) was advertised in Paris. One week earlier, a film critic had pointed out the startling difference in the current status of the two men: "Charlot on landing in England had been carried in triumph, whilst Fatty has been imprisoned in America and must confront an accusation of homicide." "*Charlot a debauché Fatty*," *Le Courrier Cinématographique*, no. 39 (September 24, 1921), 63; Patati et Patata, "Propos Cinématographiques—Charlot porté en triomphe et Fatty accusé d'un crime," *Le Cinématographie Francaise*, no. 150 (September 17, 1921), 78.

13. "'Charlot' à Paris," *Le Figaro*, September 19, 1921, 2; "Charlot rentre à Paris pour prêter son concours à la fête du Trocadéro," *Le Petit Parisien*, October 4, 1921, 2; "Charlot nous quitte . . . par la voie des airs," *Le Petit Parisien*, October 7, 1921, 3.

14. Louis Delluc, "Charlie Chaplin à Paris," in *Louis Delluc: Ecrits cinématographiques*, vol. 1: *Le Cinéma et les Cinéastes*, ed Pierre Lherminier (Cinémathèque Française, 1985), 150–55; Louis Delluc, "Charlot à Paris," *Cinéa*, no. 23 (October 14, 1921), reprinted in *Louis Delluc: Ecrits cinématographiques*, vol. 2: *Cinéma et Cie*, ed. Pierre Lherminier (Cinémathèque Française, 1986), 317.

15. "How I wish that I had learned French," Chaplin wrote in his account of his European trip. "I feel hopelessly sunk, because after about three sentences in French I am a total loss so far as conversation is concerned." Chaplin, *My Trip Abroad*, 103. One report of the interview he gave on first arriving at Cherbourg had Chaplin claiming to speak French "like a Spanish cow." "Charlot en Europe—Une Interview à Bord de l'*Olympic*," *Le Petit Parisien*, September 10, 1921, 3.

16. See, for example, Henry Barde, "En prenant un cocktail avec Charlot," *L'Homme Libre*, September 20, 1921, 1.

17. Boisyvou, "Comment je n'ai pas interviewé Charlot," *L'Intransigeant*, September 21, 1921, 1.

18. Maland, *Chaplin*, 65; Chaplin, *My Trip Abroad*, 7–8.

19. Max Massot, "Charlot est à Paris—ses projets, ses impressions et ses idées," *Le Journal*, September 19, 1921, 1.

20. Marguerite Jeanne Japy Steinheil (1869–1954) was a courtesan of the Belle Epoque. A mistress of President Félix Faure, she was allegedly making love with him when he died in February 1899. In May 1908, her husband Adolphe Steinheil and her mother were both found murdered in the Steinheil residence in Paris's 15th arrondissement. Marguerite was accused of the crimes, but her trial ended in acquittal on November 14, 1909. Chaplin had been in Paris with the Karno troupe in the autumn of 1909 and obviously heard—and remembered—some of the discussions of the case. See Armond Lanoux, *Madame Steinheil, ou, "La Connaissance du président"* (Grasset, 1983); Frédéric Delacourt, *L'Affaire Steinheil* (Editions de Vecchi, 2006).

21. Massot, "Charlot est à Paris," 1. Parts of this conversation with Chaplin (but not his comments on Bolshevism) were confirmed by another journalist who was present. Georges Martin, "Avec Charlot—Une promenade avec Charlot," *Le Petit Journal*, September 19, 1921, 1.

22. "Charlot arrive à Paris," *L'Humanité*, September 19, 1921, 1; "N'avez-vous pas vu Charlot?," *L'Humanité*, September 20, 1921, 2.

23. "Charlot bolchevik," *L'Humanité*, September 21, 1921, 1.

24. Clément Vautel, "Mon Film," *Le Journal*, September 23, 1921, 1.

25. A. Nangris, "Charlot bolchevik," *La Libre Parole*, September 24, 1921, 3.

26. Jacques Barty, "Charlot Voyage," *L'Homme Libre*, September 23, 1921, 1.

27. "Charlot bolcheviste," *Le Figaro*, September 22, 1921, 4.

28. Adrian Vély, "Charlot bolchevik," *Le Gaulois*, September 22, 1921, 1.

29. Alfred Varella, "Charlot Communiste," *Le Journal du Peuple*, September 22, 1921, 2. In September 1920, a year before Chaplin's arrival in France, one cinema magazine had already hinted at the contradiction between his alleged left-wing views and his wealth. "We are assured," it was claimed in *Le Cinéma et l'Echo du Cinéma Réunis*, "that Charlie Chaplin, who however has not complained about his fortune, has just proclaimed himself an out-and-out socialist." "Pauvre Charlot," *Le Cinéma et l'Echo du Cinéma Réunis*, no. 432 (September 17, 1920), 1.

30. Pierre Mualdez, "Propos d'un Paria," *Le Libertaire*, September 30–October 7, 1921, 2. *Le Libertaire*, at the time of Mualdez's article, was much preoccupied with campaigning for the retrial of Italian anarchists Nicola Sacco and Bartolomeo Vanzetti, who had been found guilty by a

Massachusetts jury on July 14, 1921, of two murders. See "Pour Sacco et Vanzetti," *Le Libertaire*, September 16–23, 1921, 1; "Sauvons Sacco et Vanzetti," *Le Libertaire*, September 23–30, 1921, 1.

31. *Pravda*, published in Moscow, was the official organ of the Soviet Communist Party until 1991.

32. Saint-Eloi, "Charlot bolchevik," *Le Peuple*, September 23, 1921, 2; Saint-Eloi, "Il n'y a pas que Charlot," *Le Peuple*, September 25, 1921, 2. Gassier was a co-founder of the satirical magazine *Le Canard enchaîné* in 1915. A political cartoonist who worked for *L'Humanité* and several other publications, he would not long remain a member of the new Communist Party he joined in 1920. Méric, a former anarchist who had written for *Le Libertaire*, was briefly a member of the editorial committee of *L'Humanité* but by 1921 had already become disenchanted with the centralization of the party. See "Henri Paul Gassier," *Spartacus Educational*, https://spartacus-educational.com/ARTgassier.htm and "Le 10 mai 1876, naissance de Victor Meric," *Ephéméride Anarchiste*, www.ephemanar.net/mai10.html, both accessed November 15, 2024.

33. See Maxwell Adereth, *The French Communist Party: A Critical History (1920–1984)* (Manchester University Press, 1984), 22–28.

34. Robinson, *Chaplin: His Life and Art*, 279–82, quotation from 282; Lynn, *Charlie Chaplin and His Times*, 255; "Charlot voyage," *Le Temps*, September 13, 1921, 3; "119 Years of Excellence and Splendour," The Ritz London, accessed November 15, 2024, https://www.theritzlondon.com/about-the-ritz/history/.

35. Robinson, *Chaplin: His Life and Art*, 282–83.

36. Chaplin, *My Trip Abroad*, 105; Charles Chaplin, *My Autobiography* (Bodley Head, 1964), 296–97.

37. "'Charlot' Arrive à Paris Incognito," *Le Petit Parisien*, September 19, 1921, 1.

38. Massot, "Charlot est à Paris," 1.

39. "'Charlot' Arrive à Paris Incognito," 1; Paul Cordeaux, "Charlie Chaplin dans son dernier film," *L'Echo de Paris*, September 19, 1921, 1; "'Charlot' est à Paris" and "Une interview de 'Charlot,'" *L'Eclair*, September 19, 1921, 1; "Cinq minutes avec Charlot sur le quai de la gare," *L'Homme Libre*, September 19, 1921, 3; Saint-Réal, "Charlot est dans nos murs!," *Le Gaulois*, September 19, 1921, 1; "Charlot est arrivé hier soir à Paris," *L'Action Francaise*, September 19, 1921, 3.

40. "Charlot est à Paris—ses projets, ses impressions et ses idées," *Le Journal*, September 19, 1921, 1; "Charlot . . . en chair et en os est à Paris," *Le Matin*, September 19, 1921, 2; "Charlot à Paris," *La République Française*, September 20, 1921, 1; Georges Martin, "Avec Charlot—qui est à Paris," *Le Petit Journal*, September 19, 1921, 1.

41. "Nos Échos," *L'Intransigeant*, October 7, 1921, 2.

42. "Charlot a passé une bonne nuit," *Paris-Midi*, September 19, 1921, 1. For a similar comment, see Le Masque de Fer, "Échos," *Le Figaro*, September 21, 1921, 1.

43. "Charlot . . . en chair et en os est à Paris," 2.

44. A. Aulard, "La Popularité de Charlot: Est-elle Un Signe De Décadence?," *Le Peuple*, September 20, 1921, 1; cf. "Sa Moustache," *Comoedia*, March 20, 1921, 1.

45. See Fuller, *At the Picture Show*, passim.

46. Although France did not have weekly "fanzines" in the American sense until the founding of *Ciné-Mirroir, Mon Ciné*, and *Le Film complet* (all in 1922), there were already signs of change in this direction before 1921. In 1920, for example, the year after founder Henri Diamant-Berger and editor-in-chief Louis Delluc left, *Le Film* became a glossy illustrated monthly.

47. "Charlie Chaplin dans son dernier film: 'Charlot à Paris,'" *L'Echo de Paris*, September 19, 1921, 1.

48. "Charlot Cheers Rive Gauche Crowds; Then Holds Wassail in Montmartre," *New York Herald*, Paris edition, September 23, 1921, 5; "Charlot et son sourire nous quittent . . . mais pour quatre jours seulement," *Le Matin*, September 23, 1921, 2; cf. Chaplin, *My Trip Abroad*, 113.

49. Georges Dureau, "Bienvenue à Charlot," *Ciné-Journal*, no. 630 (September 10, 1921), 1–2. Dureau's comment about Arbuckle was made a week before he was arrested and charged with the murder (later reduced to manslaughter) of Virginia Rappe.

50. G.-W. Smith, "La Voie triomphale," *Ciné-Journal*, no. 631 (September 17, 1921), 8; cf. "Charlot à Londres," *Comoedia*, September 11, 1921, 3 and "Angleterre a fait à Charlot un accueil enthusiaste," *Le Petit Parisien*, September 11, 1921, 1.

51. Maurice Prax, "Pitié pour lui," *Le Petit Parisien*, September 21, 1921, 1.

52. J.-L. Croze, "Charlot est à Paris," *Comoedia*, September 20, 1921, 1.

53. "Echos," *La Libre Parole*, September 21, 1921, 1; A. Aulard, "La Popularité de Charlot," *Le Peuple*, September 20, 1921, 1; "Parti! Charlot a quitté Paris hier matin," *Le Matin*, October 8, 1921, 1.

54. Croze, "Charlot est à Paris," 1.
55. "Charlot Chez Nous," *Le Petit Parisien*, September 20, 1921, 1; "Charlot au quartier Latin," *La Liberté*, September 21, 1921, 1.
56. "Charlot quitte Paris aujourd'hui—trés satisfait de Paris et des Français," *Le Petit Journal*, September 22, 1921, 1.
57. "Echos," *La Libre Parole*, September 21, 1921, 1.
58. Chaplin, *My Trip Abroad*, 106–11; Chaplin, *My Autobiography*, 298, 300–301; Robinson, *Chaplin: His Life and Art*, 288–89; Lynn, *Charlie Chaplin and His Times*, 259–61; "Charlot Cheers Rive Gauche Crowds," 5.
59. "Charlot Interviewé par Cami," *Le Journal*, September 20, 1921, 1.
60. "Charlot dort … sure ses lauriers," *La Liberté*, September 20, 1921, 1; "Charlot Chez Nous," *Le Petit Parisien*, September 20, 1921, 2; "Carpentier Chez Charlot," *Le Petit Parisien*, September 21, 1921, 1.
61. Waldo David Frank, "Charles Chaplin: Funny Legs," *New Yorker* 1 (May 23, 1925), 9–10, quoted in Lynn, *Charlie Chaplin and His Times*, 261.
62. "Charlot Cheers Rive Gauche Crowds," 5.
63. "Charlot Chez Nous," *Le Petit Parisien*, September 20, 1921, 1; "Chaplin Lunches with Carpentier," *New York Herald*, Paris edition, September 21, 1921, 6.
64. "'Charlot'" Arrive à Paris Incognito," *Le Petit Parisien*, September 19, 1921, 1; "Charlot est à Paris," *Le Radical*, September 19, 1921, 1; "Charlot à Paris," *Le Figaro*, September 19, 1921, 2; "Charlot à Paris," *La République Française*, September 20, 1921, 1; Henry Barde, "En prenant un cocktail avec Charlot," *L'Homme Libre*, September 20, 1921, 1.
65. "Charlot dort … sur ses lauriers," *La Liberté*, September 20, 1921, 1.
66. Maurice Coriem, "Charlot est à Paris," *Le Canard enchaîné*, September 21, 1921, 1. On journalists who spoke nothing but French, see "Charlot Chez Nous," *Le Petit Parisien*, September 20, 1921, 1; Chaplin, *My Trip Abroad*, 105, 107.
67. Urbain Dhere, "Nos Lectures—Charlot," *Paris-Midi*, September 21, 1921, 2.
68. "Carpentier Chez Charlot," *Le Petit Parisien*, September 21, 1921, 1.
69. J.-L. Croze, "Charlot et ses visiteurs," *Comoedia*, September 21, 1921, 1. *The Wonder Man* was the title of a film about Carpentier that was about to be screened in France.
70. Le Masque de Fer, "Echos," *Le Figaro*, September 21, 1921, 1; cf. "Les gloires du jour," *Le Peuple*, September 21, 1921, 1.
71. Urbain Dhere, "Nos Lectures—Charlot," 2.
72. Ibid.
73. D. Mosellan, "Echos—*La popularité*," *Le Radical*, September 20, 1921, 2.
74. Aulard, "La Popularité de Charlot," 1. Aulard's article was extensively (and approvingly) quoted in other newspapers. See, for example, *L'Action*, September 21, 1921, 3; *Paris-Midi*, September 20, 1921, 3.
75. Louis Forest, "Propos d'un Parisien: Encore Charlot!," *Le Matin*, September 20, 1921, 1.
76. "Charlot s'en va," *Le Petit Parisien*, September 22, 1921, 2.
77. J.-L. Croze referred to him as "Le grand artiste américain" ("Charlot est à Paris," 1). Other French writers referred to him as "le comique américain" (Le Masque de Fer, "Echos," *Le Figaro*, September 21, 1921, 1), commented on his "very yankee smile displaying beautiful teeth" ("Charlot est à Paris," *Le Journal*, September 19, 1921, 1), or defined him as "an American, born in Great Britain" (Henry Barde, "En prenant un cocktail avec Charlot," *L'Homme Libre*, September 20, 1921, 1).
78. Theodore Zeldin, *France 1848–1945*, vol. 2: *Intellect, Taste and Anxiety* (Oxford University Press, 1977), 1083.
79. John Horne, "Demobilizing the Mind: France and the Legacy of the Great War, 1919–1939," *French History and Civilization*, 2 (2009): 105; Zeldin, *France 1848–1945*, 1084–85.
80. Marc Trachtenberg, *Reparation in World Politics: France and European Economic Diplomacy, 1916–1923* (Columbia University Press, 1980), 213–17, quotation from 218. Also see "Les pourparlers Loucheur-Rathenau," *Le Figaro*, September 25, 1921, 1; "Dernières Nouvelles—Le Règlement de la Paix," *Le Temps*, September 26, 1921, 4; "Les accords de Wiesbaden," *Le Temps*, September 30, 1921, 1; "MM. Loucheur et Rathenau se recontreront jeudi," *Le Figaro*, October 5, 1921, 1; "M. Loucheur part pour Wiesbaden," *L'Eclair*, October 5, 1921, 1; "Les réparations en nature et les entrevues Loucheur-Rathenau," *Le Temps*, October 7, 1921, 6;

"Les accords de Wiesbaden," *Le Figaro*, October 8, 1921, 1; "Bulletin du jour: L'accord de Wiesbaden," *Le Temps*, October 8, 1921, 1.

81. In early September, Loucheur wrote to Mrs. Dike, the president of CARD, thanking her for "the day I recently spent with you in the department of the Aisne, the theatre for your charitable efforts. . . . I carry with me a precise vision of the services that have been rendered to our distressed people by the organizations created through your work, which Miss Morgan and yourself wished to show me in detail." "Au Comité pour les régions dévastées—Une lettre de M. Loucheur," *Le Figaro*, September 10, 1921, 2.

82. GM, "Charlot vous attend ce soir au Trocadéro," *Le Petit Journal*, October 5, 1921, 1; "Le Gala du Trocadéro," *L'Intransigeant*, October 6, 1921, 3.

83. Chaplin, *My Autobiography*, 297–98.

84. See "Charlot Voyage—Il quitte Paris aujourd'hui . . . mais il reviendra," *Paris-Midi*, September 22, 1921, 1; "Charlot Voyage," *L'Action*, September 23, 1921, 1; "Charlot va Jouer," *Le Journal de Peuple*, September 23, 1921, 1.

85. Chaplin, *My Autobiography*, 300–301.

86. See "Charlot au Trocadéro," *Le Figaro*, October 6, 1921, 2; GM, "Charlot vous attend ce soir au Trocadéro," 1; "Le Gala du Trocadéro," 3; "Huge Audience Throngs Trocadéro to See 'Charlot' in Gala Show," *New York Herald*, Paris edition, October 6, 1921, 1. Chaplin later listed in *My Trip Abroad* (134–35) some of the distinguished people present, though he did his best to pre-empt suggestions of social snobbery by making the existence of the list ("preserved for me by my secretary") seem nearly accidental.

87. "Le gala 'Charlot' à Trocadéro," *L'Echo de Paris*, October 6, 1921, 3; GM, "Tout Paris . . . et tout New York ont acclamé Charlot," *Le Petit Journal*, October 6, 1921, 2; Jean Bastia, "La Soirée," *Comoedia*, October 7, 1921, 1; "Huge Audience Throngs Trocadéro," 1; Chaplin, *My Trip Abroad*, 134–35. Coincidentally, while Chaplin was in Paris, the date was announced for the trial of Henri Landru, the wife-murderer who would later become the basis for Chaplin's *Monsieur Verdoux*.

88. Chaplin, *My Autobiography*, 300; Delluc, "Charlot à Paris," 317. The French satirical magazine *Le Canard enchaîné* had commented earlier that Chaplin "really wishes to see Mademoiselle Sorel and he has written to this effect to the Commission of Old-Paris." "Charlot Nous Parle de la France," *Le Canard enchaîné*, September 14, 1921, 3.

89. "Charlot rentre à Paris pour prêter son concours à la fête du Trocadéro," *Le Petit Parisien*, October 4, 1921, 2; GM, "Charlot vous attend ce soir au Trocadéro," 1.

90. "Les Mondalités—Le Gala du Trocadéro," *Le Gaulois*, October 6, 1921, 2; "Huge Audience Throngs Trocadéro," 1.

91. J.-L. Croze, "Charlot est acclamé au Trocadéro par une foule immense," *Comoedia*, October 6, 1921, 1; Chaplin, *My Autobiography*, 300.

92. "Les Mondalités—Le Gala du Trocadéro," 2; "Huge Audience Throngs Trocadéro," 1; "Charlot au Trocadéro," *Le Figaro*, October 6, 1921, 2; GM, "Tout Paris . . . acclamé Charlot," 2.

93. Louis Delluc, "Cinéma—Le Gosse," *Paris-Midi*, September 21, 1921, 2. The same review was published in *Cinéa*, no. 25 (October 28, 1921).

94. J.-L. Croze, "*The Kid [Le Gosse]*," *Comoedia*, October 7, 1921, 1.

95. C.A., "Le gala 'Charlot' à Trocadéro," *L'Echo de Paris*, October 6, 1921, 3.

96. "Charlot au Trocadéro," *La Cinématographie Française*, no. 153 (October 8, 1921), 7; "Merci, Charlot!," *La Victoire*, October 7, 1921, 1. The only complaints about the gala came from those who had expected Chaplin to appear in his Charlot costume. "Charlot au Trocadéro"; J.-L. Croze, "Charlot est acclamé," 1; "La soirée Charlot au Trocadéro," *Le Peuple*, October 7, 1921, 2.

97. "Charlot nous quitte . . . par la voie des airs," 3; "Parti! Charlot a quitté Paris hier matin," 1; "Charlot Aviateur," *L'Action*, October 8, 1921, 1; "Charlot S'envole," *La République Française*, October 8, 1921, 1.

98. United Artists, "Le dernier message de Charlot," ad, dated October 7, *La Cinématographie Française*, no. 154 (October 15, 1921), 74.

99. "Charlot est à Paris: Ses projets, ses impressions et ses idées," *Le Journal*, September 19, 1921, 1.

100. Chaplin, *My Trip Abroad*, 113.

101. "Merci, Charlot!," 1.

102. See Virmaux and Virmaux, *Philippe Soupault, Ecrits de cinéma*, 55n1.

Chapter 3

1. Although *The Pilgrim* (*Le Pélerin*, First National, 1922) was released in the United States in February 1923, it was not shown in Paris until February 1925. Consequently, *A Woman of Paris* (*L'Opinion publique*, United Artists, 1923) preceded it in France, where it was first screened in April 1924.

2. Marcel Tariol, *Louis Delluc: Choix de textes de Louis Delluc, extraits de scénarios, documents, panorama critique, témoignages, filmographie, bibliographie, documents iconographiques* (Éditions Seghers, 1965), 6–11.

3. Louis Delluc, *Cinéma et cie* (Bernard Grasset, 1919), 11.

4. Francis, quoted in Eugene C. McCreary, "Louis Delluc, Film Theorist, Critic, and Prophet," *Cinema Journal* 16, no. 1 (Fall 1976): 15.

5. Tariol, *Louis Delluc*, 23, 27, 32–33, 35–39, 55–61, 177.

6. Louis Delluc, *Charlie Chaplin*, trans. Hamish Miles (Bodley Head, 1922), 19–25, originally published as *Charlot* (Maurice de Brunoff, 1921).

7. Ibid., 12.

8. Ibid., 13–14.

9. Ibid., 26.

10. Ibid., 25.

11. Robinson, *Chaplin—The Mirror of Opinion*, 50.

12. Delluc, *Charlot*, 34–35; cf. 41, 47, 62–63.

13. Ibid., 90.

14. Louis Delluc, "Notes pour moi," *Le Film*, n.s. no. 115 (May 27, 1918), 14.

15. Delluc, *Charlot*, 68. In an excellent analysis of the historical significance of Delluc's *Charlot*—bringing out in particular its influence on "realist aesthetics and auteurist criticism"—Donna Kornhaber comments that, because of its date of publication, it "appeals to modern readers" since it focuses on short films that today are often hidden "beneath the shadow of his later feature films." Yet, while she points out that Delluc "lavishes attention" on a selective number of films, she does not comment on the fact that most Keystone movies were ignored. Donna Kornhaber, "*Charlot* as Cinema: Louis Delluc and Charlie Chaplin at the Dawn of Film Criticism," *Film History* 27, no. 2 (2015): 143, 155–56.

16. Delluc, *Charlot*, 28.

17. See, for example, Louis Delluc, "La Beauté au cinéma," *Le Film* 73 (August 6, 1917), in Abel, *French Film Theory and Criticism*, 139.

18. Delluc, *Charlot*, 17, 92.

19. Ibid., 17–18, 93–94.

20. Ibid., 11, 12, 14.

21. Ibid., 12.

22. Ibid., 79.

23. Ibid., 15–16.

24. Ibid., 14–15, 69, 94–95.

25. Élie Faure, "Charlot," *L'Esprit nouveau*, no. 6 (March 15, 1921), translated by Walter Pach and reprinted as "The Art of Charlie Chaplin," *New England Review* 19, no. 2 (Spring 1998): 146–51, quotations from 148–49, 151.

26. Élie Faure, "The Art of Cineplastics" (1922), translated by Walter Pach and reprinted in Abel, *French Film Theory and Criticism*, 262.

27. Faure, "The Art of Charlie Chaplin," 146; Faure, "The Art of Cineplastics," 259.

28. Faure, "The Art of Charlie Chaplin," 147.

29. Ibid.

30. Libby Murray, "*Charlot Français*: Charlie Chaplin, the First World War, and the Construction of a National Hero," *Contemporary French and Francophone Studies* 14, no. 4 (September 2010): 422–23.

31. Jean-Paul Sartre, "Apologie pour le cinéma" (1924), in *Charlot: Histoire d'un mythe*, ed. Daniel Banda and José Moure (Flammarion, 2013), 101–2.

32. Faure, "The Art of Charlie Chaplin," 151.

33. Henri Michaux, "Notre frère Charlie" (1924), in Banda and Moure, *Charlot*, 95–100.

34. Faure, "The Art of Charlie Chaplin," 149; Lucien Fabre, "Charlot," *La Revue Hebdomadaire*, January 10, 1925, 150.

35. Fabre, "Charlot," 165.

36. Michaux, "Notre frère Charlie," 97–98. Michaux was discussing *A Night in the Show* (Essanay, 1915).

37. Michaux, "Notre frère Charlie," 98; Jan Goldstein, "Neutralizing Freud: The Lycée Philosophy Class and the Problem of the Reception of Psychoanalysis in France," *Critical Inquiry* 40, no. 1 (Autumn 2013): 40, 42–43, 59–60.

38. Michaux, "Notre frère Charlie," 98–99.

39. Paul Renard, "Les écrivains Francophones et Charlie Chaplin," *Positif—Revue mensuelle de cinéma*, June 2014, 108.

40. Jean Prévost, "Essai sur Charlot," *Le Navire d'argent*, January 1926, reprinted as "Comme l'homme primitif au milieu de la nature…," in Banda and Moure, *Charlot*, 207.

41. Ibid., 205, 207.

42. Ibid., 206.

43. Richard Schickel, *The Essential Chaplin: Perspectives on the Life and Art of the Great Comedian* (Ivan R. Dee, 2006), 76.

44. André Maurois, "La Poésie du Cinéma," *L'Art Cinématographique* 3 (1927): 14.

45. Ibid., 2–4.

46. Ibid., 16–17.

47. Ibid., 1, 19.

48. Ibid., 12–15.

49. Ibid., 3.

50. *Charlot et le Masque de Fer* (*The Idle Class*) was first reviewed in France in November 1924. See "Charlot et le masque de fer," *Les Spectacles*, November 28, 1924, 12; Félicien Faillet, "Le Cinéma—Comiques," *L'homme libre*, November 7, 1924, 2; "Au Cinéma—Les Films de la Semaine," *Paris-Soir*, November 1, 1924, 5. René Clair noted in December 1922 that *Pay Day* would "soon" be available in France. Two years later, Pierre Henry commented that this film, which had been shown "long ago" in Belgium and Switzerland, had still not been shown in France. It arrived in Paris in September 1925. René Clair, "Sous les feux du Studio," *L'Intransigeant*, December 2, 1922, 4; P[ierre] H[enry], *Cinéa-Ciné-pour-tous*, December 1, 1924, 10; G.R., "Le semaine au Cinéma—Les Nouveaux Films—*Jour de Paye*," *Le Matin*, September 25, 1925, 4.

51. See *Le Matin*, April 25, 1924, 5.

52. René Jeanne, "*L'Opinion publique*," *Le Petit Journal*, April 25, 1924, 4; P[ierre] H[enry], "La Leçon de *L'Opinion Publique*," *Cinéa-Ciné-pour-tous*, May 15, 1924, 9–10. Henry pointed out that sequences from *Life* were later used in *Charlot cambrioleur* (*Police*, Essanay, 1916) and *Les Avatars de Charlot* (*Triple Trouble*, Essanay, 1916, a compilation never authorized by Chaplin) (10).

53. Léon Moussinac, "*L'Opinion Publique* de Charlie Chaplin," *L'Humanité*, April 24, 1924, 2; H[enry], "La Leçon de *L'Opinion Publique*," 10.

54. H[enry], "La Leçon de *L'Opinion Publique*," 10.

55. See, for example, ibid.

56. Paul Gordeaux, "*L'Opinion Publique*," *L'Echo de Paris*, April 25, 1924, 4; Jeanne, "*L'Opinion publique*," 4. Interestingly, Pierre Henry blamed these "material errors" not on Chaplin himself but on unnamed "French assistants" he had entrusted "with the task of correcting the French atmosphere" ("La Leçon de *L'Opinion Publique*," 10).

57. Abel, *French Film Theory and Criticism*, 209.

58. H[enry], "La Leçon de *L'Opinion Publique*," 10–12.

59. Jean Tedesco, "D'après 'L'Opinion publique': Essai d'une Psychologie de Charles Chaplin," *Cinéa-Ciné-pour-tous*, May 15, 1924, 6–9.

60. Paul Gordeaux, "*L'Opinion publique*," *L'Echo de Paris*, April 25, 1924, 4; cf. Jacques Vivien, "Les Critiques Cinématographiques," *Le Petit Parisien*, April 26, 1924, 6.

61. Saint-Denis, "Les Films de la Semaine—*L'Opinion publique*," *Le Courrier Cinématographique*, 14th year no. 17, April 26, 1924, 15.

62. H[enry], "La Leçon de *L'Opinion Publique*," 10; cf. Gordeaux, "*L'Opinion Publique*," 4. Sadly for Purviance, the commercial failure of *A Woman of Paris* pretty much finished her acting career.

63. Gordeaux, "*L'Opinion publique*," 4; Saint-Denis, "Les Films de la Semaine—*L'Opinion publique*," 15; H[enry], "La Leçon de *L'Opinion Publique*," 10.

64. Paul Achard, "Sur la sellette—Charlie Chaplin," *Paris-Midi*, March 2, 1925, 4. Playwright Marcel Achard (1899–1934), later of the French Academy, had his first success with the play *Voulez-vous jouer avec moâ?* (1923), which focused on circus clowns. Bernard Zimmer (1893–1964),

playwright and later screenwriter, demonstrated a fascination for puppets in his first play, *Le Veux gras* (1924).

65. Jean Chataigner, "Les Films de la Semaine," *Le Journal*, February 27, 1925, 4; Paul Gordeaux, "Les Films de la Semaine—*Le Pèlerin*," *L'Echo de Paris*, February 27, 1925, 4.

66. J.P., "Le Cinéma—*Le voyage au paradis*," *Paris-Midi*, February 23, 1925, 4; Chataigner, "Les Films de la Semaine," 4. René Jeanne also compared *The Pilgrim* stylistically to Linder's *Le Roi du Cirque*, both being "made up of a series of small sketches" assembled together in a masterly way. René Jeanne, "*Le Pèlerin*," *Le Petit Journal*, March 6, 1925, 4.

67. Jeanne, "*Le Pèlerin*," 4.

68. J.P. "Le Cinéma—*Le Pèlerin*," *Paris-Midi*, February 22, 1925, 4.

69. Chataigner, "Les Films de la Semaine," 4.

70. Gordeaux, "Less Films de la Sèmaine—*Le Pèlerin*," 4; Georges Roche, "Les Nouveaux Films—*Le Pèlerin*," *Le Matin*, February 27, 1925, 4.

71. Achard, "Sur la sellette," 4.

72. François-Robert, "Le Galois au Cinéma," *Le Galois*, March 6, 1925, 4; Boisyvon, "Les dix ans de Charlot," *L'Intransigeant*, March 7, 1925, 4.

73. Dominque Janda, "From Fernando to Medrano: A Parisian Circus Epic," *Bandwagon* 62, no. 2 (2018): 6–31; Darius Milhaud, *Le Boeuf sur le Toit*, LA Phil, accessed November 16, 2024, https://www.laphil.com/musicdb/pieces/2200/le-boeuf-sur-le-toit; Donald McManus, *No Kidding! Clown as Protagonist in Twentieth-Century Theater* (University of Delaware Press, 2003), 25.

74. Émile Vuillermoz, "Courrier Cinématographique—*Le Pèlerin*," *Le Temps*, March 7, 1925, 4.

75. Philippe Sarlat, "Les Films de la Semaine," *Paris-Soir*, February 28, 1925, 5; Roche, "Les Nouveaux Films—*Le Pèlerin*," 4; Achard, "Sur la sellette," 4.

76. Gordeaux, "Les Films de la Semaine—*Le Pèlerin*," 4; Sarlat, "Les Films de la Semaine," 5; Gaston Thierry, "Les Premières de la Semaine—*La Ruée vers l'Or* réalisé et joué par Charlie Chaplin," *Paris-Midi*, September 25, 1925, 2.

77. Boisyvon, "Les dix ans de Charlot," 4.

78. Paul Gordeaux, "Le Cinéma—*La Ruée vers l'or*," *L'Echo de Paris*, September 25, 1925, 4; Philippe Sarlat, "Les Cinémas—Les Films de la Semaine," *Paris-Soir*, September 26, 1925, 5.

79. Gordeaux, "Le Cinéma—*La Ruée vers l'or*," 4; Sarlat, "Les Cinémas—Les Films de la Semaine," 5; Thierry, "Les Premières de la Semaine—*La Ruée vers l'Or*," 2.

80. G.R., "La semaine au Cinéma—Les Nouveaux Films—*La Ruée vers l'or*," *Le Matin*, September 25, 1925, 4; Sarlat, "Les Cinémas—Les Films de la Semaine," 5; Jean Chataigner, "La semaine au Cinéma—*Les Premières de l'Ecran*—*La Ruée vers l'Or*," *Le Journal*, September 25, 1925, 4; Émile Vuilllermoz, "Courrier Cinématographique—*La Ruée vers l'or*," *Le Temps*, September 26, 1925, 5; Thierry, "Les Premières de la Semaine—*La Ruée vers l'Or*," 2.

81. René Jeanne, "Les Films de la Semaine—*La Ruée vers l'Or*," *Le Petit Journal*, September 25, 1925, 4.

82. Vuillermoz, "Courrier Cinématographique—*La Ruée vers l'Or*," 5; Thierry, "Les Premières de la Semaine—*La Ruée vers l'Or*," 2.

83. Jeanne, "Les Films de la Semaine—*La Ruée vers l'Or*," 4. Pierrot, a comedy character originating in Italy, became popular in France in the seventeenth century.

84. Sarlat, "Les Cinémas—Les Films de la Semaine," 5; G.R. "La semaine au Cinéma—Les Nouveaux Films—*La Ruée vers l'or*," 4.

85. Boisyvon, "La Vie du Cinéma—Dans l'intimité de Charlie," *L'Intransigeant*, September 26, 1925, 4.

86. Gordeaux, "Le Cinéma—*La Ruée vers l'or*," 4; Chataigner, "Le Semaine au Cinéma—Les Premières de l'Ecran—*La Ruée vers l'Or*," 4; G.R. "La semaine au Cinéma—Les Nouveaux Films—*La Ruée vers l'or*," 4; Thierry, "Les Premières de la Semaine—*La Ruée vers l'Or*," 2.

87. André Suarès, "Il n'y a pas de femme clown. Vous êtes-vous demandé pourquoi?," *Comoedia*, July 3, 1926, 1.

88. Jacques de Baroncelli, "Ce Coeur Ignoble de Charlot," *Comoedia*, July 7, 1926, 1.

89. Frédéric Lefèvre, "Une heure avec Francis Carco—Poéte et Romancier," *Les Nouvelles littéraires*, August 14, 1926, 2.

90. Ibid.

91. Léon Moussinac, "Critique de Charlot," *L'Humanité*, January 23, 1927, 4.

92. André Suarès, "Charlot et son Coeur," *Comoedia*, January 15, 1927, 1.

93. Jean Tedesco, "Une Offensive Littéraire contre Chaplin," *Cinéa-Ciné-pour-tous*, January 15, 1927, 9–10.

94. Moussinac, "Critique de Charlot," 4; Jean-Napoléon-Michel in "L'Art et le Coeur de Charlot: Un débat," *Comoedia*, January 26, 1927, 5.

95. Odile Gay in "L'Art et le Coeur de Charlot," 5.

96. Jacques de Baroncelli, "Charlot dans sa cabane," *Comoedia*, February 9, 1927, 1.

97. Gabriel Trarieux, "Notre Coeur et Charlot," *Comoedia*, February 15, 1927, 1.

98. Paul Souday, "Le Cinéma n'est pas un art," *La Dépêche—Journal de la démocratie* (Toulouse), May 29, 1927, 1; Jean de Pierrefeu, "M. Souday contre le cinéma," *Les Nouvelles Littéraires*, June 11, 1927, 1; "Réponse de Paul Souday à M. Jean de Pierrefeu," *Les Nouvelles Littéraires*, June 18, 1927, 1, 5.

99. Émile Vuillermoz, "Chronique Cinématographique—*Le Cirque*," *Le Temps*, February 18, 1928, 4.

100. Maurice Huet, "Le Cinéma—*Le Cirque*," *Le Petit Parisien*, February 17, 1928, 4.

101. R[ené] J[eanne], "Le Cinéma—Les films de la semaine—*Le Cirque* (film américain)," *Le Petit Journal*, February 24, 1928, 4. Jeanne was referring to recent books about Chaplin by Edouard Ramon and Henry Poulaille.

102. Robert Spa, "*Figaro*—Cinéma—Critiques," *Le Figaro*, February 17, 1928, 6; Boisyvon, "Les films de la Semaine—*Le Cirque*, film de Charlie Chaplin," *L'Intransigeant*, February 18, 1928, 6.

103. Léon Moussinac, "Charlie Chaplin in *Le Cirque*," *L'Humanité*, February 18, 1928, 4; Léon Moussinac, "*Le Cirque* de Charlie Chaplin," *L'Humanité*, March 10, 1928, 4.

104. Moussinac, "*Le Cirque* de Charlie Chaplin," 4.

105. Raymond Berner, "Critiques—*Le Cirque*," *Le Matin*, February 24, 1928, 4.

106. Raymond Villette, "Les Cinémas—Les grandes exclusivités—*Le Cirque*," *Le Galois*, February 19, 1928, 4; Paul Gordeaux, "Le Cinéma—Les films de la semaine—*Le Cirque* (film américain)," *L'Echo de Paris*, February 17, 1928, 4.

107. Spa, "*Figaro*—Cinéma—Critiques," 6. (Though Spa confessed in the same review that he regarded *The Pilgrim* as Chaplin's "most perfect film.")

108. Vuillermoz, "Chronique Cinématographique—*Le Cirque*," 4.

109. Jeanne, "Le Cinéma—Les films de la semaine—*Le Cirque* (film américain)," 4.

110. Berner, "Critiques—*Le Cirque*," 4; Jeanne, "Le Cinéma—Les films de la semaine—*Le Cirque* (film américain)," 4.

111. Jeanne, "Le Cinéma—Les films de la semaine—*Le Cirque* (film américain)," 4; Gordeaux, "Le Cinéma—Les films de la semaine—*Le Cirque* (film américain)," 4; Spa, "*Figaro*—Cinéma—Critiques," 6.

112. Jeanne, "Le Cinéma—Les films de la semaine—*Le Cirque* (film américain)," 4.

113. Jacques Vivien, "Le Cinéma—Critique cinématographique," *Le Petit Parisien*, February 24, 1928, 5; Jeanne, "Le Cinéma—Les films de la semaine—*Le Cirque* (film américain)," 4; Spa, "*Figaro*—Cinéma—Critiques," 6.

114. Berner, "Critiques—*Le Cirque*," 4; Vivien, "Le Cinéma—Critique cinématographique," 5.

115. Gordeaux, "Le Cinéma—Les films de la semaine—*Le Cirque* (film américain)," 4; Spa, "*Figaro*—Cinéma—Critiques," 6; Boisyvon, "Les films de la Semaine—*Le Cirque*, film de Charlie Chaplin," 6.

116. Vuillermoz, "Chronique Cinématographique—*Le Cirque*," 4; Vivien, "Le Cinéma—Critique cinématographique," 5; Villette, "Les Cinémas—Les grandes exclusivités—*Le Cirque*," 4.

117. Berner, "Critiques—*Le Cirque*," *Le Matin*, 4. Boisyvon similarly noted that "the scenes develop logically" ("Les films de la Semaine—*Le Cirque*, film de Charlie Chaplin," 6).

118. Suarès made no reference in his two articles to written words in the form of intertitles. In his critique of Souday's similar argument regarding the primacy of words, Jean de Pierrefeu pointed out that the movements and facial expressions of the screen actor were supplemented by "the announcement on the screen indicating the theme." Jean de Pierrefeu, "Mr. Souday contre le cinéma," *Les Nouvelles littéraires*, June 11, 1927, 1.

Chapter 4

1. Sydney Chaplin, "Foreword," in Lita Grey Chaplin and Jeffrey Vance, *Wife of the Life of the Party* (Scarecrow Press, 1998), ix; Lynn, *Charlie Chaplin and His Times*, 309–10.

2. The text of the divorce complaint is printed in full at the end of Chaplin and Vance, *Wife of the Life of the Party*, Lita's second published autobiography. On the points summarized here, see 132–35, 138–40, 142–46, 150, 158, 161.

3. Ibid., 133–34, 136–38, 141–42, 144. The five actresses were Edna Purviance, Pola Negri, Claire Windsor, Peggy Hopkins Joyce, and Merna Kennedy.

4. Ibid., 137–38. The "girl" was Andrea Gatesbry.

5. Maland, *Chaplin and American Culture*, 94–95.

6. Ibid., 98–99.

7. Ibid., 99–103; Robinson, *Chaplin: His Life and Art*, 375.

8. "Surrealist Manifesto—Hands Off Love," *Transition*, no. 6 (September 1927): 155–65; *La Révolution surréaliste*, nos. 9–10 (October 1, 1927), 1–6. Since Cunard's translation of Aragon's French was rather eccentric, the translation used for analysis here is that in Paul Hammond, ed., *The Shadow and Its Shadow: Surrealist Writings on the Cinema*, 2nd ed. (Polygon, 1991), 183–92.

9. "Hands Off Love," in Hammond, ed., *The Shadow and Its Shadow*, 184.

10. Ibid., 183, 185, 189.

11. Ibid., 184.

12. Ibid., 188.

13. Ibid., 189–90. For the sequence referred to by Aragon, see *The Count* (12:25 to 13:10).

14. "Hands Off Love," in Hammond, ed., *The Shadow and Its Shadow*, 189.

15. Ibid., 187, 189.

16. William S. Rubin, *Dada and Surrealist Art* (Harry N. Abrams, 1968), 132.

17. Louis Aragon, *The Libertine*, trans. Jo Levy (1924; John Calder, 1987), 10–11.

18. Paul Éluard, "D. A. F. de Sade, écrivain fantastique et révolutionnaire," *La Révolution Surréaliste*, no. 8 (December 1, 1926), quoted in Gérard Durozoi, *History of the Surrealist Movement*, trans. Alison Anderson (University of Chicago Press, 2002), 161; cf. Aragon, *The Libertine*, 16–17.

19. "Recherches sur la sexualité," *La Révolution Surréaliste*, no. 11 (March 15, 1928): 32–40. The fifteen were Louis Aragon, Jacques Baron, Jacques-André Boiffard, André Breton, Marcel Duhamel, Max Morise, Pierre Naville, Marcel Noll, Benjamin Péret, Jacques Prévert, Raymond Queneau, Man Ray, Georges Sadoul, Yves Tanguy, and Pierre Unik.

20. "Quelle sorte d'espoir mettez-vous dans l'amour?," *Le Révolution Surréaliste*, no. 12 (December 15, 1929): 65–76. The twelve were Maxime Alexandre, Louis Aragon, Jacques Baron (who declined to give a view), André Breton, Robert Desnos, Paul Éluard, Max Ernst, Jean Genbach, Camille Goemans, Paul Nougé, Georges Sadoul, and Pierre Unik.

21. Louis Aragon et al., "Manifesto of the Surrealists Concerning *L'Âge d'or*," trans. Paul Hammond, in Hammond, *The Shadow and Its Shadow*, 182–89. The seven were Maxime Alexandre, Aragon, Breton, Éluard, Benjamin Péret, Georges Sadoul, and Pierre Unik.

22. Albert Valentin, *L'Art cinématographique IV* (Librairie Félix Alcan, 1927), trans. Paul Hammond, in Hammond, *The Shadow and Its Shadow*, 106.

23. Leon S. Roudiez, "The Case of Louis Aragon and Surrealism," *French Review* 26, no. 2 (December 1952): 101.

24. André Breton, "Manifesto of Surrealism" (1924), California State University, Sacramento, 1999, https://www.csus.edu/indiv/o/obriene/art109/readings/manifestoofsurrealism.pdf.

25. Jack L. Spector, *Surrealist Art and Writing 1919–1939* (Cambridge University Press, 1997), 162–63. Analyzing the "return to order" in France after the First World War, Amy Lyford sees the misogyny that characterized many male surrealists as heavily influenced by their contemporary anxieties and ambivalences. Amy Lyford, *Surrealist Masculinities: Gender, Anxiety and the Aesthetics of Post–World War I Reconstruction in France* (University of California Press, 2007), *passim*.

26. On this point, see Neil Cox, "Critique of Pure Desire, Or When the Surrealists Were Right," in *Surrealism—Desire Unbound*, ed. Jennifer Mundy (Tate, 2001), 256–57; Spector, *Surrealist Art and Writing 1919–1939*, 162.

27. "Hands Off Love," 191.

28. Philippe Soupault, "The 'U.S.A.' Cinema," *Broom: An International Magazine of the Arts* 5, no. 2 (September 1923): 68; Robert Desnos, *Paris-Journal*, April 6, 1923, cited in Richard Abel, "The Contribution of the French Literary Avant-Garde to Film Theory and Criticism (1907–1924)," *Cinema Journal* 14, no. 3 (Spring 1975): 23.

29. Robert Desnos, "Avant-garde Cinema," in Abel, *French Film Theory and Criticism*, 430.

30. Richard Abel, "American Film and the French Literary Avant-Garde (1914–1924)," *Contemporary Literature* 17, no. 1 (Winter 1976): 101–2.

31. See https://www.gutenberg.org/ebooks/56801, accessed January 25, 2026. The book itself would not be published until 1921. Louis Aragon, *Anicet ou le panorama, roman* (Éditions de la Nouvelle Revue Française, 1921).

32. Jacques Vaché to André Breton, November 14, 1918, in Hammond, *The Shadow and Its Shadow*, 53.

33. Louis Aragon, "Charlot Sentimental," *Le Film*, n.s. 105 (March 1 or 18, 1918): 11.

34. Ibid.

35. Louis Aragon, "Charlot Mystique," *Nord-Sud*, no. 15 (May 1918), in Olivier Barbarant, ed., *Ouuvres poétiques complètes*, vol. 1 (Gallimard, 2007), 5–6.

36. Wolfgang Babilas, *Études sur Louis Aragon* (Nodus, 2000), 360.

37. Caroline Nataf, "Les poètes surréalistes et leur rapport au cinéma dans les années Vingt" (MA thesis, University of Paris IV–Sorbonne, 2003–4), 83.

38. Philippe Soupault, "Une vie de chien," *Littérature*, no. 4 (June 1919): 20, translated in Soupault, "The 'U.S.A.' Cinema," 67.

39. Twelve years after the first appearance of this comment on *The Immigrant*, Soupault republished much of it (63–64) in his book *Charlot*. This was a beautifully written imaginary biography of Charlot based on his films. Unlike Soupault's earlier comments, *Charlot* did summarize filmic narratives. The key movies referred to (though never by name) are *Easy Street* (*Charlot policeman*, Mutual, 1917) (39–42); *One A.M.* (*Charlot rentre tard*, Mutual, 1916) (42–43); *The Vagabond* (*Charlot musicien*, Mutual, 1916) (46–58); *The Kid* (*Le Gosse*, First National, 1921) (66–72); *The Immigrant* (*Charlot voyage*, Mutual, 1917) (22–23, 81–98); *Shoulder Arms* (*Charlot soldat*, First National, 1918) (107–18); *The Adventurer* (*Charlot s'évade*, Mutual, 1917) and *The Pilgrim* (*Le pélerin*, First National, 1922) (127–44); *The Gold Rush* (*La Ruée vers l'or*, United Artists, 1925) (145–60]; and *The Circus* (*Le Cirque*, United Artists, 1928) (169–92). Soupault's Charlot has "the soul of a vagabond" (3). He can never remain in one place "for he knows that beyond, further away, something new awaits" (13). He is distrusted as a marginal figure, frequently stealing food to survive (16–17, 35), and is often harassed by cops (24, 26–27, 67–68, 171–73). He tries, temporarily, all kinds of jobs to earn a living but finds discipline hard and always wants to escape constraints by following "the broad highway" (33–34, 120). His romances are ultimately doomed because "he prefers to be alone and to be unattached" (120). Soupault's life of Charlot in a series titled "The Great Fable—Chronicles of Imaginary Characters" was a deeply affectionate portrait of a favorite screen personality, conceived by the author as "a very fervent homage to Charlie Chaplin." Philippe Soupault, *Charlot* (Librairie Plon, 1931).

40. Philippe Soupault, "Charlot Voyage," *Littérature*, no. 6 (August 1919): 22, translated in Soupault, "The 'U.S.A.' Cinema," 68.

41. Herbert S. Gershman, *The Surrealist Revolution in France* (University of Michigan Press, 1974), 34.

42. See, for example, Richard Abel, "Exploring the Discursive Field of the Surrealist Scenario Text," in *Dada and Surrealist Film*, ed. Rudolf E. Kuenzli (MIT Press, 1996), 58–71.

43. Yvan Goll, "The Chaplinade: A Film Poem," *Massachusetts Review* 6, no. 3 (Spring–Summer 1965): 501–14.

44. Clinton J. Atkinson and Arthur S. Wensinger, "An Introductory Note," in Goll, "The Chaplinade," 499.

45. Michel Sanouillet, *Dada in Paris*, trans. Sharmila Ganguly (MIT Press, 2009), 6–9.

46. Ibid., 69.

47. Tristan Tzara to André Breton, January 6, 1919, in ibid., 332, 58.

48. André Breton to Tristan Tzara, January 22 and January 24, 1919, in Sanouillet, *Dada in Paris*, 332–34; *Dada 4/5*, May 15, 1919, 12.

49. Tristan Tzara to André Breton, March 30, 1919, in Sanouillet, *Dada in Paris*, 338; *Littérature*, no. 1, March 1919, 22, 24; *Littérature*, no. 5, July 1919, 10–13.

50. "La seule expression de l'homme moderne," 1919–20, Kunsthaus Zürich, https://digital.kunsth aus.ch/viewer/fullscreen/21706/; André Breton to Tristan Tzara, June 12, 1919, in Sanouillet, *Dada in Paris*, 344. A few months later, Paul Éluard described Breton himself as resembling a "tragic Charlot." Paul Draule [Éluard], "Présentations de circonstance," *Cannibale*, no. 1 (April 25, 1920): 17.

51. Gaëtan Picon, *Surrealists and Surrealism, 1919–1939* (Skira/Rizzoli, 1977), 37.

52. André Gide, who was among those present, later recalled, "Some young people, solemn, stilted, tied up in knots, got up on the platform and as a chorus declaimed insincere inanities." See

"Société des Artistes Indépendants," *Art and Popular Culture Encyclopedia*, accessed November 20, 2024, https://www.artandpopularculture.com/Salon_des_Artistes_Ind%C3%A9penda nts#1920.2C_the_emergence_of_Dada.

53. Maurice Nadeau, *The History of Surrealism*, trans. Roger Shattuck (Harvard University Press, 1989), 62.

54. Michel Sanouillet, *Dada in Paris*, ed. Anne Sanouillet, trans. Sharmila Ganguly (MIT Press, 2009), 109–10.

55. Tristan Tzara, "Memoirs of Dadaism," in Edmund Wilson, *Axel's Castle: A Study of the Imaginative Literature of 1870 to 1930* (Charles Scribner's Sons, 1932), 305.

56. Matthew Josephson, *Life Among the Surrealists: A Memoir by Matthew Josephson* (Holt, Rinehart and Winston, 1962), 124.

57. Ibid., 123.

58. Ibid.

59. "Liquidation," *Littérature*, no. 18 (March 1921): 1. Those on the "least popular" list included those the Dadaists opposed or looked down upon. They included symbolist poets Henri de Régnier (1) and Paul Fort (6); nineteenth-century poets and writers Alphonse de Lamartine (14), Alfred de Musset (15) and Émile Zola (17); contemporary writers Anatole France (2), Roman Roillard (5), and Charles Maurras (11), founder of the right-wing newspaper *L'Action Française*; Voltaire (10), presumably because of his faith in reason; and Marshall Foch (3) and the Unknown Soldier (Soldat inconnu) (9) for their association with the First World War (24).

60. Ibid., 24.

61. Ibid.

62. The exception was Pink Pills for Pale People (Pilules Pink), a popular patent medicine of the time (Ibid.).

63. Ibid.

64. Ibid., 1–7.

65. Ibid., 3–5.

66. Nadeau, *The History of Surrealism*, 52–53.

67. Sanouillet, *Dada in Paris*, 185–94, 233–53; "semi-failure" and "determining the directives" both on 235.

68. Nadeau, *The History of Surrealism*, 68.

69. "Lâchez tout," *Littérature*, no. 2 (April 1, 1922): 10.

70. Louis Aragon, "Projet d'histoire littéraire contemporaine," *Littérature*, n.s no. 4 (September 1, 1922): 3. The first item in the second period (1914–18) was listed as "Cinema, Charlot and the Vampires."

71. Sanouillet, *Dada in Paris*, 209–15.

72. Ibid., 211; Ruth Brandon, *Surreal Lives: The Surrealists, 1917–1945* (Macmillan, 1999), 162–63; André Breton, "Interview du Professeur Freud à Vienne," *Littérature*, 2nd series 1 (March 1, 1922): 19.

73. André Breton, "Manifesto of Surrealism" (1924), trans. A. S. Kline, accessed February 5, 2026, https://www.poetsofmodernity.xyz/klineasmanifesto.php, 7–8. In practice, Breton was familiar with other writers than Freud on the same issues. Later he would claim that his ideas on "the recording of dreams and free association" could be traced back to his own experiments on mentally ill men at a hospital in St. Dizier, in northeast France, during the war. Joost Haan, Peter J. Koehler, and Julien Bogousslavsky, "Neurology and Surrealism: André Breton and Joseph Babinski," *Brain: A Journal of Neurology* 135 (2012): 3831–32; André Breton, *Conversations: The Autobiography of Surrealism* (1952; Marlow, 1993), *passim*.

74. André Breton, "Entrée des Médiums," *Littérature*, n.s. no. 6 (November 1, 1922): 1–16. The word "surrealism" appears on pages 1 and 2.

75. Josephson, *Life Among the Surrealists*, 214, 216–20, quotation from 220.

76. Helena Lewis, *Dada Turns Red: The Politics of Surrealism* (Edinburgh University Press, 1990), 71.

77. Sanouillet, *Dada in Paris*, 35; Guillermo de Torre to Tristan Tzara, aerogram, 1920, Collection Bibliothèque Jacques Doucet, fonds Tzara, Paris, in Jennifer Wild, "The Automatic Choice of the Modern Tramp: Chaplin and the Parisian Avant-Garde," *Early Popular Visual Culture* 8, no. 3 (August 2010): 275. It is not known to which text Torre was referring.

78. Richard Abel, "The Contribution of the French Literary Avant-Garde to Film Theory and Criticism (1907–1924)," *Cinema Journal* 14, no. 3 (Spring 1975): 28.

79. Ibid., 28–29.

80. Abel, "American Film and the French Literary Avant-Garde," 97, 109.

81. Aragon, quoted in Sanouillet, *Dada in Paris*, 73.

82. Benjamin Péret, for example, hailed Chaplin as demonstrating in *The Gold Rush* (UA, 1925) "the individual effort each person makes to escape . . . from the terrible obsession of one's daily bread" and suggested that *The Pilgrim* (First National, 1922) showed once more how Chaplin, "hounded by the police, had been obliged . . . to deal with the lackeys of capitalism." Péret quoted in Durozoi, *History of the Surrealist Movement*, 161.

83. Constance Brown Kuriyama, "Chaplin's Impure Comedy: The Art of Survival," *Film Quarterly* 45, no. 3 (Spring 1992): 29.

84. Charles Musser, "Work, Ideology, and Chaplin's Tramp," in *Resisting Images: Essays on Cinema and History*, ed. Robert Sklar and Charles Musser (Temple University Press, 1990), 38, 40, 50–51.

85. Louis Aragon, "Du sujet," *Le Film*, 6th year, n.s. 149 (January 22, 1919), reprinted in Bernard Leuilliot, ed., *Chroniques/Aragon*, vol. 1: *1918–1932* (Stock, 1998), 39–43, in particular 42. Breton had taken Gide's book away with him during the war; his first poem published by Tzara in the *Dada* magazine, as already noted, was titled "Pour Lafcadio."

86. Marcel Raval (1921; my translation) in "Opinions et jugements sur *Anicet ou le panorama, roman*," University of Muenster, accessed November 20, 2024, https://www.unimuenster.de/LouisAragon/werk/frueh/anicet_m.htm.

87. Louis Aragon, *Anicet ou le Panorama* (Éditions de la Nouvelle revue française, 1921), 47, here in "Surrealism, Dadaism, Chaplinism, Bojan Jović," , trans. Đorđe Čolić.

88. Tom Gunning, "Chaplin and the Body of Modernity," *Early Popular Visual Culture* 8, no. 3 (August 2010): 238, 240.

89. Haan et al., "Neurology and Surrealism," 135, 3835.

90. Ibid., 3832, 3834,

91. Louis Aragon and André Breton, "Le Cinquantenaire de l'hysterie," *La Révolution Surréaliste*, March 15, 1928, translated in Rae Beth Gordon, "From Charcot to Charlot: Unconscious Imitation and Spectatorship in French Cabaret and Early Cinema," *Critical Inquiry* 27, no. 3 (Spring 2001): 549.

92. Jean Epstein, "Magnification," in Abel, *French Film Theory and Criticism* 238.

93. Gordon, "From Charcot to Charlot," 523, 529.

94. Haan et al., "Neurology and Surrealism," 3833.

95. Robert Desnos, "Le Rêve et le cinéma," *Paris-Journal*, April 27, 1923, translated in Abel, "The Contribution of the French Literary Avant-Garde to Film Theory and Criticism," 39.

96. André Breton, "As in a Wood," in Hammond, *The Shadow and Its Shadow*, 81. Breton did note, however, that some films—including "the first Chaplins"—were able to secure his and Vaché's attention.

97. Ibid.

98. Ibid.

99. André Breton, "First Manifesto of Surrealism: 1924," trans. A. S. Kline, *Poets of Modernity*, accessed November 20, 2024, https://www.poetsofmodernity.xyz/POMBR/French/Manifesto.php.

100. Haan et al., "Neurology and Surrealism," 3832.

101. Ibid., 3832–33.

102. In "First Manifesto of Surrealism: 1924," trans. A. S. Kline, Breton described *Les Champs magnétiques* (*Magnetic Fields*) as "the first purely surrealist work."

103. Abel, "American Film and the French Literary Avant-Garde," 105.

104. Henri Michaux, "Surréalisme," *Le Disque Vert*, 4th series, 1 (January 1925): 86, cited in "Surrealism, Dadaism, Chaplinism, Bojan Jović," *Surrealism*, accessed November 20, 2024, http://nadrealizam.rs/en/in-focus/research-surrealism-dadaism-chaplinism.

105. Nadeau, *The History of Surrealism*, 135–36.

106. Ibid., 117–18.

107. Ibid., 127–32, 135–38, 141, 153.

108. Jeremy Stubbs, "Obituary: Pierre Naville," *The Independent* (London), June 3, 1993.

109. Nadeau, *The History of Surrealism*, 153, 162, 203; Mikkel Bolt Rasmussen, "The Situationist International, Surrealism, and the Difficult Fusion of Art and Politics," *Oxford Art Journal* 27, no. 3 (2004): 373–74.

110. In 1932, the final break between Breton and Aragon occurred when Breton refused to go along (as Aragon ironically was prepared to do) with the PCF's condemnation of the erotic

freedom endorsed in an article by Salvador Dalí. For Breton not to have done so, argues Annie le Brun, "would have meant a complete reversal of the values represented in . . . 'Hands Off Love.'" Annie le Brun, "Desire—A Surrealist 'Invention,'" in *Surrealism—Desire Unbound*, ed. Jennifer Mundy (Tate, 2001), 301.

111. Benjamin Péret, "Against Commercial Cinema," *L'Age du cinéma*, no. 1 (March 1951), in Hammond, *The Shadow and Its Shadow*, 63.
112. On Aragon's break with the surrealists, see Nadeau, *The History of Surrealism*, 175–82.
113. Robinson, *Chaplin: His Life and Art*, 578; Chaplin, *My Autobiography*, 512.
114. Jean-Louis Bédouin, "Chaplin, the Copper's Nark," *Le Libertaire*, November 20, 1952, in Hammond, *The Shadow and Its Shadow*, 193.
115. "Finis les pieds plats," reprinted in Gérard Berréby, ed., *Documents relatifs à la fondation de l'internationale situationniste* (Éditions Allia, 1985), 262, translated by Mikkel Bolt Rasmussen in "The Situationist International," 368.
116. Rasmussen, "The Situationist International," 368–69.
117. Ibid., 369.
118. "Les lettristes disavouent les insultes de Chaplin," reprinted in Berréby, *Documents*, 147, translated in Rasmussen, "The Situationist International, 369–70.
119. "Position de l'internationale lettriste," reprinted in Berréby, *Documents*, 151, translated in Rasmussen, "The Situationist International," 370.
120. Rasmussen, "The Situationist International," 368–69, quotation from 369.
121. Ibid., 370, 380, quotation from 380.
122. Ibid., 368–71, 380–81, 384.
123. Ironically, the Situationists' extreme language in their attack on Chaplin and surrealism echoed that of the surrealists challenging the literary/artistic orthodoxy of their own day. See, for example, their 1924 pamphlet, *Un cadavre* (*A Corpse*) denouncing Anatole France after his death (Nadeau, *The History of Surrealism*, 95–96, 233–37).

Chapter 5

1. "Charlot sera cet après-midi l'hôte de Paris," *Paris-Midi*, March 22, 1931, 1; "Charlie Chaplin doit arriver cet après-midi à 14 h. 25 à la gare de Lyon," *Le Journal*, March 22, 1931, 1. There were similar stories in *Le Figaro*, *Le Matin*, *Le Petit Parisien*, and *Le Populaire*.
2. Louis Chevreuse, "L'arrivée de Charlot à Paris," *Le Figaro*, March 23, 1931, 1; "Les Parisiens sont 'venus' en foule acclamer Charlot," *Le Quotidien*, March 23, 1931, 1; "A la gare de Lyon," *Le Journal*, March 23, 1931, 1; "Charlie Chaplin est arrivé à Paris," *L'Homme Libre*, March 23, 1931, 1; "Charlot est à Paris," *Le Peuple*, March 23, 1931, 1; "Charlot à Paris," *L'Ère Nouvelle*, March 23, 1931, 3.
3. "Charlie Chaplin a été reçu par les flics," *Le Populaire*, March 23, 1931, 1.
4. Marcel Carné, "L'hommage du peuple de Paris à Charlie Chaplin," *Ciné Magazine*, 11th year no. 4 (April 1931): 10–11; "Les Parisiens sont 'venus' en foule acclamer Charlot," *Le Quotidien*, March 23, 1931, 1; A. de G., "Charlie Chaplin est à Paris," *L'Intransigeant*, March 23, 1931, 1.
5. "Hier, une foule considérable a accueilli 'Charlot' à la gare de Lyon," *L'Humanité*, March 23, 1931, 1.
6. Carné, "L'hommage du peuple de Paris à Charlie Chaplin," 11; "Charlot à Paris," *L'Ère Nouvelle*, March 23, 1931, 3; "Parisians Smother 'Charlot' on First Visit in 10 Years," *Herald Tribune*, Paris edition, March 23, 1931, 1; "A la gare de Lyon," *Le Journal*, March 23, 1931, 2.
7. "Charlot à Paris," *L'Ère Nouvelle*, March 23, 1931, 3; D.C., "Charlie Chaplin est arrivé hier à Paris," *L'Echo de Paris*, March 23, 1931, 1.
8. "À l'hotel Crillon," *L'Echo de Paris*, March 23, 1931, 1; "Charlot est arrivé à Paris," *Le Matin*, March 23, 1931, 2; Gatson Thierry, "Comment 'Il' reçut les journalistes parisiens," *Paris-Midi*, March 23, 1931, 1.
9. "L'accueil enthousiaste de Charlot à Paris," *Le Petit Parisien*, March 23, 1931, 2; "Charlot est arrivé à Paris," 2; "Parisians Smother 'Charlot' on First Visit in 10 Years," 3.
10. "Charlot à Paris," *Le Petit Journal*, March 23, 1931, 1.
11. Carné, "L'hommage du peuple de Paris à Charlie Chaplin," 12.
12. "L'accueil de Paris à Charlie Chaplin," *Pour Vous*, no. 123 (March 26, 1931): 3. An anonymous young woman on the metro, interviewed by a writer for *Pour Vous* who noticed her reading about Chaplin's Parisian reception in *L'Intransigeant*, provided a degree of corroboration for Maurois's view, confessing, "Charlot moves me because he is good, sensitive and unhappy in love. Fate and the world are unjust towards him. But I like him better this way." "Pourquoi et comment Charlot nous émeut-il?," *Pour Vous*, no. 124 (April 2, 1931): 2.
13. Ibid.

14. "La journée de Charlot," *Le Petit Journal*, March 24, 1931, 3; "Charlie Chaplin a déjeuné chez M. Aristide Briand," *Le Journal*, March 24, 1931, 1.

15. "Charlie Chaplin a déjeuné hier avec M. Aristide Briand," *Le Matin*, March 24, 1931, 2, 1; "Charlie Chaplin a déjeuné hier au Quai d'Orsay," *Le Petit Parisien*, March 24, 1931, 2; "La journée de Charlot," *Le Petit Journal*, March 24, 1931, 3.

16. "Charlot a déjeuné chez M. Briand," *L'Ère Nouvelle*, March 24, 1931, 1.

17. See Gertrude Atherton, *The Living Present*, Gutenberg, accessed November 22, 2024, http://www.gutenberg.org/files/14197/14197-h/14197-h.htm#BI_XIII_5.

18. For a list of those attending the lunch, see "Au Quai d'Orsay," *Le Temps*, March 24, 1931, 6; "Charlie Chaplin chez M. Briand," *Le Figaro*, March 24, 1931, 2; "Chaplin Leaves for Boar Hunt," *New York Herald*, Paris edition, March 24, 1931, 1.

19. "Charlie Chaplin a déjeuné hier avec M. Aristide Briand," 2.

20. "La réception de Charlie Chaplin au Quai d'Orsay," *Le Journal*, March 24, 1931, 2; "Charlie Chaplin a déjeuné hier avec M. Aristide Briand," 2.

21. "Échos—Charlot au Quai d'Orsay," *L'Avenir*, March 28, 1931, 2.

22. Charlie Chaplin, *A Comedian Sees the World*, ed. Lisa Stein Haven (University of Missouri Press, 2014), 68.

23. "Charlie Chaplin a déjeuné hier avec M. Aristide Briand," 3; "Charlie Chaplin a déjeuné hier au Quai d'Orsay," 2; "La réception de Charlie Chaplin au Quai d'Orsay," 2.

24. "Hier, une foule considérable a accueilli 'Charlot' à la gare de Lyon," 1.

25. André Villeneuve, "La Chronique des Spectacles . . . IV. Charlot," *L'Action Française*, March 27, 1931, 8.

26. "Mon Ciné informations," *Mon Ciné*, no. 473 (March 12, 1931): 12; cf. "Variétés—Les Souvenirs de Charlot," *L'Ère Nouvelle*, April 5–6, 1931, 2.

27. "Nos Échos," *Mon Ciné*, no. 476 (April 2, 1931): 13.

28. Cami, "Je suis l'ami de Chaplin, non son manager," *Ciné-Journal*, no. 1126 (March 27, 1931): 2; "Variétés—Les Souvenirs de Charlot," 2; René Pignères, "Les Parisiens en foule sont venues à la gare de Lyon acclamer Charlie Chaplin," *Le Journal*, March 23, 1931, 2.

29. A. de G., "Charlie Chaplin déjeuner au Quai d'Orsay," *L'Intransigeant*, March 24, 1931, 1; "Nos Échos," 13.

30. "Paris a fait à Charlie Chaplin un accueil triomphal," *Hebdo-Film*, no. 787 (March 28, 1931): 4; cf. "Charlie Chaplin a déjeuné hier avec M. Aristide Briand,", 2; "Charlie Chaplin a déjeuné hier au Quai d'Orsay," 2; "Charlot a été reçu hier au Quai d'Orsay," *Le Peuple*, March 24, 1931, 1.

31. "Variétés—Les Souvenirs de Charlot," 2.

32. "Nos Échos—On dit que. . . ," *L'Intransigeant*, March 29, 1931, 2; "Charlie Chaplin a reçu hier la Légion d'honneur," *Le Petit Journal*, March 28, 1931, 1.

33. "Charlie Chaplin chevalier de la Légion d'honneur," *Le Journal*, March 28, 1931, 1; "La Legion d'honneur à Charlie Chaplin," *L'Echo de Paris*, March 28, 1931, 1; "La Legion d'honneur à Charlie Chaplin," *Le Petit Parisien*, March 28, 1931, 1; "Charlot à la croix," *L'Ère Nouvelle*, March 28, 1931, 1.

34. "Charlie Chaplin a reçu hier la Légion d'honneur," 1; " 'Je suis ému au delà de toute expression' déclare Charlie Chaplin en recevant la Légion d'honneur," *Paris-Midi*, March 28, 1931, 1.

35. "Nos Échos—On dit que. . . ," 2.

36. " 'Je suis ému au delà de toute expression' déclare Charlie Chaplin en recevant la Légion d'honneur," 1.

37. "La Légion d'honneur à Charlie Chaplin," *La Victoire*, March 31, 1931, 3.

38. Lieutenant-Colonel Faye, "La dévalorisation de la Légion d'honneur," *L'Echo de Paris*, March 24, 1931, 4.

39. Jean Lecoq, "Nos Échos," *Le Petit Journal*, March 30, 1931, 2.

40. L[ucie] D[erain], "Coups de Fusils," *Ciné-Journal*, no. 1128 (April 17, 1931): 1–2. S.V., probably a pseudonym for Derain, had argued three weeks earlier that Méliès had pioneered many of the cinematographical things done by Chaplin, that it was "with the equipment of [Joseph Jules] Debrie that Chaplin's films were shot," that Pierre Noguès had discovered the slow-motion effects used so amusingly at times by Chaplin, and that Jourion had founded the trade and industry in movies that had aided the brilliant career of Chaplin's films in France. Comment by S.V. in response to Cami, "Je suis l'ami de Chaplin, non son manager," 2.

41. Ogouz cited in L[ucie] D[erain], "Coups de Fusils," *Ciné-Journal*, no. 1128 (April 17, 1931): 1.

42. Lecoq, "Nos Échos," *Le Petit Journal*, March 30, 1931, 2.

43. "Nos Échos—Legion d'honneur," *Mon Ciné*, no. 476 (April 2, 1931): 13.

44. Pierre Scize, "Charlie Chaplin déjeune avec Aristide Briand," *Le Canard enchaîné*, no. 769 (March 31, 1931): 1–2.

45. "Charlie Chaplin chasse le sanglier au château de duc de Westminster," *Paris-Midi*, March 24, 1931, 1; Chaplin, *A Comedian Sees the World*, 67.

46. A. de G., "Charlie Chaplin déjeuner au Quai d'Orsay," 1; "Charlot chasse," *L'Ère Nouvelle*, March 25, 1931, 2; "Charlie Chaplin a déjeuné hier au Quai d'Orsay," 2; "Charlot en Normandie," *La Victoire*, March 25, 1931, 1.

47. Chaplin, *A Comedian Sees the World*, 76–77.

48. Ibid., 79–83; René Pignères, "Charlot chasse le sanglier chez le duc de Westminster," *Le Journal*, March 25, 1931, 3–4; M.R., "Charlot, Charlie . . . Charlie, Charlot," *La Liberté*, March 25, 1931, 3; "'Charlot' a chassé a courre," *Le Matin*, March 25, 1931, 1. According to several newspapers, Chaplin was sufficiently revived by the massage to go dancing in a nightclub afterward. "Charlie Chaplin se repose. . . ," *Le Petit Parisien*, March 26, 1931, 2; "Comment Charlie Chaplin s'est enfin reposé," *Le Matin*, March 29, 1931, 2.

49. *New York Herald*, Paris edition, March 27, 1931, 1; "Le roi des Belges arrive ce matin à 11 h. 18 à la gare du Nord," *Paris-Midi*, March 26, 1931, 1; "Le roi Albert était, hier, l'hôte de Paris," *Le Figaro*, March 27, 1931, 1; Chaplin, *A Comedian Sees the World*, 71; "Nos Echos," *L'Intransigeant*, March 28, 1931, 2.

50. Chaplin, *A Comedian Sees the World*, 72–73; "Charlot invite le roi des Belges à Hollywood," *Paris-Midi*, March 27, 1931, 3; "Nos Echos," *L'Intransigeant*, March 28, 1931, 2.

51. "Charlie Chaplin est parti hier soir pour Nice," *Le Journal*, March 31, 1931, 2.

52. "Charlot à Nice," *Le Matin*, April 1, 1931, 2; Robinson, *Chaplin: His Life and Art*, 432; Chaplin, *My Autobiography*, 382.

53. "Charlot a été acclamé par la foule à son arrivée à Nice," *La Victoire*, April 1, 1931, 1.

54. Hetty died during the postwar influenza pandemic of 1919.

55. "Charlot ne peut s'arracher à l'enthusiasme des Niçois," *Paris-Midi*, April 1, 1931, 1; Robinson, *Chaplin: His Life and Art*, 432.

56. "Charlot à Nice," *Le Matin*, April 1, 1931, 2; "Charlie Chaplin présidera au couronnement de la reine de Nice," *Paris-Midi*, April 2, 1931, 3.

57. Berty, "C'est à Monte-Carlo que Charlot assistera à la première des 'Lumières de la Ville,'" *Paris-Midi*, April 5, 1931, 1.

58. Chaplin, *A Comedian Sees the World*, 85; "Charlot ne peut s'arracher à l'enthusiasme des Niçois," 1; "Comment il fit connaissance du roi de Suède," *Paris-Midi*, April 2, 1931, 3.

59. Chaplin, *A Comedian Sees the World*, 85.

60. Lynn, *Charlie Chaplin*, 68.

61. Chaplin, *A Comedian Sees the World*, 87–89, 92–94, 97–98.

62. Ibid., 85.

63. Ibid., 85–86.

64. Berty, "C'est à Monte-Carlo que Charlot assistera à la première des 'Lumières de la Ville,'" 1.

65. Berty, "À Monte-Carlo de hautes personnalités assistaient à la première du film de Charlot," *Paris-Midi*, April 8, 1931, 1; "La Saison de Monte-Carlo," *Le Figaro*, April 12, 1931, 4; "Chaplin Given Big Ovation at Monte Carlo Film Show," *New York Herald*, Paris edition, April 9, 1931, 8.

66. Chaplin, *A Comedian Sees the World*, 86; Berty, "À Monte-Carlo de hautes personnalités assistaient à la première du film de Charlot," 1; "Charlot se fait attendre à la première de son film 'Les Lumières de la Ville,'" *La Victoire*, April 10, 1931, 2; "Echos," *Ciné-Journal*, no. 1129 (April 17, 1931): 3. The Duke does not seem to have been affected by the experience. Almost eighty-one at the time of the Monte Carlo première, he would live until January 1942, only a few weeks short of his ninety-second birthday.

67. Scott Eyman, *Charlie Chaplin vs. America: When Art, Sex and Politics Collided* (Simon & Schuster, 2023), 65.

68. Chaplin, *A Comedian Sees the* World, 105; Robinson, *Chaplin: His Life and Art*, 436. Lady Furness had recently been replaced in the Prince of Wales's affections by Wallis Simpson, another American divorcée for whom Edward, by this stage king, would give up his throne in 1936.

69. Thierry, "Comment 'Il' reçut les journalistes parisiens," 1.

70. Jean Stelli, "Et maintenant parlons un peu de Charlie Chaplin," *La Cinématographie Française*, no. 649 (April 11, 1931): 18.

71. P.G., "Charlie Chaplin est arrivé hier à Paris," *L'Echo de Paris*, March 23, 1931, 1.

72. "Charlot à Paris," *Le Petit Journal*, March 23, 1931, 2.

73. Maurice Bourdet, "L'accueil enthousiaste de Paris à Charlot," *Le Petit Parisien*, March 23, 1931, 2.

74. "Charlot à Paris," *Le Petit Journal*, March 23, 1931, 1.

75. Thierry, "Comment 'Il' reçut les journalistes parisiens," 1; Paul Achard, "Charlie Chaplin, Curieux Homme," reprinted from *L'Ami du Peuple* in *La Victoire*, March 25, 1931, 3.

76. "Charlot à Paris," *Le Petit Journal*, March 23, 1931, 2–3; Lucie Derain, "Charlie Chaplin en France," *La Cinématographie Française*, no. 647 (March 28, 1931): 41. The reporter for *L'Echo de Paris* similarly referred to "a kind of combination of inanities." P.G., "Charlie Chaplin est arrivé hier à Paris," 1.

77. P.G., "Charlot à Paris," *L'Echo de Paris*, March 23, 1931, 3; Carné, "L'hommage du peuple de Paris à Charlie Chaplin," 12; Achard, "Charlie Chaplin, Curieux Homme," 3.

78. Achard, "Charlie Chaplin, Curieux Homme," 3.

79. Ibid.

80. P.G., "Charlot à Paris," 3; Thierry, "Charlot reçoit les journalistes parisiens," *Paris-Midi*, March 23, 1931, 3; Derain, "Charlie Chaplin en France," 41.

81. "Charlot à Paris," *Le Petit Journal*, March 23, 1931, 3.

82. P.G., "Charlot à Paris," 3.

83. Carné, "L'hommage du peuple de Paris à Charlie Chaplin," 12.

84. "Charlot à Paris," *Le Petit Journal*, March 23, 1931, 3.

85. Jean Pascal, "Editorial," *Ciné Magazine*, 11th year no. 4 (April 1931): 1.

86. "Les lumières de la Ville," *La Courrier Cinématographique*, 22nd year nos. 12 and 13 (March 30, 1931): 46; Pascal, "Editorial," 1.

87. "Les lumières de la Ville," 46.

88. Robinson, *Chaplin: His Life and Art*, 421.

89. Ibid., 415.

90. "Comment une jeune étudiante roumaine fut sacrée 'star' par Charlie Chaplin," *Le Petit Journal*, March 27, 1931, 1; "Charlot fait une heureuse," *Le Quotidien*, March 28, 1931, 1; "Comment Charlot decouvrit sa nouvelle étoile," *La Liberté*, March 28, 1931, 1; "'Je suis ému au delà de toute expression' déclare Charlie Chaplin en recevant la Légion d'honneur," 1; "Avant de partir pour Hollywood, Mlle Floriselle Constantinesco la jeune partenaire que Charlot a découverte en Europe veut passer à Paris son examen de 'sciences politiques,'" *Paris-Midi*, March 28, 1931, 2; "Chaplin Is Guest of King Albert," *New York Herald*, Paris edition, March 27, 1931, 3.

91. "La partenaire de Charlie," *Paris-Midi*, April 7, 1931, 6.

92. Charles Omessa, "En passant . . . Publicité," *La Liberté*, April 7, 1931, 1; Charles Omessa, "En passant . . . Rectification," *La Liberté*, April 10, 1931, 1.

93. Jean Berty, "Avant de quitter Venise, Charlie Chaplin parle à l'envoyé de *Paris-Midi* des ses projets, du cinéma et de la France," *Paris-Midi*, March 21, 1931, 1, 3.

94. Pignères, "Les Parisiens en foule sont venues à la gare de Lyon acclamer Charlie Chaplin," 1–2. A similar "interview" on the Paris train, in which Chaplin again spoke fluent French, appeared anonymously in *Le Matin*. "The Prince des Mimes—Charlot est arrivé à Paris—En bavardant dans le train avec Charlie Chaplin," *Le Matin*, March 23, 1931, 1–2.

95. "Charlie Chaplin arrive aujourd'hui à Paris," *Le Populaire*, March 22, 1931, 1.

96. "Hier, une foule considérable a accueilli 'Charlot' à la gare de Lyon," 1; "Charlot à Paris," *L'Humanité*, March 22, 1931, 3.

97. André de Reusse, "Lettre ouverte à Charlie Chaplin, esquire," *Hebdo*, no. 787 (March 28, 1931 [misprinted as 1932]): 1–2. Jean Stelli, in answer to Reusse, argued that few of the businessmen or stars of French cinema had paid tribute to Lumière either. Jean Stelli, "Et maintenant parlons un peu de Charlie Chaplin," *La Cinématographie Française*, no. 649 (April 11, 1931): 18.

98. Reusse, "Lettre ouverte à Charlie Chaplin, esquire," 1–3; Jacques Malthête, ed., *Georges Méliès, l'illusioniste fin de siècle? Actes du colloque de Cerisy-la-Salle, 13–22 August 1996* (Presses Sorbonne Nouvelle, 1997), 93; "Sa Vie," *Georges Méliès*, accessed November 22, 2024, www.melies.eu/bio.html.

99. Achard, "Charlie Chaplin, Curieux Homme," 3.

100. Ibid. Chaplin's friend, the cartoonist Cami, explained the incident differently: learning that Achard was traveling with a party of French journalists, all of whom wished to see him, Chaplin fled to San Francisco to watch a game of rugby football. Jean Pujade, "Le Voyage de Charlie Spencer Chaplin—Interview avec Cami ou 'Charlot s'évade,'" *Le Populaire*, March 27, 1931, 2.

101. Susan Hayward, *French National Cinema* (Routledge, 1993), 23, 135; "L'enfant de l'amour Release Info," IMDb, accessed November 23, 2024, www.imdb.com/title/tt0207453/releaseinfo.

102. Hayward, *French National Cinema*, 23–24.

103. Thompson and Bordwell, *Film History*, 224.

104. *La Cinématographie Française*, no. 647 (March 28, 1931): 61.

105. Hervé Lauwick, "Parlons des 'parlants,'" *Le Petit Journal*, March 26, 1931, 1.

106. Robert de Thomasson, "Colette regrette le cinéma muet," *Pour Vous*, no. 121 (March 12, 1931): 3.

107. Edmond Epardaud, "Que veut le Public?," *Cinéma*, April 1931, n.p.

108. "Le directeur de cinéma dont les appareils sonores marchent mal . . . vous éviterez un sort semblable . . . en choisissant un NALPAS," *La Cinématographie Française*, no. 649 (April 11, 1931): n.p.

109. Marcel Pagnol, "Cinematurgy of Paris," *Cahiers du film*, no. 1 (December 15, 1933), translated in *French Film Theory and Criticism: A History/Anthology, 1907–1939*, vol. 2: *1929–1939*, ed. Richard Abel (Princeton University Press, 1988), 129, 131–32.

110. "Parisians Flocking to Chaplin Picture," *New York Herald*, Paris edition, April 10, 1931, 2.

111. "Chronique Théâtrale-La Musique," *L'Evénement*, April 18–19, 1931, 2.

112. "Ciné," *Le Canard enchaîné*, no. 772 (April 15, 1931): 4 (cf. "*Les lumières de la ville* ont fait, hier soir, de brillants débuts," *Paris-Midi*, April 8, 1931, 2); Jean-Michel Pagès, "Charlie Chaplin dans *Lumières de la ville*," *CinéMonde*, no. 130 (April 16, 1931): 248.

113. G.I., "Les Films de la Semaine—Les Lumières de la ville," *La Liberté*, April 11, 1931, 4.

114. Marcel Lapierre, "Cinéma—Les Lumières de la Ville," *Le Peuple*, April 10, 1931, 2; Émile Vuillermoz, "Les 'Lumières de la ville,'" *Le Temps*, April 11, 1931, 5; Pierre Desclaux, "*Les lumières de la ville*—Un Nouveau Film de Charlie Chaplin," *Mon Ciné*, no. 475 (March 26, 1931): 7.

115. Pierre Henry, "La carrière de Charles Chaplin," *Cinéa et Ciné Pour Tous Réunis*, no. 13 (March 1931): 9. One consequence of all the publicity for *City Lights* was to stimulate interest in Chaplin's earlier films: the *New York Herald* noted that screenings of *The Kid* in Paris had "been attracting large audiences." "The Silver Screen," *New York Herald*, Paris edition, April 22, 1931, 9.

116. Jean le Meur, "Charlot et l'art muet," *Le Radical*, April 5, 1931, 4.

117. L[ucie] D[erain], "La présentation au Tout-Paris de 'Les Lumières de la Ville,'" *La Cinématographie Française*, no. 649 (April 11, 1931): 14.

118. Lucie Derain, "Les Lumières de la Ville," *Le Quotidien*, April 10, 1931, 4. On the first sequence as a parody of or satire on the talkie, also see, for example, Vuillermoz, "Les 'Lumières de la Ville,'" 5; "Les Lumières de la Ville," *La Liberté*, April 11, 1931, 4; "Devant l'écran—Critique Cinématographique—Charlot dans 'Les Lumières de la Ville,'" *L'Avenir*, March 28, 1931, 2.

119. Jean Pascal, "Les Lumières de la Ville," *Hebdo-Film*, no. 789 (April 11, 1931): 17–18; André de Reusse, "L'autre son de cloche," *Hebdo-Film*, no. 790 (April 18, 1931): 1–3.

120. L[ucie] D[erain], "Les Lumières de la Ville," *Ciné-Journal*, no. 1129 (April 17, 1931): 26.

121. Lucie Derain, "Les écrans de la semaine—Les Lumières de la Ville," *Le Quotidien*, April 10, 1931, 4.

122. Jacques Vivien, "Critique Cinématographique," *Le Petit Parisien*, April 10, 1931, 5. For the parallel with *Voile de bonheur*, see Paul Gordeaux, "Les Lumières de la Ville," *L'Echo de Paris*, April 10, 1931, 8.

123. Yvan Noé, "Charlot et le théâtre français," *L'Intransigeant*, April 12, 1931, 6.

124. "Les Films du Mois," *Le Cinéopse*, no. 140 (April 1931): 207.

125. Alexandre Arnoux, "Le Retour de Charlot—Les Lumières de la Ville," *L'Intransigeant*, April 11, 1931, 6.

126. Marcel A. Crance, "Réflexions sur un film de Chaplin," *Hebdo-Film*, no. 790 (April 18, 1931): 21. Crance was implicitly criticizing those, such as Reusse and Derain, who had also opposed Chaplin's award of the Légion d'honneur.

127. Ibid.

128. Jean Proudhomme, "Les Lumières de la Ville," *Le Matin*, April 10, 1931, 4; Jacques Bernier, "Une grande première: Le présentation de *City Lights*," *Ciné-Miroir*, no. 314 (April 10, 1931): 235.

129. Jorge Felice, "Les Lumières de la Ville," *Le Courrier Cinématographique*, 22nd year no. 16 (April 18, 1931): 9; Pascal, "Les Lumières de la Ville," 17; Paul Gordeaux, "Les Lumières de la Ville," *L'Echo de Paris*, April 10, 1931, 8.

130. Jean Chataigner, "Les Lumières de la Ville," *Le Journal*, April 10, 1931, 4.

131. Pascal, "Les Lumières de la Ville," 17; Robert de Beauplan, "Les Lumières de la ville," *La Petite Illustration Cinématographique*, no. 523 (April 11, 1931): 41; Felice, "Les Lumières de la Ville."

132. Felice, "Les Lumières de la Ville," 9; René Pigneres, Les Lumières de la Ville," *La République*, April 10, 1931, 4.

133. Felice, "Les Lumières de la Ville," 9.

134. J.-P. Gelas, "A propos de 'Les Lumières de la Ville,'" *L'Action Française*, April 10, 1931, 6; Proudhomme, "Les Lumières de la Ville," 4; Bernier, "Une grande première," 235.

135. Charles Jouvet, "Les Lumières de la Ville et quelques films," *Le Populaire*, April 10, 1931, 4; Marcel Sauvage, "Les lumières de la Ville," *Pour Vous*, April 9, 1931, 8.

136. Léon Moussinac, "Les lumières de la Ville," *L'Humanité*, March 12, 1931, 4.

137. Gordeaux, "Les Lumières de la Ville," 8; Richard Pierre-Bodin, "Figaro Film—Marigny—Les lumières de la Ville," *Le Figaro*, April 12, 1931, 6.

138. Gelas, "A propos de 'Les Lumières de la Ville,'" 6.

139. Ibid.

140. Gordeaux, "Les Lumières de la Ville," 8.

141. Maland, *Chaplin and American Culture*, 127–33.

142. "Chaplin Leaves for Boar Hunt," 1.

143. "Charlot a parlé politique," *Paris-Midi*, March 24, 1931, 5.

144. "Parisians Smother 'Charlot' on First Visit in 10 Years," 3.

145. On his 1931 visit, Chaplin quickly picked a quarrel with Cami, and their friendship dissolved. Robinson, *Chaplin: His Life and Art*, 431–32; Lynn, *Charlie Chaplin and His Times*, 349.

146. Carné, "L'hommage du peuple de Paris à Charlie Chaplin," 12; Maurice Huet, "Le repos de Charlot," *Le Petit Parisien*, March 27, 1931, 5.

147. Lucette Benissier, "Courrier imaginaire—Lettre à M. Charlie Chaplin," *Pour Vous*, no. 123 (March 23, 1931): 2. Alfred de Musset (1810–1857) was a French poet, novelist, and dramatist.

148. Pierre Paraf, "De l'Anschluss à Charlot," *La République*, March 25, 1931, 1.

149. Edmond Jaloux, "Charlot," *Le Temps*, March 20, 1931, 3; Noé, "Charlot et le théâtre français," 6.

Chapter 6

1. Charles Chaplin, *My Trip Abroad* (Harper, 1922), 7–8.

2. Lynn, *Charlie Chaplin and His Times*, 347–48; Robinson, *Chaplin: His Life and Art*, 456–57.

3. Robinson, *Chaplin: His Life and Art*, 423–24.

4. Lynn, *Charlie Chaplin and His Times*, 352; Robinson, *Chaplin: His Life and Art*, 427, 433, 438.

5. Robinson, *Chaplin: His Life and Art*, 458; Simon Louvish, *Chaplin: The Tramp's Odyssey* (Faber and Faber, 2009), 256.

6. Lorenzo Turrent Rozas, "Charlie Chaplin's Decline," *Living Age*, June 1, 1934, 319–22, www.unz.org/Pub/LivingAge-1934jun-00319.

7. Ad, *La Cinématographie Française*, no. 898 (January 18, 1936): 3.

8. Paul Gordeaux pointed out that "five years, in cinema, is quite something. In five years, new spectators have appeared for whom the only great comedians are M. Fernandel, Lucien Baroux, W. C. Fields and Eddie Cantor!" He was happy to see that young members of the audience, seeing Charlot for the first time, had been among the most enthusiastic spectators. Paul Gordeaux, "Le Cinéma—Les Films de la Semaine—Temps modernes," *L'Echo de Paris*, March 20, 1936, 4.

9. "La Chanson de Charlie Chaplin en *Temps Modernes*," *La Cinématographie Française*, no. 912 (April 25, 1936): 20; René Lehmann, "Cinéma—Les films nouveaux. Marigny.—*Les Temps Modernes*," *L'Intransigeant*, March 15, 1936, 9.

10. Henri Jeanson, "*Les Temps Modernes*—Silence! Voici Charlie Chaplin," *Le Canard Enchaîné*, March 18, 1936, 1; Jean Marguet, "La Critique—*Les Temps Modernes*," *Le Petit Parisien*, March 21, 1936, 6.

11. Émile Vuillermoz, "Le Cinéma—Chronique—*Les Temps Modernes*," *Le Temps*, March 21, 1936, 5.

12. Émile Cerquant, "Au Cinéma—*Temps Modernes*," *L'Humanité*, March 21, 1936, 4.

13. Jeanson, "*Les Temps Modernes*—Silence! Voici Charlie Chaplin." Cf. Gilbert Bernard, "Les Nouveaux Films—Marigny. *Les Temps Modernes*," *Le Matin*, March 15, 1936, 5; Jean Vidal, "Anticipation," *Pour Vous*, no. 383 (March 19, 1936): 8.

14. Lehmann, "Cinéma—Les films nouveaux. Marigny—*Les Temps Modernes*."

15. Marguet, "La Critique—*Les Temps Modernes*."

16. Charles Jouet, "Cinéma—*Les Temps Modernes*," *Le Populaire*, March 20, 1936, 4; Raymond Lange, "Charlot For Ever—*Réflexions sur 'Temps Modernes,'*" *Pour Vous*, no. 383 (March 12, 1936): 2.

17. Roger Karl (Sannois), "La parole est aux spectateurs—Temps Modernes," *Pour Vous*, no. 388 (April 23, 1936): 6.

18. "Demain, au théâtre Marigny—*Modern Times*," *Le Matin*, March 13, 1936, 4.

19. Gordeaux, "Le Cinéma—Les Films de la Semaine—Temps modernes."

20. X, "*Le Temps Modernes*—Tragi-comédie sonore," *La Cinématographie Française*, no. 907 (March 21, 1936): 12.

21. François Vinneuil, "Les Spectacles—L'Écran de la Semaine," *L'Action Française*, March 20, 1936, 4.

22. Jean Laury, "Le Films Nouveaux—Marigny. *Modern Times*—Un amoncellement désordonné de trouvailles," *Le Figaro*, March 15, 1936, 5; Lange, "Charlot For Ever—*Réflexions sur 'Temps Modernes'*"; Maurice Bessy, "Le vagabond dans l'engrenage des Temps modernes," *Cinémonde*, no. 387 (March 19, 1936) 183.

23. Bernard, "Les Nouveaux Films—Marigny—*Les Temps Modernes*." The reviewer in *La Cinématographie Française* defended the episodic character of Chaplin's movie in different terms. "A film of Charlie Chaplin," he wrote, "goes beyond common means of assessment. This is why we cannot reproach him for having totally neglected the unity of action and the connection between his varied scenes" (X, "*Le Temps Modernes*—Tragi-comédie sonore").

24. Jean Cocteau, *My Contemporaries*, trans. and ed. Margaret Crosland (Chilton Book Company, 1968), 86.

25. Vuillermoz, "Le Cinéma—Chronique—*Les Temps Modernes*."

26. X, "*Le Temps Modernes*—Tragi-comédie sonore"; "Le Cinéma: Les Films que nous verrons—A propos des *Temps Modernes*," *Le Figaro*, March 12, 1936, 5.

27. "Demain, au théâtre Marigny—*Modern Times*," *Le Matin*, March 13, 1936, 4. Also see Jeanson, "*Les Temps Modernes*—Silence! Voici Charlie Chaplin."

28. "Le Cinéma: Les Films que nous verrons—À propos des *Temps Modernes*," *Le Figaro*, March 12, 1936, 5. One critic disliked the song on the grounds that Chaplin was a silent actor who ought to have remained a mime artist. M. Despa, "On a présenté—À Marigny," *Le Courrier Cinématographique*, 27th year no. 12 (March 28, 1936): 6.

29. "La Chanson de Charlie Chaplin en *Temps Modernes*," *La Cinématographie Française*, no. 912 (April 25, 1936): 20.

30. Kristin Thompson and David Bordwell, *Film History: An Introduction* (McGraw Hill, 1994), 9.

31. "René Clair, *À Nous la Liberté*," in Michel Margairaz and Danielle Tartakowsky, *"L'avenir nous apppartient": Une histoire du front populaire* (Larousse, 2006), 16.

32. See, for example, R. C. Dale, *The Films of René Clair*, vol. 1: *Exposition and Analysis* (Scarecrow Press, 1986), 205.

33. X, "*Les Temps Modernes*—Tragi-comédie sonore"; cf. Gordeaux, "Le Cinéma—Les Films de la Semaine—Temps modernes."

34. Marguet, "La Critique—*Les Temps Modernes*."

35. Pierre Billard, *Le mystère René Clair* (Plon, 1998), 187; David Robinson, "Clair, Chaplin et l'affaire *Les Temps Modernes/À Nous la Liberté*," in *René Clair ou le Cinéma à la lettre*, ed. Noël Herpe and Emmanuelle Toulet (Association française de recherche sur l'histoire du cinéma, 2000), 191.

36. Robinson, "Clair, Chaplin et l'affaire," 193.

37. Sadoul, *Vie de Charlot*, 118, 245.

38. Robinson, "Clair, Chaplin et l'affaire," 197.

39. In the sequence, Lucie (Dolly Davis) imagines Jean's face superimposed on the face of a dog.

40. Dale, *The Films of René Clair*, 72n7.

41. Celia McGerr, *René Clair* (Twayne, 1980), 66–67, 84, 104, 116. Pierre Billard also described Émile "as a natural child of Charlot" (*Le mystère de René Clair*, 184).

42. Robinson, "Clair, Chaplin et l'affaire," 194.

43. Ibid., 194–95.

44. Billard, *Le mystère René Clair*, 185. One film fan anticipated much of Billard's argument in 1936. In the correspondence column of film magazine *Pour Vous*, Jacques Loew of Paris wrote, "People have often spoken of the influence of Chaplin on René Clair. . . . But to be influenced does not mean to imitate. . . . Chaplin, we give you the right to re-do the 'gag' of the mass-production line

which was close to being inevitable since you were working on the same theme, but then, the parallels of the factory and the prison, and above all the game of rugby . . . why, master, have you borrowed from your pupil?" Jacques Loew, "La parole est aux spectateurs—Temps modernes," *Pour Vous*, no. 389 (April 30, 1936): 10.

45. Billard, *Le mystère René Clair*, 185. The difference, Billard suggested, was that Clair's film had been produced in four months for four million francs; Chaplin's had involved three years' work and had cost around fifty times as much (185).

46. Clair quoted in McGerr, *René Clair*, 104.

47. Robinson, "Clair, Chaplin et l'affaire," 192; Billard, *Le mystère René Clair*, 187.

48. Robinson, "Clair, Chaplin et l'affaire," 195–97. It might be noted that Chaplin faced numerous suits claiming plagiarism during his career as a filmmaker. These suits often failed or were dismissed by the courts, though he did agree to pay Orson Welles for first proposing the idea for what would become Chaplin's *Monsieur Verdoux* (1947). Robinson, *Chaplin*, 519–20.

49. Jouet, "Cinéma—*Les Temps Modernes*."

50. Edward Shorter and Charles Tilly, *Strikes in France 1830–1968* (Cambridge University Press, 1974), 127; Margairaz and Tartakowsky, "*L'avenir nous apppartient*," 234.

51. Shorter and Tilly, *Strikes in France*, 127, 132, 136.

52. *Modern Times* was shown at the Rexy in Lille and in Calais, where it played at both the Alhambra and the Familia theaters, advertised by a giant eighteen-meter-long publicity sign, during the June strikes. Jac, "À Lille, Roubaix, Tourcoing," *La Cinématographie Française*, no. 921 (June 27, 1936): 131; Jac, "Les 'Meilleurs Résultats' à Calais," *La Cinématographie Française*, no. 921 (June 27, 1936): 131. It had "marked the real beginning of the season" in Nancy. "L'Exploitation à Nancy—Le Films devant le public," *La Cinématographie Française*, no. 944 (December 5, 1936): 12. Among films presented for two weeks, it was the best earner of the year in Toulouse and the third most successful film as a whole in Limoges. "À Toulouse—Quelques Résultats Comparatifs," *La Cinématographie Française*, no. 947 (December 26, 1936): 172; "À Limoges," *La Cinématographie Française*, no. 947 (December 26, 1936): 182.

53. Shorter and Tilly, *Strikes in France*, 132. *Modern Times* was first shown in Le Havre on April 29 at the Nouvel Empire. In June it played successfully at the Alhambra. M[arcel] L[agneaux], "La présentation des 'Temps Modernes' au Havre," *La Cinématographie Française*, no. 915 (May 16, 1936): 15; Marcel Lagneaux, "Au Havre," *La Cinématographie Française*, no. 921 (June 27, 1936): 126. In Rouen it was one of the three greatest successes—by a wide margin— of films shown in June. L. Cary, "À Rouen," *La Cinématographie Française*, no. 921 (June 27, 1936): 129.

54. Ginette Vincendeau, "The Popular Cinema of the Popular Front," in *La vie est à nous: French Cinema of the Popular Front, 1934–1938*, ed. Ginette Vincendeau and Keith Reader (BFI/ National Film Theatre, 1986), 80, 95–97.

55. Goffredo Fofi, "The Cinema of the Popular Front in France (1934–38)," *Screen* 13, no. 4 (Winter 1972–73): 10.

56. Ibid., 50n34; Julian Jackson, *The Popular Front in France: Defending Democracy, 1934–38* (Cambridge University Press, 1988), 142; Raymond Durgnat, *Jean Renoir* (Studio Vista, 1975), 131. Despite being banned from cinemas, *La vie est à nous* continued to be shown to leftists in private screenings prior to the elections. See Elizabeth Grottle Strebel, "French Social Cinema and the Popular Front," *Journal of Contemporary History* 12, no. 3 (July 1997): 507–8.

57. Fofi, "The Cinema of the Popular Front," 10–11.

58. Jackson, *The Popular Front in France*, 97–99.

59. Ibid., 85, 99.

60. Ibid., 102, 104.

61. Ibid., 99–100, 107. There was a sequence in Renoir's banned film, *La vie est à nous*, about an older worker who was dismissed because he couldn't meet new production targets as enforced by a deeply unsympathetic *chronométreur* (141).

62. Ibid., 103.

63. Fofi, "The Cinema of the Popular Front," 10–11. Among such right-wing supporters, Fofi identified film writer Robert Brasillach, who would be executed for collaborating with the Germans and supporting Vichy during the Second World War, and film critic François Vinneuil (47–48n18).

64. Jean Renoir, "An Actor Named Charlot," in Renoir, *My Life and My Films*, trans. Norman Denny (Atheneum, 1974), 41–43.

65. Elizabeth Grottle Strebel, "Renoir and the Popular Front," *Sight and Sound* 49, no. 1 (Winter 1979–80): 38; cf. Fofi, "The Cinema of the Popular Front," 14–15; Jackson, *The Popular Front in France*, 140.

66. Jonathan Buchsbaum, "Toward Victory: Left Film in France, 1930–35," *Cinema Journal* 25, no. 3 (Spring 1986): 32, 34–35, 52n83; Jackson, *The Popular Front in France*, 141; Abel, *French Film Theory and Criticism*, 2:153.

67. Abel, *French Film Theory and Criticism*, 2:153–54.

68. Pascal Ory, "De 'Ciné-Liberté' à la Marseillaise: Espoirs et limites d'un cinéma libéré (1936–1938)," *Le mouvement social*, no. 91 (April–June 1975): 154.

69. Fofi, "The Cinema of the Popular Front," 17.

70. Christopher Faulkner, *The Social Cinema of Jean Renoir* (Princeton University Press, 1986), 80.

71. Strebel, "Renoir and the Popular Front," 36.

72. Jean Renoir, "À propos de Temps Modernes," *Ciné-Liberté*, 1st year no. 1 (May 20, 1936): 1.

73. *Paris-Presse*, April 3, 1945, 3; also see *Ce Soir*, April 3 1945, 1.

74. Monique Berger, "*Le Dictateur*," *Le Populaire*, February 21, 1945; Didier Daix, "Les Spectacles de Paris—'Le Dictateur,'" *Ce Soir*, April 6, 1945, 2.

75. Jean Néry, "Les Spectacles—*Le Grand Dictateur*," *Le Monde*, April 12, 1945, 3.

76. Bernard Zimmer, "Les Spectacles—Une satire politique de Chaplin: *Le Grand Dictateur*," *Paris-Presse*, April 21, 1945, 2; Berger, "*Le Dictateur*"; Robinson, *Chaplin: His Life and Art*, 656–57.

77. Jean Romeis, "Charlot et son Dictateur," *Concorde*, May 1, 1945.

78. See references to critics who thought this way in Gabriel Audisio, "Le Tragi-Comédie du Grand Dictateur," *Action*, no. 32 (April 13, 1945): 9; Néry, "Les Spectacles—*Le Grand Dictateur*"; Zimmer, "Les Spectacles—Une satire politique de Chaplin: *Le Grand Dictateur*," 2.

79. Romeis, "Charlot et son Dictateur."

80. Audisio, "Le Tragi-Comédie du Grand Dictateur"; G. Damas, "Le Dictateur," *Témoinage Chrétien*, August 6, 1945.

81. G. Joly, "Les Spectacles—*Le Dictateur*—Charlie Chaplin ou le Revanche de l'Homme," *L'Aurore*, April 12, 1945, 2.

82. Although the statistics produced by the Centre National de Cinématographie cover the number of spectators between 1945 and 1999, most of those spectators were in the months after a film's opening. *The Great Dictator* was by some distance the most popular film in France in 1945: it had 8,028,720 spectators, 2,246,086 of them in the city of Paris (Paris-ville). Its closest competition was Jean Dréville's *La Cage aux Rossignols*, the story of a teacher in a reform school introducing his pupils to music, which attracted 5,085,489, with 1,539,628 in Paris. In third place was Marcel Carné's *Les Enfants du Paradis*, set in the early nineteenth-century world of Parisian theater, with 4,768,505, including 1,938,603 from Paris. In fourth was Christian-Jacque's version of *Carmen*, with 4,277,813 spectators, including 959,294 Parisians. Simon Simsi, *Ciné-Passions: 7e art et industrie de 1945 à 1999* (Éditions Dixit, 2000), 2.

83. Zimmer, "Les Spectacles—Une satire politique de Chaplin: *Le Grand Dictateur*," 2.

84. Gilbert Badia, "*Le grand dictateur* avec Charlie Chaplin," *La Marseillaise*, April 12, 1945; Romeis, "Charlot et son Dictateur."

85. François Chalais, "*Le Grand Dictateur*," *Carrefour*, June 14, 1945.

86. Daix, "Les Spectacles de Paris—'Le Dictateur.'"

87. Luc Estang, "*Le Dictateur*," *Les Etoiles*, July 17, 1945. G. Damas noted that the public "knows just the right time to stop laughing" in the final stages of the film. G. Joly noted, however, that the barber's final speech was greeted with an ovation. Damas, "*Le Dictateur*"; Joly, "Les Spectacles—*Le Dictateur*."

88. The first comparison made by a French film critic between Hitler's mustache and Charlot's fake one appears to have been made in 1936. Maurice Bourdet, "Est-ce Charlot? Est-ce Chaplin?," *Cinémonde*, no. 389 (April 2, 1936): 225.

89. Estang, "*Le Dictateur*."

90. Gabriel Audisio described Chaplin's "simulated German" as "a tremendous verbal invention" ("Le Tragi-Comédie du Grand Dictateur").

91. "Listen to the hoarse sounds from his throat," declared François Chalais. "Words strike the face which are neither English nor German but a caricature of vocabulary, a sonorous miming of which Mr. Chaplin is the astonishing master" ("*Le Grand Dictateur*").

92. Bernard Zimmer, "*Le grand dictateur*," *La Bataille*, April 26, 1945; Damas, "*Le Dictateur*."

93. Badia, "*Le grand dictateur* avec Charlie Chaplin"; René Jeanne, "Le Retour de Charlot—*Le Dictateur*, au Gaumont-Palace," *La France au Combat*, April 12, 1945, 5; Zimmer, "Les Spectacles—Une satire politique de Chaplin: *Le Grand Dictateur*."

94. Joly, "Les Spectacles—Le Dictateur—Charlie Chaplin ou la Revanche de l'Homme"; Zimmer, "Les Spectacles—Une satire politique de Chaplin: *Le Grand Dictateur*," 2. Critics such as Joly and Zimmer appear to have based their comments primarily on the second of Capra's seven documentaries (1942–45): *The Nazis Strike* (1943).

95. Audisio, "Le Tragi-Comédie du Grand Dictateur." One later account suggested that the seventeen meetings between Hitler and Mussolini were distinguished by rivalry and continual showmanship between the two. See Santi Corvaja, *Hitler and Mussolini: The Secret Meetings*, trans. Robert L. Miller (Enigma, 1999).

96. Chalais, "*Le Grand Dictateur*."

97. Badia, "*Le grand dictateur* avec Charlie Chaplin"; Daix, "Les Spectacles de Paris—'Le Dictateur.'"

98. Zimmer, "*Le grand dictateur*."

99. Jean Sollies suggested that "the character of Charlot . . . fits into Jewish folklore." "A being on the margin," he appeared to evoke the legendary Wandering Jew of medieval tradition. Jean Sollies, "Le Grand Dictateur," *Gavroche: Revue d'histoires populaires*, February 12, 1945. On Chaplin's alleged Jewishness, also see Audisio, "Le Tragi-Comédie du Grand Dictateur."

100. Berger, "*Le Dictateur*"; Badia, "*Le grand dictateur* avec Charlie Chaplin"; Zimmer, "*Le grand dictateur*.".

101. Zimmer, "*Le grand dictateur*"; Romeis, "Charlot et son Dictateur."

102. Daix, "Les Spectacles de Paris—'Le Dictateur'"; Damas, "*Le Dictateur*"; Néry, "Les Spectacles—*Le Grand Dictateur*."

103. Chalais, "*Le Grand Dictateur*"; Sollies, "*Le Grand Dictateur*."

104. Néry, "Les Spectacles—*Le Grand Dictateur*." Daix also thought the scenario "not very solidly constructed" ("Les Spectacles de Paris—'Le Dictateur'").

105. Néry, "Les Spectacles—*Le Grand Dictateur*."

106. Jeanne, "Le Retour de Charlot—Le Dictateur, au Gaumont-Palace."

107. Ibid.

108. Audisio, "Le Tragi-Comédie du Grand Dictateur."

109. See, for example, ibid.

110. Joly, "Les Spectacles—Le Dictateur—Charlie Chaplin ou la Revanche de l'Homme."

111. Audisio, "Le Tragi-Comédie du Grand Dictateur"; Jeanne, "Le Retour de Charlot—Le Dictateur, au Gaumont-Palace."

112. Zimmer, "*Le grand dictateur*."

113. See, for example, Sollies, "Le Grand Dictateur"; Audisio, "Le Tragi-Comédie du Grand Dictateur."

114. Joly, "Les Spectacles—Le Dictateur—Charlie Chaplin ou la Revanche de l'Homme"; Audisio, "Le Tragi-Comédie du Grand Dictateur."

115. Sollies, "Le Grand Dictateur"; Audisio, "Le Tragi-Comédie du Grand Dictateur."

116. Jeanne, "Le Retour de Charlot—Le Dictateur, au Gaumont-Palace"; Audisio, "Le Tragi-Comedie du Grand Dictateur."

Chapter 7

1. Robinson, *Chaplin: His Life and Art*, 571–72; Lynn, *Charlie Chaplin and His Times*, 483, 488; Robinson, *Chaplin: The Mirror of Opinion*, 137.

2. Scott Eyman cites an article by right-wing journalist Westbrook Pegler in December 1942 in which Pegler raised the issue of "why Charlie Chaplin has been allowed to stay in the United States about 40 years without becoming a citizen." By January 1944, an aide to FBI head J. Edgar Hoover was discussing the possibility of his deportation after the war. In 1947, John E. Rankin demanded Chaplin's deportation in a speech in the House of Representatives. Eyman, *Charlie Chaplin vs. America*, 132–33, 165, 202, quotation from 133.

3. Robinson, *Chaplin: His Life and Art*, 572.

4. Ibid., 512–13, 517–18, 520–22; Lynn, *Charlie Chaplin*, 413–19, 423–28, 432–38; Maland, *Chaplin and American Culture*, 197–201.

5. Robinson, *Chaplin: His Life and Art*, 522–24; Lynn, *Charlie Chaplin*, 436–37; Maland, *Chaplin and American Culture*, 202–5.

6. Robinson, *Chaplin: His Life and Art*, 522, 524–28; Maland, *Chaplin and American Culture*, 201–2, 205–6; Lynn, *Charlie Chaplin*, 437–38.

7. Maland, *Chaplin and American Culture*, 207–20.

8. Robinson, *Chaplin: His Life and Art*, 575.

9. Maland, *Chaplin and American Culture*, 265.

10. Lynn, *Charlie Chaplin*, 390–91.

11. Robinson, *Chaplin: His Life and Art*, 485–86. Under the title "Rhythm: A Story of Men in Macabre Movement," this had first been published in *Script Magazine* in January 1938. For the text, see the Charlie Chaplin Archive, accessed November 27, 2024, http://www.charliecha plinarchive.org/en/collection/cerca/rhythm-a-story-of-men-in-macabre-movement-charles-chaplin.

12. Robinson, *Chaplin: His Life and Art*, 489.

13. Lynn, *Charlie Chaplin*, 419–23; Robinson, *Chaplin: His Life and Art*, 515–17; Maland, *Chaplin and American Culture*, 186–94, quotation from 193–94.

14. Lynn, *Charlie Chaplin*, 422–23; Maland, *Chaplin and American Culture*, 194.

15. Robinson, *Chaplin: His Life and Art*, 538–43; Lynn, *Charlie Chaplin*, 359–60.

16. Robinson, *Chaplin: The Mirror of Opinion*, 129. Robinson uses "McCarthyism" here as a shorthand description for militant anticommunism. Senator Joseph R. McCarthy did not emerge as a leader in this campaign until after his speech at Wheeling, West Virginia, in February 1950.

17. Maland, *Chaplin and American Culture*, 232.

18. David Bell and Byron Criddle, "The Decline of the French Communist Party," *British Journal of Political Science* 19, no. 4 (October 1989): 517. Also see Richard F. Kuisel, "Coca-Cola and the Cold War: The French Face Americanization, 1948–1953," *French Historical Studies* 17, no. 1 (Spring 1991): 101–2.

19. John Flower, "The American Dream—or Nightmare: Views from the French Left, 1945–1965," *French Cultural Studies* 20, no. 1 (2009): 48.

20. Ibid., 49.

21. Kuisel, "Coca-Cola and the Cold War," 101–2; Flower, "The American Dream—or Nightmare," 49.

22. Flower, "The American Dream—or Nightmare," 49–50.

23. Robinson, *Chaplin: His Life and Art*, 538–42.

24. Maland, *Chaplin and American Culture*, 259–61.

25. Robinson, *Chaplin: His Life and Art*, 545, 547.

26. Lynn, *Charlie Chaplin and His Times*, 466, 468–70. Also see Eyman, *Charlie Chaplin vs. America*, 233–38.

27. Maland, *Chaplin and American Culture*, 268, 273–75, quotation from 273. In *Charlie Chaplin vs. America*, Scott Eyman cites an FBI report dated one month after the cancelation of Chaplin's reentry permit in 1952 which concluded that "besides the FBI, Army and Navy Intelligence, the Internal Revenue Service, the Central Intelligence Agency, the Department of State, and the U.S. Postal Service had all been surveilling Chaplin at one time or another" (14). Bureaucratic surveillance of this kind preceded the events of the 1940s and did not end with Chaplin's effective expulsion from the United States: the Bureau of Investigation (predecessor of the FBI) opened a file on him in 1922. The FBI and State Department continued to monitor his mail and visitors after he had settled in Switzerland, while the Immigration and Naturalization Service as late as 1959 was still investigating Chaplin to ensure it would be able to block any attempt he might make to reenter the United States (57, 299, 314).

28. "Ça recommence: Pas de viande à Paris cette semaine…," *L'Humanité*, April 15, 1947, 1.

29. L. Gabriel-Robinet, "Sans les communistes," *Le Figaro*, May 7, 1947, 1.

30. See "Après les résolutions du Vel d'Hiv' Metro: La parole est au gouvernement 'Grève générale dans la région parisienne si les conditions de la C.G.T. no sont pas acceptées," *Paris-Presse*, October 21, 1947, 1; "Ramadier Entre Deux Feux: La victoire R.P.F. et l'agitation sociale," *Paris-Presse*, October 21, 1947, 1.

31. "Un Français sur trois a voté communiste! 31% des voix à notre Parti au lieu de 28% aux élections du 10 novembre 1946," *L'Humanité*, October 21, 1947, 1.

32. "'Disparition du centrisme' estime-t-on aux Etats-Unis," *Le Figaro*, October 21, 1947, 4; "Le département d'État ne s'attendait pas à une victoire de R.P.F.," *Le Monde*, October 22, 1947, 8.

33. "Deux Millions dans la Lutte," *L'Humanité*, November 27, 1947, 1; "20 fédérations comptant plus de 4 millions de syndiqués ont formé un comité national de grève," *L'Humanité*, November 28, 1947, 1; "Métro: Arrêt Total," *L'Humanité*, December 2, 1947, 1; "Fiers de leur grève de trois semaines, militants en tête, les travailleurs, conscients de leur force, ont repris leur place à l'usine et au chantier," *L'Humanité*, December 11, 1947, 1.

34. Maldwyn A. Jones, *The Limits of Liberty: American History 1603–1980* (Oxford University Press, 1983), 519.

35. "Le projet Truman est approuvé par la commission des affaires étrangères de la Chambre," *Le Monde*, April 18, 1947, 2; "Le Sénat américain adopte le plan Truman d'aide à la Grèce et à la Turquie," *Le Monde*, April 24, 1947, 1; "Le Congress des Etats-Unis a approuvé définitivement le programme d'aide à la Grèce et à la Turquie," *Le Figaro*, May 16, 1947, 3; "Le Président Truman a signé la loi d'aide a la Grèce et a la Turquie," *Le Monde*, May 24, 1947, 2.

36. Jones, *The Limits of Liberty*, 519–20; Eliot Sorel and Pier Carlo Padoan, *The Marshall Plan: Lessons Learned for the 21st Century* (OECD, 2008), 15–16.

37. "M. Lovett: 'Pas d'aide américaine à une France communiste,'" *France-Soir*, December 6, 1947, 2.

38. Henri Pierre, "La lutte contre le terrorisme raciste et le communisme," *Le Monde*, January 30, 1947, 2.

39. "L'offensive anticommuniste bat son plein," *Le Monde*, March 28, 1947, 2; "Un manifeste du parti communiste," *Le Monde*, March 29, 1947, 2; "L'offensive anticommuniste," *Le Monde*, April 1, 1947, 2; "Le cabinet divisé sur l'action anticommuniste," *Le Monde*, April 5, 1947, 2.

40. "La discussion de la nouvelle législation ouvrière," *Le Monde*, May 16, 1947, 2; "650,000 manifestants à New-York contre les lois antiouvrières du Président Truman," *Ce Soir*, June 12, 1947, 1; "600,000 New-Yorkais manifestent contre les lois antiouvrières," *L'Humanité*, June 12, 1947, 1.

41. "Ecrans et studios," *Le Figaro*, October 22, 1947, 4; "Petit dépêches de l'étranger-Etats-Unis," *Le Monde*, October 22, 1947, 2; "Chasse aux artistes démocrats à Hollywood," *L'Humanité*, October 24, 1947, 4; "Adolphe Menjou Procureur," *Le Monde*, October 24, 1947, 2.

42. "'Pas de communistes chez moi nous sommes Américains 100%' déclare Walt Disney à la commissions des activités antiaméricaines," *Le Figaro*, October 26–27, 1947, 3.

43. "Ecrans et studios," *Le Figaro*, October 24, 1947, 4; "Ecrans et studios," *Le Figaro*, October 23, 1947, 4. Also see "Adolphe Menjou Procureur," 2; René Buzelin, "Menjou s'en va-t-en guerre…," *Le Canard enchaîné*, October 29, 1947, 3.

44. "Dans 'Monsieur Verdoux' Charlie Chaplin tue le vagabond éternel pour créer un personnage distingué," *Paris-Presse*, April 13–14, 1947, 1, 3; "Charlot est 'mort'—Vive Chaplin," *Ce Soir*, April 11, 1947, 1; "Monsieur Verdoux? Mon premier vrai Landru provoque la mobilisation de la police montée," *L'Aurore*, April 13–14, 1947, 2.

45. Donald Ducky, "Monsieur Verdoux ou Charlot contre Monsieur Tout-le-Monde," *Le Canard enchaîné*, April 23, 1947, 3.

46. "La première mondiale de 'Monsieur Verdoux' a eu lieu hier a New-York," *Ce Soir*, April 13–14, 1947, 4; "Première à Broadway de 'Monsieur Verdoux' le Landru de Charlie Chaplin," *Paris-Presse*, April 13–14, 1947, 3.

47. Donald Ducky, "Monsieur Verdoux ou Charlot contre Monsieur Tout-le-Monde," 3; "Charlie Chaplin parle de 'Monsieur Verdoux,'" *Le Figaro*, April 16, 1947, 4; "Dans 'Monsieur Verdoux' Charlie Chaplin tue le vagabond éternel pour créer un personnage distingué," 1.

48. Huguette ex-MICRO, "Bouts de pellicule," *Le Canard enchaîné*, April 16, 1947, 4.

49. "Dans 'Monsieur Verdoux' Charlie Chaplin tue le vagabond éternel pour créer un personnage distingué," 3.

50. Donald Ducky, "Monsieur Verdoux ou Charlot contre Monsieur Tout-le-Monde," 3.

51. Ibid. The writer also cited approvingly the pro-Chaplin comments at the conference of "an intelligent critic who loves the cinema," a reference to Philip Agee.

52. "Hollywood et la politique," *Le Figaro*, May 20, 1947, 4.

53. "'Expulsons Charlie Chaplin' demande un représentant démocrate américain," *Le Figaro*, June 14, 1947, 3. Also see "Charlie Chaplin sera-t-il expulsé des États-Unis?," *L'Humanité*, June 14, 1947, 3; "Charlot indésirable aux U.S.A.?," *L'Aurore*, June 14, 1947, 2; "'Expulsons Chaplin des États-Unis' demande le député américain John Rankin," *Ce Soir*, June 14–15, 1947, 1.

54. "Charlot indésirable aux U.S.A.?," 2.

55. "'Expulsons Charlie Chaplin' demande un représentant démocrate américain," 3; "Charlie Chaplin sera-t-il expulsé des États-Unis?," 3.

56. Henri Pierre, "Charlot indésirable?," *Le Monde*, June 17, 1947, 1.

57. "'Expulsons Chaplin des États-Unis' demande le député américain John Rankin," 1; "Charlie Chaplin sera-t-il expulsé des États-Unis?," 3.

58. "'Monsieur Verdoux' Le Dernier Film de Charlie Chaplin est interdit dans un Etat américain," *Ce Soir*, June 14–15, 1947, 4. Although *Ce Soir* claimed that the film had been banned "in the state of Tennessee," the ban—taken on the initiative of controversial Memphis censor Lloyd T. Binford—applied only to the city of Memphis.

59. Pierre, "Charlot indésirable?," 1.

60. Ibid.

61. Maland, *Chaplin and American Culture*, 221, 223, 225; Lynn, *Charlie Chaplin*, 440.

62. Lynn, *Charlie Chaplin*, 439–40, 460. Gerhard Eisler's testimony to the committee—setting the pattern for what would happen later in the year to the "Hollywood Ten"—degenerated into a shouting match with Chairman J. Parnell Thomas. On the initiative of freshman congressman Richard M. Nixon, the House of Representatives voted with near unanimity to cite him for contempt of Congress (460).

63. Lynn, *Charlie Chaplin*, 464.

64. "Hanns Eisler," Wikipedia, accessed November 27, 2024, http://en.wikipedia.org/wiki/Hanns _Eisler.

65. Maland, *Chaplin and American Culture*, 256, 261. Eisler denied membership in the Communist Party.

66. Lynn, *Charlie Chaplin*, 460–61. Unlike his two fellow defendants, Gerhard Eisler escaped a jail term by fleeing to Europe.

67. "Charlie Chaplin s'est adressé à Picasso," *L'Humanité*, December 9, 1947, 1.

68. Chaplin, *My Autobiography*, 512–13; Robinson, *Chaplin: His Life and Art*, 578–79.

69. Charles S. Chaplin Jr., *My Father, Charlie Chaplin* (1960), quoted in Robinson, *Chaplin: His Life and Art*, 547.

70. "Charlie Chaplin s'est adressé à Picasso," 1.

71. In the wake of the Picasso telegram, Chaplin continued to campaign against the attempt to deport Hanns Eisler and his wife. When the deportation warrant was issued in February 1948, he offered financial assistance to the couple, and the U.S. government allowed them to leave voluntarily once they promised never to return. Lynn, *Charlie Chaplin*, 461.

72. Robinson, *Chaplin: His Life and Art*, 547–48; Maland, *Chaplin and American Culture*, 269.

73. Charlie Chaplin, "J'en ai assez d'Hollywood," *L'Action*, December 24–30, 1947, 6. The article in *L'Action* was a translation of a piece that had first appeared on December 7, 1947, in the left-wing British newspaper, *Reynolds' News*.

74. Ibid.

75. Ibid.

76. Lynn, *Charlie Chaplin*, 459; Maland, *Chaplin and American Culture*, 240.

77. Robinson, *Chaplin—The Mirror of Opinion*, 129.

78. Maland, *Chaplin and American Culture*, 240–41.

79. Ibid., 250–51. The film ran for a very respectable four weeks at both the Gaumont-Palace and the Rex in Paris. See *La Cinématographie Française*, no. 1245 (February 7, 1948): 26.

80. "Region de Sud-Est," *La Cinématographie Française*, no. 1245 (February 7, 1948): 7; "L'Explotation Sud-Ouest-Bordeaux" and "Toulouse," *La Cinématographie Française*, no. 1251 (March 20, 1948): 18–19; "L'Exploitation Française-Strasbourg," "Dijon-Les Bonnes Recettes," "Marseille/Les Belles Recettes," "Nantes," Montpellier," *La Cinématographie Française*, no. 1252 (March 27, 1948): 81, 83, 84, 86–88; "Region de Sud-Est-Marseille," "Les Succès des Agences de Distribution," *La Cinématographie Française*, no. 1256 (April 24, 1948): 10; "Tarbes-Region de Sud-Ouest," *La Cinématographie Française*, no. 1257 (April 30, 1948): 14; "L'Exploitation: Avignon," *La Cinématographie Française*, no. 1258 (May 8, 1948): 8; "L'Exploitation: Lyon," "L'Exploitation: Strasbourg," "L'Exploitation: Metz," *La Cinématographie Française*, no. 1259 (May 15, 1948): 20, n.p.; "L'Exploitation: Nice," *La Cinématographie Française*, no. 1260 (May 22, 1948): 15.

81. See, for example, Monique Berger, "Charles Chaplin succède à Charlot—L'acteur de genie a suivi la marche du temps—La version doublée trahit *Monsieur Verdoux*," *Le Populaire*, January 13, 1948, 1; Louis Chavet, "Charlie Chaplin dans *Monsieur Verdoux*: Hélas! 'Charlot' s'éloigne de plus en plus. . . ," *Le Figaro*, January 15, 1948, 4; "Les Films que vous pourrez voir cette semaine," *L'Aurore*, January 14, 1948, 2; "M. Verdoux en danger," *L'Action*, January 6, 1948, 9.

82. Jean Antoine, "Le 'Doublage' qui n'était qu'un moyen peut-il devenir un art?," *Paris-Presse*, January 20, 1948, 2. Antoine defended popular playwright-screenwriter Marcel Achard, criticized by other critics and fined two thousand francs for translating Chaplin's words into French (2).

83. Jean Renoir, "Chaplin Among the Immortals," *Screen Writer* 3, no. 2 (July 1947): 1–4.

84. André Bazin, "Pastiche et postiche ou le néant pour une moustache," *Esprit* (1945), reprinted in Bazin, *Charlie Chaplin* (Petite bibliothèque des Cahiers du cinéma, 2000), 32–36.

85. André Bazin, "Monsieur Verdoux ou le martyre de Charlot," *L'Ecran Français*, no. 131 (December 30, 1947): 4, translated in Jean-Richard Rene Bodon, *Andre Bazin's "Charlie Chaplin": An Annotated Translation and Analysis of Text Based on Methods Derived from "De la Politique des Auteurs"* (University Microfilms, 1985), chap. 2, 58.

86. Ibid., 54–58.

87. Nathalie Moffat, "A Hollywood, avec Charlie Chaplin," *Les Temps Modernes* 2 (December 1946): 561–64.

88. Nathalie Moffat, "Monsieur Verdoux," *Les Temps Modernes* 2 (July 1947): 176–80.

89. André Bazin, "The Myth of Monsieur Verdoux," in Bazin, *What Is Cinema?*, trans. Hugh Gray (University of California Press, 1971), 2, quotation from 103.

90. André Bazin, "Defense de 'Monsieur Verdoux,'" *Les Temps Modernes* 3 (December 1947): 1115–22; André Bazin, "Le mythe de M. Verdoux," *Revue du Cinéma* 2 (January 1948): 2–25, in Bazin, *What Is Cinema?*, 2:102–23.

91. Bazin, "The Myth of Monsieur Verdoux," 103.

92. Ibid., 104–5.

93. Ibid., 111–12.

94. Ibid., 105.

95. Ibid., 112.

96. Ibid., 103–4.

97. Ibid., 114–16.

98. Ibid., 117.

99. Ibid., 116–17.

100. Ibid., 118–19. Bazin later changed his mind about *Modern Times*, which he hailed as "one of the best of Charlie's full-length films—perhaps the best, along with *City Lights*" (118–19). For Bazin's reappraisal of *Modern Times*, see his "Le temps rend justice aux *Temps modernes*," *Arts*, no. 485 (October 13, 1954), reprinted in Bazin, *Charlie Chaplin*, 27–31.

101. Bazin, "The Myth of Monsieur Verdoux," 119–20.

102. Ibid., 120.

103. An amusing sideshow to the arrival of *Monsieur Verdoux* in Paris was that a real bank employee called Henri Verdoux tried unsuccessfully to prevent the film's distribution, claiming it was defamatory. Marcel Idzkowski and Claude Helly, "Monsieur Verdoux (de Paris) intente un procès à Monsieur Verdoux (de Hollywood) alias Charlie Chaplin," *Paris-Presse*, January 14, 1948, 2; "M. Verdoux veut faire interdire 'Monsieur Verdoux,'" *France-Soir*, January 14, 1941, 1.

104. Robert Pilati, "Petit bonhomme vit encore: Monsieur Verdoux ou la vengeance de Charlot," *Ce Soir*, January 18–19, 1948, 2.

105. Ibid.; P.R., "*Monsieur Verdoux*," *La Cinématographie Française*, no. 1242 (January 17, 1948): 14.

106. Interim [Gustave Joly], "*Monsieur Verdoux*," *L'Aurore*, January 13, 1948, 2.

107. Citoyen Cane, "Le Cinéma: Salut à Chaplin!," *Le Canard enchaîné*, January 14, 1948, 4.

108. Monique Berger, "Il ne leur manquait que la parole . . . Charles Chaplin succède à Charlot," *Le Populaire*, January 13, 1948, 1, BiFi Collection.

109. Jean Thevenot, "*Monsieur Verdoux*: Dans son dernier film Charlie Chaplin a-t-il tué Charlot?," *Jeunesse ouvrière*, no. 967 (March 27–April 3, 1948), BiFi Collection.

110. Pierre Kast, "*Monsieur Verdoux*," *L'Action*, no. 173 (January 21–27, 1948): 11.

111. Pilati, "Petit bonhomme vit encore," 2.

112. Ibid.

113. Guy Leclerc, "*Monsieur Verdoux*: Révolte et défaite de Charlot!," *L'Humanité*, January 18–19, 1948, 4.

114. Hervé Lauwick, "L'écran: *Monsieur Verdoux*," *Noir et Blanc*, no. 155 (January 28, 1948), BiFi Collection.

115. H. Michel, "*Monsieur Verdoux* ou la fin de Charlot," *Education nationale*, January 10, 1948, BiFi Collection.
116. Louis Chavet, "Charlie Chaplin dans 'Monsieur Verdoux': Hélas! 'Charlot' s'éloigne de plus en plus…," *Le Figaro*, January 15, 1948, 4.
117. Claude Hervin, "*Monsieur Verdoux*," *Paris-Presse*, January 17, 1948, 2.
118. Henry Magnan, "Charles Chaplin et *Monsieur Verdoux*," *Le Monde*, January 20, 1948, 4.
119. Ibid.
120. Henri Queffelec, "*Monsieur Verdoux*," *La Bataille*, January 21, 1948, 6.
121. Sadoul, *Vie de Charlot*, 150–51. There was apparently no response to this nomination from the Norwegian parliament.
122. Christine de Rivoyre, "Charlie Chaplin à Cherbourg," *Le Monde*, September 23, 1952, 12. According to Rivoyre, twenty-two of the sixty journalists were British (and would remain on the *Queen Elizabeth* for the final leg of its voyage to Southampton), and although there were few American journalists present, five of United Press's star reporters had been flown over to cover the Chaplin story (12).
123. Léo Sauvage, "Charlie Chaplin joue sur le 'Queen Elizabeth' un sketch comique digné de ses meilleurs films," *Le Figaro*, September 19, 1952, 4; "Charlie Chaplin menacé de ne pouvoir rentrer aux EtatsUnis," *L'Humanité*, September 20, 1952, 1; "Mesures fascistes: Le gouvernement Américain ouvre une enquête contre Charlie Chaplin," *L'Humanité*, September 22, 1952, 1.
124. Henry Neel, "'Je ne veux pas faire de révolution, je veux seulement faire encore quelques films' nous déclare Charlie Chaplin à son arrivée à Cherbourg," *Le Figaro*, September 23, 1952, 10; Christine de Rivoyre, "Avec Charlie Chaplin sur le pont du *Queen Elizabeth*," *Le Monde*, September 24, 1952, 7; M.-L.B., "A Cherbourg sur le 'Queen Elizabeth' j'ai vu Charlot 'indésirable,'" *L'Humanité*, September 23, 1952, 1–2.
125. Neel, "'Je ne veux pas faire de révolution,'" 10; M.-L.B., "A Cherbourg sur le 'Queen Elizabeth,'" 1–2; Rivoyre, "Avec Charlie Chaplin sur le pont du *Queen Elizabeth*," 7. In his autobiography, Chaplin remembered that although the journalists "were sympathetic, the ordeal was dreary and exhausting" (*My Autobiography*, 502).
126. Chaplin, *My Autobiography*, 501.
127. Neel, "'Je ne veux pas faire de révolution,'" 10; M.-L.B., "A Cherbourg sur le 'Queen Elizabeth,'" 6 (quotation).
128. Rivoyre, "Avec Charlie Chaplin sur le pont du *Queen Elizabeth*," 7.
129. "Mesures fascistes," 3.
130. P.R., "Charles Chaplin est arrivé mercredi à Paris," *La Cinématographie Française*, no. 1490 (November 1, 1951): 5; Christine de Rivoyre, "Charlie Chaplin à Paris," *Le Monde*, October 30, 1952, 9.
131. Pierre Macaigne, "J'ai failli le voir," *Le Figaro*, October 30, 1952, 6. In fact, Paul Carrière noted in *Le Figaro*, there were two separate delegations. One, of "auteurs," also included two screenwriters–film directors (André Berthomieu, Jan-Paul Le Chanois), screenwriter Louis Chavance, and composer of film music Georges Van Parys. The other, of film critics, also included Jean-Pierre Barrot, René Jeanne, Denis Martin, Claude Mauriac, and Jean Nery. Most of them were prevented from reaching Chaplin by the police cordon. Paul Carrière, "D'Orly à la Place Vendôme," *Le Figaro*, October 30, 1952, 6.
132. Carrière, "D'Orly à la Place Vendôme," 6.
133. Macaigne, "J'ai failli le voir," 1, 6.
134. Carrière, "D'Orly à la Place Vendôme," 6.
135. Olivier Merlin, "La journée de la 'presse,'" *Le Monde*, October 31, 1952, 7.
136. Rivoyre, "Charlie Chaplin à Paris," 7.
137. Ibid.; Carrière, "D'Orly à la Place Vendôme," 6.
138. Rivoyre, "Charlie Chaplin à Paris," 9.
139. "M. André Marie remettra cet après-midi la rosette à Chaplin," *Le Figaro*, October 31, 1952, 6; Chaplin, *My Autobiography*, 508–10, quotations from 509.
140. C[hristine] de R[ivoyre], "Charlie Chaplin, Officier de la Légion d'honneur," *Le Monde*, November 2–3, 1952, 7.
141. Christine de Rivoyre, "Charlie Chaplin à Paris: La présentation privée de 'Limelight,'" *Le Monde*, November 1, 1952, 9. According to Rivoyre, those present at the Biarritz from the world of French film included directors Jacques Becker, Robert Bresson, Louis Dequin, Julien

Duvivier, Jean Grémillon, Marcel L'Herbier, and Nicole Vedrès; screenwriters Marcel Aymé, Philippe Hériat, Henri Jeanson, and Noël-Noël; composer Georges Auric; and all the principal film critics (9).

142. It had already been announced that there would be no gala performance in advance of the film's public release. P.R., "Charles Chaplin sera à Paris le 30 courant pour présenter 'Limelight,'" *Le Cinématographie Française*, no. 1489 (October 25, 1952): 1.

143. Rivoyre, "Charlie Chaplin à Paris: La présentation privée de 'Limelight,'" 9.

144. P.R., "Charles Chaplin est arrivé mercredi à Paris," 5; Rivoyre, "Charlie Chaplin à Paris: La présentation privée de 'Limelight,'" 9.

145. P.R., "Charles Chaplin est arrivé mercredi à Paris," 5. Chaplin recalled in his autobiography that the American ambassador was notably absent. One French journalist reported, however, that the ambassador, James Dunn, had been present at the Legion of Honor ceremony earlier in the day. Chaplin, *My Autobiography*, 510; R[ivoyre], "Charlie Chaplin, Officier de la Légion d'honneur," 7.

146. R[ivoyre], "Charlie Chaplin, Officier de la Légion d'honneur," 7.

147. Chaplin, *My Autobiography*, 507, 510–11. For newsreel coverage of Chaplin at the Comédie Française, see British Pathé, "Selected Originals: C'est Charlie! Aka Charles Chaplin in Paris (1952)," https://www.youtube.com/watch?v=JbG_XnJ8UrQ or http://www.britishpathe.com/video/cest-charlie-aka-charles-chaplin-in-paris/query/vincent, both accessed November 27, 2024.

148. P.R., "Charles Chaplin: Officier de la Légion d'Honneur," *La Cinématographie Française*, no. 1491 (November 8, 1951): 4; "Charlie Chaplin a été reçu par les acteurs parisiens," *Le Monde*, November 5, 1951, 9.

149. Chaplin, *My Autobiography*, 512. Chaplin claimed in his autobiography that he had already made up his mind not to return to the United States but had not confided this to Crocker or anyone else, reasoning, "I still had property there which I had not yet disposed of" (512).

150. Ibid., 512–13; Robinson, *Chaplin: His Life and Art*, 578–79.

151. P.R., "Charles Chaplin, Officer de la Legion d'Honneur," 4; Pol Ferjac, "Le dernier film de M. Chaplin," *Le Canard enchaîné*, November 5, 1952, 1.

152. Christine de Rivoyre, "Charlot fait homme," *Le Monde*, October 31, 1952, 1.

153. "Nous avons aussi nos clowns, cher Monsieur Chaplin!," *Le Canard enchaîné*, October 29, 1952, 1.

154. Georges Raven, "En Courant—Libérez Charlot," *Le Figaro*, October 31, 1952, 1.

155. See, for example, R.D., "Le 81e Film de Charlie Chaplin (63 ans)," *Radio-Cinéma-Télévision*, July 27, 1952; Kira Appel, "*Limelight* (sombre drame) a redonné à Charlot sa jeunesse," *France-Soir*, August 16, 1952; both in BiFi Collection.

156. Harry Robinson, "Ce que fut la répétition générale du film *Limelight* à Londres," *Les Lettres Françaises*, October 15, 1952; Wilbur G. Landrey, "*Limelight*," *L'Aurore*, October 15, 1952; both in BiFi Collection.

157. "La princesse Margaret verra ce soir *Limelight* dont la presse londonienne a eu la primeur," *Combat*, October 15, 1952, BiFi Collection. Cf. "Première mondiale de *Limelight*," *L'Humanité*, Ocober 15, 1952, BiFi Collection.

158. "Les critiques anglais sont déroutés par *Limelight* qui les a fait plus pleurer que rire," *Libération*, October 16, 1952, BiFi Collection.

159. J.P., "Après les larmes Chaplin connait son 'heure de verité,'" *Combat*, October 18, 1952; Henry Magnan, "Charlie Chaplin a été longuement acclamé lors du gala de présentation de *Limelight* à Londres," *Le Monde*, October 17, 1952, BiFi Collection.

160. Kléber Haedens, "*Limelight* a obtenu hier son passeport pour l'éternité," *Paris-Press/L'Intransigeant*, November 1, 1952; R.-M. Arlaud, "*Les Feux de la rampe (Limelight)*, *Combat*, October 31, 1952; both in BiFi Collection.

161. Monique Berger, "Triomphe de Charlie Chaplin: *Limelight*," *Populaire Dimanche*, November 9, 1952, 9; Georges Sadoul, "*Limelight (Les feux de la rampe)*: Une tragédie optimiste," *L'Humanité*, October 31, 1952, 2; Simone Dubreuilh, "*Limelight* est un message d'amour," *Libération*, October 31, 1952, BiFi Collection.

162. André Bazin, "*Limelight*, ou la mort de Molière [*Limelight*, or the Death of Molière]," *France-Observateur*, no. 130 (November 6, 1952), in Bazin, *What Is Cinema?*, 2:124.

163. Berger, "Triomphe de Charlie Chaplin," 9; Janine Bouissounouse, "Dans *Limelight* . . . le genie de Charlie Chaplin atteint le sommet de la grandeur tragique," *Ce Soir*, November 1, 1952, 1, BiFi Collection; Bazin, *What Is Cinema?*, 2:127.

164. Sadoul, "*Limelight* (*Les feux de la rampe*)," 2.

165. Haedens, "*Limelight* a obtenu hier son passeport pour l'éternité." Simone Dubreuilh noted that in *Limelight* "for the first time . . . Chaplin dies at the end of a film" ("*Limelight* est un message d'amour"). While Verdoux's execution is not shown in the film, the final scene has him being led away to the guillotine.

166. Bouissounouse, "Dans *Limelight*," 1; Claude Garson, "*Limelight* ou 'Les Feux de la Rampe,'" *L'Aurore*, October 31, 1952, 2; Claude Mauriac, "*Limelight*," *Le Figaro Litteraire*, November 8, 1953; all from BiFi Collection.

167. Christine de Rivoyre, "Le presentation privée de *Limelight*," *Le Monde*, November 1, 1952, BiFi Collection.

168. Bazin, "*Limelight*, or the death of Molière," *What Is Cinema*, 2:125–27.

169. Bazin, "Si Charlot ne meure . . . [If Charlot Hadn't Died]," *Cahiers du cinéma*, no. 17 (November 1952), in Bodon, *André Bazin's "Charlie Chaplin*," 82, 84, 86.

170. Ibid., 83, 86. With this reference to Chaplin's "own old face," Bazin was clearly thinking of the moment in *Limelight* when Chaplin took off Calvero's makeup to reveal the face of a sixty-three-year-old.

171. Mannoni, cited in P.P., "Revue de Presse—Charlot ambassadeur," *Le Populaire de Paris*, November 1–2, 1952, 2, BiFi Collection.

172. P.R., "*Limelight*," *La Cinématographie Française*, no. 1491 (November 8, 1952): 12; Pierre Laroche, "Le Coeur 'Ignoble' de Charlot," *Le Canard enchaîné*, November 5, 1952, 4; both in BiFi Collection.

173. Berger, "Triomphe de Charlie Chaplin," 9.

174. P.R., "*Limelight*," 12; Michel de Saint-Pierre, "Le Cinéma: *Limelight*," *Temoignage Chrétien*, October 17, 1952; both in BiFi Collection.

175. André Lang, "*Limelight* (Les Feux de la rampe)," *France-Soir*, November 1, 1952, 6; Garson, "*Limelight* ou 'Les Feux de la Rampe,'" 2; Bouissounouse, "Dans *Limelight*," 1; all in BiFi Collection.

176. Berger, "Triomphe de Charlie Chaplin," 9; P.R., "*Limelight*," 12; Bouissounouse, "Dans *Limelight*," 1; all in BiFi Collection.

177. Andé Bazin, "Grandeur de Limelight [The Grandeur of *Limelight*]," *Esprit* 21, no. 201 (April 1953), in Bazin, *What Is Cinema?*, 2:128.

178. Laroche, "Le Coeur 'Ignoble' de Charlot," 4; Garson, "*Limelight* ou 'Les Feux de la Rampe,'" 2; Pierre-Jean Guyo, "*Limelight* ou Chaplin tel qu'en lui-même. . . ," *La Croix*, November 11, 1952; all from BiFi Collection.

179. Jean-José Richer, "Témoignages sur *Limelight*," *Cahiers du cinema*, no. 18 (December 1952): 33, BiFi Collection.

180. Ibid., 33–34. Bazin pointed out that, while melodrama is "defined by the absence of ambiguity," the character Calvero "is ambiguity itself" ("The Grandeur of *Limelight*," 129). For other criticisms of the interpretation of *Limelight* as a melodrama, see Anon., "*Limelight*, de Charles Chaplin, un chef d'oeuvre shakespearian," *Lettres Françaises*, November 13, 1952 and Nicole Vedrès, "Témoignages sur *Limelight*," *Cahiers du cinema*, no. 18 (December 1952): 23; both in BiFi Collection.

181. Richer, "Témoignages sur *Limelight*," 34.

182. Guyo, "*Limelight* ou Chaplin tel qu'en lui-même."

183. Saint-Pierre, "Le Cinéma: *Limelight*."

184. Bazin, "The Grandeur of *Limelight*," 129. Bazin commented that, even with all the publicity generated by Chaplin himself as a "traveling salesman" for the movie, the distributor failed to secure his aim of half a million admissions. Yet, as a writer for *L'Aurore* pointed out, the price of admission in the four large Paris cinemas that were "exclusively" showing the film was a very high three hundred francs (itself down from the five hundred francs initially proposed). "This sum," he judged, whatever the merits of the film itself, "will be prohibitive for the mass of everyday spectators." Bazin, "The Grandeur of *Limelight*," 128–29; Le Strapontin, "La première exclusivité parisienne de *Limelight* rapportera 150 millions," *L'Aurore*, November 4, 1952, 2, BiFi Collection.

185. Georges Rouquier, "Témoignages sur *Limelight*," *Cahiers du cinema*, no. 18 (December 1952): 25, BiFi Collection; Bazin, "The Grandeur of *Limelight*," 132.

186. André Michel, "Témoignages sur *Limelight*," *Cahiers du cinéma*, no. 18 (December 1952): 24, BiFi Collection.

187. Bazin, "The Grandeur of *Limelight*," 130–32.

188. P.R., "Festival Chaplin en Sorbonne," *La Cinématographie Française*, no. 1497 (December 20, 1952): 4.

Chapter 8

1. Sadoul, *Vie de Charlot*, 257–58.

2. "Le film de Chaplin *Un Roi à New York* est présente demain à Londres en première mondiale," *L'Aurore*, September 9, 1957, BiFi Collection.

3. "Première mondiale de *Un Roi à New York*," *L'Humanité*, September 11, 1957; "Attaqué par la presse Américaine Chaplin se défend," *Le Monde*, September 12, 1957; both in BiFi Collection.

4. Sadoul, *Vie de Charlot*, 186. For a thoughtful review by the London correspondent of *Le Monde*, see Jean Wetz, "*Un Roi à New-York*: Un excellent Charlot, mais un mauvais Chaplin," *Le Monde*, September 12, 1957, BiFi Collection.

5. Lynn, *Charlie Chaplin and His Times*, 506; Maland, *Chaplin and American Culture*, 321–22.

6. Marthe-Louise Lévy, "*Un roi à New-York* est un film gai, mais…," *Populaire-Dimanche*, October 13, 1957, BiFi Collection.

7. Sadoul, *Vie de Charlot*, 260.

8. "Chaplin à son public: 'Mon film attaque la politique; comment peut-on m'accuser de politique," *Combat*, October 25, 1957, 4; Jean de Baroncelli, "Quand Paris reçoit 'Un Roi,'" *Le Monde*, October 26, 1957, 9; both in BiFi Collection.

9. Robinson, *Chaplin: His Life and Art*, 591.

10. "Cette Nuit au Gaumont-Palace: 4,500 Parisiens divisés sur le nouveau film de Chaplin *Un Roi à New York*," *L'Aurore*, October 25, 1957, 4; Baroncelli, "Quand Paris reçoit 'Un Roi,'" 9; "Chaplin à son public'"; all in BiFi Collection.

11. "Cette Nuit au Gaumont-Palace," 4.

12. Baroncelli, "Quand Paris reçoit 'Un Roi,'" 9; "Cette Nuit au Gaumont-Palace," 4; both in BiFI Collection.

13. See Bodon, *André Bazin's Charlie Chaplin*, 98n17.

14. André Bazin, "Un roi à New York," *France-Observateur*, no. 390 (October 31, 1957), in Bazin, *Charlie Chaplin*, 102–4; André Bazin, "Une Roi à New York," *Education Nationale*, November 1, 1957, BiFi Collection.

15. Bazin, "Un roi à New York," in Bazin, *Charlie Chaplin*, 102–3. Bazin confessed he had been "bored stiff" for three-quarters of the second part (103). Also see Bazin, "Une Roi à New York," *Education Nationale*.

16. Bazin, *Charlie Chaplin*, 102–3; Bazin, "Une Roi à New York," *Education Nationale*.

17. Bazin, *Charlie Chaplin*, 105–6.

18. Claude Brulé, "Les Nouveaux Spectacles—*Un Roi à New York*," *Paris-Presse/L'Intransigeant*, October 27–28, 1957, 7; Jean de Baroncelli. "*Un Roi à New-York* de Charlie Chaplin," *Le Monde*, October 27, 1957; both in BiFi Collection.

19. Armand Monjo, "*Un Roi à New-York* de Charlie Chaplin," *L'Humanité*, October 25, 1957, 2, BiFi Collection. Also see Claude Garson, "Satire antiaméricaine avec Chaplin dans *Un Roi à New York*," *L'Aurore*, October 26–27, 1957, 4, BiFi Collection.

20. Garson, "Satire antiaméricaine avec Chaplin dans *Un Roi à New York*," 4.

21. Baroncelli argued that the caviar–turtle soup sequence represented a return to classical Chaplin comedy in which one "known object" was associated with another known object "*Un Roi à New-York* de Charlie Chaplin"). To Claude Garson, it was "perhaps the best moment in the film" ("Satire antiaméricaine avec Chaplin dans *Un Roi à New York*," 4). Even Louis Chauvet, generally critical of the film itself, assured his readers they would enjoy this sequence. Louis Chauvet, "*Un Roi à New York*," *Le Figaro*, October 25, 1957, 12. All from BiFi Collection.

22. Jean Dutourd, "Le Cinéma: Le Roi Chaplin," *Carrefour*, October 30, 1957. Also on this sequence, see Monjo, "*Un Roi à New-York* de Charlie Chaplin," *L'Humanité*, October 25, 1957, 2 and Garson, "Satire antiaméricaine avec Chaplin dans *Un Roi à New York*," 4. All from BiFi Collection.

23. Dutourd, "Le Cinéma: Le Roi Charles"; Monjo, "*Un Roi à New-York* de Charlie Chaplin," 2; Garson, "Satire antiaméricaine avec Chaplin dans *Un Roi à New York*," 4. Simone Dubreuilh saw the fake dinner party sequence as comparable to the eating machine scene in *Modern Times* and hailed it as "the summit of the comedy in *A King in New York*." Simone Dubreuilh, "*Un Roi à New York*," *Libération*, October 26, 1957. All from BiFi Collection.

24. Monjo, "*Un Roi à New-York* de Charlie Chaplin," 2; Garson, "Satire antiaméricaine avec Chaplin dans *Un Roi à New York*," 4.

25. J. P. Vivet, "*Un Roi à New York*," *L'Express*, October 31, 1957; Dubreuilh, "*Un Roi à New York*"; both from BiFi Collection.

26. Chauvet, "*Un roi à New York*," 12. Robert Benayoun similarly commented that "the sequences about TV, which have nothing new about them . . . do not stand comparison with, shall we say, Kazin." Robert Benayoun, "Charlot règle ses comptes: *Un Roi à New York*," *Demain*, November 14, 1957, BiFi Collection.

27. Dubreuilh, "*Un Roi à New York*"; Dutourd, "Le Cinéma: Le Roi Charles"; Baroncelli, "*Un Roi à New-York* de Charlie Chaplin.".

28. "A Londres, Devant le Nouveau film de Charlie Chaplin," *Le franc-tireur*, September 11, 1957; Benayoun, "Charlot règle ses comptes"; both from BiFi Collection.

29. Baroncelli, "*Un Roi à New-York* de Charlie Chaplin"; Monjo, "*Un Roi à New-York* de Charlie Chaplin," 2; Benayoun, "Charlot règle ses comptes."

30. Monjo, "*Un Roi à New-York* de Charlie Chaplin," 2.

31. Brulé, "Les Nouveaux Spectacles—*Un Roi à New York*," 7; Vivet, "*Un Roi à New York*."

32. Marthe Louis-Lévy, "*Un Roi à New-York* est un film gai, mais"; Jeander, "*Un Roi à New York*," *Le Canard enchaîné*, October 30, 1957, 4; both in BiFi Collection. Roland Barthes published an essay on Minou Drouet in *Mythologies* (Éditions du Seuil, 1957). Also see Ann Jefferson, *Genius in France: An Idea and Its Uses* (Princeton University Press, 2014), 183–92.

33. Baroncelli, "*Un Roi à New-York* de Charlie Chaplin." R.-M. Arlaud noted on similar lines that Chaplin had evaded a "settling of accounts" with HUAC. R.-M. Arlaud, "Le Film du Jour: *Un Roi à New-York*," *Combat*, October 27, 1957, BiFi Collection.

34. Roger Fressoz, "Un Roi à New-York," *Témoignage chrétian*, November 8, 1957, BiFi Collection.

35. Garson, "Satire antiaméricaine avec Chaplin dans *Un Roi à New York*," 4. Garson asserted that "McCarthyism" lasted only two years in the United States compared to the repressions of Stalin, which lasted much longer. In reality, Joseph R. McCarthy's career as an anticommunist campaigner began with his speech at Wheeling, West Virginia, in February 1950 and effectively ended with his censure by the U.S. Senate in December 1954. "McCarthyism," however, was often used as a generic term to refer to American anticommunism, which had a long history both before and after the rise and fall of McCarthy himself.

36. Brulé, "Les Nouveaux Spectacles—*Un Roi à New York*," 7. The Hungarian uprising of 1956 was a mass revolt by many Hungarians against the communist regime in their country and its subordination to the Soviet Union. It was violently suppressed by Soviet troops and tanks, with thousands of Hungarians killed and injured.

37. Vivet, "*Un Roi à New York*"; Dutourd, "Le Cinéma: Le Roi Chaplin."

38. Garson, "Satire antiaméricaine avec Chaplin dans *Un Roi à New York*," 4; François Gault, "Un Roi à New York," *Le Coopérateur de France*, October 10, 1957; Fressoz, "*Un Roi à New-York*"; all in BiFi Collection.

39. Brulé, "Les Nouveaux Spectacles—*Un Roi à New York*," 7.

40. Chauvet, "*Un Roi à New York*," 12.

41. André Lang, "*Un Roi à New-York* (Un pétard dans une blague)," *France-Soir*, October 26, 1957, 8, BiFi Collection.

42. François Truffaut, "*Un Roi à New York* est un film génial," *Arts*, October 30, 1957, BiFi Collection.

43. Jean Mitry, "Les films de Charlot," special issue, *Images et Son*, April 1957. An updated version of this was later published by Mitry as *Tout Chaplin* (Editions Atlas, 1972). In a brief introduction to this latter work, Mitry claimed that—since Delluc in 1921 and (much more briefly) Theodore Huff in the French version of his book on *Charlie Chaplin* (NRF, 1953)—no other works had attempted to offer such a full summary of Chaplin's films (9).

44. Jean Mitry, *Charlot et la "Fabulation" chaplinesque* (Éditions Universitaires, 1957).

45. Pierre Leprohon, *Charlot ou la naissance d'un mythe* (Éditions Corymbe, 1935); Jean Epstein, "La naissance d'un mythe," *Corymbe*, January–February 1935, reprinted in Epstein, *Écrits sur le cinéma* (Seghers, 1974), 1:239–41; Barthelémy Amengual, "Evolution et signification du mythe de Charlot" and "Travail et Culture," in *L'Education Populaire en Algérie* (Algiers, 1950); Barthelémy Amengual, "Le mythe de Charlot," *Raccords* 2 (Autumn 1951): 21–24. Also see Jean Duvignaud, "Le Mythe Chaplin," *Critique*, no. 84 (May 1954): 389–99.

46. William Gilcher, "Jean Mitry," in Gilcher et al., "Four Tributes: Jean Mitry, Jay Leyda, George Pratt, Jacques Ledoux," *Film History* 2 (1988): 393–94; J. Dudley Andrew, "The Film Theory of Jean Mitry," *Cinema Journal* 14, no. 3 (Spring 1975): 1–2.

47. See "Avertissement," in Mitry, *Charlot et la "Fabulation" chaplinesque*, n.p.

48. Ibid., 25–26. Although Mitry was correct in claiming (26) that the classic appearance of Charlot (derby hat, tight-fitting jacket, baggy trousers, big shoes, and a cane) did not emerge

immediately, he ignored the point that the Tramp figure was present in both *Mabel's Strange Predicament* and *Kid Auto Races at Venice*, respectively the second and third Keystone films Chaplin completed in 1914 (though they were released in reverse order).

49. Films in these categories, according to Mitry, included *Tango Tangles, The Face on the Bar Room Floor*, and *Tillie's Punctured Romance* (all Keystone, 1914); *A Night Out, In the Park*, and *A Night in the Show* (all Essanay, 1915); and *One A.M* and *The Cure* (both Mutual, 1916–17) (ibid., 26–27).

50. Ibid., 26.

51. Sadoul, *Vie de Charlot*.

52. Barthélemy Amengual, "Le mythe de Charlot: Un débat mal conduit," *Positif—Revue mensuelle de cinéma*, no. 499 (September 2002): 81.

53. Mitry, *Charlot et la "Fabulation" chaplinesque*, 28–31.

54. Ibid., 33, 53.

55. Ibid., 33–34.

56. Luc Moullet, "Jean Mitry, *Charlot et la 'Fabulation' Chaplinesque*," *Cahiers du cinéma*, no. 73 (July 1957): 57. Moullet's unidentified thirteen studies of Chaplin (almost certainly an underestimate) probably included the works by Louis Delluc (1921), Robert Florey (1927), Edouard Ramond (1927), Henry Poullaille (1927), Pierre Leprohon (1935), Maurice Bessy and Robert Florey (1952), and Georges Sadoul (1952). To Moullet, Mitry's analysis was much deeper than that offered by these earlier studies because it traced the evolution of Chaplin's art as a film director through "rigorous and detailed analyses" of his whole output, making clear how its features evolved over time.

57. Mitry, *Charlot et la "Fabulation" chaplinesque*, 24.

58. Ibid., 34, 54–55.

59. Ibid., 49.

60. Ibid., 49–50.

61. Ibid., 50–52.

62. Ibid., 56.

63. Ibid., 55–58, 60–61, 67–68.

64. Sadoul, *Vie de Charlot*, 195.

65. Chaplin, *My Autobiography*.

66. Sadoul, *Charlie Chaplin*, 196–97. Also see "Chaplin: Un petit monsieur très satisfait," *Arts*, no. 69 (January 18–24, 1967); M. Aubriant, "Une Comtesse de Hong-Kong," *Paris-Presse*, January 19, 1967; both in BiFi Collection.

67. Sadoul, *Vie de Charlot*, 199.

68. Robinson, *Chaplin: His Life and Art*, 438, 440–41.

69. When Goddard filed for divorce against Chaplin in Mexico in 1942, she claimed that they had been married in China in 1936. But, as Scott Eyman comments, "no marriage license has ever turned up" (*Charlie Chaplin vs. America*, 83).

70. Robinson, *Chaplin: His Life and Art*, 482. The character of Natascha also bears a considerable resemblance to the beautiful Russian emigrée "Skaya," whom Chaplin wrote about meeting in a famous Montmartre restaurant during his Paris visit of 1921 (*My Trip Abroad*, 124–27).

71. Robinson, *Chaplin: His Life and Art*, 607–17; Lynn, *Charlie Chaplin*, 515–18; Eyman, *Charlie Chaplin vs. America*, 330–34.

72. On the press conference, see "Charlie Chaplin aime sa 'Comtesse,'" *France-Soir/Paris-Presse/ L'Intransigeant*, January 13, 1967; "Les bruits de la ville," *Le Nouvel Observateur*, no. 114 (January 18–25, 1967); Paul Carriére, "Charlie Chaplin défend sa 'Comtesse,'" *Le Figaro*, January 12, 1967; Samuel Lachize, "Charlie Chaplin à Paris," *L'Humanité*, January 12, 1967; Jean Rochereau, "*La Comtesse de Hong-Kong*? Mais c'est mon meilleur film affirme Chaplin," *La Croix*, January 13, 1967; all in BiFi Collection.

73. Claude Mauriac, "Une comtesse de Hong-Kong," *Figaro littéraire*, January 19, 1967, BiFi Collection. Mauriac claimed he felt "humiliated" because he had not yet seen the film.

74. Carriére, "Charlie Chaplin défend sa 'Comtesse'"; "Les bruits de la ville"; "Charlie Chaplin aime sa 'Comtesse'"; Lachize, "Charlie Chaplin à Paris"; Rochereau, "*La Comtesse de Hong-Kong*?"

75. Carriére, "Charlie Chaplin défend sa 'Comtesse'"; Robert Chazal, "*La comtesse de Hong-Kong* (La ruée vers le zéro)," *France-Soir*, January 14, 1967; both in BiFi Collection.

76. Carriére, "Charlie Chaplin défend sa 'Comtesse'"; "Charlie Chaplin aime sa 'Comtesse'"; Rochereau, "*La Comtesse de Hong-Kong*?"

77. Odile Grand, "Chaplin a conquis le Tout-Paris avec sa *Comtesse de Hong-Kong*," *L'Aurore*, January 13, 1967; "Chaplin: 'Dommage que la première de *La comtesse de Hong-King* n'ait pas eu lieu à Paris," *France-Soir*, January 14, 1967; both in BiFi Collection.

78. "Les bruits de la ville—La Ruée vers Loren," *Le Nouvel Observateur*, no. 114, January 18–25, 1967, BiFi Collection.

79. Grand, "Chaplin a conquis le Tout-Paris avec sa *Comtesse de Hong-Kong*."

80. Michèle Fabron, "Charlot, c'est flou!," *Minute*, January 19, 1967, BiFi Collection.

81. Jean de Baroncelli, "La Comtesse de Hong-Kong," *Le Monde*, January 15–16, 1967, BiFi Collection.

82. Louis Chauvet, "La Comtesse de Hong-Kong," *Le Figaro*, January 14–15, 1967, BiFi Collection. A writer in *L'Aurore* interviewed Deval himself and the playwright pointed out that Chaplin might have seen *La Prétentaine* at a performance in Switzerland, where he lived, and darkly suggested that it would not be the first time Chaplin had committed plagiarism. *City Lights*, Deval alleged, had its origins in French writer-director Jean Sarment's play *The Most Beautiful Eyes in the World* (1927). "Cette comtesse qui trouble Jacques Deval," *L'Aurore*, January 30, 1967. Also see Henry Rabine, "*La Comtesse de Hong-Kong*," *La Croix*, January 23, 1967; both in BiFi Collection.

83. Chauvet, "La Comtesse de Hong-Kong."

84. Michel Aubriant, "Chaplin a metamophosé Sophia Loren," *Candide*, January 23, 1967; Samuel Lachize, "*La Comtesse de Hong Kong* est un grand film! Chaplin n'a pas démérité de Charlot," *L'Humanité*, January 16, 1967; Henry Chapier, "*La Comtesse de Hong-Kong*," January 15, 1967; all in BiFi Collection.

85. "*La Comtesse de Hong-Kong*, film de Charles Chaplin," *Carrefour*, January 25, 1967; Claude Brulé, "Moi, j'adore le film de Chaplin," *Candide*, January 16, 1967; Michel Duran, "*La comtesse de Hong-Kong* (Charlot dessous)," *Le Canard enchaîné*, no. 2413 (January 18, 1967): 7; all in BiFi Collection.

86. Mauriac, "*Une comtesse de Hong-Kong*."

87. "*La Comtesse de Hong-Kong* par Charles Chaplin," *Nouvelles littéraires*, January 19, 1967, BiFi Collection.

88. Rabine, "*La Comtesse de Hong-Kong*." On this repetition, also see Pierre Billard, "Chaplin est resté à quai," *L'Express*, January 16–22, 1967, BiFi Collection.

89. Gérard Guegan, "Les comptes de la comtesse," *Cahiers du cinéma*, no. 188 (March 1967): 61; Fabron, "Charlot, c'est flou!"; Chazal, "*La comtesse de Hong-Kong*" (La ruée vers le zéro)."

90. V. Volmarez, "Lettre ouverte à Charles Chaplin," *Aux Ecoutes*, February 19, 1967, BiFi Collection.

91. "*La Comtesse de Hong-Kong*," *Nouvelles littéraires*, January 19, 1967; "*La comtesse de Hong-Kong*, film de Charles Chapin," *Carrefour*, January 25, 1967; Chauvet, "La Comtesse de Hong-Kong"; all in BiFi Collection.

92. Fabron, "Charlot, c'est flou!"; Mauriac, "*Une comtesse de Hong-Kong*."

93. See, for example, Anon., *Le Populaire*, February 7, 1967, BiFi Collection.

94. Billard, "Chaplin est resté à quai"; Régine, "Le culot de Charlot," *Arts*, January 25–31, 1967, BiFi Collection.

95. Chazal, "*La comtesse de Hong-Kong* (La ruée vers le zéro)."

96. Brulé, "Moi, j'adore le film de Chaplin." In "*La comtesse de Hong-Kong* (La ruée vers le zéro)" Chazal also suggested that Loren's "taxi-girl" symbolized the "poor and persecuted" whom Charlot had always defended.

97. Claude Garson, "*La Comtesse de Hong-Kong*," *L'Aurore*, January 15, 1967, BiFi Collection. An anonymous writer in the socialist newspaper *Populaire* suggested that the "billionaire" in *Countess* was much less realistic than the millionaire in *City Lights*. Anon., untitled review, *Populaire*, February 7, 1967, Bifi Collection.

98. Carriére, "Charlie Chaplin défend sa 'Comtesse'"; Baroncelli, "*La comtesse de Hong-Kong*."

99. Lachize, "Charlie Chaplin à Paris"; Carriére, "Charlie Chaplin défend sa ''Comtesse''"; "Charlie Chaplin aime sa 'Comtesse.'". Also see "Les bruits de la ville," 30–31.

100. Chazal, "*La comtesse de Hong-Kong* (La ruée vers le zéro)"; Chauvet, "*La comtesse de Hong-Kong*."

101. Gérard Guegan, "Les comptes de la comtesse," *Cahiers du cinéma*, no. 188 (March 1967): 61.

102. "*La Comtesse de Hong-Kong* par Charles Chaplin."

103. Billard, "Chaplin est resté à quai."

104. Brulé, "Moi, j'adore le film de Chaplin"; Henry Chapier, "*La Comtesse de Hong-Kong* de Charlie Chaplin," *Combat*, January 15, 1967, BiFi Collection.

105. Rabine, "*La Comtesse de Hong-Kong*"; Jean-Louis Bory, "Les pirouettes de Robby et Grilletto," *Le Nouvel Observateur*, January 25–31, 1967, 44, BiFi Collection.

106. Volmavez, "Lettre ouverte à Charles Chaplin"; Billard, "Chaplin est resté à quai"; Brulé, "Moi, j'adore le film de Chaplin."

107. Lynn, *Charlie Chaplin and His Times*, 518–19; Robinson, *Chaplin: His Life and Art*, 619–20, 627–28; Eyman, *Charlie Chaplin vs. America*, 345–46; Sadoul, *Charlie Chaplin*, 262, 266.

108. Robinson, *Chaplin: His Life and Art*, 622.

109. François Truffaut, "Préface" to *Charlie Chaplin* (Petite bibliothèque des Cahiers du cinéma, 2000), 9; Elaine Woo, "Studio Exec Helped Bring Chaplin and His Films Back to U.S.", *Los Angeles Times*, October 1, 2011, https://www.washingtonpost.com/local/obituaries/studio-exec-helped-bring-chaplin-and-his-films-back-to-us/2011/09/29/gIQAN5aQDL_story.html.

110. Truffaut, "Préface" to *Charlie Chaplin*, 9; Sadoul, *Vie de Charlot*, 262.

111. Robinson, *Chaplin: His Life and Art*, 620; Woo, "Studio Exec Helped Bring Chaplin and His Films back to U.S."

112. Robinson, *Chaplin: His Life and Art*, 620–621; Lynn, *Charlie Chaplin*, 521; Maland, *Chaplin and American Culture*, 337; Eyman, *Charlie Chaplin vs. America*, 336–37.

113. Robinson, *Chaplin: His Life and Art*, 621; Eyman, *Charlie Chaplin vs. America*, 338.

114. Truffaut to Eric Rohmer, 1971, in *François Truffaut: Letters*, ed. Gilles Jacob and Claude de Givray, trans. Gilber Adair (Faber and Faber, 1989), 367; Truffaut, "Préface" in *Charlie Chaplin*, 9.

115. René Rousseau, "La soirée d'ouverture," *Le Figaro*, May 13, 1971, 20; Jean de Baroncelli, "Hommage à Charlie Chaplin pour l'ouverture du XXVe Festival de Cannes," *Le Monde*, May 14, 1971, 27; "Cannes plus brillante que Hollywood pour la soirée inaugurale de Festival," *L'Aurore*, May 12, 1971, 12; all in BiFi Collection.

116. Three more were invited but decided not to come: Ingmar Bergman from Sweden, the director most honored by Cannes over the years, and two men who had both been given awards for filming *Othello*: American-born Orson Welles (1952) and Russian Sergei Yutkevich (1956). "Cannes jour 'J': Des prix d'excellence aux plus fidèles," *France-Soir*, January 13, 1971, 13; "Cannes plus brillante que Hollywood pour la soirée inaugurale de Festival," 12; Baroncelli, "Hommage à Charlie Chaplin pour l'ouverture du XXVe Festival de Cannes," 27; all in BiFi Collection.

117. Rousseau, "La soirée d'ouverture," 20; "Cannes plus brillante que Hollywood pour la soirée inaugurale de Festival," 12; Guy Teisseire, "A la soirée inaugurale Chaplin est redevenu Charlot avec la canne du ministre," *L'Aurore*, May 13, 1971, 14, BiFi Collection.

118. See Festival de Cannes, "Homage to Charlie Chaplin," May 12, 1971, http://fresques.ina.fr/festival-de-cannes-en/fiche-media/Cannes00416/homage-to-charlie-chaplin.html.

119. Rousseau, "La soirée d'ouverture," 20; Robert Chazell, "Charlie Chaplin est redevenu Charlot pour la soirée d'ouverture," *France-Soir*, May 14, 1971, 15, BiFi Collection.

120. INA, "Homage rendu par Jacques Duhamel à Charlie Chaplin," May 12, 1971, http://www.ina.fr/video/I00014516.

121. Jonathan Rosenbaum, "Moviegoing at Cannes: Classics Without Labels," *Village Voice*, June 17, 1971, https://jonathanrosenbaum.net/2023/12/moviegoing-at-cannes-classics-without-labels/.

122. Jeffrey Vance, *Chaplin: Genius of the Cinema* (Harry M. Abrams, 2003), 355.

123. Lynn, *Charlie Chaplin and His Times*, 524–25.

124. Ibid., 523; Candice Bergen, *Knock Wood* (Simon and Schuster, 2014), 205–6. In her autobiography, Bergen referred to Schneider using the pseudonym "Robin."

125. Anthony Holden, *The Oscars: The Secret History of Hollywood's Academy Awards* (Warner Books, 1994), 14, 78, 81, 94.

126. He would share the Best Original Dramatic Score with Raymond Rasch and Larry Russell for *Limelight* in 1952 (ibid., 595).

127. Ibid., 377.

128. Lynn, *Charlie Chaplin and His Times*, 523.

129. Maland, *Chaplin and American Culture*, 338; Eyman, *Charlie Chaplin vs. America*, 341.

130. Bergen, *Knock Wood*, 206–7; AP, "On This Day: 3 April 1972," YouTube, https://www.youtube.com/watch?v=4ecT8X3o4A8.

131. Vance, *Chaplin: Genius of the Cinema*, 355.

132. McCandlish Phillips, "Chaplin Salute Fills Philharmonic Hall," *New York Times*, April 5, 1972, 38. Phillips also noted the presence at Philharmonic Hall of Mo Rothman, who had arrived in New York a week earlier and—the reporter shrewdly commented—"stands in a singularly good position to turn all the current attention centered on Mr. Chaplin into cash flow" (38).

133. See AP, "USA: Mayor John Lindsay Presents Charlie Chaplin with Handel Medallion," April 6, 1972, YouTube, https://www.youtube.com/watch?v=37CsURkH5s0.

134. Bergen, *Knock Wood*, 208.

135. Maland, *Chaplin and American Culture*, 339; Lynn, *Charlie Chaplin and His Times*, 523.

136. Lynn, *Charlie Chaplin and His Times*, 531–32; Maland, *Chaplin and American Culture*, 339; Oscars, "Charlie Chaplin's Honorary Award: 44th Oscars (1972)," YouTube, https://www.youtube.com/watch?v=J3Pl-qvA1X8.

137. Robinson, *Chaplin: His Life and Art*, 622, 624.

138. Glenn Myrent and Georges P. Langlois, *Henri Langlois: First Citizen of Cinema*, trans. Lisa Nesselson (Twayne, 1995), 244; Patrick Olmeta, *La Cinémathèque Française de 1936 à nos jours* (CNRS Éditions, 2000), 123.

139. Myrent and Langlois, *Henri Langlois*, 266.

140. On the whole controversy, see Olmeta, *La Cinémathèque Française*, 119–48; Antoine de Baecque and Serge Toubiana, *Truffaut: A Biography*, trans. Catherine Temerson (Knopf, 1999), 235–40.

141. Myrent and Langlois, *Henri Langlois*, 267–68.

142. Ibid., 214; Olmeta, *La Cinémathèque Française*, 154.

143. "Les lumières de Chaillot," *Cinéma 68*, no. 129 (October 1968), quoted in Olmeta, *La Cinémathèque Française*, 154.

144. Richard Roud, *A Passion for Film: Henri Langlois and the Cinémathèque Française* (Viking Press, 1983), 15; Myrent and Langlois, *Henri Langlois*, 13–14.

145. Langlois, quoted in Myrent and Langlois, *Henri Langlois*, 22–23.

146. Roud, *A Passion for Film*, 26–27.

147. Myrent and Langlois, *Henri Langlois*, 39.

148. Roud, *A Passion for Film*, 27–28; Myrent and Langlois, *Henri Langlois*, 42, 48.

149. On the consequences of the Occupation for Langlois and his colleagues, see Olmeta, *La Cinémathèque Française*, 73–79.

150. Myrent and Langlois, *Henri Langlois*, 80–81.

151. Sadoul, *Charlie Chaplin*, 118, 245. Norbert Aping, while arguing that the film was not formally banned in Nazi Germany, notes that it nevertheless became "impossible to show" it (*Charlie Chaplin and the Nazis*, 219–26, quotation from 226).

152. Myrent and Langlois, *Henri Langlois*, 109.

153. See P.R., "Festival Chaplin en Sorbonne," *La Cinématographie Française*, no. 1497 (December 20, 1952): 4.

154. Roud, *A Passion for Films*, 108–115, quotation from 108.

155. Myrent and Langlois, *Henri Langlois*, 146–48, quotation from 148.

156. Ibid., 215.

157. Marie-Guy Baron, "Les baisers de Charlot au public de *Monsieur Verdoux*," *France-Soir*, September 14, 1973; G.T., "*Monsieur Verdoux* à la Cinémathèque: Le public debout acclame Chaplin," *L'Aurore*, September 9, 1973; both in BiFi Collection.

158. Myrent and Langlois, *Henri Langlois*, 301. On the exhibition, out of which grew Langlois's Museum of Cinema (1975), see Olmerta, *La Cinémathèque Française*, 155–56.

159. Baron, "The baisers de Charlot," *France-Soir*, September 14, 1973, BiFi Collection. For a (sadly silent) film of Chaplin at the Cinémathèque, see Henri Langlois, "Visite de Charlie Chaplin à la Cinémathèque française," 1973, Cinémathèque, https://www.cinematheque.fr/henri/film/122208-visite-de-charlie-chaplin-a-la-cinematheque-francaise-anonyme-1973/.

160. Myrent and Langlois, *Henri Langlois*, 301.

161. Baron, "The baisers de Charlot"; Samuel Lachize, "Les chefs-d'oeuvre n'ont pas de rides: *Monsieur Verdoux* de Charlie Chaplin," *L'Humanité*, September 15, 1973, BiFi Collection.

162. Henry Chapier, "*Monsieur Verdoux* de Charles Chaplin: L'evangile de l'éternel révolté," *Combat*, September 14, 1973. On the modernity of *Monsieur Verdoux*, also see Jean de Baroncelli, "Le retour de *Monsieur Verdoux*," *Le Monde*, September 14, 1973; both in BiFi Collection.

163. "*Monsieur Verdoux* de Charlie Chaplin," *La Croix*, October 1, 1973, BiFi Collection.

164. Ibid.; Baroncelli, "Le retour de *Monsieur Verdoux*."

165. Albert Cervoni, "Le retour de Verdoux," *France Nouvelle*, September 25, 1973, BiFi Collection.

166. Lachize, "Les chefs-d'oeuvre n'ont pas de rides"; G.T., "*Monsieur Verdoux* à la Cinémathèque: le public debout acclame Chaplin," *L'Aurore*, September 13, 1973, BiFi Collection.

167. G.T., "*Monsieur Verdoux* à la Cinémathèque"; Lachize, "Les chefs-d'oeuvre n'ont pas de rides."

168. "Quand Charlot attaque," *Nouvel Observateur*, no. 464 (October 1, 1973), BiFi Collection; Cervoni, "Le retour de Verdoux"; Chapier, "*Monsieur Verdoux* de Charles Chaplin."

169. Baroncelli, "Le retour de *Monsieur Verdoux*."

170. "*Monsieur Verdoux* de Charlie Chaplin"; Michel Duran, "*Monsieur Verdoux* (Toujours vert, toujours dur)," *Le Canard enchaîné*, September 12, 1973, BiFi Collection; Lachize, "Les chefs-d'oeuvre n'ont pas de rides.".

Afterword

1. Louis Delluc, "Beauty in the Cinema," in Abel, *French Film Theory and Criticism*, 1:139.

2. Élie Faure, "Charlot," *L'Esprit Nouveau*, no. 6 (March 15, 1921), translated and reprinted as "The Art of Charlie Chaplin," *New England Review* 19, no. 2 (Spring 1998): 151.

3. Jean Renoir, "An Actor Named Charlot," in Renoir, *My Life and My Films*, trans. Norman Denny (Atheneum, 1974), 41–43; "De Charlot à Chaplin," interview with Jean Mitry in Joël Magny and Noël Simsolo, *Chaplin aujourd'hui* (Petite bibliothèque des Cahiers du cinéma, 2003), 21.

4. Morvan Lebesque, "Un Roi à New York," *Le Canard enchaîné*, November 6, 1957, BiFi Collection.

5. Myrent and Langlois, *Henri Langlois*, 13–14, 301.

6. Delluc, *Charlie Chaplin*, 11–12, 14–15. Also in 1921, Ricciotto Canudo, an Italian film theorist living in Paris, argued that film was the new "seventh art," following on from the six traditional arts, which he identified as architecture, sculpture, painting, music, poetry, and dance.

7. See Abel, *French Film Theory and Criticism*, 1:99–100.

8. Paul Souday, "Le Cinéma n'est pas un art," *La Dépêche—Journal de la démocratie* (Toulouse), May 29, 1927, 1; Jean de Pierrefeu, "M. Souday contre le cinéma," *Les Nouvelles Littéraires*, June 11, 1927, 1; André Maurois, "La Poésie du Cinéma," *L'Art Cinématographique* 3 (1927): 1, 19.

9. Sadoul, *Vie de Charlot*, 239.

10. Robinson, *Chaplin*, 375.

11. Sadoul gives a partial list of the twenty-four signatories of the protest: author-director Louis Jouvet, opera singer Françoise Rosay, stage and film actor André Luguet, actor-director Jean-Louis Barrault and his actress wife Madeleine Renaud, the polymath Jean Cocteau, artist Henry Matisse, poet-novelist Louis Aragon and his wife translator Elsa Triollet, Belgian film director-screenwriter-actor Jacques Feyder, writer Louis Martin-Chauffier, author-dramatist Francis Carco, composer George Auric, and writer Henry Malberbe (*Vie de Charlot*, 149). The *Washington Post* reported that the protest was signed by Picasso himself and twenty-three others. "Picasso, Others Protest Eisler Deportation," *Washington Post*, December 12, 1947, C13.

Note on Sources

1. Carr, *Charlie Chaplin: A Political Biography from Victorian Britain to Modern America* (New York: Routledge, 2017), 2.

2. Abel, *French Film Theory and Criticism: Vol. 1, 1907-1939*, 95.

3. Ibid.

4. Ibid., 96, 196–97, quotation from 196.

5. Waverly Root, *The Paris Edition 1927-1934* (San Francisco: North Point Press), 57.

6. Abel, *French Film Theory and Criticism: Vol. 1, 1907-1939*, 196 (quotation) and 322.

Index